TEACHER'S HANDBOOK

CONTEXTUALIZED LANGUAGE INSTRUCTION

Judith L. Shrum
Eileen W. Glisan

Heinle and Heinle Publishers
A Division of Wadsworth, Inc.
Boston, Massachusetts 02116 USA

The publication of *Teacher's Handbook* was directed by the members of the Heinle & Heinle Secondary School Publishing team:

Editorial Director: Janet Dracksdorf
Production Editor: Pamela Warren
Developmental Editor: Margaret Potter
Marketing Manager: Elaine Uzan Leary

Also participating in the publication of this text were:

Publisher: Stanley J. Galek
Editorial Production Manager: Elizabeth Holthaus
Manufacturing Coordinator: Jerry Christopher
Interior Design and Composition: Greg Johnson
Cover Design: Hannus Design Associates
Illustrators: Jim Roldan and Len Shalansky

Manufactured in the United States of America

ISBN 0-8384-40614

10   9   8   7   6   5   4   3   2   1

Printed in the United States of America

Heinle & Heinle is a division of Wadsworth, Inc.

Contents

TEXT PERMISSIONS

We wish to thank the authors, publishers and holders of copyright for their permission to reprint the following:

"Procedures for an Official Oral Proficiency Interview.", "Phases of Listening to Authentic Input in Spanish: A descriptive study." (1992), "Beyond Form Based Drill and Practice: Meaning Enhancing CALL on the Macintosh." (May 1992), "Choosing and Using Video Texts. (1990)", "Spanish for Native Speakers: Frierian and Vygotskian Perspectives." (1990), "An Etiquette for the Non-Supervisory Observation of L2 classrooms." (May 1992), "Reducing Composition Errors: An Experiment." (April 1984), The ACTFL Oral Proficiency Interview Tester Training Manual." (1989), "ACTFL Newsletter" (Spring 1992), "An Investigation of Students' Perspectives on Anxiety and Speaking." (1990), courtesy of *ACTFL Foreign Language Annals*.

"Toward Cultural Proficiency.", courtesy of Winter 1992 Newsletter, Northeast Conference on the Teaching of Foreign Languages.

"Writing as a Process.", courtesy of *The French Review*: Vol. 63, No. 1

"Wechelspiel.", courtesy of Langenscheidt Publishers Inc.

"Cajun Telephone Stomp Song from Cajun Conja.", courtesy of Michael Doucit/Rhino Records and Orange Sunrise/Dosay Publishing.

"Integrating Video and CALL in the curriculum: The Role of the ACTFL Guidelines.", "Modern Media in Foreign Language Education: Theory and Implementation.", "Applying Pedagogical Principles to CALL Software Development.", courtesy of The National Textbook Company.

"Strategies for Teaching the Composition Process.", courtesy of Koch and Brazil (1978), by The National Council of Teachers in English, reprinted with permission.

"Semantic Mapping: Classroom Applications.", reprinted with permission of Joan Heimlich and The International Reading Association.

"Children Moving.", courtesy of George Graham et al. by permission of the Mayfield Publishing Company (1987).

"Languages and Children—Making the Match.", courtesy of Foreign Language Instruction in the Elementary School by Helena Anderson-Curtain and Carol Ann Pesola by Addison-Wesley Publishing Company (1988).

"Adult Language Learning Styles and Strategies in an Intensive Training Setting." (1990), "Technology in the Service of Language Learning." (1991), courtesy of *The Modern Language Journal,* The University of Wisconsin Press.

"Déjeuner du Matin.", courtesy of Jacques Prévert, Gallimard Publishers (1949).

"Chesterfield County Public Schools Observations/Foreign Language Form.", courtesy of Jane Baskerville.

"Building Competency Through the Improving of Thinking Skills.", courtesy of the Milwaukee Public Schools (1985).

"Task Oriented Creative Writing with système-D.", courtesy of *The CALICO Journal,* Duke University (March 1990).

"Curriculum Unit From Grade 4.", "Sample Jigsaw Activity for four groups of Students." courtesy of the Pittsburgh Public Schools (1992).

"Teaching a Second Language: Guide for the Student Teacher." (1980), "Research on Cultural Diversity and Second Language Learning. A national center for educators." (Sept.1991), courtesy of The Center for Applied Linguistics, ERIC Clearinghouse.

"French Department Curriculum.", courtesy of the Shaler Area School District.

"Cueing Thoughtful Questions and Discussions.", "Chart: Strategies to extend student thinking found in Kuykendall.", courtesy of the Maryland State Department of Education, Language and Learning Improvement Branch (1989).

"Elementary School Foreign Language Program Goals.", courtesy of The Center for Applied Linguistics (1985).

"Planning for Instruction in the Immersion Classroom.", courtesy of Lorenz and Met (1989).

"El Mundo.", courtesy of Mónica Péres (1989).

Acknowledgements

We gratefully recognize the influence of our students, our colleagues, our publisher, and our families on the thinking that resulted in this book. The work and experiences of many educators formed the basis from which the case study portion of the *Handbook* was developed. We are especially grateful to Dr. Robert Small, formerly at Virginia Polytechnic Institute and State University, currently Dean of Education at Radford University, whose book, *A Casebook for English Teachers* (Small and Strzepek 1988), provided a model for the cases. Without a doubt, we could never offer sufficient thanks to the teachers and students whose work became part of the case studies presented here. Some of these experiences are our own, while others are those we have observed during more than a half-century of combined teaching and research in language education. We hope that the case studies adequately reflect the valiant efforts of good teachers.

Throughout our work in creating this *Handbook,* many individuals served as sounding boards for our ideas and brought numerous new insights to the chapters. We owe special gratitude to Richard Donato, University of Pittsburgh, for his careful reading of the entire book, his helpful suggestions and additions, his willingness to pilot the chapters, and his enthusiastic support of our work. We thank Thekla Fall of the Pittsburgh Public Schools, for contributing many of the appendices and for making helpful suggestions. In addition, in our own work and in the work of others, we notice that good teaching is filled with renewed commitment to students and their learning, revisited goals, and reflection. To this end, we are grateful for the candid input and shining examples of effective teaching offered by the teachers who participated in Dr. Shrum's graduate course, "Advanced Curriculum and Instruction: The Teaching and Learning Processes in Foreign Language Education."

Several colleagues deserve special thanks for work that appears as actual chapters or portions of chapters in the *Handbook.* Bonnie Adair-Hauck (University of Pittsburgh), Richard Donato (University of Pittsburgh), and Philomena Cumo (Carlynton High School, Pittsburgh, Pennsylvania) contributed in Chapter 6 a unique and forward-looking view of a whole language approach to teaching grammar. Virginia Scott, from Vanderbilt University, drew upon her expertise with *systéme-D* to write a case study for Chapter 12.

We are grateful to our editor, Janet Dracksdorf of Heinle and Heinle Publishers, for her patience and commitment of time and effort to supervise the many aspects of publication of this volume. In addition, we wish to thank production editor Pam Warren and her staff, all of whom worked under very tight deadlines. We are grateful for the constructive comments and attention to detail by Donald Pharr, the copy editor, and to the following reviewers, who helped shape our ideas:

Margaret Azevedo, Stanford University

Jane Baskerville, Chesterfield County Schools, Virginia

Peggy Boyles, Putnam City Schools, Oklahoma City, Oklahoma

R. Marshall Brannon, Foreign Language Education Consultant, Virginia
    Department of Education

Richard Donato, University of Pittsburgh

Greg Duncan, Georgia Department of Education

John Gutiérrez, Pennsylvania State University

Todd Hughes, doctoral student, University of Pennsylvania

Anne Jensen, Campbell Unified School District, California

Sally Magnan, University of Wisconsin

Ingeborg McCoy, Southwest Texas State University

Virginia Murillo, San Francisco Unified School District

Anne Nerenz, Eastern Michigan University

Mel Resnick, University of North Carolina

Finally, we wish to thank our families for the role they played in maintaining our mental stability, sharpening our wits, and offering gentle wisdom. Among those we wish to thank for such generous gifts are Roy and Nina Glisan, and Alexander Cuthbert. This book is especially dedicated to Elaine Shrum and, in memoriam, to Paul Shrum.

Judith Shrum
Virginia Polytechnic Institute
and State University

Eileen W. Glisan
Indiana University
of Pennsylvania

Small, R. and J. E. Strzepek. *A Casebook for English Teachers*. Belmont, CA: Wadsworth, 1988.

Preface

The information and activities designed for this *Handbook* are developed around the central theme of **contextualizing** language instruction. Language that is introduced and taught in **context** presents real situations that encompass all aspects of a conversational exchange: the physical setting, the purpose of the exchange, the roles of the participants, the socially acceptable norms of interaction, in addition to the medium, topic, tone, and register of the exchange (Hymes 1974). Each chapter of the *Handbook* assists language professionals as they develop a contextualized approach to language teaching that is based on meaningful language use, real communication, and interaction among language learners. The teaching examples and case studies in the *Handbook* offer a broad perspective of diverse teaching circumstances in elementary, middle/intermediate/junior high schools, high schools and beyond. Further, the teaching examples are offered for various languages to show that the principles underlying contextualized instruction are constant for the many age groups represented and the languages that are taught.

This *Handbook* enables foreign language teachers to use current theories about learning and teaching as a basis for reflection and practice. Teachers are active decision makers who use opportunities to apply theory through observing classroom interaction, designing and teaching their own lessons, and making appropriate decisions in a wide variety of situations that confront them daily. Developing foreign language teachers use many information sources as they reflect upon their teaching and make decisions: competence in the second language; knowledge of how the target language is taught; application of subject knowledge to actual teaching; application of research findings to classroom teaching; clinical experience; and knowledge of the means by which teaching effectiveness is examined within the school context (Lange 1990). Accordingly, this *Handbook* presents theoretical findings concerning key aspects of language teaching, together with observational episodes, micro-teaching situations, and case studies in order to assist beginning teachers as they develop their teaching approaches and experienced teachers as they update their theoretical knowledge and teaching practices. This *Handbook* assists teachers in their "… intellectual, experiential, and attitudinal growth …," a key process in teacher development (Lange 1990, p. 250).

The *Handbook* uses the "multiple activities" approach to teacher preparation as advocated by Gebhard, Gaitan, and Oprandy (1990), in order to develop the investigative and decision-making skills needed to foster professional growth for novice and experienced teachers. In this model, teachers grow through interaction with other professionals by means of "(1) teaching a class; (2) observing the teaching act; (3) conducting investigative projects of teaching; and (4) discussing teaching in several contexts" (Gebhard, Gaitan, and Oprandy 1990, p. 16). Accordingly, novice and experienced teachers using this *Handbook* will find structured and open-ended opportunities to observe classroom teaching, and to plan and conduct micro-teaching lessons, in light of the theory and information discussed in each chapter. A variety of case studies and related activities provides interesting opportunities to investigate and discuss effective classroom practice. Indeed, novice and experienced teachers can strengthen their individual approaches to teaching by observing, investigating, discussing ideas, teaching and relating these activities to one another.

The flexible nature of the *Handbook* offers the possibility of a number of uses: as a primary methodology textbook used with other supplementary information and materials provided by the instructor; as a reference book; as an introduction to professional foreign/second language teacher education; as a practical follow-up to courses in the historical and theoretical knowledge base of foreign/second language acquisition. Methodology instructors will be able to link specific activities to the sequence of their syllabus or related textbook by using the index that lists topics along with their corresponding micro-teaching activities and case studies.

■ Organization of the *Handbook*

The *Handbook* consists of twelve chapters: the first chapters present topics of a more general nature, and later chapters proceed to more specific technique-oriented issues. Chapter 1 explores the role of contextualized input and output in the language learning process including a presentation of key theoretical frameworks that focus on the importance of meaningful input and output in acquiring language. In Chapter 1, the **Observe and Reflect** section will start teachers thinking about and observing the teaching and learning of languages. Chapter 2 examines an integrative approach to language instruction in which language is presented and taught in meaningful contexts. In Chapter 3, teachers will learn how to organize content for instruction by means of long- and short-range planning.

Special attention is given in Chapters 4 and 5 to foreign/second language learners in elementary and middle/intermediate/junior high schools. The unique cognitive and maturational characteristics of learners at these two levels respond best to particular approaches and strategies. An approach utilized with older adolescents, for example, may be inappropriate for young children. However, as will be highlighted throughout the chapters, many techniques can be adapted for use across instructional levels. The information in Chapters 4 and 5 is introduced in terms of the interaction between learning and the developmental stages of children, the possible effects on language learning, and implications for teaching. Teachers will explore the cognitive and maturational differences between the elementary and middle school child and the adolescent learner and develop lessons appropriate to these cognitive levels.

Chapters 6–9 offer many opportunities for teachers to design lessons for teaching grammar, listening, reading, speaking, and writing, all within real language contexts and appropriate to students at various levels of instruction. In Chapter 6, teachers will explore an approach for contextualizing grammar instruction through the use of whole language and guided participatory teaching. Chapter 7 presents ideas for developing listening and reading skills through the use of authentic input and building of strategies. In Chapter 8, teachers explore strategies for teaching speaking through meaningful contexts and opportunities for classroom interaction. Chapter 9 presents ideas for integrating writing into language instruction through techniques such as writing across the curriculum, process-oriented writing, and peer editing.

Chapter 10 presents ideas for how teachers might handle other factors concerning student diversity that affect classroom language learning, such as: learning styles; learning disabilities; characteristics of being "at-risk" or "gifted"; and a variety of cultural, ethnic, and racial backgrounds. In Chapter 11, teachers explore various alternatives for evaluating learner progress, including contextualized test formats and techniques that go beyond paper-and-pencil tests. Finally, Chapter 12 illustrates the role of technology in teaching language within a communicative, contextualized framework.

▍Chapter Organization

Each chapter of the *Handbook* is organized into three sections:

1. *Conceptual Orientation.* It grounds teaching practices in a valid body of research and theoretical knowledge. This section briefly describes the theoretical principles underlying the language learning observation, teaching tasks and case studies presented later in the chapter. The section is a summary of what is known about topics in language teaching and includes references to the original research sources for additional in-depth study or review.

2. *Observe and Reflect/Teach and Reflect.* The **Observe and Reflect** (Chapter 1) and **Teach and Reflect** (all subsequent chapters) sections highlight practical elements of learning how to teach and contain two guided observations and two teaching episodes respectively. Each observation or micro-teaching situation integrates the theoretical orientation to give novice teachers an opportunity to implement pedagogically sound teaching techniques within the environment of a methods class. These micro-teaching situations can also be useful for experienced teachers attempting to learn new techniques. Discussion questions following each teaching or observation situation will help teachers integrate certain teaching techniques into personal teaching approaches.

3. ***Discuss and Reflect.*** This section provides two case studies, presenting real situations experienced by foreign language teachers at various levels of instruction. The case studies offer teachers the opportunity to link the theoretically grounded practices explored in the first two sections of each chapter with the reality of teaching circumstances found in schools. Every day foreign language teachers commonly face challenges, like those presented in the case studies, challenges that may arise out of mismatches between teaching goals, student preparedness, and academic tasks, or out of institutional goals that are inconsistent with teaching goals. The **Discuss and Reflect** section includes two types of cases: those that present teaching situations that *support* the theoretical bases featured in the chapter and those that present problematic teaching situations that are *inconsistent* with the theory and rationale of the chapter. The cases present the information necessary to enable teachers to read the case and the referenced materials and prepare a resolution of the case for class discussion. Often the cases include many details about teachers and/or teaching situations so that readers might decide which details contribute the most to resolving the case.

    Case Study Pedagogy. The case study approach was recommended by the Task Force on Teaching as a Profession (Carnegie Forum on Education and the Economy) in their report entitled *A Nation Prepared: Teachers for the 21st Century* (1986). The approach utilized in the case study presentation is based on certain aspects of three models of teacher supervision: (1) Freeman's (1982) alternative supervision model; (2) Cogan's (1973) collaborative or "clinical" supervision model; and (3) a nondirective supervision model (Copeland 1982; Freeman 1982; Dowling and Sheppard 1976). First of all, readers are given maximum guidance as they reflect upon the situations and attempt to analyze them. In the first several chapters of the *Handbook,* teachers are given a list of alternatives that represent plausible solutions to the problem or challenge presented in the teaching situation. The class discussion of each alternative assists readers in developing their own approaches to the case.

    Secondly, *Handbook* users are encouraged to collaborate with their peers and the instructor as they discuss the alternatives and/or the development of their own approaches to the situations. Sharing ideas within the classroom greatly facilitates the problem-solving process. Teachers are also encouraged to consult other referenced works for additional information that will assist them in formulating sound approaches to the case development. *Handbook* users may choose from among the suggested references or consult others recommended by their instructor.

    Thirdly, as readers become increasingly more familiar with case study exploration, they are asked to assume greater responsibility for developing their own solutions to the problems and challenges presented in the cases, on the basis of the information provided in the chapter, class discussions, and previously acquired knowledge and experience. *The Handbook* is designed to be used as a practical reference, a reflective planning notebook. Space is provided for notes, and for writing plans and thoughts as a springboard for discussion. This feature personalizes the *Handbook* for each user, and encourages reflection in writing. Thus, the entire process leads teachers to develop their own problem-solving abilities while preparing them to reflect on their own teaching and classroom situations.

Additional Resources

The *Handbook* contains a collection of useful materials and sources of information that foreign language teachers use and consult regularly:

- the ACTFL Proficiency Guidelines
- a listing of sources for materials and information
- a list of professional organizations and agencies
- a list of professional publications
- a set of performance standards for foreign language teachers
- an instructional evaluation form used in school a district
- a contract or letter of expectation for use by student teachers and cooperating teachers or between peer coaches and/or mentors
- other supporting material for the *Handbook* chapters

REFERENCES

Carnegie Corporation. *A Nation Prepared: Teachers for the 21st Century*. New York: Carnegie Corporation, 1986.

Cogan, M. *Clinical Supervision*. Boston: Houghton Mifflin, 1973.

Copeland, W. "Student Teachers' Preference for Supervisory Approach." *Journal of Teacher Education* 33 (1982): 32–36.

Dowling, G., and K. Sheppard. "Teacher Training: A Counseling Focus." Eds. J. Fanselow and R. Crymes. *On TESOL '76*. Washington, D.C.: TESOL, 1976.

Freeman, D. "Observing Teachers: Three Approaches to In-Service Training and Development." *TESOL Quarterly* 16 (1982): 21–28.

Gebhard, J., S. Gaitan, and R. Oprandy. "Beyond Prescription: The Student Teacher as Investigator." Eds. J.C. Richards and D. Nunan. *Second Language Teacher Education*. Cambridge: Cambridge University Press (1990): 16–25.

Hymes, D. *Foundation of Sociolinguistics*. Philadelphia: University of Pennsylvania, 1974.

Lange, D. "A Blueprint for a Teacher Development Program." Eds. J. Richards and D. Nunan. *Second Language Teacher Education*. Cambridge: Cambridge University Press (1990): 245–268.

CHAPTER 1

Understanding the Role of Contextualized Input and Output in the Language Learning Process

Chapter One presents a summary of several major theoretical positions that stress the importance of contextualized input and output in the language learning process. The theories selected for discussion are those that continue to receive much attention from scholars in the field.[1] You will apply your understanding of these theories by completing two observations of individuals using language. The case studies included in this chapter present real teaching situations, offering you the chance to use theory to explain the events and to formulate your own responses to them.

CONCEPTUAL ORIENTATION

As McLaughlin (1987) suggests, theories of language learning can help us to: (1) understand data obtained in empirical studies; (2) transform the meaning of what we know; and (3) predict where theories are leading in terms of further research and practice. In our discussion, we will use the term "second language acquisition" as Ellis defined it: "... the subconscious or conscious processes by which a language other than the mother tongue is learnt in a natural or a tutored setting" (Ellis 1986, p. 6). However, in your reading of other research, you may encounter the term "foreign language learning" to refer to formal classroom instruction outside of the geographical region where it is commonly spoken and "second language acquisition" used to refer to acquiring another language within one of the regions where the language is commonly spoken.

■ The Role of Input: Krashen's Input Hypothesis

Although there are many differences between first and second language acquisition, research clearly indicates that both first and second language learners need large amounts of contextualized, meaningful input in order to acquire

---

[1]This summary reviews key characteristics of the theories presented; if you want more information about certain theories, consult the bibliography included at the end of the chapter.

language. Children acquire their first language by hearing it spoken by family and friends in a variety of communicative events and by interacting with others in activities such as games and storytelling. Second language learners who have opportunities to actively understand natural language, such as in face-to-face conversation, acquire language more quickly and more successfully than learners exposed exclusively to meaningless exercises that focus on structure alone (Lightbown 1985). One theory that has served as the catalyst for further research in this area is Krashen's *Input Hypothesis,* which suggests that acquisition in the classroom occurs only when language is presented under certain conditions, that is, when learners receive optimal comprehensible input that is interesting, a little beyond their current level of competence, *not* grammatically sequenced, and given in an environment where students are "off the defensive" (Krashen 1982, p. 127). Perhaps the most controversial claim made by Krashen concerns the type of input necessary for acquisition to take place. Krashen (1982) defines acquisition as a subconscious "picking up" of rules as in the L1 acquisition process while learning, by contrast, is a conscious focus on knowing rules. According to Krashen, acquisition, *not* learning, leads to real communication.

The Role of Negotiation of Meaning: The Variable Competence Model

A number of researchers, however, have questioned Krashen's claim that second language learners utilize primarily "acquired, subconscious" knowledge rather than "learned, conscious" knowledge in real communication. The *Variable Competence Model,* as developed by Bialystok (1982), Ellis (1988), and Tarone (1983), for example, suggests that learning occurs through use of a continuum between subconscious, automatic processes and conscious, analytic processes. The learner may activate either automatic, unanalyzed processes or non-automatic, analytic processes as necessary given the particular type of discourse being carried out. Learners may utilize "primary processes," drawing on automatic rules, when engaging in unplanned, spontaneous discourse and "secondary processes," drawing on non-automatic rules, when engaging in consciously pre-planned discourse. In a spontaneous situation, learners might speak without referring subconsciously to language rules. For example, asking someone his or her name in Spanish can be accomplished by beginning learners without consciously thinking through the use of reflexive verbs. On the other hand, in pre-planned speaking events, learners might draw upon formal language rules as they prepare their discourse. For example, explaining to a doctor what happened when you sprained your ankle could require the conscious use of reflexive verbs and past tenses. Of course, in any given language-use situation, non-automatic processes and automatic processes may operate in concert.

According to Ellis (1988), this view accounts for the individual variation in the language of a second language learner as different types of knowledge and procedures are activated in different communicative contexts. For example, in certain situations, a learner might use a given structure with apparent mastery, while in other situations he or she might demonstrate an incomplete understanding of the structure. Language development occurs as a result of the acquisition of new rules through participation in various types of communicative acts and the ability to activate either conscious or unconscious knowledge for use in unplanned discourse. According to Ellis (1988), "Rapid development along the 'natural' route occurs when the learner has the chance to negotiate meaning in unplanned discourse" (p. 186). While both Krashen and Ellis present different views of the processes involved in L2 acquisition, the evidence convincingly indicates that the ability to verbalize a language rule does not signify that the language learner can use it in communication (Lightbown 1985). Further, some evidence suggests that the processing of mechanical drills, which is different from the way in which communicative language is processed, does not promote language acquisition (Lightbown 1983).

The Role of Interaction: Long's Interaction Hypothesis

We have seen that Krashen's Input Model is based upon the need for comprehensible input while the Variable Competence Model stresses the importance of the negotiation of meaning in the acquisition process. According to Long (1983), input can be made "comprehensible" in three ways:

- by simplifying the input, i.e., using familiar structures and vocabulary;
- by using linguistic and extra-linguistic context, i.e., familiar structures, background knowledge, gestures; and
- by modifying the interactional structure of conversation.

This third element is the basis of Long's (1981) *Interaction Hypothesis*, which takes into account both input and learner production in promoting acquisition. Long (1983) maintains that speakers make changes in their language as they interact or "negotiate meaning" with each other. Speakers negotiate meaning to avoid conversational trouble which is the result of the speaker's planning for the conversation; or to revise language when trouble occurs. This negotiation is often spontaneous and may alter the course of the discussion. Long's theory implies that learners cannot simply listen to input, but that they must be active conversational participants who interact and negotiate the type of input they receive in order to acquire language.

Vygotsky's Zone of Proximal Development

Work done by L. S. Vygotsky, a social psychologist, also highlights the importance of social interaction in acquiring language. Vygotsky's views on learning and development in children differ markedly from those of Piaget for whom learning and mental development are independent processes. According to Piaget (1979), learning does not affect the course of development since maturation precedes learning. In this framework, the learner must be cognitively ready to handle certain learning tasks. In Vygotsky's (1978) view, however, learning *precedes* maturation. The learner brings two levels of development to the learning task: an actual developmental level, representing what the learner can do, and a potential developmental level, representing what the learner will be able to do in the future. Through interaction with others, the learner progresses from the "actual developmental level" to the "potential developmental level". Between the two levels is the learner's *Zone of Proximal Development*, which Vygotsky defined as "the distance between the actual developmental level as determined by independent problem solving and the level of potential development as determined through problem solving under adult guidance or in collaboration with more capable peers" (1978, p. 86). Figure 1 (Faltis 1990) illustrates the zone or ZPD. In this process, the potential development level of

FIGURE 1 The Zone of Proximal Development

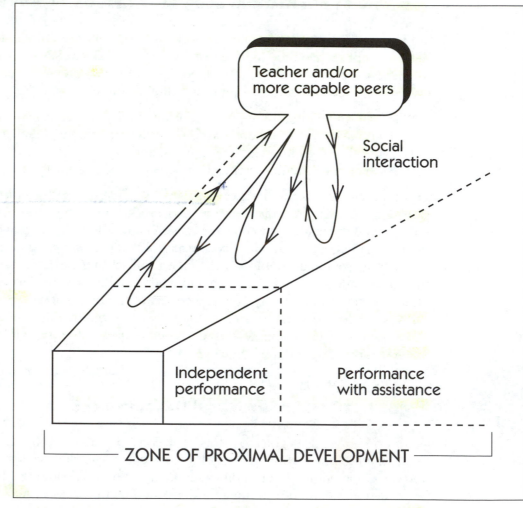

Source: Faltis 1990.

the learner becomes the next actual developmental level as a result of the learner's interaction with others and the expanding of cognitive abilities. In terms of second language acquisition, Vygotsky's theory implies that, while students need a great deal of contextualized input, acquisition may be contingent on cooperative, meaningful interaction.

■ The Role of Output: Interlanguage Theory

Selinker (1974) has defined *interlanguage* as an individual linguistic system created by second language learners as a result of five cognitive processes: (1) interference from the native language; (2) effect of instruction (approach, rules provided by teacher, classroom activities, etc.); (3) overgeneralization of target language rules (application of rules to contexts where they don't apply); (4) strategies involved in second language learning, such as rote memorization, use of formal rules, and guessing in context; and (5) strategies involved in second language communication, such as circumlocution, use of gestures, appeal for assistance from a conversational partner.

As learners process input and acquire language, evidence indicates that there may be predictable sequences in both first and second language acquisition, in which certain structures are acquired before others (Lightbown 1985). In the second language classroom, studies have shown that students acquire structures in a particular order that may not parallel the order in which they were taught (VanPatten 1986). For example, in his study of the acquisition of the two Spanish copulas *ser* and *estar,* VanPatten (1985) found that *ser* is acquired early in the learning process and is overgeneralized to other contexts requiring the *to be* construction.

Research continues to examine the relationship between learner errors in grammar, vocabulary, and syntax and reactions by native speakers to those errors. Due to the wide variety of speech and writing samples that researchers have used, it is difficult to clearly interpret the many studies done to analyze native speaker reactions. Research by Chastain (1980), Galloway (1980), Guntermann (1978), Gynan (1984), and others indicates that individual errors may not be detrimental to communication between learners and native speakers. What may be more important, however, is the learner's ability to negotiate meaning with his or her conversational partner until the message is conveyed (Savignon 1983).

Swain's Output Hypothesis

While many studies have focused on the role of input, Swain (1985) has suggested that output is extremely important in the acquisition process, as it: (1) pushes students to find other means for expressing a message when communication breakdown occurs; (2) moves the learner from semantic processing, which is a focus on the meaning of key content words, characteristic of the early stages of second language acquisition, to syntactic processing, which is a focus on structural features; and (3) enables the learner to test out hypotheses about the second language, that is, to correct and/or revise individual language rules.

■ The Role of Affect

Other variables that may influence the degree of success in learning another language are those pertaining to *affect,* such as motivation, anxiety, personality, and attitude. The *Affective Filter Hypothesis,* as proposed by Dulay and Burt (1977), relates these affective factors to the second language acquisition process. Krashen (1982) maintains that acquisition can occur only in the presence of certain affective conditions: i.e., the learner is motivated, self confident, and has a low level of anxiety. Krashen proposes that, when these conditions are present, comprehensible input is received, passes through the filter, and is used most effectively by the learner. When these conditions are not present, the affective filter becomes high and prevents the input from passing through and from being used effectively. According to Stevick (1976), the language classroom can encourage low filters by promoting low anxiety among students and keeping them "off the defensive" (cf. Krashen, 1982, p. 127).

Evidence suggests that personality or cognitive styles also affect second-language learning; these factors include the willingness to take risks, skill in social interactions, and attitude toward the target language, among others (Wong-Fillmore 1985; Young 1990). A number of these variables will be discussed in greater detail in Chapter 10.

■ Implications of the Research for Classroom Teaching

The research findings described above point to several implications concerning classroom language instruction. Acquisition may be facilitated by providing for the following elements in the classroom:

- comprehensible input in the target language;
- opportunities for students to negotiate meaning in the target language;
- opportunities for students to interact communicatively with one another in the target language;
- a non-threatening environment that encourages self-expression.

OBSERVE AND REFLECT

The following two activities will enable you to examine the classroom from the perspective of the real world.

EPISODE ONE
Observing a Child Interacting in His/Her Native Language

Observe a small child between the ages of 2 1/2 and 3 who is interacting with one or more other people (parent, older siblings, etc.) in his/her native language. Observe for at least one hour, paying particular attention to the child's use of language. Use the observation guide provided below to focus your attention during the observation. Afterwards, reflect on the observation by answering the questions in the guide.

EPISODE TWO
Observing a Beginning Language Class

Now observe a beginning language learning classroom in an elementary or secondary school. Use the same questions presented in the observation guide below as you observe the students interacting in the foreign language. Answer the questions after your observation.

OBSERVATION GUIDE
Use of Language in an Acquisition or Learning Mode

Novice = child or classroom learner
Expert = caretaker, older individual, teacher

1. What is the topic of conversation? Why are the expert and novice speaking?
2. When does the novice participate in the conversation? To answer questions? To ask questions? To provide additional information?
3. What kinds of questions does the expert ask?
4. How does the expert react to what the novice says?
5. How does the expert help the novice when the novice has trouble expressing an idea?
6. What happens when the expert and novice do not understand each other?
7. What kind of language errors do you notice?
8. What does the expert do when the novice makes a language mistake?

Think about the theories presented in this chapter and describe four important implications for classroom teaching as you see them.

_____

_____

_____

_____

_____

_____

As a language learner, have you experienced teaching approaches that were based upon one or more of these implications? Explain.

_____

_____

_____

_____

_____

As you reflect upon the classroom you visited in Episode Two (or any other observation you have made), describe the role of input, output, and meaningful interaction as you observed it.

_____

_____

_____

_____

_____

_____

_____

DISCUSS AND REFLECT

The following case studies will give you insight into the ways foreign language teachers struggle with the relationship between functional, contextualized language teaching and the more traditional approach emphasizing grammatical accuracy.

CASE STUDY 1
Poor Exam Results

Ms. Baker, a beginning teacher, has just concluded the first half of the academic year and is in the process of conducting mid-year examinations with her Spanish I classes. During the initial in-service days at the beginning of the school year, she studied the goals for Spanish I as set forth in the Curriculum Guide for her school system. She thought it was good that the goals included a variety of functions and contexts in which students were to produce Spanish. She asked her fellow teachers what was expected of the students by the end of the year; they answered, "You have to finish ten chapters of the book."

Now, at mid-year, she is reflecting on the progress her students have made. She has finished the first five chapters of the textbook and has done her best to provide opportunities for students to use the language in a variety of functions and contexts. Ms. Baker has followed fairly closely the organization of the textbook, teaching the grammatical structures and vocabulary that were presented. Because she feels that accuracy is important, she corrected students' errors as they were made so that they would acquire the correct forms. She discussed the finer grammatical points with students in English, drilled them in structured practice exercises in the target language, and later provided opportunities for communicative activities. The oral target language input she provided to students consisted of the taped dialogues in the textbook program and her own personalized questions.

Now, during the course of the oral and written exams, Ms. Baker is growing more and more frustrated with the exam results. Only a few of her students were able to correctly use some of the grammatical structures studied extensively in class. She is asking herself why her students are not using these structures naturally and with a high degree of accuracy on the exams.

Which of the following changes could Ms. Baker make to her teaching approach? Explore the advantages and disadvantages of each.

1. She could focus more on error correction and place more emphasis on using the language accurately, perhaps by weighting the grading of exams to include more points for accuracy.
2. She could suggest to her department that they cover fewer chapters in the textbook in order to have more time to practice individual grammatical points.
3. She could give students more responsibility for correcting their own errors through techniques such as peer correction and peer editing.
4. She could alter her high expectations of grammatical accuracy at this level and focus mainly on meaning.
5. She could review the Curriculum Guide to better understand how to make the primary focus of her teaching language functions and contexts, rather than grammatical accuracy.

Now that you have discussed the possible reasons why Ms. Baker's students are not performing to her satisfaction on the exams, develop your own rationale according to one or more of the theories presented in this chapter: the Input Hypothesis, the Variable Competence Model, the Interaction Hypothesis, the Vygotskian framework, the Interlanguage Theory, the Output Hypothesis, or other affective/motivational factors.

To prepare the case:

- Consult these sources for information about how language is learned:
  Chapters 5 and 8 in Larsen-Freeman and Long (1991)
  Chapters 5 and 6 in Ellis (1990)
  Chapter 3 in Brown (1987)
  Chapters 6 and 7 in McLaughlin (1987)
  Chapters 1 and 2 in Richard-Amato (1988)
- Read a journal article for insights into language learning and teaching (such as VanPatten 1992).

Now, write a brief description of what *you* would do if you were Ms. Baker in the situation described above.

_____

_____

_____

_____

_____

In the second episode of this chapter's *Observe and Reflect* section, you observed a beginning language learning class. Compare what you observed to the description of Ms. Baker's classroom approach as discussed in the case study.

_____

_____

_____

_____

_____

CASE STUDY 2
Conducting a Cooperative Learning Task

Mr. Flitchum has been teaching high school German for ten years in the Smith River School District. His approach to teaching German has been a traditional grammar-based one and he has not changed many aspects of his teaching since he began his career. His classes are teacher-centered: he presents grammar rules, has students do mechanical exercises to learn the structures, and does some communicative practice as time permits. Approximately every other week, his students read a short text dealing with some aspect of German culture and answer comprehension questions. Mr. Flitchum uses little spoken German in the classroom except for conducting the grammar practice.

Midway through the year, however, Mr. Flitchum decided to try out some new ideas he had learned at a recent workshop for language teaching. The workshop presented various techniques for teaching communicative language use and involving students more in creative self-expression. Since the chapter students were working with included vocabulary dealing with family, Mr. Flitchum decided to have students interview one another in pairs in order to find out certain information about each other's families. He presented the task in English: "Choose a partner and interview one another in German to find out: how many people are in the immediate family; what their relationships are; what their occupations are; and what they look like." He gave them fifteen minutes to complete the interviews. However, as Mr. Flitchum began to circulate around the room, he found that students were confused: they had no idea how to form the questions in German; they were madly going through verb charts and vocabulary lists in their books; and they seemed to dislike the idea of working together in pairs.

Explore the following alternatives that Mr. Flitchum could have used:

1. He could have asked students to write out the questions for homework and use them in class the next day to conduct the interviews.
2. He could have introduced the activity by giving examples of some questions students might form for use in the interviews.
3. He could have integrated grammar practice with functional use by providing more opportunities for students to use each grammar point through communicative use and interaction.
4. He could have provided more input in German through such strategies as presenting an authentic video of native speakers of German describing their families.

After having discussed the alternatives above, formulate your own list of probable causes for the difficulties Mr. Flitchum's students are experiencing. Base your rationale on the theories presented in this chapter dealing with the role of input/output and social interaction.

_____

_____

_____

_____

_____

_____

To prepare the case:

- Consult the following sources dealing with pair/group work and student interaction:
  Chapter 49 in Cross (1991)
  Chapters 10 and 13 in Chastain (1988)
  Chapter 12 in Richard-Amato (1988)
  Johnson & Johnson (1987)
- Observe a language lesson in which students are interacting with one another.

Now imagine that you are Mr. Flitchum:

1. What would you do as you sense that students are having difficulties with the interviews?

_____

_____

_____

_____

_____

_____

2. What elements of your teaching would you begin to change as you learn more about current research in second language acquisition and its implications?

_____

_____

_____

_____

_____

_____

3. Interview an experienced language teacher and discuss the kinds of changes that he or she has made over the years to update his/her approach to teaching. Describe these changes below.

_____

_____

_____

_____

_____

_____

_____

_____

_____

_____

REFERENCES

Bialystok, E. "On the Relationship Between Knowing and Using Forms." *Applied Linguistics* 3 (1982): 181–206.

Brown, H.D. *Principles of Language Learning and Teaching*. Englewood Cliffs, NJ: Prentice Hall, 1987.

Chastain, K. "Native Speaker Reaction to Instructor-Identified Student Second-Language Errors." *Modern Language Journal* 64 (1980): 210–15.

Chastain, K. *Developing Second Language Skills*. San Diego, CA: Harcourt Brace Jovanovich, 1988.

Chomsky, N. *Rules and Representations*. New York: Columbia University Press, 1980.

Cross, D. *A Practical Handbook of Language Teaching*. London: Cassell Villiers House, 1991.

Dulay, H., and M. Burt. "Remarks on Creativity in Language Acquisition." Eds. M. Burt, H. Dulay, and M. Finnochiaro. *Viewpoints on English as a Second Language*. New York: Regents, 1977.

Ellis, R. *Understanding Second Language Acquisition*. Oxford: Oxford University Press, 1986.

Ellis, R. *Classroom Second Language Development*. Englewood Cliffs, NJ: Prentice Hall, 1988.

Ellis, R. *Instructed Second Language Acquisition*. Oxford: Basil Blackwell Ltd., 1990.

Faltis, C. "Spanish for Native Speakers: Freirian and Vygotskian Perspectives." *Foreign Language Annals* 23 (1990): 117–126.

Galloway, V.B. "Perceptions of the Communicative Efforts of American Students of Spanish." *Modern Language Journal* 64 (1980): 428–433.

Gleason, J.B. *The Development of Language*. Columbus, OH: Charles E. Merrill Publishing Company, 1985.

Guntermann, G. "A Study of the Frequency and Communicative Effects of Errors in Spanish." *Modern Language Journal* 62 (1978): 249–253.

Gynan, S.N. "Attitudes Toward Interlanguage: What Is The Object of Study?" *Modern Language Journal* 68 (1984): 315–321.

Johnson, D.D., and R.T. Johnson. *Learning Together and Alone: Cooperation, Competition, and Individualization*. Englewood Cliffs, NJ: Prentice Hall, 1987.

Krashen, S. *Principles and Practice in Second Language Acquisition*. Oxford: Pergamon Press, 1982.

Larsen-Freeman, D., and M.H. Long. *An Introduction to Second Language Acquisition Research*. White Plains, NY: Longman, 1991.

Lightbown, P. "Exploring Relationships Between Developmental and Instructional Sequences in L2 Acquisition." Eds. H. W. Seliger and M. H. Long. *Classroom Oriented Research in Second Language Acquisition*. Rowley, MA: Newbury House, 1983.

Lightbown, P. "Great Expectations: Second-Language Acquisition Research and Classroom Teaching." *Applied Linguistics* 6 (1985): 173–189.

Long, M.H. "Input, Interaction and Second Language Acquisition." Ed. H. Winitz. *Native Language and Foreign Language Acquisition*. Annals of the New York Academy of Sciences No. 379. New York: Academy of Sciences (1981): 259–178.

Long, M.H. "Native Speaker/Non-Native Speaker Conversation in the Second Language Classroom." Eds. M. A. Clarke and J. Handscomb. *On TESOL '82: Pacific Perspectives on Language Learning and Teaching*. Washington, D.C.: TESOL, 1983.

McLaughlin, B. *Theories of Second-Language Learning*. London: Edward Arnold, 1987.

Piaget, J. *The Development of Thought*. New York: Viking, 1979.

Richard-Amato, P.A. *Making It Happen—Interaction in the Second Language Classroom*. White Plains, NY: Longman, 1988.

Savignon, S. *Communicative Competence: Theory and Classroom Practice*. Reading, MA: Addison-Wesley, 1983.

Schulz, R.A. "Second Language Acquisition Theories and Teaching Practice: How Do They Fit?" *Modern Language Journal* 5 (1991): 17–26.

Selinker, L. "Interlanguage." Eds. J.H. Schumann and N. Stenson. *New Frontiers in Second-Language Learning*. Rowley, MA: Newbury House, 1974.

Stevick, E. *Memory, Meaning, and Method*. Rowley, MA: Newbury House, 1976.

Swain, M. "Communicative Competence: Some Roles of Comprehensible Input and Comprehensible Output in Its Development." Eds. S. Gass and C. Madden. *Input in Second Language Acquisition*. Rowley, MA: Newbury House, 1985: 235–253.

Tarone, E. "On the Variability of Interlanguage Systems." *Applied Linguistics* 4 (1983): 142-163.

Terrell, T.D. "A Natural Approach to Second Language Acquisition." *Modern Language Journal* 61 (1977): 325–337.

VanPatten, B. "The Acquisition of *Ser* and *Estar* by Adult Classroom Learners: A Preliminary Investigation of Transitional Stages of Competence." *Hispania* 68 (1985): 399–406.

VanPatten, B. "Second Language Acquisition Research and the Learning/ Teaching of Spanish: Some Research Findings and Implications." *Hispania* 69 (1986): 202–216.

VanPatten, B. "On Babies and Bathwater: Input in Foreign Language Learning." *Modern Language Journal* 71 (1987): 156–164.

VanPatten, B. "Second-Language Acquisition Research and Foreign Language Teaching, Part I." *Association of Departments of Foreign Languages Bulletin* 23 (1992): 52–56.

Vygotsky, L.S. *Mind in Society: The Development of Higher Psychological Processes*. Cambridge, MA: Harvard University Press, 1978.

Young, D.J. "An Investigation of Students' Perspectives on Anxiety and Speaking." *Foreign Language Annals* 23 (1990): 539–553.

Wong-Fillmore, L. "Second Language Learning in Children: A Proposed Model." Eds. R. Eshch and J.Z. Provenzano. *Issues in English Language Development*. Rosslyn, VA: National Clearinghouse for Bilingual Education, 1985.

CHAPTER 2

Contextualizing and Integrating Language Instruction

This chapter presents ideas for implementing an integrative approach to language instruction, through which language is presented and taught in meaningful contexts for the purpose of communicating. As defined in the Preface, language that is introduced and taught *in context* presents real situations that encompass the physical setting, the purpose of the exchange, the roles of the participants, and the socially acceptable norms of interaction, in addition to the medium, topic, tone, and register of the exchange (Hymes 1974). Grammatical structures that might otherwise be devoid of context become an integral part of the communicative acts that occur in contexts.

In this chapter, you will explore several options for teaching grammar in context. Strategies such as top-down teaching, content-based instruction, and the use of culturally and linguistically authentic materials will be discussed. You will have the opportunity to design a contextualized lesson and to develop ideas for implementing content-based instruction. In one of the case studies, you will learn how two teachers explore the nature of contextualized textbook exercises. In the second case study, you will see how a teacher of ESL develops a top-down approach to teaching a lesson. This chapter provides the foundation for subsequent chapters that examine the teaching of each skill.

CONCEPTUAL ORIENTATION

For decades, elementary school teachers have been combining language and content through techniques such as storytelling, games, role plays, and, more recently, integration of subject areas such as mathematics and geography. However, at later levels of instruction, we have become quite adept at separating linguistic form from content and culture. Indeed, methods such as ALM and cognitive code have advocated separation of skills and a discrete-point approach to the teaching of grammar. In describing current-day pedagogical practice, Kramsch warns that "By being taught as text, discourse has been decontextualized and is now taught according to structuralist principles of language learning" (1991, p. 198). Bialystok (1983) notes that this decontextualization may be the cause of the difficulty experienced by both children and adults in acquiring a second language.

■ The Importance of Context

The research has confirmed the important role context plays in enabling language learners to process and produce a foreign or second language (Swaffer, Arens, and Byrnes 1991; Smith 1985). Simply put, the more familiar the context, the easier it is to understand it and function within it. Further, for information to be meaningful, learners must be able to link or relate it to knowledge they already have (Minsky 1982). Learners use various kinds of background knowledge as they attend to a message within a given context (Smith 1985; Goodman 1972). For example, they use their knowledge of the foreign language, their own knowledge and personal experiences, and their understanding of how discourse, such as conversation and newspaper articles, is organized (Omaggio 1986). A great deal of the recent literature in teaching listening and reading has focused on ways to prepare students for the comprehension task and to help them use context to activate background knowledge (Swaffer, Arens, and Byrnes 1991; Glisan 1988).

The introduction of teaching language in order to achieve proficiency-based outcomes has also underscored the importance of meaning and context in comprehension and production. The guidelines developed by the American Council on the Teaching of Foreign Languages (ACTFL) and the Educational Testing Service (ETS) define what language users are able to do with the language at various stages. (See Appendix A1.) In the last ten years, many professionals have grasped the idea of using the proficiency definition of what it means to know a language for purposes of organizing instruction. (See Appendix A2 for a historical overview of the development of the proficiency concept.) The proficiency model defines language ability in terms of three criteria: (1) functions: linguistic tasks performed such as asking for information, narrating past activities, or expressing opinions; (2) contexts/contents: the settings in which one uses language, e.g., informal settings, transactional situations, formal settings, together with the topics or themes of conversation, such as topics related to self and to immediate environment (family, shopping, transportation, restaurant, etc.), concrete topics of personal and general interest, and abstract topics; and (3) accuracy: the precision of the message in terms of fluency, grammar, vocabulary, pragmatic competence, pronunciation, sociolinguistic competence (Buck, Byrnes, and Thompson 1989). Meaning and contextualized practice form the foundation for an approach that seeks to develop proficiency.

■ The Traditional Bottom-Up Approach: Skill-Based Approaches

Historically, foreign languages have been taught in the U.S. by means of a "bottom-up" approach: students learn grammar rules and vocabulary and then later practice using them in communication. Rivers (1983) has used the term *skill-getting* to refer to the type of practice that helps students learn grammatical formations; for example, mechanical drills, such as substitution or transformation drills, focus students' attention on correct forms without requiring them to attend to the message itself. In the *skill-using* phase, students use the learned structures in communicative activities designed to focus their attention on meaningful interaction. Littlewood (1980) has suggested that classroom practice activities be sequenced so that meaning increasingly receives more focus. In his model, activities progress through the following stages: (1) primary focus on form; (2) focus on form, plus meaning; (3) focus on meaning, plus form; and (4) primary focus on meaning (cf. Omaggio, 1986, p. 95). The basic dichotomy between mechanical and communicative practice has remained relatively intact in language textbooks since the eras of both the Audiolingual and the Cognitive methods. However, the dichotomy's usefulness for the language learner has not gone unquestioned, as researchers continue to pose questions such as (1) How can we best lead students through the skill-getting phase (Cook 1982)? and (2) How do we bridge the gap between skill-getting and skill-using (Chastain 1987)?

The recent focus on more meaningful, contextualized teaching has prompted some changes in the traditional bottom-up mechanical/communicative format of textbook exercises. In his review of textbook exercise formats, Walz found that current textbooks are "contextualizing" mechanical or skill-getting exercises in a wide variety of ways such as by (1) connecting exercise sentences with the same situation or theme; (2) providing a context for the exercise in the form of information concerning people, activities, or descriptions; and (3) combining cultural aspects with language practice within the exercise (1989, p. 161). Walz also points out that textbook authors seem to have different ideas of what "contextualization" of an exercise means: "Contextualization, especially with respect to mechanical drills, does not seem to be the same as creating a context, which is the topic and situation of a communicative act that are necessary for understanding" (1989, p. 162). Indeed many "contextualized" exercises are simply disguised mechanical drills that do not require students to understand meaning in order to complete them. Walz recommends that textbook authors develop exercise contexts that *must* be understood in order to accomplish the task. Further, Walz (1989) suggests that: (1) sentences in mechanical drills be related in meaning and be introduced with a brief title in the directions; (2) contextualized meaningful drills have short directions and force students to make a choice when responding; and (3) most activities be communicative, with the students' experience and opinions forming the context.

■ A Top-Down Approach: Theme- and Task-Based Approaches

Although far from being conclusive, recent studies in the teaching of grammar have pointed to the possible benefits of a "top-down" or "whole language" approach to language instruction, through which students manipulate language to communicate thoughts by using higher level skills before attending to discrete language structures with the use of lower level skills. By means of activities such as negotiation of meaning and joint problem solving with the teacher and classmates, students "participate in a more complex task than the students are capable of producing by themselves" (Adair-Hauck 1992, p. 7). Therefore, meaning and context take the front seat in this "performance before competence" approach, which reflects how first-language learners acquire language (Cazden 1981). You will learn in a later chapter the specific implications of this phenomenon for the teaching of grammar. Anderson (1984) proposes four criteria for judging a whole language approach to language teaching. Language learning should (1) include meaningful, natural language; (2) include whole language, not language fragments; (3) be functional; and (4) be learned in a meaningful context.

How does one implement a top-down or whole language approach? Within the thematic unit being taught, the teacher might present a "text" to the class for the purpose of helping students understand its meaning while discussing it to the extent possible. This "text" can be a story that is told, an authentic taped conversation or short reading, a piece of realia (for example, a postcard, a letter, or an invitation), or any verbal input given by the teacher. For example, in a chapter dealing with travel, students might (1) listen to a public service announcement that gives advice to travelers; (2) read an advertisement on taking a cruise; or (3) listen to a story about a family vacation. If the vocabulary and grammar have been appropriately matched to the theme, then these initial authentic contexts contain examples of structures and words used naturally. For example, in a Spanish version of the contexts given above, appropriate grammatical structures found would include future tense, the prepositions *por* and *para,* and the subjunctive used with adverbial expressions.

As students attend to the initial context, they are given tasks for demonstrating understanding of main ideas and/or particular details, such as selecting the main idea from a list of alternatives, creating a possible title for the text, responding to true-false statements, and finding specific pieces of information. The teacher leads the class in discussion for the purpose of relating new information to previously learned information, for heightening understanding of the text, or, in the case of a story, for recreating the text. While the text may contain new vocabulary and grammatical structures, students cope with the unknown by negotiating meaning with the teacher—that is, by asking questions, requesting clarification, and gleaning meaning from the context itself. Through exploration of the text, students indirectly learn vocabulary and grammar that can later become the focus of more directed and personalized practice. Thus, a unit/chapter plan for integrating skills and culture might feature the following organization:

Level of Instruction: Intermediate high school/college
Context: Travel
Functions: Making travel plans, getting a hotel room, discussing means of transportation

1. Students listen to an authentic conversation between an airline employee and a traveler; students explore main ideas through discussion and true-false questions.

2. Students read an authentic advertisement on taking a cruise; they explore main ideas and offer their opinions.

3. Students listen to the teacher describe in the target language the forms of transportation in several target culture countries and difficulties caused by pollution. Students see pictures and discuss information with the teacher.

4. Students practice new vocabulary, most of which they heard or read in one of the steps above, by means of a Total Physical Response (TPR) activity and interviews with classmates.

5. Students practice grammatical structures that were seeded in the initial contexts. Grammar is practiced in context by means of guided and open-ended activities and self-expression.

6. Students listen to an authentic conversation between a hotel clerk and a guest; they explore main ideas and some details, and use this as a context for discussion and role play.

7. Students read an advertisement dealing with renting a car while vacationing; same activities are done as in #6 above.

8. Synthesis activities are used to bring together all skills and information in the unit/chapter: role plays, original conversations using the theme of travel, written compositions and letters. Students read and explore a longer magazine article dealing with housing options when traveling abroad and listen to and explore a longer segment dealing with an airline advertisement. In exploring these longer segments, students are guided through them by means of various steps, ranging from identifying main ideas to expressing opinions and writing compositions.

The teacher/student interactive relationship described above is an element of what Jones calls "cognitive instruction," through which students process information in meaningful ways, take responsibility for their own learning, and become independent learners (1986, p. 7). According to Jones (1986), this type of instruction can substantially alter the capability of the learner, especially the low-achieving student. As students and teacher work together to understand and explore new contexts through a "scaffolding" process, the teacher shows learners how to use various strategies to solve tasks (Duffy and Roehler 1986). Bruner's (1983) comments concerning first-language development are also applicable to second language acquisition. According to Bruner, "One sets the game, provides a scaffold to assure that the child's ineptitudes can be rescued or rectified by appropriate intervention, and then removes the scaffold part by part as the reciprocal structure can stand on its own" (1983, p. 60). According to Donato (forthcoming), students can also provide scaffolding for each other's linguistic production. As described in Chapter 1, several researchers maintain that this type of social interaction is vital to language acquisition (Vygotsky 1978; Long 1983). A more interactive approach to language teaching also offers numerous opportunities for learners to develop and use a variety of strategies for understanding and creating language.

This approach to the lesson involves top-down processing, because students attend to the whole language when they attempt to construct meaning and deal with the unknown. This approach is the opposite of the bottom-up approach, in which students first learn discrete grammatical structures and vocabulary and then later practice them in contextualized activities. While top-down processing is still a new area of research, preliminary studies point to the likelihood that students of a top-down or whole language approach may be able to acquire language at a higher and more successful rate than in the traditional bottom-up approach (Adair-Hauck 1992). One of the reasons for this may be that a bottom-up approach often allows little time in the unit for contextualized practice, since most of the time is spent in analyzing small segments of language.

Characteristics of the "Text" as Input

As described earlier, a top-down approach utilizes whole language in the form of an initial oral or written text that provides the context or theme of the unit. Oller (1983) maintains that certain kinds of texts are more easily internalized than others. According to Oller's Episode Hypothesis, "text (i.e., discourse in any form) will be easier to reproduce, understand, and recall, to the extent that it is motivated and structured episodically" (1983, p. 12). Episodic organization refers to the motivation (affect) and logical organization of the text. A text that has motivation has an apparent purpose, holds the attention and interest of the listener or reader, introduces a conflict of some sort, and is not dull and boring. A text that is logically sequenced has the characteristics of a good story and connects meaningfully to our experience in the world. Unfortunately, many language textbooks contain poorly motivated and illogically sequenced texts and dialogues that do not reflect real-world language or situations, although they usually contain multiple examples of the grammar being presented!

Read the following example of a dialogue taken from a 1985 beginning-level Spanish textbook. Does it reflect logical organization and motivation? Does it captivate the interest of the reader?

Juana, la estudiosa
TIMOTEO: Los caballos están corriendo. ¿Quieres verlos?
Juana:　　No, gracias. Estoy leyendo. Van a darnos un examen mañana.
TIMOTEO: ¿Sigues asistiendo a la escuela?
JUANA:　　No, hombre. Estoy tomando unos cursos especializados en la ciudad.
TIMOTEO: A ti te gusta estudiar. A mí, no.

[English translation]

Studious Juana
TIMOTEO: The horses are running. Do you want to see them?
JUANA:　　No, thanks. I'm reading. We're going to have an exam tomorrow.
TIMOTEO: Are you still going to school?
JUANA:　　No way! I'm taking some specialized courses in the city.
TIMOTEO: You like to study. I don't.

Compare the dialogue above to the following conversation that students hear on tape. The conversation comes from a 1991 intermediate-level Spanish textbook program (Glisan and Shrum 1991).

Ud. va a escuchar una conversación telefónica entre Teresa y Roberto. Hablan de sus planes para esta noche.

TERESA: ¿Diga?

ROBERTO: Hola, Teresa. Te habla Roberto.

TERESA: Hola, Roberto. ¿Cómo estás?

ROBERTO: Yo, bien. ¿Y tú?

TERESA: Un poco cansada hoy.

ROBERTO: Mira, ¿quieres ir al cine conmigo esta noche?

TERESA: Eh...me encantaría, pero, de verdad que estoy un poquito cansada. Esta mañana tuve un examen.

ROBERTO: Sí. Mira, eh, así que ¿no quieres ir al cine?

TERESA: Bueno, la verdad, la verdad, tengo que reconocer que es que hay una telenovela esta noche...mi telenovela preferida y quiero quedarme a ver la televisión.

ROBERTO: O sea...o sea que eso de la, del cansancio es pura excusa.

Teresa: Mitad, sólo.

ROBERTO: Ajá. A mí no me gusta la televisión. Sobre todo durante la telenovela pasan demasiados comerciales.

TERESA: Pero cuando estás cansado es la mejor manera de relajarte.

ROBERTO: Bueno sí, pero yo prefiero hacer ejercicio o algo así para relajarme.

TERESA: Y además, también hay programas educativos muy interesantes.

ROBERTO: ¿En la televisión?

TERESA: Sí.

ROBERTO: Pero muy de vez en cuando. Entonces, mira, si tú te vas a quedar a ver la televisión, yo creo que voy a llamar a Fausto y Eliana a ver si ellos quieren ir.

TERESA: Me parece una buena idea. Yo...iré otro día.

ROBERTO: O.k. Muy bien. Chau, pues.

TERESA: Gracias por llamarme.

ROBERTO: O.k., chau.

TERESA: Adiós.

[English translation]

TERESA: Hello?

ROBERTO: Hi, Teresa. It's Roberto.

TERESA: Hi, Roberto? How are you?

ROBERTO: I'm fine. And you?

TERESA: A little tired today.

ROBERTO: Hey, do you want to go to the movies with me tonight?

TERESA: Uh...I'd love to, but I'm really a little tired. This morning I had an exam.

ROBERTO: Yes. Look, then, you don't want to go to the movies?

TERESA: Well, the truth is that there's a soap opera on tonight...my favorite soap opera and I want to stay home to watch it.

ROBERTO: Then this thing about being tired is just an excuse.

TERESA: Half, only.

ROBERTO: Aha! I don't like television. Above all during the soap opera there are too many commercials.

TERESA: But when you're tired it's the best way to relax.

ROBERTO: Well yes, but I prefer to exercise or something like that to relax.

TERESA: And in addition, there are also very interesting educational programs on t.v.

ROBERTO: On t.v.?

TERESA: Yes.

ROBERTO: But very seldom. Then, look, if you're going to stay home to watch t.v., I think I'm going to call Fausto and Eliana to see if they want to go.

TERESA: That seems like a good idea to me. I'll...go another day.

ROBERTO: O.k. Very good. Bye, then.

TERESA: Thanks for calling me.

ROBERTO: O.k., bye.

TERESA: So long.

How does the second conversation reflect a typical organization of a real conversation on the phone? Is the conversation motivated? What type of conflict is introduced? Does it leave the listener wondering about anything at the end of the conversation?

In discussing the implications of the Episode Hypothesis for language teaching, Oller states that "...perhaps second language teaching would be more successful if it incorporated principles of good story writing along with the benefits of sound linguistic analysis" (1983, p. 12).

As suggested earlier in the chapter, authentic materials should be used in the introductory "text" presented to students. Villegas Rogers and Medley have defined authentic materials as "... language samples—both oral and written—that reflect a naturalness of form, and an appropriateness of cultural and situational context that would be found in the language as used by native speakers" (1988, p. 468). Through exploring these materials, students have the opportunity to see and hear real language with a purpose. Another convincing reason to use authentic samples is for their richness in cultural content. Because these texts are prepared for native speakers, they reflect the details of everyday life in a culture, as well as its societal values. Galloway and Labarca suggest that "no textbook culture note on the Hispanic family, for example, can replace the study of authentic birth or christening, wedding and death announcements, where, under the observable linguistic conventions, lie the rituals of events, the connotations of rites of passage, the meaning of 'family,' and the dynamic nature of culture" (1990, p. 139). We often have difficulty integrating culture into our teaching because we have stripped language of its authenticity and hence its culture. In Chapter 7, you will learn more about the use of authentic materials for listening and reading.

■ Content-Based Instruction

Another vehicle for contextualizing language teaching is through content-based instruction (CBI), which has been widely implemented in FLES (Foreign Language in the Elementary School) and ESL (English as a Second Language) programs. Leaver and Stryker have defined a content-based instructional approach as one in which "... language proficiency is achieved by shifting the focus of the course from the learning of language per se to the learning of subject matter" (1989, p. 270). They cite four characteristics of CBI:

1. Organization of the curriculum is taken from the subject matter such as social studies, history, business, economics, etc.
2. Core matter should be primarily authentic.
3. Students use the foreign language to learn new information and to evaluate that information.
4. The topics, content matter, and activities should correspond to the cognitive, linguistic, and affective needs of students.

Content-based instruction became the foundation of immersion and foreign language programs for K-12 students as early as the 1960s. Its success in immersion programs in Canada has been widely documented (Lambert 1984). Many post-secondary programs have implemented CBI, particulary in intermediate- and advanced-level courses. Lafayette and Buscaglia (1985) have described a successful project that "pushed down" subject-matter instruction to the second year of college study. French students who completed a fourth-semester French civilization course attained significant gains in listening, speaking, and writing, while their traditional counterparts achieved significant progress in listening and writing only.

Glisan and Fall note that "the content-based instruction found in elementary immersion programs utilizes a key educational principle that advances all learning—increased time on task" (1991, p. 11). They suggest implementing CBI at the high school level by offering content-based electives such as art, physical education, and music, in addition to foreign language classes. Students enjoy success with these courses because they receive concrete, visual, and manipulative practice that aids comprehension (Glisan and Fall 1991). CBI also has been shown to result in enhanced motivation, self-confidence, language proficiency, and cultural literacy (Leaver and Stryker 1989).

TEACH AND REFLECT

In these activities, you will face the challenge of using a textbook whose instructional approach is inconsistent with the principles outlined in the previous section of this chapter. You will also have the opportunity to design a content-based advanced course using the principles described in this chapter.

EPISODE ONE
Contextualizing the Teaching of a Past Tense Grammar Point

You are beginning a new unit/chapter that introduces a past tense in your target language. Unfortunately, your textbook is an outdated one that is organized around grammar points and has little contextual support. Vocabulary is included for leisure-time activities. Your task as you plan is to

1. Find a context in which the past tense can logically be studied. You might build on the theme of the given vocabulary.
2. Identify the linguistic functions: what will students be able to do by the end of the chapter/unit? Address all skills and cultural understanding.
3. Identify what kind of introductory texts can be presented in a top-down fashion. Include a description of a listening segment and a short reading that might be used. Your instructor may ask you to actually design these texts. How do these texts rate according to Oller's (1983) Episode Hypothesis? How would students explore them?
4. What other vocabulary and grammar would you need to present in addition to past tense given the context being practiced? Remember that at least some of the vocabulary and grammar should appear in the texts presented in the chapter.

EPISODE TWO
Developing a Content-based Level Five Foreign Language Class

You are a high school foreign language teacher whose teaching assignment for next year includes a level five class. This is the first time that your program has had enough students for level five, and you want to make the course a valuable experience that will motivate other students to take it in the future. You are thinking about designing a content-based course instead of a skills-based one. What are some possibilities for incorporating content at this level in the high school curriculum? Write a two-paragraph course description that incorporates content. Include the kinds of activities students would do as well as expected outcomes. Your instructor may ask you to work with one or two classmates on this assignment.

DISCUSS AND REFLECT

In these case studies, you will see how teachers view various forms of contextualized exercises and how an ESL teacher helps her learners learn language for use in the contexts in which they live and work.

CASE STUDY 1
A Look at Contextualized Exercises in Textbooks

The Livingston Community School District adopts new textbooks every seven years. This year, textbooks will be ordered for the French program. Two of the five French teachers were given the task of examining new textbook series for French I–IV and selecting the best three to be presented to the entire French faculty. Mr. Wallace will begin his third year of teaching next year. He was given this task because his students and their parents continue to praise his teaching. Mrs. Moulin has been teaching French I and II for 22 years at one of the district's middle schools. She has kept abreast of developments in pedagogy over the years and is considered a good teacher by students and fellow teachers.

In their initial meeting about textbook selection, the two teachers agree that the textbook they choose should have the following characteristics:

- present vocabulary in context
- contain concise grammatical explanations
- contain authentic reading and listening segments
- use many illustrations and photos
- present grammar practice in contextualized exercises
- feature grammatical structures necessary for carrying out linguistic functions in context

However, as they examine each first-year textbook, Mr. Wallace and Mrs. Moulin soon discover that there is a wide variety in the types of "contextualized" practice exercises presented in today's textbooks. In order to expedite their textbook selection task, they decided to identify the different types of exercises they find and examine the manner in which they are contextualized. They find that their top three texts contain three different contextualized exercise types that offer students the opportunity to practice the linguistic function of "making comparisons." The exercises appear below, along with the title of the chapter in which they are presented.

FIGURE 1 Sample Textbook Exercises

Chapitre 16: Achetons des fruits et des légumes!

F. Make comparisons, using the expressions **plus de**, **moins de**, and **autant de**.

Nelly: 3 cousins	Bénédicte: 6 cousins	Georgette: 5 cousins
Étienne: 12 cousins	Liliane: 6 cousins	Hervé: 9 cousins

MODÈLE: Comparez Étienne et Liliane.
  Étienne a plus de cousins que Liliane.

1. Comparez Nelly et Bénédicte.	4. Comparez Bénédicte et Étienne.
2. Comparez Georgette et Nelly.	5. Comparez Hervé et Georgette.
3. Comparez Liliane et Bénédicte.	6. Comparez Hervé et Étienne.

Source: Bragger and Rice 1989.

[English translation]
Chapter 16: Let's buy some fruit and vegetables!

F. Make comparisons, using the expressions **more than**, **less than,** and **as much of**.

Nelly: 3 cousins	Bénédicte: 6 cousins	Georgette: 5 cousins
Étienne: 12 cousins	Lilliane: 6 cousins	Hervé: 9 cousins

MODEL: Compare Étienne and Liliane.
  Étienne has more cousins than Liliane.

1. Compare Nelly and Bénédicte.	4. Compare Bénédicte and Étienne.
2. Compare Georgette and Nelly.	5. Compare Hervé and Georgette.
3. Compare Liliane and Bénédicte.	6. Compare Hervé and Étienne.

FIGURE 1 Sample Textbook Exercises *(continued)*

Chapitre 3: La vie des jeunes

EXERCICE 16. Le mode de vie de la famille Dumont nous permet de comparer les façons de vivre aux Etats-Unis et en France. Utilisez les éléments indiqués pour formuler des phrases comparatives.

1. un appartement français / être / grand / un appartement américain
2. un repas chez McDonald's / être / long / un repas français
3. les devoirs français / être / difficile / les devoirs américains
4. le week-end en France / être / long / le week-end américain
5. les examens américains / être / difficile / les examens français
6. les disques en France / être / cher / les disques américains
7. un vélo / être / rapide / une moto
8. les voitures américaines / être / gros / les voitures françaises

Source: St. Onge, St. Onge, Kulick and King 1991.

[English translation]

Chapter 3: Young lifestyles

EXERCISE 16. The lifestyle of the Dumont family allows us to compare the way of life in the United States and France. Use the following structure to formulate comparative phrases.

1. a french apartment / is / large / an american apartment
2. a french meal at McDonald's / is / long / a french meal
3. french homework / is / difficult / american homework
4. the weekend in France / is / long / the weekend in America
5. american exams / are / difficult / french exams
6. record albums in France / are / expensive / record albums in America
7. a bicycle / is / fast / a motorbike
8. American automobiles / are / big / French automobiles

Chapitre 7: La famille

EXERCICE 5. ***Plus ou moins.*** *(More or less.)* Compose sentences to compare the following items. Use the list of adjectives provided or your imagination.

âgé	beau	indépendant
amusant	introverti	individualiste
cultivé	conformiste	idéaliste
sportif	sympathique	réservé
rapide	dynamique	équilibré
ouvert	intelligent	sensible
vieux	attirant	sérieux
mignon	bon	???

1. mon père/ma mère
2. ma voiture/la voiture de mon copain
3. mon groupe préféré/les Rolling Stones
4. un film comique/un film d'épouvante
5. mon(ma) camarade de chambre/mon (ma) meilleur(e) ami(e)
6. un restaurant français/un restaurant américain
7. un voyage en avion/un voyage par le train
8. la génération de mes parents/ma génération

Source: St. Onge and Terry 1986.

FIGURE 1 Sample Textbook Exercises *(continued)*

[English translation]
Chapter 7: The Family

EXERCISE 5. *More or less.* Compose sentences to compare the following items. Use the list of adjectives provided or your imagination.

age	beautiful	independent
funny	introverted	individualist
cultured	conformist	idealist
competitive	sympathetic	reserved
fast	dynamic	stable
open	intelligent	sensible
old	attractive	serious
sweet	good	???

1. my father / my mother
2. my car / my friends car
3. my favorite group / the Rolling Stones
4. a film comedy / a horror movie
5. my roommate / my best friend
6. a french restaurant / an american restaurant
7. a plane ride / a train trip
8. my parents' generation / my generation

Ask yourself these questions:

1. What comments might Mr. Wallace and Mrs. Moulin make as they discuss whether or not the exercises are "contextualized?"
2. Imagine that a textbook presents a sequence of practice exercises dealing with the function of "making comparisons," in which the tasks are ordered from mechanical practice initially to progressively more communicative language use, as in Littlewood's (1980) model. Where would each of these three exercises fit best according to Littlewood's sequencing of activities presented on page 25 of this chapter? Explain your rationale.
3. How does the use of "contextualization" in each exercise address the suggestions offered by Walz (1989), as described earlier in this chapter?

To prepare the case:

■ Read Walz (1990) for an in depth review of contextualized language practice in foreign language textbooks.

■ Find a textbook written in the 1960s, one written in the early 1980s, and one written in the 1990s. Compare the three on these points:
   • meaningful contexts for presentation of language
   • sequencing of practice exercise in terms of student tasks
   • strategies to help students interact with and use the language presented

  Describe the differences and similarities you find. Trace the changes in our understanding of how people learn languages, and show how these changes are reflected in the three textbooks you have examined.

Select two current foreign language textbooks in the language you teach. Identify one linguistic function—such as asking questions, making comparisons, or describing in the past—that is presented and practiced in each text. Analyze the presentation and practice in terms of contextualization.

Now write a brief description of your own views concerning contextualization of language practice. How will your philosophy guide your selection of new textbooks?

_____

_____

_____

_____

_____

_____

Review the three exercises that present practice of the function "making comparisons." How might this function be taught in a top-down fashion in your target language? Use the suggestions provided earlier in this chapter and your own ideas to develop a plan.

_____

_____

_____

_____

_____

_____

_____

_____

CASE STUDY 2
Developing a Top-down ESL Lesson

Ms. Combes teaches an advanced class of English as a Second Language for the English Language Institute in a northeastern state. Learners in her class speak Portuguese and Arabic. For the most part, they earn their living from commercial fishing, from working in restaurants, or from helping to develop computer software.

When the class began, the students told Ms. Combes that their biggest problem was listening to and understanding English as it was spoken to them by local native speakers and in the media. Ms. Combes decided to use taped segments from radio and television and recorded conversations of people in the community to help her students develop the necessary skills for listening in context.[1]

As Ms. Combes planned the unit that presented the linguistic function/context of "ordering a meal," she decided to use a top-down approach and begin with an authentic conversation. She obtained permission from a restaurant owner to record the conversational exchanges between two college students having dinner and their waiter. A transcription of the taped segment appears below. Ms. Combes now needs to plan how she will use the conversation as a basis for developing a lesson.

[Transcription of the taped conversation at the restaurant]

WAITER: Good evening, and welcome to the Red Snapper Restaurant. May I bring you anything to drink?

CLAUDIA: Sure. Do you have any diet sodas?

WAITER: Yes, Diet Coke and Slice.

CLAUDIA: Diet Coke please.

HEATHER: I'll just have some water. Claudia, are you sure you don't want water instead? They say the Nutra Sweet in diet sodas is really bad for you.

CLAUDIA: No, I hate drinking a lot of water. Besides, I don't drink that much pop.

WAITER: I'll be right back with your drinks. Here are the menus.

CLAUDIA: Gee, I hope we can find some low-cal entrees on the menu. We've been exercising like crazy to get into shape! These restaurants use so much fat in their cooking.

HEATHER: Oh, look, they do have a section on the menu called "On the lighter side." These salads only have 400 calories.

WAITER: Here's your water ... and here's your Diet Coke. Let me tell you about our specials for today. Our catch of the day is the golden trout, served with a butter sauce. The second special is fresh lobster, served with rice.

CLAUDIA: No, no, we don't want anything too fattening. We'd like something low in fat but high in fiber ... like these salads. I think I'll have the shrimp salad, but could you put some lemon juice on it instead of salad dressing?

WAITER: Hmm ... lemon juice ... I suppose so.

HEATHER: I'd like the Caesar's salad with the vinaigrette dressing, but on the side please.

WAITER: Of course ...

HEATHER: Gee, Claudia, do you think this waiter thinks we're weird since we're being so picky about our food?

---

[1] Thanks to Mrs. Dee Messinger for the inspiration for this case.

CLAUDIA: Don't worry about it! Maybe he's just having a bad evening.
A few minutes later ...
WAITER: Here you are, ladies ... your salads. I don't suppose you'd like bread.
HEATHER: Maybe, if you have light butter.
WAITER: I don't think we do. Do you two always watch everything you eat? I think you can afford to splurge every once in a while!
CLAUDIA: We do, but we're trying to lose a few pounds, so we're being extra careful.
WAITER: I'll check on the butter ...
CLAUDIA: Heather, look! Isn't that guy who just came in from our health club? Do you think he'll remember us?
HEATHER: Maybe ... Oh, great ... Look ... He's with our aerobics instructor.
CLAUDIA: It figures, doesn't it?

Ask yourself these questions:

1. What types of background knowledge might students need to understand the conversation?
2. What type of pre-listening work might be done in order to prepare students for the listening task?
3. What kinds of vocabulary and common grammatical structures are found in the conversation? Which words and structures might be most important in this context?
4. What types of cultural information would students learn from this conversation?
5. How might comprehension be checked?
6. How might students be engaged in speaking and writing as a follow-up to listening?
7. What types of reading texts might Ms. Combes select as the unit is continued?
8. What types of synthesis activities might be used in order to integrate all skills and information?
9. How does this taped conversation in the restaurant rate according to Oller's (1983) Episode Hypothesis?

To prepare the case:

- Read the article by Enright (1986) about using contexts.
- Read pages 196-204 in Richard-Amato (1988) dealing with integrating the skills in teaching.
- Read Chapter 6 in Scarcella and Oxford (1992) on integrating language skills.
- Read Chapter 1 in Oller (1983) about the Episode Hypothesis.
- Find a first-year textbook that presents lessons with an initial listening or reading segment and examine the manner in which grammar and vocabulary are taught.

Write a brief introduction for Ms. Combes' restaurant conversation in which you set the scene so that students will understand the context in which the conversation takes place.

_____

_____

_____

_____

_____

_____

_____

_____

Now select a grammar point from a textbook for beginning, intermediate, or advanced learners of the foreign language you teach. Describe how the grammar is contextualized in terms of functions, contexts, and practice activities.

_____

_____

_____

_____

_____

_____

_____

_____

_____

Offer your suggestions for how you might contextualize this particular grammar point—for example, by means of an initial taped segment, other functions and/or contexts, other types of practice activities, etc.

_____

_____

_____

_____

_____

_____

_____

_____

_____

REFERENCES

Adair-Hauck, B. *Instructional Mediation: Restructuring Foreign Language Explanations*. Unpublished manuscript, 1992.

Anderson, G. S. *A Whole Language Approach to Reading*. Lanham, MD: University Press of America, 1984.

Bialystok, E. "Inferencing: Testing the 'Hypothesis Testing' Hypothesis." Eds. H. W. Seliger and M. H. Long. *Classroom Oriented Research in Second Language Acquisition*. Rowley, MA: Newbury, 1983: 104–123.

Bragger, J., and D. Rice. *On y va*. Boston, MA: Heinle and Heinle, 1989.

Bruner, J. *Child's Talk: Learning to Use Language*. New York: Norton, 1983.

Buck, K., H. Byrnes, and I. Thompson. *The ACTFL Oral Proficiency Interview Tester Training Manual*. Hastings-on-Hudson, NY: ACTFL, 1989.

Cazden, C. B. "Performance Before Competence: Assistance to Child Discourse in the Zone of Proximal Development." *Quarterly Newsletter of the Laboratory of Comparative Human Cognition* 3 (1981): 5–8.

Chastain, K. "Examining the Role of Grammar Explanation, Drills, and Exercises in the Development of Communication Skills." *Hispania* 70 (1987): 160–166.

Cook, V. "Structure Drills and the Language Learner." *Canadian Modern Language Review* 38 (1982): 321–329.

Donato, R. "Collective Scaffolding in Second Language Learning." Eds. J. P. Lantolf and G. Appel. *Vygotskian Approaches to Second Language Acquisition*. Norwood, NJ: Ablex, 1993: forthcoming.

Duffy, G. G., and L. R. Roehler. "The Subtleties of Instructional Mediation." *Educational Leadership* 43 (1986): 23–27.

Enright, D. S. "Use Everything You Have To Teach English: Providing Useful Input to Young Language Learners." Eds. P. and D. S. Enright. *Children and ESL: Integrating Perspectives*. Washington, DC: Teachers of English to Speakers of Other Languages, 1986: 115–162.

Galloway, V., and A. Labarca. "From Student to Learner: Style, Process, and Strategy." Ed. D. W. Birckbichler. *New Perspectives and New Directions in Foreign Language Education*. Lincolnwood, IL: National Textbook Company, 1990: 111–158.

Glisan, E. W. "A Plan for Teaching Listening Comprehension: Adaptation of an Instructional Reading Model." *Foreign Language Annals* 21 (1988): 9–16.

Glisan, E. W., and T. F. Fall. "Adapting an Elementary Immersion Approach to Secondary and Postsecondary Language Teaching: The Methodological Connection." Ed. J. K. Phillips. *Building Bridges and Making Connections*. Burlington, VT: Northeast Conference on the Teaching of Foreign Languages, 1991: 1–29.

Goodman, K. "Reading: A Psycholinguistic Guessing Game." Eds. L. Harris and C. Smith. *Individualizing Reading Instruction: A Reader*. New York: Holt, Rinehart, and Winston, 1972.

Hymes, D. *Foundation of Sociolinguistics*. Philadelphia: University of Pennsylvania, 1974.

Jones, B. F. "Quality and Equality Through Cognitive Instruction." *Educational Leadership* 43 (1986): 4–11.

Kramsch, C. "The Order of Discourse in Language Teaching." Ed. B. Freed. *Foreign Language Acquisition Research and the Classroom*. Lexington, MA: D.C. Heath, 1991: 191–204.

Lafayette, R., and M. Buscaglia. "Students Learn Language Via a Civilization Course—A Comparison of Second Language Classroom Environments." *Studies in Second Language Acquisition* 7 (1985): 323–342.

Lambert, W. "An Overview of Issues in Immersion Education." *Studies on Immersion Education: A Collection for United States Educators*. Sacramento, CA: California State Department of Education, 1984.

Leaver, B. L., and S. B. Stryker. "Content-Based Instruction for Foreign Language Classrooms." *Foreign Language Annals* 22 (1989): 269–275.

Littlewood, W. T. "Form and Meaning in Language Teaching Methodology." *Modern Language Journal* 64 (1980): 441–445.

Minsky, M. "A Framework for Representing Knowledge." Ed. J. Haugeland. *Mind Design*. Cambridge, MA: MIT Press, 1982.

Oller, J., Jr. "Some Working Ideas for Language Teaching." Eds. J. Oller, Jr., and P. A. Richard-Amato. *Methods that Work*. Rowley, MA: Newbury House Publishers, Inc., 1983: 3–19.

Omaggio, A. *Teaching Language in Context*. Boston, MA: Heinle and Heinle, 1986.

Richard-Amato, P. A. *Making It Happen—Interaction In The Second Language Classroom*. New York: Longman, 1988.

Rivers, W. *Communicating Naturally in a Second Language*. Chicago: University of Chicago Press, 1983.

Scarcella, R., and R. Oxford. *The Tapestry of Language Learning*. Boston, MA: Heinle and Heinle, 1992.

Smith, F. *Reading Without Nonsense*. New York: Teachers College Press, 1985.

St. Onge, S., and R. M. Terry. *Vous y êtes!* Boston, MA: Heinle and Heinle, 1986.

St. Onge, S., R. St. Onge, K. Kulick, and D. King. *Intéraction*. Boston, MA: Heinle and Heinle, 1991.

Swaffar, J., K. M. Arens, and H. Byrnes. *Reading for Meaning: An Integrated Approach to Language Learning*. Englewood Cliffs, NJ: Prentice Hall, 1991.

Villegas Rogers, C., and F. W. Medley, Jr. "Language With a Purpose: Using Authentic Materials in the Foreign Language Classroom." *Foreign Language Annals* 21 (1988): 467–478.

Walz, J. "Context and Contextualized Language Practice in Foreign Language Teaching." *Modern Language Journal* 73 (1989): 160–168.

3 Organizing Content and Planning Lessons

In this chapter, you will learn how to use long- and short-range planning to organize the content that you want to teach throughout the year. You will have the opportunity to explore unit and daily lesson plans and design long- and short-range objectives. This work will serve as a basis for your preparation of lessons in subsequent chapters. You will read about and discuss the process that experienced foreign/second language teachers follow as they prepare lesson plans and write objectives. In the case studies, you will see some mismatches: the first between a teacher's and his administrator's view of the purposes for the same class, and the second between student purposes for learning and the structure of a course.

CONCEPTUAL ORIENTATION

Most schools are part of a statewide educational system that establishes mission statements and purposes for education for all students in that state. Such statements are often expressed in the form of guiding principles, such as "*Every child* has the right to the essential learning experiences that form a sound educational foundation, and every child can learn successfully from these experiences" (Virginia Board of Education 1992, p. 2). Such broad statements are transformed into expectations for students' accomplishments in specific skills or areas of study. Generally, such statements are developed by or with the consent of the groups of people who use the educational system. Private schools also comply with a set of goals established by the organization or group of individuals that directs the school.

As a beginning teacher, you will probably receive a written foreign language curriculum guide that outlines the content students are expected to learn by the end of the year and that is consistent with the general purposes described for the entire school system and for the statewide curriculum. Curriculum guides are generally optional, although some states monitor their implementation more than others. Historically, curriculum guides have been usually nothing more than a list of the textbook's table of contents, consisting of a series of grammar points and sometimes including vocabulary themes, such as weather expressions, numbers, kinship terms, etc. This approach to curriculum design reflects the traditional focus on language structure rather than on language use.

■ Design of Objectives: Focus on Learner Outcomes

More recently, curriculum design has given increasing attention to learner outcomes in terms of the competencies and skills students should acquire. Richards (1990) describes three current models for development of program objectives: (1) skills-based objectives; (2) content-based objectives; and (3) proficiency-based objectives.

Skills-Based Objectives. The curriculum planner describes the competencies that represent functional ability in a specific skill but are "independent of specific settings or situations" (Krahnke 1987, p. 49). In listening, for example, we might expect students to have developed the following "microskills" upon completion of a given course:

- understand the gist and main ideas of authentic listening texts in familiar contexts;
- detect the mood of the message and determine to a degree the feelings of the speakers;
- use the context and familiar words in order to understand unfamiliar parts of the message.

The use of skills-based objectives may be most helpful in long-term planning as teachers establish to what degree students can function within each skill area.

Content-Based Objectives. The curriculum planner describes specific functions that students should be able to perform within specific content areas. For example, within the theme or topic "Family," the learner should be able to

easier for students →

- describe immediate family members in terms of their relationships (mother, sister, etc.);
- describe the physical and personality characteristics of members of the immediate family;
- provide biographical information about immediate family members, such as age, residence, occupation;
- describe the activities and interests of family members.

Proficiency-Based Objectives. The curriculum planner might use proficiency criteria in two ways.

First, the ACTFL guidelines can be used to establish a performance level to be attained by the end of a given program. For example, teachers might establish "Intermediate Mid" as the minimal speaking performance level to be attained by the end of a four-year high school sequence of study. In this case, the ACTFL guidelines would be used to develop goal statements that describe Intermediate Mid proficiency. For example, general goal statements can be used to describe what the student should be able to do at this level:

- ask and answer questions related to personal needs and familiar topics;
- participate in short conversations and express basic courtesy;
- successfully handle a number of uncomplicated situations necessary for survival in the target culture.

It is important to note that, while the guidelines can be helpful in establishing performance expectations, they cannot be used verbatim as goal statements since they are written as *assessment* descriptors for testers. The guidelines, particularly at the lower levels, tend to describe in detail negative aspects of performance, or what the speaker cannot do well. For example, in assessing the speech of an Intermediate Mid speaker, the guidelines state that "... speech may continue to be characterized by frequent long pauses, since the smooth incorporation of even basic conversational strategies is often hindered as the speaker struggles to create appropriate language forms" (ACTFL Proficiency Guidelines 1989, p. 2). Although the ACTFL guidelines are not suitable as statements of objectives, they can be used to develop performance outcomes as shown in the goal statements above, which describe targeted learner outcomes in terms of an Intermediate Mid level of proficiency.

Second, teachers might use proficiency principles for both unit and daily planning. Expected learner outcomes can be defined in terms of the *functions* learners can perform, the specific *contexts* in which they can use the language, and the *accuracy* of their language (Buck, Byrnes, and Thompson 1989). Bragger (1985) suggests using these three criteria in a daily syllabus or plan as a way to organize lesson design. For example, here are some objectives outlined for a Spanish lesson:

Function: Expressing likes and dislikes
Context: Leisure-time activities
Accuracy: Use of the verbal expression *me gusta/no me gusta* ("I like/don't like"); use of appropriate vocabulary dealing with sports and leisure-time activities; understandable pronunciation.

In this type of plan, there may be several functions that address proficiency in various skills areas and cultural understanding as well. Allen (1985) has suggested the integration of culture topics appropriate to each context and function under study in the syllabus. For example, the study of the thematic unit "weather" might integrate culture in the following manner:

- Students learn about the weather patterns in various geographical regions where the target language is spoken.
- Students learn about the weather characteristic of different seasons.
- Students compare the weather in one country during a particular season with the weather in another country in the same or different season.
- Students study a written text of a weather report/forecast that corresponds to the conditions indicated on the map of a given country that they used as a point of departure of the lesson; they identify equivalents in the written text for the oral expressions they have learned.

■ Students study written texts of weather reports/forecasts corresponding to the conditions indicated on their maps of a country, representing different print media (newspapers, magazines); they note the differences and attempt to explain them (p. 157).

Appendix A3 is Allen's (1985) sample culture-based syllabus for a beginning-level French course, which identifies a possible sequence of contexts for communication, grammatical structures, and cultural topics that could be integrated well with the language syllabus. The culture topics appear in three categories: (1) those dealing with surface features of the target culture, with primary emphasis on behavior; (2) those pertaining to daily life in the target culture—habits, patterns of living, etc.; and (3) those dealing with a more conceptual level, with attention to political, social, economic, cultural institutions and patterns, and with the challenges currently facing the people of that culture. Each stage of learning in the syllabus features a convergence of theme or topic, grammar, and function. In the beginning stage, isolated facts and concrete topics related to behavior are matched to elementary grammatical structures such as interrogative and negative forms, and linguistic functions such as asking questions. In a later stage, abstract topics are matched to structures such as the subjunctive in French which the learner uses in order to hypothesize and support an opinion. The convergence of these factors serves as a process through which students are able to acquire a set of behaviors, a body of knowledge, and a set of skills that facilitate learning about the target culture and their own cultures as well (Allen 1985).

■ Year-Long or Course-Long Curriculum Planning[1]

At some point in your teaching career, you will be involved in writing curricula for a language program. Since long-term objectives must be valid regardless of which textbook is used, teachers should write a curriculum for any given level without reference to a particular textbook. The text should be adapted to reflect the objectives rather than vice versa.

MacDonald has identified three steps in undertaking course-level planning:

1. Identifying (or reviewing) the central goals and purposes of the program or course you will be teaching.
2. Selecting course content, then organizing and sequencing to make it as coherent and teachable as possible.
3. Determining the amount of time to be spent on the various topics in the sequence. (1991, p. 66).

In the first step, language teachers identify the *broader skills* they want students to acquire in terms of listening, reading, speaking, writing, and cultural under-

---

[1]Cole and Miller (1985) present a detailed description of how they developed a proficiency-oriented curriculum at the secondary level. Their article is extremely helpful to teachers designing or redesigning their curriculum to be more learner-centered.

standing. (Cultural understanding may cover a broad area, including everyday life-styles, the arts of a culture, geography, history, and so on.) Within this framework, a reading skill that a teacher describes might be the ability to identify main ideas in familiar printed material such as advertisements and magazine articles.

As a second step, the teacher selects themes or contexts and *linguistic functions,* together with the grammar and vocabulary that students need to learn in order to attain the end-of-the-year goals. This course content is then organized and sequenced according to the ability level of students and the complexity of the language. Third, teachers decide how much *time* will be spent on each theme or topic. Appendix A4 is an example of an excerpt from a year-level long-range plan.

Unit Planning

In addition to course-level or year-long planning, you will also design the units of instruction to be presented throughout the year. A unit is usually a series of related lessons around a theme or particular context. Some examples include family, shopping and bargaining, and daily routine/school activities. While units may correspond to unit divisions in the textbook, teachers often adapt the text in order to include other material and/or address the needs of learners more effectively.

MacDonald suggests four basic steps in planning units of instruction:

1. Identifying the main purposes of the unit
2. Producing a content outline for the unit
3. Determining types of learning outcomes to be promoted
4. Selecting teaching strategies and activities (1991, p. 76).

In step one, language teachers determine why a particular unit should be taught. For example, the main purpose of the unit on "Vacations and Travel" might be to enable students to make travel arrangements and take a trip to a foreign country.

In step two, language teachers identify the content of the unit in terms of its topics, vocabulary, and grammar. For example, in the unit on "Vacations and Travel," some of the topics might include means of transportation, bus and metro routes, directions for getting around a city, or lodging. The vocabulary would consist of the words and expressions necessary for each topic. The grammar would consist of structures that students need in order to perform the unit tasks; for example, in this unit, future time might be necessary in order to plan a vacation.

In step three, specific learner outcomes are defined for the four skills and cultural understanding. The following is an example of a set of outcomes for the unit on "Vacations and Travel": The student will be able to follow verbal directions around the city (listening); buy an airline ticket (speaking); get from one place to another by following a subway map (reading and culture); fill out an application for a passport (writing); discuss various possibilities for lodging (speaking, listening, culture).

In step four, teachers decide how the content will be organized into chunks for daily lessons and determine which techniques or strategies can best be used to help students learn the material. Subsequent chapters of the *Handbook* will present a variety of teaching techniques, and, through your own experience and innovation, you will continue to add strategies to your repertoire.

The Appendix includes an example of an elementary school unit plan (Appendix A5) and a high school unit plan (Appendix A6), both of which are prepared in somewhat different formats. However, note that both unit plans have a similar organization in that they describe content, performance outcomes, and specific grammar and vocabulary.

■ Daily Lesson Planning

Working from the broader unit plans, language teachers organize the material to be presented in daily lessons. Perhaps the most important aspect of planning a daily lesson is to identify the objective(s) that you want to achieve by the end of the class period. Effective objectives describe what students will be able to do in terms of observable behavior and when using the foreign language. For example, the objective may focus on students' ability to accomplish some linguistic function—to communicate some real information. Objectives use action verbs that represent desired student behavior. Verbs such as *learn* or *understand* are generally too vague for use in objectives. You may find it helpful to refer to Appendix A7 for Bloom's Taxonomy of Thinking Processes, which contains a list of action verbs that can be used in writing objectives. Objectives should also contain an indication of the realistic context in which students will be able to use the target language that they learn. Objectives should not consist of a listing of textbook exercises, although these may be a part of the instructional strategies. Which of the following are appropriate lesson objectives?

1. The student will learn about modes of transportation.
2. The teacher will present ways to tell time.
3. The student will describe his or her family.
4. The student will understand how to form the future tense.
5. The student will identify numbers given in a taped airline announcement.

must be measureable!

As a novice teacher, you will undoubtedly need to design daily lesson plans that are more detailed in order to help guide you through the teaching process. Some school districts use the lesson format proposed by Hunter and Russell (1977). This model, which can be used for both lesson planning and observation, provides the following optional elements of lesson design:

- Anticipatory set: what the teacher does at the beginning of the class to get students' attention and relate previous work to today's lesson.
- Objective and purpose: how the teacher communicates the objective(s) to students.
- Input: how the teacher provides the knowledge and skills needed for today's lesson.
- Modeling: how the teacher shows students what they are to do.
- Checking for understanding: how the teacher monitors students' understanding.
- Guided practice: how the teacher provides opportunities for students to practice using the new knowledge/skills under supervision.
- Independent practice: how the teacher provides opportunities for students to practice using the new knowledge/skills independently (Hunter, 1984).

The Hunter Model describes teacher behavior in each phase. Richard-Amato (1988) adapted the Hunter Model in order to focus more on student participation and input. Her model, as presented below, describes the role of both teacher and students.

FIGURE 1 Lesson Design: Adaptation of the Hunter Model

LESSON PHASE	ROLE OF TEACHER	ROLE OF STUDENTS
I. Perspective (opening)	Asks what students have learned in previous lesson Previews new lesson	Tell what they've learned previously Respond to preview
II. Stimulation	Prepares students for new activity Presents attention grabber such as picture or song	Relate activity to their lives Respond to attention grabber
III. Instruction/ Participation	Presents activity Checks for understanding Encourages involvement	Do activity Show understanding Interact with others
IV. Closure	Asks what students have learned Previews future lessons	Tell what they've learned Give input on future lessons
V. Follow-up	Presents other activities to reinforce same concepts Presents opportunities for interaction	Do new activities Interact with others

Source: Adaptation of Richard-Amato 1988.

You may want to use the Richard-Amato model as you prepare your micro-teaching lessons in subsequent chapters. If you use this format, your written daily lesson plans might be organized as follows:

(handwritten margin note: plan for lesson at: verbs)

(handwritten margin note: 45 min.)

I. Objective(s): Students will be able to ...
II. Materials: text, pictures, audiotapes, realia, etc.
III. Procedures:
   A. Perspective
   B. Stimulation
   C. Instruction/Participation
   D. Closure
   E. Follow-up
IV. Self-Evaluation (to be completed after lesson is taught)

TEACH AND REFLECT

These activities are designed to help you use the information from the previous section of this chapter to formulate goals and lesson plans.

EPISODE ONE
Writing Chapter Objectives

Select a chapter from a textbook for the foreign language you teach, as recommended by your instructor. Assume that this chapter fits into one of your unit plans.

1. Write two objectives for each skill (listening, speaking, reading, and writing) and cultural understanding.
2. Explain how these objectives are a part of your year-long curriculum plan.

EPISODE TWO
Writing daily lesson objectives

Use the same sample chapter that you used in Episode One. Design objectives for the first two daily lessons that you present from this chapter. Remember that your objectives should reflect observable behavior. Brainstorm a list of possible techniques that you might use to achieve these objectives. You might think back to strategies you observed in your class visitations and/or other experiences you have had in foreign language classrooms.

DISCUSS AND REFLECT

The case studies here show you how one teacher communicated daily goals to his students and how another teacher learned how to address her students' goals.

CASE STUDY 1
Two Views of Reality

Mrs. Gardner, the principal of George Washington High School, observed the French I class taught by Mr. Pointreau during first period. It is now second period, Mr. Pointreau's planning period, and he is meeting with Mrs. Gardner to discuss her conclusions:

MRS. G.: That was a very good class, Mr. Pointreau. You have a nice way of managing your class time so that the students are all on task and using French. I noticed that you always write your objective on the board in the upper left-hand corner. Why do you do that?

MR. P.: Well, I thought it was a good way to communicate to the students what they will be doing during the class. It serves as an "advance organizer[2]," a way of organizing instruction so that students know where they're going during the lesson. I just started using it this year to see how it would work.

MRS. G.: Well, yes, that's great. How is it working for you?

MR. P.: Well, at first I wrote too much. I wrote out the whole objective from my lesson plan. Then I shortened it to only the grammar point, but then students couldn't see the relationship between the communicative activities we did in class and the language structures they need to use to communicate. Now I write something like what you saw today: accepting/refusing invitations, *conditionnel*. The students thought it was funny at first, but now they look up at the board when they come in the room to see what we'll be up to during the period.

Ask yourself these questions:

1. What did Mr. Pointreau hope to gain by writing the objective on the board?
2. On what principles of learning did he base his action?
3. Are there other ways he could gain the same results?
4. What problems might result because of this strategy?

What do you think of the following alternatives for focusing student attention on Mr. Pointreau's objective?

1. Have a drawing on a poster or an overhead transparency so that students see it when they come into the classroom. The drawing uses thought bubbles to show two scenes of a boy inviting a girl to go to the movies with him. In one scene she accepts the invitation; in another she refuses.
2. Ask students about the last time anyone invited them to go somewhere. Then ask them when they last invited someone to go somewhere. See how many of the necessary words they can guess.

---

[2]Ausubel recommends the use of *advance organizers,* that is, "appropriately relevant and inclusive introductory materials that are maximally clear and stable … introduced in advance of the learning material itself, used to facilitate establishing a meaningful learning set. … *Organizers are presented at a higher level of abstraction … and inclusiveness than the new materials to be learned.*" Ausubel, (Novak and Hanesian, 1978, pp. 170–171, italics in original.)

3. Tell the students that today they are going to learn how to use the conditional tense.
4. Tell the students that today they are going to learn how to accept and refuse invitations.
5. Start class by checking the homework, then telling students to open their books to the page that shows the conjugation for the conditional tense or the vocabulary for invitations.

To prepare the case:

■ Read Chapter 3 in Freiberg and Driscoll (1992) to find ways to organize instruction and to set objectives.

Now write a description of the considerations that you think are important when writing objectives:

_____

_____

_____

_____

_____

_____

Write three questions you would ask yourself as you think about writing long- and short-range objectives.

_____

_____

_____

_____

_____

_____

_____

Describe two ways your teachers have communicated to you their objectives for daily lessons.

_____

_____

_____

_____

_____

_____

_____

_____

CASE STUDY 2
Finding Students' Purposes for Learning

Ms. Kelly teaches English as a Second Language in a factory on a Native American reservation in the southwestern United States. Her class of eight adult students meets daily for an hour, and then she has another half hour of individual time with each student during the day. The students live and work within an English-speaking environment; Ms. Kelly's task is to teach them to read and write. In September, when she began her job, Ms. Kelly noted that the book that the plant manager had chosen for the students consisted of seven chapters, each 20 pages long. The semester was 15 weeks long, so that meant she and her students would spend two weeks on each chapter, with about five days for testing and cultural activities.

It is now the beginning of October, and Ms. Kelly has been reviewing the progress of her class. They appear to be right on schedule, having "covered" Chapters 1 and 2. The students' grades on her teacher-made tests have been good, and the students appear to have learned what is in the textbook. Ms. Kelly has noticed that their reading is still slow and full of hesitation and mispronunciation, and they don't recognize words from their reading when they see them in other written materials, such as newspaper articles. To make matters worse, the students have been complaining in their half-hour individual time that their reading and writing lessons are boring and that they are not learning anything. In an effort to encourage them and show them how much they really have learned, Ms. Kelly began pointing out their successes to them, but their complaints continued.[3]

_____

[3]Thanks to Susan Franks (1992) for the inspiration for this case.

Ask yourself these questions:

1. Is the course learner-centered? That is, does it address learner needs?
2. What do you think about the way Ms. Kelly matched the course content to the available time?
3. What could be the students' purpose for learning how to read and write English if they can already speak it well enough to live and work? Are there other people who may know what the learners need?
4. What situations would require these adult learners to read and write?

What do you think of the following suggestions for Ms. Kelly?

1. Add worksheets to the students' daily assignments.
2. Interview the students to find out what they want and need to learn to read and write, then build lesson plans around their goals.
3. Find another book that is more interesting to the students.
4. Interview the plant manager to find out more specifically what materials the students need to be able to read and write.

To prepare the case:

- Read Chapter 12 of Richard-Amato (1988), dealing with planning lessons.
- Read Cole and Miller (1985) for information about how to design a learner-centered language curriculum.
- Consult the following sources for information about literacy skills: Hosenfeld (1984) and Freire and Macedo (1987).

Now write a description of Ms. Kelly's problem.

_____

_____

_____

_____

_____

_____

_____

_____

_____

Talk with an experienced foreign language teacher and find out what student needs he or she thinks about when planning lessons.

_____

_____

_____

_____

_____

_____

_____

List three things you would do if you were Ms. Kelly to improve your lesson planning.

_____

_____

_____

_____

_____

_____

_____

_____

REFERENCES

ACTFL Proficiency Guidelines. Yonkers, NY: The American Council on the Teaching of Foreign Languages, 1989.

Allen, W. W. "Toward Cultural Proficiency." Ed. A. Omaggio. *Proficiency, Curriculum, Articulation: The Ties That Bind.* Middlebury, VT: Northeast Conference on the Teaching of Foreign Languages, 1985: 137–166.

Ausubel, D. P., J. D. Novak, and H. Hanesian. *Educational Psychology: A Cognitive View.* New York: Holt, Rinehart and Winston, 1978.

Bragger, J. "The Development of Oral Proficiency." Ed. A. Omaggio. *Proficiency, Curriculum, Articulation: The Ties That Bind.* Middlebury, VT: Northeast Conference on the Teaching of Foreign Languages, 1985.

Buck, K., H. Byrnes, and I. Thompson. *The ACTFL Oral Proficiency Interview Tester Training Manual.* Hastings-on-Hudson, NY: ACTFL, 1989.

Cole, C., and F. Miller. "Developing a Proficiency-Oriented Curriculum at the Secondary Level." *Foreign Language Annals* 18 (1985): 463–468.

Franks, S. *A Whole Language Curriculum for Nonreading, Limited English Proficient Native American Adult Factory Workers.* Blacksburg, VA: Doctoral Dissertation, 1992.

Freiberg, H. J., and A. Driscoll. *Universal Teaching Strategies.* Boston: Allyn and Bacon, 1992.

Freire, P., and D. Macedo. *Literacy: Reading the Word and the World.* South Hadley, MA: Bergin and Garvey, 1987.

Hosenfeld, C. "Case Studies of Ninth Grade Readers." Eds. J. C. Alderson and A. H. Urquhart. *Reading in a Foreign Language.* London: Longman Group, 1984: 231–249.

Hunter, M., "Knowing, Teaching and Supervising." Ed. P. Hosford. *Using What We Know About Teaching.* Alexandria, VA: Association for Supervision and Curriculum Development, 1984: 169–192.

Hunter, M. and D. Russell. "How Can I Plan More Effective Lessons?" *Instructor* 87 (1977): 74–75.

Krahnke, K. *Approaches to Syllabus Design for Foreign Language Teaching.* Englewood Cliffs, NJ: Prentice-Hall, 1987.

MacDonald, R. E. *A Handbook of Basic Skills and Strategies for Beginning Teachers.* White Plains, NY: Longman Group Ltd., 1991.

Richard-Amato, P. A. *Making It Happen—Interaction in the Second Language Classroom.* New York: Longman, 1988.

Richards, J. C. *The Language Teaching Matrix.* New York: Cambridge University Press, 1990.

Virginia Board of Education. *The Virginia Common Core of Learning.* (September 17, 1992 Discussion Draft) Richmond, VA: Virginia Board of Education, 1992.

Broadening the Language Arts Experience for Elementary School Learners

In this chapter, you will explore ways to teach language at the elementary school level. Several types of program models will be used to incorporate language instruction so that it meets various goals. You will design a content-based elementary school lesson and plan several components of a lesson, based on the language-experience approach to reading. You may want to consider how the strategies presented here for teaching language at the elementary school level might be adapted for use at the middle/junior high and high school levels of instruction. In the case studies, you will see how two teachers implemented French in their physical education and first grade classrooms.

CONCEPTUAL ORIENTATION

The past decade has brought about a renewed interest in the teaching of foreign languages to young children. Research in second language acquisition has pointed to the benefits of a longer, sustained period of language study that begins as early as possible (Dulay, Burt, and Krashen 1982). The studies suggest that: (1) learners learn more quickly if exposure to the target language is rich and meaningful; (2) an initial silent phase helps students internalize language, minimize errors, and improve pronunciation; (3) learners who are relaxed and confident learn faster; (4) correction of grammatical errors does not seem to enable students to avoid them; and (5) learners who begin language study before puberty tend to attain a higher level of proficiency than those who begin later (Dulay, Burt, and Krashen 1982). Young children have a high success rate with foreign language because they are able to mimic sounds and intonation patterns well, they are curious about different sounds and codes, and they are not self-conscious (Lipton 1991). Some studies have suggested that the age of ten is also a critical time in the development of attitudes toward people of other cultures (Lambert and Klineberg 1967). Foreign language educators would probably agree that early exposure to language helps students learn to

teacher modeling

listen and communicate, broadens their cultural awareness, and, if integrated within the elementary curriculum, can help students attain greater success with their basic skill areas.

The Elementary School Learner

The Swiss psychologist Jean Piaget described two stages in the development of children ages three to ten:

- preoperational (ages 3-7): children view themselves as the center of the universe; they need to have concrete experiences that build upon their developing intellectual skills;
- concrete operational (ages 7-10): children still need concrete experiences, but they can solve problems more logically; they can think beyond the idea of "self" (Wadsworth 1971).

According to the Canadian educator Kieran Egan (1979), children ages four/five to nine/ten are in the "mythic" stage of development, in which they make sense of the world by responding in terms of their emotions, such as love, hate, fear, joy; and morals, such as good or bad. In order to plan effective learning experiences for children in the mythic stage, Egan suggests experiences that

1. enable students to interpret what they are learning in terms of their emotions and broad moral categories;
2. initially build new information in terms of contrasting qualities: big/little, good/bad;
3. illustrate clear, unambiguous meaning, such as good or evil.

Since children in the mythic stage are open to imagination and make-believe, Egan suggests the use of storytelling as an effective technique for instruction. The use of the technique will be discussed later in the chapter.

Figure 1 illustrates the physical, cognitive, and social characteristics of children ages five through ten.

Program Models

As school districts across the nation are examining ways to "push down" language instruction to the elementary school level, they are faced with the need to choose from several different program models. Selection of a program model may be based on one or more of the following factors: (1) objectives of language instruction; (2) time available for language instruction during the school

FIGURE 1 Developmental Characteristics of Children Ages 5–10

AGE	PHYSICAL	COGNITIVE	SOCIAL
5/6	• large and small motor skills still developing • very active • short attention span • fatigue easily	• need concrete objects as base for experience • still learning bulk of language • limited by "centration" • can classify along one dimension • think in terms of associating words with meanings	• egocentric • uninhibited • friendly • need structure • need praise • see self as physical traits • interact with peers more as friends • enjoy fantasy play
7/8	• refining large and small motor skills • longer attention span • on task longer	• greater ability to reason • interest in how/why relationships • reading and writing • language may be ahead of concepts • can construct a series (small to big) • can classify hierarchically • still need concrete experiences	• more separate sense of self • more reflective • go by rules • stronger friendships
9/10	• skills well developed	• reading and writing well established • can classify along more than one dimension • can think logically • can "conserve" • analyze work critically • still need concrete experiences	• increased autonomy • sensitive to differences • friendships are important and peer-oriented (same sex) • judgmental

Source: Rhodes, Curtain, & Haas 1990.

day; (3) teachers available and qualified to teach foreign language to children. Figure 2 presents the types of language programs and the goals and percent of class time spent in the foreign language per week.

In the language immersion model, either total or partial, designated elementary content areas such as mathematics, science, and geography are taught by means of the foreign language. Curtain and Pesola (1988) cite four primary goals of immersion instruction: (1) functional proficiency in the second language; (2) mastery of subject-content material of the curriculum; (3) cross-cultural understanding; and (4) achievement in English language arts comparable to or surpassing the achievement of students in English-only programs. In immersion teaching, language is not grammatically sequenced, but follows the

FIGURE 2 Elementary School Foreign Language Program Goals

Program Type	Percent of Class Time Spent in FL per Week	Goals
TOTAL IMMERSION Grades K–6 (continuous)	50–100% (Time spent learning *subject matter* taught in FL; language learning *per se* incorporated as necessary throughout curriculum)	To become functionally proficient in the foreign language (to be able to communicate on topics appropriate to age almost as well as native speakers) To master subject content taught in the foreign language To acquire an understanding of and appreciation for other cultures
PARTIAL IMMERSION Grades K–6 (continuous)	approx. 50% (Time spent learning *subject matter* taught in FL; language learning *per se* incorporated as necessary throughout curriculum)	To become functionally proficient in the foreign language (to a lesser extent than is possible in total immersion) To master subject content taught in the foreign language To acquire an understanding of and appreciation for other cultures
CONTENT-ENRICHED FLES Grades K–6 (continuous)	15–50% (Time spent learning language *per se* as well as learning subject matter in the FL)	To acquire proficiency in listening, speaking, reading, and writing the foreign language To master subject content taught in the foreign language To acquire an understanding of and appreciation for other cultures
FLES Grades K–6 (continuous)	5–15% (Time spent learning language *per se*)	To acquire proficiency in listening and speaking (degree of proficiency varies with the program) To acquire an understanding of and appreciation for other cultures To acquire some proficiency in reading and writing (emphasis varies with the program)
FLEX Grades K–6 (not continuous)	approx. 5% (Time spent learning language and about language—sometimes taught mostly in English)	To develop an interest in foreign languages for future language study To learn basic words and phrases in one or more foreign languages To develop careful listening skills To develop cultural awareness

Source: Adapted by Curtain and Pesola (1988) with permission from Nancy Rhodes Center for Applied Linguistics.

sequence of the elementary curriculum and the communicative needs of the students. The errors that are corrected are those that interfere with meaning. Reading instruction is based upon previously mastered oral language.

FLES (Foreign Language in the Elementary School) is often used to refer in general to any type of language program at the elementary school level. However, Figure 2 uses FLES to refer to "pull-out" language programs, in which the language is taught one to five times per week for 20 minutes to an hour. In the more traditional type of FLES program, the focus is on the language and culture rather than on subject-content. The "content-enriched" FLES programs feature some integration of subject-content and foreign language instruction.

FLEX (Foreign Language Exploratory) programs feature short periods of language instruction at the elementary or middle school levels. The goal of these programs is to motivate young students to study a foreign language by introducing them to the language learning process and exploration of a new culture.

■ FLES Programs of the Past and Present

While elementary school language programs are being developed at an increasing rate, the profession is trying to avoid the problems experienced by the FLES programs of the 1960s. The heyday of audiolingualism brought with it a burst of enthusiasm, albeit short-lived, for elementary school language instruction. Unfortunately, despite government funding and public support, the new elementary school programs declined rapidly after 1964. Lipton (1990) cites six primary reasons for the demise of the FLES programs of the 1960s: (1) FLES programs promised too much linguistic fluency in too short a time; (2) FLES programs grew too rapidly, without careful planning; (3) there was little articulation with and support by secondary school teachers; (4) there were few qualified teachers who had both command of the language and knowledge of the elementary school student; (5) there were too many songs, dances and games, and students were unaware of their progress; and (6) foreign language was separated from the rest of the elementary curriculum.

However, there are many indications that today's elementary school language programs will not repeat the mistakes of the past. The revolution in language teaching over the past two decades has affirmed the importance of communicative language teaching. New programs are emphasizing content-based learning that provides an integrated place for language in the elementary school curriculum. Culture and global connections are becoming integral components of the foreign language curriculum. New teacher training programs are enabling elementary school teachers to acquire proficiency in a foreign language and expertise in integrating language instruction into their curricula. (See Appendix A8 for a Teacher Observation Guide.) More effective teaching materials that contextualize language instruction are appearing.

■ Techniques

Elementary school foreign language teaching features the use of a wide variety of techniques designed to actively involve students in language use. Since space permits the description of only a few of the most salient techniques, you may find it helpful to consult one or more of the references listed at the end of this chapter in order to explore other techniques in greater detail.

In Chapter 2, you learned about the general concept of content-based instruction. CBI is, of course, an integral component of immersion instruction. However, content-based lessons can also be designed in FLES or "content-enriched "FLES" programs. These lessons provide the means for contextualizing instruction and for integrating foreign language and elementary subject-content. In planning immersion lessons, the Montgomery County Public Schools (Maryland) have designed two types of objectives according to the linguistic skills needed, subject-content material, and cognitive skills necessary to perform tasks. *Content-obligatory* objectives consist of the vocabulary, grammar, and language functions required for comprehension and mastery of a concept. The elementary school curriculum is used to identify these objectives. *Content-compatible* objectives include the vocabulary, grammar, and language functions that may be integrated logically into the content of a lesson but are not required for understanding or mastery of a concept (Lorenz and Met 1989). In Appendix A9, you will find a partial lesson plan for a Grade 1 mathematics lesson with these two kinds of objectives illustrated.

At the elementary school level, listening is used as the vehicle through which students first begin to acquire language. Many studies have shown the benefits of providing an initial period of instruction in which students listen to input without being forced to respond in the target language (Winitz and Reeds 1973; Postovsky 1974). Through techniques such as the Total Physical Response (TPR) (Asher 1986), students in an acquisition-rich environment demonstrate understanding by responding physically to oral commands, then progress gradually to productive use. In addition to physical responses, in the beginning stages students give yes-no answers, choose the correct word, or manipulate visuals while listening to input. This "comprehension before production" stage allows students to "bind" or mentally associate input with meaning and instills the self-confidence necessary for producing language (Terrell 1986).

In Chapter 3, you learned ways to contextualize language instruction by presenting an initial authentic oral or written segment. At the elementary school level, teachers use children's stories to provide an integrated-skills approach to acquisition. The teacher tells the story a number of times over an extended period of time, while also showing pictures and using gestures and mime to demonstrate meaning. After students hear the story numerous times, they are then involved through TPR and acting out story parts. Story mapping may be used to help students recall and visually organize the various story elements—people, places, actions, and descriptions (Heimlich and Pittelman 1986). A sample story map appears in Appendix A10.

Children's literature from the countries where the target language is spoken serves as an excellent source for story texts and provides another avenue for integrating culture into the program. In addition to helping students experience culture, authentic literature can serve as the foundation for a whole-language curriculum and appeals to children in Egan's (1979) mythic stage of learning, as described earlier. Pesola (1991) suggests the use of both folktales and contemporary children's literature in the elementary school classroom. Folktales, which present cultural information and describe solutions to human challenges, make effective stories since they come from a culture's oral tradition. Contemporary children's literature lets young students identify with the feelings and moral challenges faced by story characters (Pesola 1991).

One of the ways in which the transition is made to reading from hearing a story or attending to other oral input is through the use of the language experience chart approach. This technique uses previously learned oral language as the basis for practicing reading and writing skills. The context is an experience that is shared by the class such as a field trip, story, film, or cultural experience. This technique features the following steps: (1) the teacher provides target language input that describes the shared experience, in a top-down fashion as described in Chapter 2; (2) the teacher checks comprehension through TPR and questions requiring one-word and then longer responses; (3) students retell the story or experience with the teacher's help as the teacher writes their account on large "language experience chart" paper (lined paper on an easel); (4) students copy this version into their notebooks; and (5) this permanent record is used for a variety of reading and writing tasks (Hansen-Krening 1982; Allen 1970; Hall 1970). The language-experience chart approach has been used with success by both first- and second-language learners (Dixon and Nessel 1983). This technique is particularly helpful to poor readers, who benefit from the progression from listening and speaking (while experiencing) to reading and writing.

The elementary school teacher uses a repertoire of techniques for actively involving children in learning. Through cooperative learning, in which students interact with one another in pairs and small groups in order to accomplish a task together, opportunities for using the target language are significantly increased. Research on cooperative learning by Johnson and Johnson (1987) suggests that the benefits of group and pair work include higher retention and achievement, development of interpersonal skills and responsibility, and heightened self-esteem and creativity. Other strategies used to provide hands-on experiences include the use of games, songs, rhymes, finger plays, role plays, and demonstrations (see Curtain and Pesola [1988] for more information).

Another avenue for providing individual or small-group practice is the use of learning centers, which add variety and interest. The learning center is a designated area of the classroom that contains materials and directions for a specific learning task such as a game, listening activity, or reading. It may be a desk or group of desks, bulletin board, or computer center, but it always attracts attention because of its bright colors or attractive use of shapes and pictures (Glisan and Fall 1991). The learning center should be thematically arranged, contain instructions for self-pacing, and allow for a range of student ability and interest levels.

Culture is a key component in a content-based elementary school language program, for here it is integrated with all subjects in the curriculum.

Crawford-Lange and Lange suggest that teachers develop a process for teaching culture that

1. makes the learning of culture a requirement.
2. integrates language learning and culture learning.
3. allows for the identification of a spectrum of proficiency levels.
4. addresses the affective as well as the cognitive domains.
5. considers culture as a changing variable rather than a static entity.
6. provides students with the skill to re-form perceptions of culture.
7. provides students with the ability to interact successfully in novel cultural situations.
8. exemplifies that participants in the culture are the authors of the culture.
9. relates to the native culture.
10. relieves the teacher of the burden of being the cultural authority (1984, p. 146).

As described earlier in this chapter, the use of authentic literature can be an effective way to introduce many elements of cultural heritage in the classroom. The teaching of thematic units such as "Nutrition" or "Holidays" also provides the opportunity to present visual materials that show certain characteristics of the target culture; photographs, magazine pictures, and realia obtained from the target culture are rich in cultural information. Pesola suggests the following activities for integrating culture within the elementary school content areas:

- *Social Studies:* create banners or other items for display reflecting symbols used to represent the target city; celebrate a holiday important in the target city, preferably one that is not celebrated locally, or at least not celebrated in the same way.
- *Mathematics and Science:* Apply the concepts of shapes and symmetry to the folk arts and other visual arts from the target culture; use catalogs from the target culture for problem-solving mathematics activities involving budgeting and shopping.
- *Art and Music:* Replicate authentic crafts from the target culture in classroom art activities; incorporate typical rhythms from the target culture in the development of chants and rhymes reinforcing new vocabulary and concepts (1991, pp. 341–343).

See Pesola (1991) for a wealth of other ideas on ways to integrate culture with these content areas.

Just as acquiring a language means more than knowing about its linguistic system, understanding another culture involves more than learning facts about it. Rosenbusch (1992) suggests the development of "global units" to help elementary school students develop a global perspective and deeper awareness of key issues in the target culture. For example, she describes a global unit dealing with "Housing," in which students compare housing in the native and target cultures through activities such as viewing and discussing slide presentations and making drawings, graphs, and housing models to illustrate similarities and differences. Students can gain a deeper awareness of the target culture by means of experiences in which they role play authentic situations or participate in "fantasy experiences" (Curtain and Pesola 1988). For example, Curtain and Pesola (1988) describe an airplane fantasy experience in which children pretend that they are taking a trip, acting out each phase from checking in baggage to finding their seats to landing. A truly integrated elementary school program carefully connects language and culture and provides many opportunities for students to learn about the culture through contextualized instruction and meaningful interaction.

TEACH AND REFLECT

At some point in your career, you may be called upon to work with young children. In this chapter, you have explored a variety of ideas for how to teach languages to elementary school learners. Many of the techniques for teaching languages to young children may also be adapted for use with adolescent and adult learners. The following activities will help you design a content-based elementary school lesson and a language experience lesson for storytelling.

> **EPISODE ONE**
> **Designing a Content-based Elementary School Lesson**
>
> Design a content-based lesson that addresses one of the following learner outcomes:
>
> | | |
> |---|---|
> | *Grade 1 Mathematics* | The student will identify halves, thirds, and fourths of a region or set. |
> | *Grade 1 Science* | The student will classify objects by size, shape, and color. |
> | *Grade 1 Science* | The student will make accurate observations using the senses. |
> | *Grade 4 Mathematics* | The student will measure length (km and mm). |
> | *Grade 4 Science* | The student will observe and label the parts of green plants. |
> | *Grade 4 Science* | The student will identify and describe some features and characteristics of the planets of our solar system. |
>
> (Objectives are from *Milwaukee Public Schools Outcome-Based Education,* cited by Curtain and Pesola 1988.)

Assume that your lesson would be 15–20 minutes in length and that this is the first day on this topic. Use the lesson plan format presented in Chapter 3, being sure to include both content-obligatory and content-compatible objectives, as described earlier in this chapter and as exemplified in Appendix A9. Plan your presentation and two or three student activities. As you plan the lesson, keep in mind the following ideas:

1. Design a lesson that is appropriate, given the developmental characteristics of your students (consult Figure 2 in this chapter).
2. Present *oral* language, not written.

3. Involve students in *hands-on* activities from the start of the lesson.
4. *Do not lecture* or overwhelm students with information they don't understand. They learn by being involved actively.
5. *Use the target language.* Make yourself understood by using realia, gestures, and mime.
6. *Check comprehension* often through TPR or short-response questions.

Your instructor may ask you to present a 5–8 minute segment of this lesson to the class.

> **EPISODE TWO**
> **Developing a Storytelling Lesson**
>
> Design a 15/20-minute storytelling lesson, in which you present a story that is familiar to the children from their native culture (such as *Goldilocks and the Three Bears*) or a simple, authentic children's story or folktale. Prepare visuals and realia as necessary for depicting meaning. Follow the suggestions given in this chapter for presenting the story orally and incorporating student involvement. Prepare a lesson plan, remembering that this is the first day on the story. Your instructor may ask you to present all or part of your story to the class. Be prepared to discuss how you would use the language experience chart approach to progress to reading after spending much time working with the oral version of the story.

DISCUSS AND REFLECT

In these case studies, you will see how two teachers implemented French in the physical education and academic content of their first grade curriculum.

> **CASE STUDY 1**
> **Combining Physical Education and French**
>
> Amy Guilderson and Georges Arnault have been teaching at the elementary school in Milford City for two years, ever since they began their teaching careers. Amy teaches physical education, and Georges teaches first grade. Georges is of French descent and grew up speaking French at home. Amy studied French in college and completed a semester-long study abroad experience in France prior to graduating from college. Amy enjoys the opportunity to speak French with Georges.
>
> While having lunch together one day, they began talking about teaching their students some French. Georges had been reading some recent journal articles that presented the idea of combining foreign language and content-area instruction. They wondered what would happen if certain elements of physical education classes were taught in French. Excitedly, they launched into their experiment and agreed that Amy would use French to teach some lessons in physical education to the students in Georges' first grade class for a trial period of two weeks.
>
> The students in Georges' first grade class were normally scheduled to meet with Amy for thirty minutes twice a week for a total of one hour per week. On the

other three days of the week, the students normally went to art and music classes during that time period. Amy had planned that, during the two week period, students would begin to develop the motor skills required for dribbling a ball. They would begin to learn how to control large balls by bouncing them in place and then by running after them as they bounced them. She thought that this would be an enjoyable setting in which to begin the use of French.

Here is an excerpt from a physical education book Amy uses frequently to help her outline her lessons. Figure 3 shows the levels of skill development for dribbling, and Figure 4 shows some of the things Amy would already know about how to teach dribbling at the precontrol skill level. Most of Amy's learners are at the precontrol level, although some of them have demonstrated that they can do one or two of the control level tasks.

FIGURE 3 Skill Theme Development Sequence

DRIBBLING

Proficiency Level

Using Harlem Globetrotters' dribbling/passing routines
Playing small-group basketball
Dribbling and throwing at a target
Playing Dribble/Pass Keep Away
Dribbling and passing in game situations
Dribbling and passing with a partner
Playing Dribble Tag
Playing Now You've Got It, Now You Don't
Dribbling against opponents—group situations
Starting and stopping; changing directions quickly while dribbling

Utilization Level

Dribbling against an opponent: one on one
Dribbling around stationary obstacles
Dribbling in different pathways
Dribbling while changing directions
Dribbling and changing speed of travel

Control Level

Dribbling and traveling
Dribbling in different places around the body while stationary
Dribbling with the body in different positions
Dribbling continuously while switching hands
Dribbling at different heights

Precontrol Level

Dribbling with one hand
Striking down (dribbling) continuously with both hands
Striking a ball down and catching it

Source: Graham, Holt-Hale, and Parker 1987.

FIGURE 4 Precontrol Level

At the precontrol level, we give children opportunities to strike a ball down repeatedly without losing the ball from self-space. The children should use their fingers and a flexed wrist action rather than holding the whole hand rigidly. Relatively light balls—eight-inch plastic playground balls—that bounce true (they aren't lopsided) are best for introducing children to dribbling. Be careful when inflating balls: Too much air equals too much bounce for control.

ACTIVITIES LEADING TO SKILL DEVELOPMENT

Striking a Ball Down and Catching It

Bounce the ball down in front of you so it rebounds directly up to you.

- Bounce the ball with two hands.
- ❏ Bounce the ball hard enough so it will rebound slightly above your waist height. Too much force makes the ball bounce over your head; with insufficient force, the ball won't come back up.
- ❏ Place your fingertips directly on top of the ball and push down. A push out will make the ball bounce away from you.

Striking Down (Dribbling) Continuously with Both Hands

Bounce the ball down with both your hands so it rebounds up and then push down again so the bounce continues. This continuous bounce is called a *dribble*.

- ❏ Push the ball with your fingertips, not your flat palm.
- ❏ Stand with your feet shoulder width apart to avoid bouncing the ball on your feet.
- Practice until you can dribble the ball five times without losing control of it.

Dribbling with One Hand

Dribble the ball with one hand, like a basketball player.

- ❏ You can move your feet slightly to avoid dribbling on your toes, but stay close to your self-space position.
- ❏ Stand with your knees bent, leaning *slightly* forward to create clear space for dribbling.
- ❏ Remember to push the ball directly down.
- ❏ Push hard enough on each contact for the rebound to reach waist height.
- Count the number of times you can dribble without losing control: Catch the ball, bounce it on your toes, move it out of your space.
- On the signal, begin dribbling with one hand. Continue dribbling in self-space until the signal to stop is given.
- Dribble the ball with your other hand. Let's review the clues for success:

1. How high should the ball rebound?
2. How do you keep the ball from traveling forward and away from you?
3. How do you avoid dribbling on your toes?

Have children repeat each task with their nondominant hand throughout all levels of skill. The proficient basketball player is equally skilled with each hand.

Source: Graham, Holt-Hale, and Parker 1987.

As one of her first planning tasks, Amy needed to decide what type of language in French she would need to use to teach students how to dribble a ball. First, she made a list of the functions, or communicative tasks, that she and her students would need to perform as they communicated during instruction. Now she is ready to make a corresponding list of the language used to perform those functions. She knows that the physical education tasks her students are learning to perform are concrete, and she can easily demonstrate them while giving instructions in French, counting bounces, asking questions, and commenting about good performance. She will show her list to Georges and ask him to help her make sure that the French is correct and that she is pronouncing it accurately.

Ask yourself these questions:

1. Identify the context in which Amy will teach her students French.
2. How might Amy justify to her students this integration of French? How might she prepare them for the task ahead?
3. How will Amy know whether she should continue the two-week venture with French? What are some possible extensions of her program?

To prepare the case:

■ Interview a first grade physical education teacher to find out what students learn at that level. Compare your findings with those of other students in your class.
■ Read Chapter 10 in Curtain and Pesola (1988), dealing with planning for instruction.

Imagine that you are Amy and that you are developing your list of linguistic functions and corresponding language in French. You have just completed the list of functions that appears below. Now develop the language necessary to perform those functions. Use the target language you teach. You may find it helpful to consult a native-speaker friend or colleague for verification of the language.

Lesson on Dribbling: Linguistic Functions/Specific Language

<u>Language to Be Used by Teacher</u>

Function: giving directions

    Specific language: _____

_____

_____

_____

Function: asking questions

    Specific language: _____

_____

_____

Language to Be Used by Teacher and Students

Function: greeting/leave-taking

    Specific language: _____

_____

_____

Function: counting

    Specific language: _____

_____

_____

Function: requesting clarification

    Specific language: _____

_____

_____

Function: expressing courtesy

    Specific language: _____

_____

_____

What implications for high school teachers of French emerge from this description of teaching French in a physical education context? How will you incorporate the lessons of this case into your teaching?

_____

_____

_____

_____

_____

_____

_____

_____

_____

CASE STUDY 2
Teaching First Grade Content in French

Amy Guilderson and Georges Arnault implemented a two-week trial of teaching physical education through French in one of the Milford City elementary schools, as described in Case Study 1. Inspired by Amy's success, Georges decided to teach some aspect of his elementary school content to his first graders in French. Since he grew up speaking French, he felt he had the language capability to do so. He also knew how to teach young children, having taught in the Milford City elementary schools for two years.

Georges asked Amy for a list of the words his students had learned from her, for he had been hearing his students exchange greetings in French for several days. He also had noticed that, on occasion, when they needed to count something, they counted in French. He was pleased that the students had learned how to use expressions of politeness such as "excuse me" and "it's your turn" in French. They also knew how to ask someone what his or her name was and how to introduce themselves and their friends. Georges selected a portion of the content he would have taught in English over the next few weeks, and decided to teach some of it in French. He thought it might be interesting to incorporate some use of French in the mathematics portion of his class day. One of the upcoming curricular goals that he would be addressing was that students should be able to identify halves, thirds, and fourths of a region or set by the end of the year. He thus wanted to teach the most concrete and visually graphic portions of each day's math lesson in French.

Ask yourself these questions:

1. What are some dos and don'ts Georges should keep in mind as he teaches his students this math content?
2. What types of concrete experiences might work best in teaching halves, thirds, and fourths of a region or set?
3. How might Georges sequence activities involving listening, speaking, reading, and writing over the two-week period?

To prepare the case:

- Talk with an elementary school teacher to find out how this particular math skill is generally taught to first graders.
- Read Chapter 10 of Curtain and Pesola (1988), dealing with planning for instruction.
- Read Met (1991) for ideas about teaching content through language.
- Read Chapter 8 in Lipton (1992), dealing with approaches used in teaching language at the elementary school level.

Imagine that you are Georges and are planning your first lesson to teach this math concept. What is the content-obligatory language students will need to know? What is the content-compatible language you have selected?

Content-obligatory _____

_____

_____

_____

_____

Content-compatible _____

_____

_____

_____

_____

Do you think Georges and Amy are justified in their enthusiasm concerning teaching portions of the first grade curriculum in French? Using what you learned in this chapter, describe the academic and social benefits and disadvantages of their plan. Be sure to discuss the possible reactions learners might have, what the learners' parents will think about the plan, and what school administrators are likely to think about it.

_____

_____

_____

REFERENCES

Allen, R. V. *Language Experience in Reading*. Chicago: Encyclopaedia Britannica Press, 1970.

Asher, J. J. *Learning Another Language Through Actions: The Complete Teachers' Guidebook*. Los Gatos, CA: Sky Oaks Publications, 1986.

Crawford-Lange, L. M., and D. L. Lange. "Doing the Unthinkable in the Second-Language Classroom: A Process for the Integration of Language and Culture." Ed. T. V. Higgs. *Teaching for Proficiency, the Organizing Principle*. Lincolnwood, IL: National Textbook Company, 1984: 139–177.

Curtain, H. A. "Methods in Elementary School Foreign Language Teaching." *Foreign Language Annals* 24 (1991): 323–329.

Curtain, H. A., and C. A. Pesola. *Languages and Children—Making the Match*. Reading, MA: Addison-Wesley, 1988.

Dixon, C., and D. Nessel. *Language Experience Approach to Reading (and Writing): Language Experience Reading for Second Language Learners*. Hayward, CA: Alemany Press, 1983.

Dulay, H., M. Burt, and S. Krashen. *Language Two*. New York: Oxford University Press, 1982.

Egan, K. *Educational Development*. New York: Oxford University Press, 1979.

Glisan, E. W., and T. F. Fall. "Adapting an Immersion Approach to Secondary and Postsecondary Language Teaching: The Methodological Connection." Ed. J. K. Phillips. *Building Bridges and Making Connections*. Burlington, VT: Northeast Conference on the Teaching of Foreign Languages, 1991: 1–29.

Graham, G., S. A. Holt-Hale, and M. Parker. *Children Moving*. Palo Alto, CA: Mayfield Publishing Company, 1987.

Hall, M. A. *Teaching Reading as a Language Experience*. Columbus, OH: Merrill, 1970.

Hansen-Krening, N. *Language Experiences for All Students*. Reading, MA: Addison-Wesley, 1982.

Heimlich, J. E., and S. D. Pittelman. *Semantic Mapping: Classroom Applications*. Newark, DE: International Reading Association, 1986.

Johnson, D., and R. Johnson. *Learning Together and Alone: Cooperation, Competition, and Individualization*. Englewood Cliffs, NJ: Prentice Hall, 1987.

Lambert, W. E., and O. Klineberg. *Children's Views of Foreign People*. New York: Appleton-Century-Crofts, 1967.

Lambert, W. E., and G. R. Tucker. *Bilingual Education of Children: The St. Lambert Experiment.* Rowley, MA: Newbury House, 1972.

Lipton, G. C. "A Look Back ... A Look Ahead." *Hispania* 73 (March 1990): 255–258.

Lipton, G. C. "FLES (K-8) Programs for the Year 2000 ..." *Hispania* 74 (December 1991): 1084–1086.

Lipton, G. C. *Practical Handbook to Elementary Foreign Language Programs.* Lincolnwood, IL: National Textbook Company, 1992.

Lorenz, E. B., and M. Met. *Planning for Instruction in the Immersion Classroom.* Montgomery County Public Schools, MD, 1989.

Met, M. "Learning Language Through Content: Learning Content Through Language." *Foreign Language Annals* 24 (1991): 281–295.

Milwaukee Public Schools Outcome-Based Education, Grades One and Four, for Mathematics, Science, and Social Studies. Milwaukee Public Schools, 1987.

Pesola, C. A. "Culture in the Elementary School Foreign Language Classroom." *Foreign Language Annals* 24 (1991): 331–346.

Pesola, C. A., and H. A. Curtain. "Elementary School Foreign Languages: Obstacles and Opportunities." Ed. H. S. Lepke. *Shaping the Future: Challenges and Opportunities.* Northeast Conference on the Teaching of Foreign Languages, 1989: 41–59.

Postovsky, V. "Effects of Delay in Oral Practice at the Beginning of Second Language Learning. *The Modern Language Journal* 58 (1974): 5–6.

Rhodes, N., H. A. Curtain, and M. Haas. "Child Development and Academic Skills in the Elementary School Foreign Language Classroom." Ed. S. Magnan. *Shifting the Instructional Focus to the Learner.* Northeast Conference on the Teaching of Foreign Languages, 1990: 57–92.

Rosenbusch, M. H. "Is Knowledge of Cultural Diversity Enough? Global Education in the Elementary School Foreign Language Program." *Foreign Language Annals* 25 (1992): 129–136.

Swaffar, J., K. M. Arens, and H. Byrnes. *Reading for Meaning: An Integrated Approach to Language Learning.* Englewood Cliffs, NJ: Prentice Hall, 1991.

Terrell, T. D. "Recent Trends in Research and Practice: Teaching Spanish." *Hispania* 68 (1986): 193–202.

Wadsworth, B. J. *Piaget's Theory of Cognitive Development.* New York: David McKay, 1971.

Winitz, H., and J. Reeds. "Rapid Acquisition of a Foreign Language by the Avoidance of Speaking." *International Review of Applied Linguistics* 11 (1973): 295–317.

5 Integrating Language Study in the Middle School Curriculum

This chapter will explore ways to teach language at the middle school level. You will learn about the cognitive, physical, and social-emotional development of the middle school-aged child and the resulting implications for classroom instruction. Ideas will be presented for conducting language learning experiences within a learner-centered classroom and for integrating language study into the middle school curriculum. You will have the opportunity to design lessons appropriate for the middle school learner. You might want to think about how these techniques can also be used at the high school level of instruction. In the case studies, you will see how two teachers strive to change certain aspects of their teaching in order to address the instructional and affective needs of middle school learners.

CONCEPTUAL ORIENTATION

The teaching of foreign language at both the elementary and secondary levels in the United States has received enthusiastic support at various historical periods. However, prior to the last five years, little attention was paid to the teaching of foreign language to junior high or middle school students. Current emphasis on teaching language at this level is due in part to two factors: (1) a growing change in approach to teaching 11- to 14-year-old learners and (2) an attempt to begin language learning experiences as early as possible so that students benefit from a longer, uninterrupted period of language study.

Early in the twentieth century, the concept of the three-year junior high was adopted. This was to provide (1) attention to the needs of adolescents; (2) exploration of a wide variety of subjects; (3) individualization of teaching; and (4) better articulation between elementary and secondary education (Melton 1984). As junior high schools were developed, however, many of them abandoned this original philosophy and became very similar to senior high schools. In 1920 Briggs stressed the importance of three key concepts—individualization, exploration, and articulation—in teaching the middle-level student. These ideas have become the foundation for middle-level education, which today has taken on various organizational forms, from the traditional 7–8 grade junior high to the 7–8–9 grade intermediate school to the 6–7–8 grade middle school. (See Adair-Hauck [1992] for a description of three recently developed middle school models.)

Despite the evidence that the middle-school learner is different from his or her elementary and secondary counterparts, there is no empirical evidence that the grade-level organization affects learning or achievement (Johnston 1984). What seems to be most important is the quality of the middle-level program in providing opportunities for students to explore not only many subjects, but also many approaches within a subject (Melton 1984). Middle schools of the 1990s provide opportunities for students to explore content through a variety of experiences, such as discussion, discovery, experimentation, and cooperative learning. According to Nerenz, "... good middle-level education allows students to experience old things in new ways and entirely new fields of learning in varied ways" (1990, p. 95).

The Middle-Level Learner

Eichhorn (1966) has termed learners ages 11 to 14 as "transescents." The middle school child is different from the elementary and high school learner because of the many physical, cognitive, and emotional changes that happen to him or her within a short period of time. Middle school learners are a diverse student group. As Mead maintains, they are "... more unlike each other than they have ever been before or ever will be again in the course of their lives" (1965, p. 10). Rapidly occurring physical changes often accompany periods of restlessness and variable attention span (Nerenz 1990). Middle-level learners are aware of their physiological changes and become preoccupied with self-image. Nerenz (1990) has suggested that these feelings often make students sensitive to typical classroom discussions concerning physical descriptions, daily routines with reflexive verbs, vocabulary for parts of the body, comparisons of clothing sizes, body dimensions, and other similar topics that refer to appearance.

Egan (1979) characterizes middle school students as "romantic learners" who enjoy knowledge for its own sake, bringing a great deal of curiosity to the classroom. Middle school learners demonstrate a wide diversity of skills and abilities since, according to Maynard, intellectual development from one learner to the next "... ranges from the pre-operational cognitive level through the concrete level to the formal mature level of abstract thinking" (1986, p. 21). Research by Epstein and Toepfer (1978) indicates that children between the ages of 11 and 13 1/2 experience a progressively slower period of brain growth, which may make them less able to acquire new cognitive skills and handle complex thinking processes. According to research by Piaget (1972) and Elkind (1974), the age of 13 generally begins the stage of formal, abstract mental operations.

The research of Egan (1979), Wiseman, Hunt, and Bedwell (1986), Lipsitz (1980), Andis (1981), and Johnston (1984) has revealed that the middle-level learner views issues as either right or wrong, demonstrates a strong sense of justice and will work conscientiously for an important cause, is fascinated with the extremes of what exists and what is known, is able to memorize and retain massive amounts of detail, strives to define himself or herself as an individual, and gains identity by becoming part of a group. Indeed, if tapped appropriately in the classroom, the cognitive, social, and affective characteristics of middle school learners could serve to enhance their ability to acquire a foreign language.

Teaching Approaches and Techniques for Middle School Instruction

What is the ideal middle school environment? According to Beane (1986), it is one in which the adults are "nice"; that is they know students' names and are interested in them as individuals. The curriculum should be lively, and should contain activities that vitalize ideas through doing, making, creating, building, and dramatizing. Learners should have frequent opportunities to work together in pairs or in small groups. In their summary of the research on characteristics of effective middle school teachers, Johnston and Markle (1979) noted that, among other qualities, these teachers have a positive self-concept; demonstrate warmth; are optimistic, enthusiastic, flexible, and spontaneous; accept students; demonstrate awareness of developmental levels; use a variety of instructional activities and materials; use concrete materials and focused learning strategies; incorporate indirectness in teaching; and incorporate "success-building" behavior in teaching.

In her discussion of the role of foreign language in the middle school curriculum, Adair-Hauck has suggested that a successful language program "... will relate curricular objectives with the *needs* of the middle school learner" (1992, p. 15). The information presented here concerning the middle school learner points to the following curricular implications:

1. The classroom should be *student-centered,* with students encouraged to take risks, negotiate meaning, try new learning strategies, express their ideas, respect different points of view, interact with peers, and feel a sense of accomplishment and success.
2. The curriculum should be a *functionally based* one, rather than grammatically based, so that language is presented in terms of its social, interactive, and communicative use.
3. A functional curriculum lends itself to a *spiral approach* to instruction in which previously taught material is re-entered and new expressions and more complex language are integrated within a familiar framework. Material is recycled by presenting language in new contexts and providing practice in various modalities of learning, such as aural, visual, and kinesthetic. A variety of classroom techniques and multimedia presentations should be used in the middle school language class.

4. To appeal to students' curiosity and fascination with adventure and drama, a top-down approach might be implemented in which *culturally appropriate myths, folktales, science fiction, and adventure stories* are presented (Byrnes 1990).

5. This stage in the students' development might also be an opportune time for *connecting language and content through content-based instruction,* by combining geography, history, social studies, and the arts (Byrnes 1990).

6. *Culture* should be taught through a focus "... not only on *what* people do but perhaps more importantly on *why* they do it that way" (Nerenz 1990, p. 108).

7. Each lesson should feature *a balance between skill-getting, skill-using, and strategy training activities* (Adair-Hauck 1992). (See Oxford's [1990] Strategy Inventory for Language Learning [SILL] through which students can become more self-confident and effective learners.)

In designing daily foreign language lessons, the top-down approach present-ed in Chapter 2 might be adapted for use at this level. A typical class might be structured in the manner presented below; each corresponding stage in Richard-Amato's (1988) model, as presented in Chapter 3, appears in parentheses:

I. **Introduction** (Perspective): a five- to seven-minute warm-up during which previously practiced material is recycled and conversation is begun.

II. **Input** (Stimulation): a ten- to fifteen-minute segment in which the teacher provides target language input as the vehicle for introducing or spiraling linguistic functions, including grammar and vocabulary, or for presenting authentic contexts such as a folktale, adventure story, realia piece, article or poem. Students demonstrate comprehension through discussion, short exercises, or recreating the context.

III. **Interaction** (Instruction/Participation): a ten-minute period in which stu-dents interact with one another in order to gain skills in using the new or spiraled material. Students communicate ideas and perform meaningful tasks in two or three short activities designed to be done in pairs or small groups.

IV. **Integration** (Follow-up): an eight- to ten-minute closing segment that fea-tures one or two synthesis activities for integrating new and old material as well as two or more skills. Synthesis activities might include role plays, games, readings, or projects, all with follow-up writing assignments.

SAMPLE LESSON PLAN
Unit: Family   Day 1: Identifying family members
Objective: The student will be able to identify family members heard within a fairy tale.
Materials: visuals, tape (optional), practice sheets for pair activity
Procedures:

I. *Introduction:* Using their summaries of yesterday's interviews that they had written up for homework, students report to the class one or two things a classmate likes or doesn't like to do in his or her leisure time. The teacher asks other students to share their opinions of the activities mentioned.

II. *Input:* Students hear the first half of a culturally authentic fairy tale or a familiar story, such as "Cinderella," that focuses on a family. This could also be a narrative about a real family. Visuals are used to demonstrate meaning. As students listen for the second time, they try to fill in missing parts, particularly those containing kinship terms, as the teacher pauses momentarily. Students complete a short multiple choice comprehension exercise.

III. *Interaction:* With a partner, students generate a list of family terms they heard in the story. They then interview a classmate about his or her family, using questions such as "How many brothers do you have?" and "Which family members do you live with?" Students ask the teacher for any new words. For homework, students will write three pieces of information they learned from the interview.

IV. *Integration:* Students read a short letter in which a pen pal describes his or her family. As they read it, they fill in missing names from a family tree.

Nerenz (1990) has also suggested a similar four-step lesson design for middle school language instruction that includes a review/preview phase, skill-getting phase, and skill-using phase, along with culminating activities that focus on reading and writing.

You have already seen that an important principle underlying the middle school curriculum is the opportunity to explore a subject from different angles. Foreign language teachers should find this aspect advantageous as they develop or expand the foreign language program. A key feature could be the integration of other subject areas into the language curriculum so that students explore certain aspects of science, geography, social studies, or art from a new angle—by using the foreign language and learning about foreign cultures. Including at least some content-based instruction provides for a smoother transition from an elementary language program and leads effectively into a more advanced-level high school program.

TEACH AND REFLECT

In the first activity, you will build on the sample lesson plan presented in the CONCEPTUAL ORIENTATION section for the first day on a unit dealing with family. In the second activity, you will extend your understanding of storytelling and design a unit with a culturally authentic story suitable for middle school learners.

EPISODE ONE
A Lesson for Day Two on the Family Unit

The chapter presented above is a sample lesson plan for the first day on the unit dealing with family. Design a 40-minute lesson that you might teach on the **second** day working with this same unit. Follow the same four-step procedure outlined earlier in this chapter. Be sure to include your lesson objectives as well as the necessary grammar and vocabulary. Your instructor may ask you to present a part of this lesson, complete with any materials you might use (for example, visuals and tapes).

EPISODE TWO
Unit and Lesson Design Around a Story, Myth, or Folktale

In Chapter 4, you designed a storytelling lesson appropriate for elementary school students. Now select a *culturally authentic* story, myth, or folktale that you will present to a middle school class in your target language. First, design a unit plan built around the story you select; use the unit plan design model presented in Chapter 3. Second, design a lesson plan for the first day on this story. Follow the four-step procedure outlined in this chapter. Be sure to include your objectives for the lesson and prepare visuals and realia to help demonstrate meaning. Your instructor may ask you to present part of your lesson to the class.

DISCUSS AND REFLECT

Viewed in terms of middle school learning situations, the first case study reveals the organization of instruction meant to help with re-entry of material and exchange of meaningful language, and the second study shows how a highly organized and efficient teacher realized the importance of some affective elements of teaching.

CASE STUDY 1
The Slinky® Approach

Mr. Freeman likes to think of the way he re-enters or recycles material for his students as the Slinky approach. One day he brought in a metal Slinky so that his class could visualize what he meant. "The metal wire in the shape of a loosely coiled spring is continuous," he explained, "just like your learning of Spanish. You will continue to build on what you know, and what you see today at the midpoint of this loop of the Slinky, you may see tomorrow at the top of the next loop, and maybe at the bottom of the next loop the day after tomorrow." He pointed to the rings on the Slinky and slid his finger along the loops as he explained further: "For instance, what we do today as new material, you'll practice in class and for homework; then we'll use it again tomorrow in a slightly different way, and combine it with other new material the third day."

For a part of his class on Wednesday, Mr. Freeman used posterboard flashcards of colors to teach his seventh grade students the colors of red, blue, yellow, black, white, orange, brown, and purple. In addition, he used swatches of cloth from his wife's sewing supplies to teach them the words for a variety of fabric designs, such as *striped, flowered,* and *checkered.* On Thursday, Mr. Freeman began his class with a warm-up designed to review the vocabulary his students had been working with. He was very proud of how well they had learned their vocabulary, as they efficiently reproduced the words for each flashcard and fabric design he showed them. This portion of the class was conducted entirely in the target language, with choral drill of the vocabulary words lasting about three or four minutes. Individual responses to color and design cue flashcards lasted about two minutes. During this six-minute instructional episode, each student had the opportunity to speak an average of ten times.

Ask yourself these questions:

1. At what level of language use are Mr. Freeman's students operating in this exercise?
2. Which of these four steps has Mr. Freeman used: Introduction, Input, Interaction, and/or Integration?
3. Nerenz (1990) outlined these steps for reading and writing in middle schools: review/preview, skill-getting, skill-using, and culminating activities. What evidence is there that Mr. Freeman may have applied this sequence to his vocabulary lessons?
4. Did Mr. Freeman use the Slinky approach, according to his own definition of it?

To prepare the case:

■ Ask an experienced teacher how he or she sequences material from one day to the next.
■ Read Nerenz (1990) for further explanation about recommended sequencing patterns.

Mr. Freeman wants to provide more opportunities for his students to interact in Spanish and to negotiate meaning. He is considering the following alternatives for integrating activities. Which offers the most opportunities to interact and share real meaning? Which offers the fewest?

1. Have five sets of flashcards for colors and designs, and have students work in pairs or trios, asking each other "What color is this?" or "What design is this?"
2. Have each student turn to a conversation partner and ask what his or her favorite color is.
3. Have students work in pairs, asking each other what color or design their own clothing is.
4. Show pairs of students how to ask each other if they have at home different items of clothing in the same design or color. Ask for descriptions of those items and others they have at home.

List three questions you could teach your students to ask of each other that would require the exchange of real, meaningful, and pertinent information about colors and designs.

_____

_____

_____

_____

_____

Here are three questions typically asked in this context. For each, give a reason why you would not want your middle school students to use these questions.

What size is your favorite item of clothing? _____

_____

How does it fit you? _____

_____

How do you look in plaid? _____

_____

Imagine that you are Mr. Freeman and you have decided to present this vocabulary in a top-down manner. Where could you obtain authentic language input? Brainstorm a list of sources of listening or reading material on this topic. Keep in mind the age of your learners.

_____

_____

_____

_____

_____

CASE STUDY 2
Orderliness with Affection

Ms. Carson has won several awards for teaching excellence in the Jefferson School District. Her high school students like her clear explanations of rules and the logical step-by-step drills they practice, leading to their written and oral production of French. For years, parents in the district have asked for French classes in Carver Middle School. This year, the school district granted their request and selected Ms. Carson to teach the classes, given her past record of success. In addition to teaching her three classes of French at Washington High School, Ms. Carson drives five miles a day to teach two first-year French classes at Carver Middle School. Since the school district uses a seven-period day, Ms. Carson has five classes, one period for travel, and a planning period.

Ms. Carson is very excited about working with young language learners. In fact, she strongly supported the parents' efforts over the years to persuade the school district to offer the French classes. During the summer, she planned her lessons for the middle school classes very carefully and has taught the first month of class in a very orderly and methodical manner. Each time the students must learn something new, Ms. Carson explains the rule and elaborates on it in great detail. She then has the students practice it by using repetition drills, substitution drills and, finally, writing drills requiring the students to fill in the blanks on practice sheets she prepares for them each night. Then she asks the students to make sentences using the new information they have learned and, finally, to interview each other using the language they have learned. Ms. Carson is a no-nonsense teacher whose classes are structured and filled with on-task activity. Ms. Carson is surprised that, after the first month of class, the students have not settled down and continue to be restless and inattentive. At Carver Middle School's Open House last week, several parents reported to Ms. Carson that the students have told them how orderly their French class is. The parents also reported that the students like Ms. Carson but do not feel that Ms. Carson likes them very much.

Ask yourself these questions:

1. How would you describe Ms. Carson's approach to language teaching?
2. Given what you know about middle school learners, what characteristics of her students might Ms. Carson need to address?
3. What effect do you think Ms. Carson's daily schedule might have on her instruction, if any?

What do you think of the following alternatives for Ms. Carson?

1. Appear before the school board and ask them to abandon the middle school program because the students are not cognitively ready for language learning.
2. Ask one of her third- or fourth-year high school students to team teach with her in the middle school since the addition of one extra person in the role of teacher will enable her to better monitor the students' behavior.
3. Use fewer repetition drills and more small group work and open discussion.
4. Study middle school curriculum and human development in order to understand the needs of middle school learners.

To prepare the case:

- ■ Recall your own school experience and a favorite teacher you had when you were age 11 to 13 1/2. Try to answer these questions:
  - • What did you like best about your teacher?
  - • What were some of the things you did in that teacher's class that you especially liked and especially didn't like?
- ■ Interview a middle school student to find out what he or she likes about the way his or her favorite teachers teach. Ask the same questions you asked yourself.
- ■ On a scale from 1-5, rank the items listed in the chart in Figure 1 from moderately anxious (1) to moderately relaxed (5), given what you know about middle school learners (Young 1990).

FIGURE 1 Ranking of Anxiety Level on Scale of 1 to 5

Moderately Relaxed				Moderately Anxious
5	4	3	2	1

_____	Read orally in class.
_____	Repeat individually after the instructor.
_____	Speak in front of the class.
_____	Read silently in class.
_____	Open discussion based on volunteer participation.
_____	Work in groups of 3 or 4.
_____	Write your work on the board.
_____	Interview each other in pairs.
_____	Present a prepared dialogue in front of the class.
_____	Compete in class games by teams.
_____	Write a composition at home.
_____	Listen to questions and write answers to the questions.
_____	Role play a situation spontaneously in front of the class.
_____	Repeat as a class after the instructor.
_____	Work on projects (i.e., newspapers, filmstrips, photo albums).
_____	Speak individually with the instructor in his/her office.
_____	Interview each other in pairs.
_____	Make an oral presentation or skit in front of the class.
_____	Do exercises in the book.
_____	Work in groups of two and prepare a skit.
_____	Repeat individually after the instructor.

Source: Young 1990.

Now compare your ranking for Figure 1 with Figure 2, which was developed from research with university-level students. Describe the similarities and differences you find in your ranking.

FIGURE 2 Activities Arranged by Anxiety Level by Means

Anxiety Level	Mean		Activity
Moderately Relaxed	4.54	1.	Read silently in class.
	4.38	2.	Repeat as a class after the instructor.
	4.05	3.	Write a composition at home.
Neither Anxious Nor Relaxed	3.94	4.	Do exercises in the book.
	3.90	5.	Work in groups of 3 or 4.
	3.69	6.	Work on projects (i.e., newspapers, film-strips, photo albums).
	3.53	7.	Compete in class games by teams.
	3.53	8.	Repeat individually after the instructor.
	3.51	9.	Open discussion based on volunteer participation.
	3.50	10.	Interview each other in pairs.
	3.30	11.	Work in groups of two and prepare a skit.
	3.26	12.	Read orally in class.
	3.13	13. 14.	Listen to questions and write answers to the questions.
	3.07	15.	Speak individually with the instructor in his or her office.
	3.02	16.	Write a composition in class.
Moderately Anxious	2.83	17.	Write your work on the board.
	2.47	18.	Present a prepared dialog in front of the class.
	2.26	19.	Give an oral presentation or skit in front of the class.
	2.23	20.	Speak in front of the class.
	2.12	21.	Role play a situation spontaneously in front of the class.

Source: Young 1990.

Describe the classroom behavior of a restless student whom you have observed. Postulate some reasons for the student's behavior.

REFERENCES

Adair-Hauck, B. "Foreign Languages in the Middle Schools: A Curricular Challenge." *Pennsylvania Language Forum* 64 (1992): 12–18.

Andis, M. F. "Early Adolescence. Skills Essential to Learning Television Project." (Working paper) Bloomington, IN: Agency for Instructional Television, 1981.

Beane, J. A. "A Human School in the Middle." *Clearing House* 60 (1986): 14–17.

Briggs, J. B. *The Junior High School.* New York: Houghton Mifflin, 1920.

Byrnes, H. "Curriculum Articulation in the Nineties: A Proposal." *Foreign Language Annals* 23 (1990): 281–292.

Egan, K. *Educational Development.* New York: Oxford University Press, 1979.

Eichhorn, D. H. *The Middle School.* New York: Center for Applied Research, 1966.

Elkind, D. *Children and Adolescents: Interpretive Essays on Jean Piaget.* 2nd. ed. London: Oxford University Press, 1974.

Epstein, H. T., and C. F. Toepfer, Jr. "A Neuroscience Basis for Reorganizing Middle School Education." *Educational Leadership* 36 (1978): 656–660.

Johnston, J. H. "A Synthesis of Research Findings on Middle Level Education." Ed. J. H. Lounsbury. *Perspectives: Middle School Education, 1964–1984.* Columbus, OH: Middle School Association, 1984.

Johnston, H. J., and G. Markle. "What Research Says to the Middle Level Practitioner." *National Middle School Association* (May 1979): 16–17.

Lipsitz, J. S. "The Age Group." Ed. M. Johnson. *Toward Adolescence: The Middle School Years.* Seventy-ninth Yearbook of the National Society for the Study of Education, pt. 1. Chicago: University of Chicago Press, 1980: 7–31.

Maynard, G. "The Reality of Diversity at the Middle Level." *Clearing House* 60 (1986): 21–23.

Mead, M. "Early Adolescence in the United States." *Bulletin of the National Association of Secondary School Principals* 49 (1965): 5–10.

Melton, G. E. "The Junior High School: Successes and Failures." Ed. J. H. Lounsbury. *Perspectives: Middle School Education, 1964-1984.* Columbus, OH: Middle School Association, 1984.

Nerenz, A. G. "The Exploratory Years: Foreign Languages in the Middle-Level Curriculum." Ed. S. Magnan. *Shifting the Instructional Focus to the Learner.* Middlebury, VT: Northeast Conference on the Teaching of Foreign Languages, 1990: 93–126.

Oxford, R. *Language Learning Strategies: What Every Teacher Should Know.* New York: Newbury House Publishers, 1990.

Piaget, J. "Intellectual Evolution from Adolescence to Adulthood." *Human Development* 15 (1972): 1–12.

Richard-Amato, P. A. *Making It Happen—Interaction in the Second Language Classroom.* White Plains, NY: Longman, 1988.

Rivers, W. *Interactive Language Teaching.* Cambridge: Cambridge University Press, 1988.

Slinky®. Milton Bradley Co., 1989.

Wiseman, D. G., G. H. Hunt, and L. E. Bedwell. "Teaching for Critical Thinking." Paper presented at the Annual Meeting of the Association of Teacher Educators, Atlanta, GA, 1986.

Young, D. J. "An Investigation of Students' Perspectives on Anxiety and Speaking." *Foreign Language Annals* 23 (1990): 539–553.

CHAPTER

6 Using a Whole Language Approach to Teach Grammar

*(This chapter was written by **Bonnie Adair-Hauck**, University of Pittsburgh; **Richard Donato**, University of Pittsburgh; and **Philomena Cumo**, Carlynton High School, Pittsburgh, Pennsylvania.[1])*

In this chapter, you will explore a whole language approach to the teaching of grammar in the foreign language classroom. A brief overview concerning the changing role of grammar instruction will be presented. You will examine the rationale for the need to present an integrative and whole language approach to grammar instruction. A model of how teachers and learners can co-construct grammar explanations in meaningful ways will be described. Suggestions will also be provided on how to create and design classroom activities that extend or expand particular grammatical structures. You will have an opportunity to examine grammar presentations in textbooks and to develop classroom activities that focus on an integrated and whole language approach to the teaching of grammar. In the case studies, you will see how one teacher attempts to teach reflexive verbs with a whole language approach and how another uses songs as the context for teaching grammar.

CONCEPTUAL ORIENTATION

Many researchers agree that formal classroom instruction of certain grammatical structures—that is, morphological inflections, function words, and syntactic word order—can be beneficial to students (Lightbown and Spada 1990; Herron and Tomasello 1992; Long 1991; Rutherford 1988; and Sharwood Smith 1988). The rationale for teaching grammar is multifaceted. First, students in middle school and high school are already literate and therefore have established expectations concerning language instruction (Celce-Murcia 1991). Grammar instruction can also be beneficial because of the fact that it raises learners' consciousness concerning the differences and similarities of L1 and L2 (Rutherford

---

[1]These individuals were asked to coauthor this chapter since their cutting-edge research in the teaching of grammar supports the *Handbook's* premise of contextualized language instruction.

1988 and Sharwood Smith 1988). In this respect, grammar instruction can be used as a "linguistic map," with reference points or "rules of thumb" to assist students as they explore the "topography" of the new language.

However, we need to remember that grammatical structures by themselves are rather useless. Like road signs, grammatical structures take on meaning only if they are situated in a context and in connected discourse. Furthermore, Krashen (1982) reminds us that grammatical structures will become internalized only if the learners are placed in a situation in which they need to use the structures for communicative purposes. Consequently, an important role of the teacher is to create learning situations in which the students feel a need to exploit the grammar in order to comprehend and communicate in the target language.

■ The Explicit/Implicit Controversy

Although many professionals agree on the benefits of some grammar instruction, *how* to teach grammar has met with little agreement. The controversy has become particularly acute with the advent of the communicative language teaching revolution, which has consistently underscored the importance of stressing meaning over form. For years, our profession has been grappling with polarized views concerning the teaching of grammar within a communicative framework. Some scholars (Higgs and Clifford 1982) advocate an explicit method of grammar instruction, with direct teacher explanations followed by related manipulative exercises. Many of us have probably experienced this method of grammar instruction, since most textbooks tend to present grammar in this fashion. Unfortunately, many of the textbooks' manipulative drills are grounded in shallow and artificial contexts, so these drills become rather meaningless to students (Walz 1989).

Another problem with explicit grammar instruction is that it advocates a direct and overt role on the part of the teacher. Consequently, this practice designates a rather passive role on the part of the students. Interaction for them is supposed to take place *after* the explanation and after plenty of structural manipulation of the grammatical elements. In Rivers' (1983) terms, "skill-getting" should be stressed before "skill-using." See Chapter 2 for a discussion on the differences between skill-getting and skill-using activities.

On the other side of the spectrum, implicit grammar explanation as espoused by Krashen (1985), Terrell (1977), and Dulay and Burt (1973) rejects the need for formal grammar analysis. These researchers argue that students can acquire language naturally if they are provided with suffcent comprehensible input from the teacher. In other words, if students are exposed to a sufficient amount of comprehensible input, they will eventually be able to hypothesize and determine the functions as well as the meanings of the linguistic forms. Theoretically, the learners should be able to do the hypothesizing on their own. (For a more thorough discussion of the implicit/explicit dichotomy, see Donato and Adair-Hauck 1992.)

However, Herron and Tomasello (1992) advise that the inductive method cannot guarantee that the learner will discover the underlying concepts or that the induced concepts will actually be correct. Furthermore, the inductive approach can be frustrating to adolescent or adult learners, many of whom have already become analytical with regard to the rules that govern their native languages. These learners intuitively yearn to speed up the learning process by consciously comparing and contrasting their own native rules to the rules that govern the new target language.

Reformulating Grammar Instruction

Although explicit and implicit teaching are clearly opposites, they share some notable deficiencies. Neither approach acknowledges the critical role of the teacher in negotiating classroom explanations, and neither approach acknowledges the contributions and backgrounds that the learners bring to the instructional setting (Tharp and Gallimore 1988). Moreover, neither approach recognizes the natural learning tendencies that occur between human beings outside the classroom. A Vygotskian approach to instruction (see Chapter 1) indicates that learning is a dynamic, reciprocal, and interactive process.[2] However, our profession has been grappling with two established methods, neither of which recognizes the mutually responsive interactions that are fundamental to learning as it occurs naturally between humans in everyday life (Brown, Collins, and Duguid 1989).

Therefore, we believe it is time for the profession to begin a serious reappraisal regarding the teaching of grammar. In this chapter, we are advocating a whole language and guided participatory approach that contrasts with traditional explicit or implicit teaching.[3] In many ways, this alternative approach may serve as a viable compromise between the explicit/implicit polarized views, as shown in Figure 1.

FIGURE 1 Whole Language and Guided Participation: An Alternative Approach to Grammar Instruction

Implicit Explanations	Guided Participation	Explicit Explanations
Learners analyze the grammar explanation for themselves.	*Teachers and learners* collaborate on and co-construct the grammar explanation.	*Teacher* provides grammar explanation for learners.

[2]All work in this area is to a greater or lesser degree rooted in the research of theorists such as Vygotsky (1978) and Leontiev (1981). For examples of recent research, see Lave (1977); Cole (1985); Newman, Griffin, and Cole (1989); and Rogoff (1990).

[3]The term *guided participation* was first coined by Barbara Rogoff (1990).

For a number of reasons that will be discussed later in this chapter, ==we believe that a whole language and guided participatory approach might hold the key to dramatic improvement in the teaching of grammar.==

Basic Principles of Whole Language Teaching

Before discussing some practical applications of this approach, we should discuss some basic principles of whole language and guided participatory teaching. Many specialists in first language development have been exploring the implications of whole language teaching for the past decade. Likewise, researchers in cognitive psychology have been investigating guided participation in the areas of science, math, and social studies. Unfortunately, foreign language education has been lagging behind these other disciplines. First we will discuss some basic principles of a whole language approach to grammar instruction, and then we will discuss how to use guided and joint problem solving to enhance grammar explanations.

As early as 1976, psycholinguist Ken Goodman stated that "==Language is language only when it is whole==" (quoted in Fountas and Hannigan 1989, p. 134). According to Goodman, the whole is always viewed as being greater than the sum of its parts, and it is the whole that gives meaning to the parts. In terms of grammar instruction, words, phrases, or sentences are not linguistic islands unto themselves; on the contrary, these linguistic elements only gain meaning when they are placed in context, and when used in conjunction with the whole. ==According to Goodman, once students experience the whole, they are then better prepared to deal with the analyses of the parts== (Fountas and Hannigan 1989).[4]

We should acknowledge that Goodman is primarily addressing the needs of first language learners. However, research in first language development has oftentimes acted as a catalyst for theoretical advancement in second language development. For example, concepts such as the importance of comprehensible input, the role of interaction, and the notion of scaffolding in both motherese and foreigner talk are all couched in the theoretical underpinnings of first language development (Ellis 1988; Hatch 1983; Hawkins 1988). Furthermore, many second language specialists are currently emphasizing the importance of content-based instruction, authentic texts for listening and reading comprehension, and the need for connected discourse in grammar instruction (Celce-Muria 1991), all of which emphasize the importance of whole language rather than fragmented speech in second/foreign language classrooms.

Conceptually, then, we need to reappraise our orientation to grammar instruction if we have too often focused on fragmented discourse and artificial

---

[4]Please note that as early as the first quarter of this century, Vygotsky and Piaget, both constructionists, stressed that the whole is always greater than and gives meaning to its parts. However, unlike Piaget, Vygotsky stressed that language and social interaction lead to cognitive development.

exercises. Many language programs stress a bottom-up approach by emphasizing the "bits and pieces" of language (sounds, vocabulary lists, verb drills, etc.). This classroom practice usually results in *non-language* that can be characterized as being unnatural, cognitively undemanding, and dull (Cummins 1984). On the other hand, a whole language approach stresses natural discourse and encourages students to comprehend meaningful and longer samples of discourse from the very beginning of the lesson.

By introducing the lesson with a whole text (for example, a story, poem, song, taped listening selection, or cartoon), the teacher is foreshadowing the grammar explanation through the use of integrated discourse that will highlight the critical grammar structures to be taught. Galloway and Labarca explain that foreshadowing of new language elements is beneficial, for it provides "learners with a 'feel' for what is to come and can help students cast forward a familiarity net by which aspects of language prompt initial recognitions and later, gradually, are pulled into the learner's productive repertoire" (1990, p. 136). In this way, the lesson highlights the functional significance of the grammatical structure before the learners' attention is focused on form. This approach agrees with Ausubel, Novak, and Hanesian's (1968) idea of using advance organizers to assist the students by providing an "anchoring framework" for the new concepts to be learned. Unlike many classroom textbooks, which may offer a group of disconnected sentences or a "contextualized" drill (Walz 1989), a whole language and guided participatory approach invites the learner to use language functionally and purposefully through integrated discourse. This practice is in agreement with Krashen's Input Hypothesis, which stresses the importance of comprehensible input that "contains structures a little beyond our current level of competence" (Krashen 1982, p. 21). As a result, from the very beginning of the lesson the teacher and learners are engaged in authentic use of language through joint problem-solving activities and interactions. By using pictures, mime, and gestures, the teacher scaffolds (see Chapter 2) and guides the learners to eventually comprehend the story or other sample of connected discourse. Once comprehension is achieved, the teacher can then turn the students' attention to various linguistic elements.

Storytelling is particularly adaptable to whole language instruction, since it is natural to tell stories orally, stressing listening comprehension, followed by role plays and then reading and writing activities. Oller (1983) reminds us that the episodic organization represented in stories aids comprehension and retention. Furthermore, using "multiple passes" and recycling the story line through picture displays, TPR activities, or role-playing scenarios deepens comprehension. The framework of the story provides a continuous flow of mental images that help the learner to eventually glean the function and the meaning of the forms. After these initial activities and interactions have helped the learners to understand the meaning of the discourse, the teacher turns the learners' attention to specific language forms or structure. This approach is in agreement with Celce-Murcia's suggestion concerning grammar instruction for ESL learners, when she states that "one of the best times for them [the students] to attend to form is *after* comprehension has been achieved and in conjunction with their production of meaningful discourse" (1985, p. 301, italics added).

■ Whole Language: A Cyclical Approach

Unlike bottom-up processing, which is traditionally linear in nature, grammar instruction using a whole language approach is cyclical, as shown in Figure 2. During the first stage of the cycle, the teacher foreshadows the grammar structure with an appropriate text. At this point, the meaning or comprehension of the text is of prime importance. The second stage is actually an extension of the first stage, since once again the emphasis is on meaning. However, the second stage differs due to an increased level of learner participation. Now the learners have a general idea of the significance of the story; consequently, they can become more participatory through TPR activities, mime, role-playing, etc. All of these activities serve to deepen comprehension for the learners. Once comprehension is achieved and meaning is understood, the teacher moves into the third stage and turns the learners' attention to focus on form, or the various linguistic elements of the grammatical structure(s). After this stage, the teacher

FIGURE 2 A Whole Language Approach to Grammar Instruction: Integrating Meaning, Form, and Function

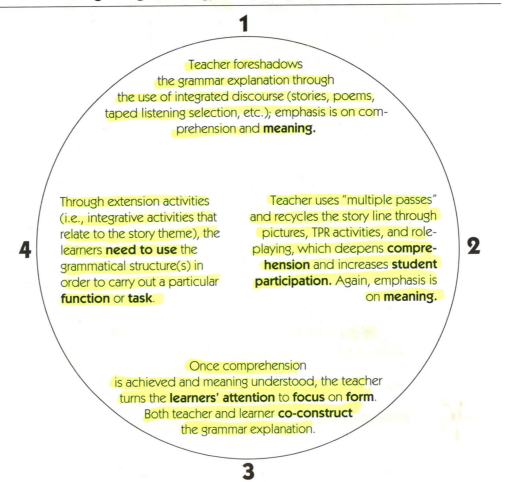

1

Teacher foreshadows the grammar explanation through the use of integrated discourse (stories, poems, taped listening selection, etc.); emphasis is on comprehension and **meaning.**

4

Through extension activities (i.e., integrative activities that relate to the story theme), the learners **need to use** the grammatical structure(s) in order to carry out a particular **function** or **task**.

2

Teacher uses "multiple passes" and recycles the story line through pictures, TPR activities, and role-playing, which deepens **comprehension** and increases **student participation.** Again, emphasis is on **meaning.**

3

Once comprehension is achieved and meaning understood, the teacher turns the **learners' attention** to **focus** on **form**. Both teacher and learner **co-construct** the grammar explanation.

Source: Adair-Hauck and Donato, in preparation.

completes the cycle by encouraging the learners to interact with integrated discourse through expansion activities such as rewriting or recreating similar stories, paired activities, or group activities. (Suggestions on how to design these activities are described on pages 100–101.) Through these extension activities, the learners become more aware of the function of the grammatical structure. That is, they learn that they can carry out a particular task or function by exploiting or using the appropriate grammatical structure. This approach is in agreement with Larsen-Freeman's (1991) suggestion that meaning, form, and function need to be "interacting dimensions" of grammar instruction.

A Model for Integrating Form in a Whole-Language Approach

Focus on form has recently become the topic of intense research and has been shown to be an important design feature of language teaching (Long 1991). This *Handbook's* theory of learning and development has emphasized the importance of creating a zone of proximal development with the learner so that what the learner requires help on today will emerge as independent, automatic performance at a later time. Grammar teaching can also be viewed in this way. It is no less an interactive process between expert and novice than any other aspect of developing communicative ability in learners. Learners need to be guided to reflect on the language they use to create their own meanings.

No language teaching should be driven by grammar instruction alone, nor should grammar instruction be literally interpreted to mean instruction on morphology (e.g., adjective or subject-verb agreement, rules for pluralization, etc.) or meaningless manipulation of forms. When the teacher focuses on form, attention is drawn to the formal properties of the language, which include its sound system, word formation, syntax, discourse markers, and devices for relating one sentence to another, to name a few; our colleagues who teach reading in the elementary schools call this form of instruction "Language Arts." Classes that focus on language form for the purpose of increasing comprehension and meaning have been shown to result in greater language gains than classes where no focus on form is available or where forms are learned as meaningless structures (Lightbown and Spada 1990). Therefore, the issue is not whether a teacher should focus on form; rather, answering the questions of *how* and *when* and in *what context* will ultimately clarify this important design feature of foreign language instruction.

The following is a model for contextualizing interactions with students about the forms of language. The model is called PACE (Donato and Adair-Hauck, in preparation), an acronym for the four steps we have developed for integrating formal instruction in the context of a whole language lesson.

P—PRESENTATION of Meaningful Language

This step represents the "whole" language you are presenting in a thematic way. It can be an interesting story (folktales and legends work well), a TPR lesson, a recorded authentic listening segment, an authentic document, or a demonstration of a real-life, authentic task—playing a sport, making a sandwich, doing a science experiment. Materials from the textbook chapter (narratives, dialogues, stories) may even be used if they are found to be interesting and episodically organized. The Presentation does *not* consist of isolated, disconnected sentences illustrating the target form in question. Rather, it is thematic, contextualized whole language intended to capture student interest and provide opportunities for the teacher to create comprehension through the negotiation of meaning (see Chapter 1). Care should also be taken to ensure that the presentation adequately represents the structure in question and that the structure is appropriate to the learners' developmental level. The structure should appear often enough during the Presentation to be salient to the students without making the language sound unnatural or stilted. Authentic stories, documents, or listening segments can guarantee naturalness and often contain naturally occurring repetitions; think about the story of Goldilocks and the three bears, for example!

The presentation should also be interactive. By scaffolding participation in the activity, teachers can guide students through the new element of the language to be learned. This guided participation may take the form of student repetitions of key phrases cued by the teacher during a storytelling session, student-teacher role reversal in a TPR activity, cloze exercises based on listening segments, or discussions that anticipate the content of a reading. The goal here is to enable students to stretch their language abilities by using the new elements of the target language in meaningful ways through the help and mediation of the teacher. This step may last for either a part of or the entire class session. For example, a storytelling lesson may contain pre-storytelling activities, dramatization, pair-work comprehension checks, or story-retelling exercises. The length of time required depends on the nature of the activity and the amount of negotiation work required to charge the language with meaning.

A—ATTENTION

This step focuses learner attention on some aspect of the language used during the Presentation activity. In this step, the teacher highlights some regularity of the language. This can be achieved in several ways. Teachers can ask questions about patterns found in a written text or about words and phrases repeated in a story. Overhead transparencies of example sentences from the Presentation can be prepared, with important words and phrases circled or underlined. The point to this step is to get learners to focus attention on the target form without needless elaboration or wasted time.

C—CO-CONSTRUCT AN EXPLANATION

Learners and teacher should be co-constructors of grammatical explanation. After learners focus attention on the target form, the teacher assists them in raising their awareness about the target structure. During this step, students are guided to hypothesize, guess, make predictions, or come to generalizations about the target form. Co-constructing an explanation requires teacher questions that are well-chosen, clear, and direct. Questions are powerful tools in the hands of teachers who can adjust their questioning "in flight" to meet the emergent understandings of their students. For example, asking students questions such as "What words do you hear or see repeated in the text, and what could they mean?," "What pattern do you see in this group of words?," and "How do certain words change as their meanings change?" is a way to help students to draw insights from the language they hear and understand. These cognitive "probes" help learners discover regular grammatical patterns, sound systems, word order, unique cultural meanings of words, or language functions. As students hypothesize and generalize about the target form, teachers build upon and extend students' knowledge without overwhelming them with superfluous grammatical detail. Hypothesis testing can also be conducted, with teachers leading learners in trying out their new knowledge by applying their generalizations to new situations. Teachers are also aware that the help they provide is graduated and may range from brief hints about the target form to explicit instruction if needed (Aljaafreh 1992).

It is important to note that, unlike guided induction techniques, which rely primarily on teacher questioning, a co-constructed explanation is not an inquisition. Rather, co-constructed explanations recognize that students may not be able to perceive the formal properties of language on the basis of the teacher's questions alone. What is obvious to an expert language user is often a mystery to the novice. A co-constructed explanation is as participatory for the teacher as it is for the students. That is, teachers need to assess the abilities of their students and assist them by providing as well as eliciting information when necessary. As Tharp and Gallimore (1988) point out, teaching is responsive assistance and cannot be reduced to series of actions to be performed in the same order in every instructional circumstance. By listening closely to learner contributions during this step, teachers can assess how much help is needed to attain the concept. In time, some learners may be able to work in small groups on their own grammar problems and report back to the class about their discoveries (Fotos and Ellis 1991).

E—EXTENSION ACTIVITY

Focus on form is only useful if this knowledge can be pressed into service by the learners in a new way at a later time. In whole language teaching, the teacher never loses sight of the "whole." Therefore, the Extension Activity provides learners with the opportunity to use their new skill in creative and interesting ways while at the same time integrating it into existing knowledge. The Extension Activity should be interesting, be related to the theme of the lesson in some way, and, most importantly, allow for creative self-expression. Extension activities are *not* work sheets on which learners use the target form to fill in blanks of disconnected sentences. Rather, they can be information-gap activities, role-play situations, dramatizations, games, authentic writing projects, paired interviews, class surveys, or simulations of real-life situations. The possibilities are endless, as long as the learners have the chance to try to use the target form in ways that they see are useful and meaningful. The Extension Activity closes the circle of the PACE lesson and puts the "whole" back into whole language teaching.

Key Elements of Whole Language Learning

Figure 3 summarizes the differences between a whole language approach and the traditional approach to the teaching of grammar. The discussion above should have led you to the conclusion that language learning is a thinking process, or from the learner's viewpoint, a guessing game. Teachers need to design cognitively demanding activities that will encourage learners to hypothesize, predict, take risks, make errors, and self-correct (Fountas and Hannigan 1989). By doing so, the learners become active participants in the learning process. All the whole language and guided participatory activities described later in this chapter have a common denominator—they all encourage the learners to be active thinkers and hypothesizers as they collaborate in language learning activities with the teacher or with their peers.

FIGURE 3 Teaching of Grammar

Whole Language/Guided Participation vs.	Traditional Approach
1. Whole language approach uses higher skills and language before moving to procedural skills.	1. Sequencing of tasks from simple to complex.
2. Instructional interaction between Teacher ("expert") and Students ("novices").	2. Little teacher/student interaction; teacher-directed explanation.
3. Richly implicit explanation (guided participation).	3. Explicit explanation of grammar.
4. Encourages performance before competence (approximations encouraged).	4. Student must master each step before going to next step (competence before performance).
5. Students participate in problem-solving process (opportunity for learners' actions to be made meaningful).	5. Students are passive learners who rarely participate in constructing the explanation.
6. Language and especially questions must be suitably tuned to a level at which performance requires assistance.	6. Few questions—mainly rhetorical.
7. Lesson operationalizes functional significance of grammatical structure before mechanical procedures take place.	7. Oftentimes the functional significance of grammatical point does not emerge until end of lesson.

Source: Adair-Hauck and Donato, in preparation.

Whether listening to a storytelling activity, co-constructing a grammar explanation, or collaborating with peers during an extension activity, the learners are actively discovering and hypothesizing about the target language. This approach concurs with Bruner's (1986) advice that students need to be cognitively challenged through the use of discovery methods. Moreover, all the classroom activities described below encourage interaction and the functional use of language by giving the learners opportunities to share information, ask questions, and solve problems collaboratively.

Finally, a distinguishing theme of whole language and a guided participatory approach to grammar instruction is that learning needs to be integrated, contextualized, and meaning-centered (Pearson 1989). In Appendix A11, we have included a sample whole language lesson to teach the past definite in French with *avoir*. The lesson begins with a story, "The Lion and the Mouse," which foreshadows the functional significance of the grammar point. Please note that all the subsequent classroom activities—for example, role-playing, paired activities to retell the story, team activities using graphic organizers—are contextualized and relate to the them of "The Lion and the Mouse." In this way, the unit is contextualized and integrated, which enables the instructional events to flow naturally. As noted earlier, integrated and meaning-centered activities facilitate comprehension and retention on the part of learners. Furthermore, the extension activities encourage learners to integrate meaning, form, and function while experiencing language in context.

It should be mentioned that creating integrated and meaning-centered activities is probably one of the most difficult aspects of whole language teaching, since many textbooks still stress context-reduced practice and fragmented materials. The activities described below will provide you with suggestions on how to incorporate integrated and whole language activities into your classroom.

■ Designing Contextualized Whole Language Activities

As noted above, creating contextualized activities is not an easy task, but it is the only way to implement, encourage, and succeed at whole language teaching. Just as most hard work brings good results, through whole language learning students are able to converse with more confidence, and their listening, reading, and writing skills improve. As they use this foreign language in real communication, it becomes less "foreign" and more a natural, integral part of their experience. If the teacher fills a student's head with grammar rules, the student will think grammar rules. If presented with real-life situations, the student will think real-life situations. The correctness of his or her use of the foreign language comes through proper varieties of practice examples and the teacher's expert guidance through this practice.

We know the best way to learn a foreign language is to live with those who speak it, and our students should be encouraged to take this step. In preparation for that event, and also for those students who will not venture beyond the foreign language classroom, there is much practice to be done with peers and with the teacher, whose responsibility it is to find or create meaningful practice.

When designing integrated and meaning-centered activities, keep in mind the following guidelines:

1. Stay within the level of your students' experience (language and culture).
2. Know your goals.
3. Design a task to reach those goals.
4. Give clear and simple instructions for each activity.
5. Vary the activities for each context.

Appendix A11 contains a variety of sample whole language activities as well as suggestions on how to create your own whole language activities.

TEACH AND REFLECT

In these activities, you will learn how to identify different approaches for the teaching of grammar, and you will design a lesson that emphasizes a whole language approach.

EPISODE ONE
Examining Grammar Presentations in Textbooks

In preparation for this activity, examine at least two textbooks in the target language. Decide whether the textbooks use an explicit or implicit approach to grammar explanation. To do so, answer the following questions for each textbook:

1. Does the textbook offer some form of grammatical analysis? If so, is the textbook advocating direct and explicit or indirect and implicit grammar explanations?

_____

_____

_____

2. When is the teacher supposed to focus the learners' attention on form or on grammatical structures—at the beginning of the chapter, middle, end, or not at all?

_____

_____

_____

3. Analyze the role assigned to the learner regarding grammar explanations. That is, is the learner a passive listener during the explanation? Is the learner supposed to be an active hypothesizer? Is the learner supposed to hypothesize alone or in collaboration with others?

_____

_____

_____

4. Now identify a particular language function, such as asking and giving directions, making purchases, or describing people or things. (Turn to the chapter that focuses on your selected language function.) How does the chapter relate language function to form? Hint: Are "skill-getting" activities emphasized before "skill-using" activities, or vice-versa?

_____

_____

_____

5. Examine the chapter to see if the learners are exposed to meaningful, integrated discourse. If so, how—through stories, poems, songs, videotapes, and drama? And when—beginning, middle, or end of chapter?

_____

_____

_____

6. In your opinion, how well does the chapter integrate (1) meaning—that is, the thoughts and ideas of the message being conveyed; (2) form—the various linguistic or grammatical elements; and (3) function—how to carry out a particular task by exploiting the appropriate grammatical structures?

_____

_____

_____

_____

7. In your estimation, is one particular dimension—meaning, form, or function—emphasized more than the others? If so, which one? Can you offer an explanation of why one dimension might be emphasized at the expense of the others?

_____

_____

_____

EPISODE TWO
Designing a Whole Language Lesson

You are now going to design a lesson that emphasizes a whole language approach to grammar instruction. First, you need to identify a particular linguistic function, for example, asking questions, making purchases, or describing people or things. Think of an appropriate context in which you would need to use this function. Then decide which structures should be incorporated into the lesson so that the learners are capable of carrying out the function. Using the following steps as guidelines, decide how you are going to PACE the whole language lesson.

1. Identify an integrated discourse sample that foreshadows the selected linguistic function, context, and accuracy structures. Remember that the "text" can be in the form of a story, poem, taped listening selection, advertisement, video-taped interview, and so on.
2. Decide what you need to do to help students comprehend the meaning of the "text." For example, will you aid the learners' comprehension if you use visuals, mime, gestures, and props? Gather all necessary supplemental materials. This phase is critical to the success of the lesson. Be **creative!**
3. Demonstrate for your fellow classmates how you plan to introduce the whole language text. Even if your classmates do not know your target language, see if you can convey the general meaning or significance of the text. (Make use of those props!)
4. Discuss how you would use "multiple passes" to recycle the story line. In other words, what kind of TPR activities, role-playing scenarios, or other activities would be appropriate to deepen the learners' comprehension? Remember that at this stage, the students will become more participatory.
5. Write a short description of how you would focus the learners' attention on form. What "hints" or "helping questions" are you going to ask? In other words, how do you plan to "co-construct" the explanation?
6. Now design at least three extension activities that relate to the selected context. (Note: Use the extension activities that are in Appendix A11 as guidelines.) These activities should create a need for the learners to use the identified accuracy structures. In doing so, the learners will develop a fuller understanding of the function of the grammar structures.

DISCUSS AND REFLECT

The following case studies will enable you to explore ways in which a whole language approach is put into practice in the classroom.

> ### CASE STUDY 1
> ### Using a Whole Language Approach to Teach Reflexive Verbs
>
> Mr. West, a French teacher, has learned about a new way to incorporate grammar teaching into a whole language lesson. He is anxious to try out this new approach since the textbook he uses, which serves as the basis of his district's curriculum, is grammar-driven. He has not yet succeeded in doing anything more than present the "grammar-rule-of-the-day" and complete the textbook exercises with his classes. Mr. West previews the chapter and sees that he will need to teach reflexive verbs. He picks a context for this new structure—the morning routine. For his presentation, Mr. West writes the French equivalent of the following sentences on the board:
>
> | | |
> |---|---|
> | I wash my son's face. | I wash myself. |
> | I get my son up. | I get up. |
> | I look at my son. | I look at myself in the mirror. |
> | I brush my son's hair. | I brush my hair. |
>
> Mr. West reads the sentences aloud, hoping that the class will perceive the non-reflexive/reflexive contrast in the two columns. The students seem bored, uninterested, and unchallenged. He then asks a question: "What do you see here?" The students are bewildered and silent until Mr. West calls on Mike. Mike says, "French sentences beginning with *Je*." "These students are clueless about these sentences and completely confused," Mr. West thinks to himself. He decides to abandon the questioning and delivers a lesson in English on the formation and use of French reflexive verbs. Because of this experience, he thinks that students are unable to think about the target language and that all that can be done to ensure "learning" is to lecture students on the rules they need to know.

Ask yourself these questions:

1. Why are the students bored and uninterested?
2. How would you evaluate Mr. West's PRESENTATION? Does it satisfy the requirements of a PRESENTATION in the PACE model? Why or why not?
3. What would you have done when Mike responded with "French sentences beginning with *Je?*"
4. How do you think the students were feeling about Mr. West's lesson?

To prepare the case:

- Review the PACE model presented in this chapter.
- Examine one or more textbooks in the language you teach to see how reflexive verbs are presented.
- Read Celce-Murcia (1985), Walz (1989), and Larsen-Freeman (1991) for further information about the role of grammar in contextualized teaching.

What type of PRESENTATION would you choose for contextualizing a lesson on reflexive verbs?

_____

_____

_____

_____

_____

_____

How would you develop this lesson?

_____

_____

_____

_____

_____

_____

_____

CASE STUDY 2
Using Songs to Foreshadow Grammar

Mr. Kruse teaches French at a suburban high school near a large Pennsylvania city. Most of his students have had little, if any, experience with other cultures, nor have they interacted with foreigners who live in the area except for visitors invited to the classroom. Their life experience and their curiosity about and interest in other cultures are very limited, as evidenced in the few, mundane questions they ask when confronted with a visitor from another country.

While in France last summer, Mr. Kruse bought several CDs, one of which was an American Cajun recording then popular in France. In an attempt to stir the interest of his students and to show French influence on American culture, Mr. Kruse decided to plan a grammar lesson using one of the songs from this recording. The words to this song follow, both in French and in English.

Cajun Telephone Stomp

O bébé, j'avais essayé
De causer aujourd'hui.
"Y avait quelque chose qui est arrivé
Et moi, j'ai commencé d'être fâché.

Sur le téléphone de l'autre côté,
"Y avait une 'tite voix mal enregistrée.
"Après le beep," c'est ça il dit,
"Laisse ton message, 'ya personne ici."

Quoi c'est ça, il dit le beep?
C'est pas Cadien, ni poli,
S'il n'est pas là, quoi faire sa voix?
O yé yaille, mon cœur fait mal.

Après dix fois avec cette voix maudite
C'a commencé de ma faire rire,
J'ai oublié à qui je veux parler
et enfin, j'ai accroché.

Cajun Telephone Stomp

O baby, I tried
To talk to you on the phone today.
Something strange happened
And I started to get mad.

On the other end of the line,
There was a little voice, a bad recording,
"After the beep," that's what it said,
"Leave your message, there's no one home."

What is this, it said "the beep?"
That's not Cajun, nor polite,
If no one's there, why is this voice?
O yé yaille, it makes me sad.

After hearing that darn voice ten times,
It started to make me laugh,
I forgot who I was calling
And finally, I hung up.

—from *Cajun Conja,* by Beausoleil

Ask yourself these questions:

1. What information concerning the recording artist might students need to know?
2. What vocabulary might students need to know in order to understand the context?

3. What work might be done in advance to prepare the students for listening to the recording?
4. What cultural information might be learned from this song?
5. What grammar might be targeted?
6. What types of activities might be designed to target the grammar?
7. What types of activities might support the Cyclical Approach to teaching this grammar?
8. What creative activities might be explored, based on this model?

To prepare the case:

- Find a music magazine in the target language, and read some articles concerning modern music.
- Read a brief history of Cajun culture and music or about the music characteristic of the target culture that you teach.
- Refer to Adair-Hauck and Donato's Cyclical Approach, presented in this chapter.
- Read pp. 91–118 of Omaggio (1986), which deal with the role of context in comprehension and learning.
- Listen to current hit songs by other recording artists.

1. Describe the differences and similarities you find in the songs you heard, emphasizing the style, content, and cultural aspects of the recordings so that students working in groups might create a song of their own.

_____

_____

_____

_____

_____

_____

_____

_____

_____

_____

2. Using a song as your context, select a grammar point and design two contextualized activities that will integrate the meaning, form, and function.

_____

_____

_____

_____

_____

_____

_____

_____

_____

_____

_____

_____

REFERENCES

Adair-Hauck, B., and R. Donato. "Foreign Language Explanations Within the Zone of Proximal Development." (in preparation).

Aljaafreh, A. "The Role of Implicit/Explicit Error Correction and the Learner's Zone of Proximal Development." Unpublished dissertation. University of Delaware, 1992.

Ausubel, D., J. Novak, and H. Hanesian. *Educational Psychology: A Cognitive View*. New York: Holt, Rinehart and Winston, 1968.

Brown, J., A. Collins, and P. Duguid. "Situated Cognition and the Culture of Learning." *Educational Researcher* 1 (1989): 32–41.

Bruner, J. *Actual Minds, Possible Worlds*. Cambridge, MA: Harvard University Press, 1986.

Celce-Murcia, M. "Making Informed Decisions About the Role of Grammar in Language Teaching." *Foreign Language Annals* 18 (1985): 297–301.

Celce-Murcia, M. "Grammar Pedagogy in Second and Foreign Language Teaching." *TESOL Quarterly* 25 (1991): 459–479.

Cole, M. "The Zone of Proximal Development: Where Culture and Cognition Create Each Other." Ed. J. V. Wertsch. *Culture Communication and Cognition: Vygotskian Perspective*. New York: Cambridge University Press, 1985: 146–161.

Cummins, J. "Language Proficiency, Bilingualism and Academic Achievement." *Bilingualism and Special Education: Issues in Assessment and Pedagogy*. San Diego, CA: College-Hill, 1984.

Donato, R., and B. Adair-Hauck. "Discourse Perspectives on Formal Instruction." *Language Awareness* 2 (1992): 73–89.

Donato, R., and B. Adair-Hauck. "A Model for Integrating Form in a Whole Language Lesson." (in preparation).

Dulay, H., and M. Burt. "Should We Teach Children Syntax?" *Language Learning* 23 (1973): 245–258.

Ellis, R. *Classroom Second Language Development*. Englewood Cliffs, NJ: Prentice Hall, 1988.

Fotos, S., and R. Ellis. "Communicating about Grammar: A Task-Based Approach." *TESOL Quarterly* 25 (1991): 605–628.

Fountas, I., and I. Hannigan. "Making Sense of Whole Language: The Pursuit of Informed Teaching." *Childhood Education* 65 (1989): 133–137.

Freeman, Y., and D. Freeman. *Whole Language for Second Language Learners*. Portsmouth, NH: Heineman Educational Books, 1992.

Galloway, V., and A. Labarca. "From Student to Learner: Style, Process and Strategy." Ed. D. Birckbichler. *New Perspectives and New Directions in Foreign Language Education*. Lincolnwood, IL: National Textbook Company, 1990: 111–158.

Goodman, K. *What's Whole in Whole Language*. Portsmouth, NH: Heineman Educational Books, 1986.

Hatch, E. *Psycholinguistics: A Second Language Perspective*. Rowley, MA: Newbury House, 1983.

Hawkins, B. *Scaffolded Classroom Interaction and Its Relation to Second Language Acquisition for Minority Children*. Unpublished Ph.D. dissertation. University of California, Los Angeles, 1988.

Herron, C., and M. Tomasello. "Acquiring Grammatical Structures by Guided Induction." *The French Review* 65 (1992): 708–718.

Higgs, T. V., and R. T. Clifford. "The Push Toward Communication." Ed. T. V. Higgs. *Curriculum, Competence, and the Foreign Language Teacher*. ACTFL Foreign Language Education Series, vol. 13. Lincolnwood, IL: National Textbook, 1982: 57–79.

Krashen, S. *Principles and Practice in Second Language Acquisition*. Oxford: Pergamon, 1982.

Krashen, S. *The Input Hypothesis*. New York: Longman, 1985.

Larsen-Freeman, D. "Teaching Grammar." Ed. M. Celce-Murcia. *Teaching English as a Second or Foreign Language*. Boston, MA: Heinle and Heinle, 1991: 279–295.

Lave, J. "Cognitive Consequences of Traditional Apprenticeship Training in West Africa." *Anthropology and Education Quarterly* 8 (1977): 177–180.

Leontiev, A. "The Problem of Activity in Psychology." Ed. J. V. Wertsch. *The Concept of Activity in Soviet Psychology*. Armonk, NY: M. E. Sharpe, 1981: 37–71.

Lightbown, P., and N. Spada. "Focus on Form and Corrective Feedback in Communicative Language Teaching." *Studies in Second Language Acquisition* 12 (1990): 429–448.

Long, M. "The Least a Second Language Acquisition Theory Needs to Explain." *TESOL Quarterly* 24 (1991): 649–666.

Newman, D., P. Griffin, and M. Cole. *The Construction Zone: Working for Cognitive Change in School*. New York: Cambridge University Press, 1989.

Oller, J., Jr. "Some Working Ideas for Language Teaching." Eds. J. Oller, Jr. and P. Richard-Amato. *Methods That Work*. Rowley, MA: Newbury House, 1983.

Omaggio, A. *Teaching Language in Context*. Boston, MA: Heinle and Heinle, 1986.

Pearson, D. "Reading the Whole-Language Movement." *Elementary School Journal* 90 (1989): 231–241.

Rivers, W. *Communicating Naturally in a Second Language*. Chicago: University of Chicago Press, 1983.

Rogoff, B. *Apprenticeship in Learning*. Oxford: Oxford University Press, 1990.

Rutherford, W. "Grammatical Consciousness Raising in Brief Historical Perspective." Eds. W. Rutherford and M. Sharwood Smith. *Grammar and Second Language Teaching*. New York: Harper, 1988.

Sharwood Smith, M. "Consciousness Raising and the Second Language Learner." Eds. W. Rutherford and M. Sharwood Smith. *Grammar and Second Language Teaching*. New York: Harper, 1988.

Terrell, T. "A Natural Approach to Second Language Acquisition and Learning." *Modern Language Journal* 61 (1977): 325–337.

Tharp, R., and R. Gallimore. *Rousing Minds to Life: Teaching, Learning and Schooling in Social Context*. New York: Cambridge University Press, 1988.

Vygotsky, L. S. *Mind in Society: The Development of Higher Psychological Processes*. Cambridge, MA: Harvard University Press, 1978.

Walz, J. "Context and Contextualized Language Practice in Foreign Language Teaching." *Modern Language Journal* 73 (1989): 161–168.

Using an Interactive Approach to Teach Listening and Reading

In this chapter, you will explore ideas for teaching listening and reading within meaningful contexts. Listening and reading processes are first discussed in terms of current theoretical frameworks. Key research findings concerning the variables involved in listening and reading comprehension are presented along with implications for classroom teaching. A model for teaching listening and reading in an interactive way is also presented. This model will help you guide your students through oral and written texts, assist them in developing comprehension strategies, and engage them in text interaction. You will have the opportunity to develop lessons for teaching authentic listening and reading texts by using the interactive model presented in the chapter. In the case studies, you will accompany four teachers as they examine the results of several teaching techniques, finding ways to verify their success and exploring ways to bring about change.

CONCEPTUAL ORIENTATION

Few would dispute the claim that comprehension is necessary in order for language acquisition to occur. In order to communicate effectively, learners must understand what is being said. To function successfully with a target language, learners depend upon their ability to comprehend the spoken and written word. Empirical studies have identified a positive relationship between listening ability and foreign language acquisition (Feyten 1991) as well as between reading ability and language acquisition (Krashen 1984; Stotsky 1983).

Historically, listening and reading skills have received less attention in language teaching than have the productive skills of speaking and writing. Due in part to a lack of knowledge about receptive skills, teachers often failed to devote explicit attention to developing listening and reading abilities, assuming that comprehension would occur on its own. More recently, however, the profession has recognized that merely exposing learners to oral or written input is not sufficient and that explicit teaching of comprehension strategies is needed (Joiner 1986).

Listening and Reading Processes

Listening and reading are active processes that require an interplay between various types of knowledge. Scarcella and Oxford (1992) have described the listening and reading processes in terms of Canale and Swain's (1980) model of communicative competence. According to this model, listeners and readers draw upon four types of competencies as they attempt to comprehend an oral or a written message:

1. grammatical competence: knowledge of morphology, syntax, vocabulary, and mechanics;
2. sociolinguistic competence: knowing what is expected socially and culturally by native speakers of the target language;
3. discourse competence: the ability to use cohesive devices such as pronouns, conjunctions, and transitional phrases to link meaning across sentences, as well as the ability to recognize how coherence is used to maintain the message's unity;
4. strategic competence: the ability to use a number of guessing strategies to compensate for missing knowledge (Scarcella and Oxford 1992).

Listeners and readers rely upon the types of knowledge described above as they perform a variety of tasks in the comprehension process. Some tasks or subskills reflect top-down processing, in which meaning is derived through the use of contextual clues and activation of personal background knowledge. These subskills include identifying key ideas and guessing meaning through a process that Goodman (1967) calls a "psycholinguistic guessing game." In his description of a top-down approach to reading, Goodman states that "Efficient reading does not result from precise perception and identification of all elements, but from skill in selecting the fewest, most productive cues necessary to produce guesses which are right the first time" (cf. Chastain, 1988, p. 223).

Other tasks or subskills reflect bottom-up processing, in which meaning is understood through analysis of language parts. Simply put, the listener or reader processes language in a sequential manner, combining sounds or letters to form words, then combining words to form phrases, clauses, and sentences of the text (Goodman 1967). Bottom-up subskills include discriminating between different sounds or letters, recognizing word-order patterns, recognizing suprasegmental patterns or sentence structures, and translating individual words.

Top-down skills are more useful in second-language processing, since reading is not based on oral language use, as is the case in the native language. Bottom-up processing can be used effectively in learning to read the native language, since oral language is already firmly in place. Therefore, in L1, orality leads to literacy, while in L2, literacy leads to and improves orality.

However, the current view of listening and reading skills is that they involve both bottom-up and top-down processing, as described above. According to Scarcella and Oxford, "Listening can best be understood as a highly complex, interactive operation in which bottom-up processing is interspersed with top-down processing, the latter involving guessing" (1992, p. 142). Similarly, in their discussion of the reading process, Swaffar, Arens, and Byrnes state that reading comprehension "… results from interactive variables that operate simultaneously rather than sequentially" (1991, p. 21). Eskey (1986) proposes an interactive model of the reading process that accounts for the interaction of the reader's different kinds of knowledge (bottom-up and top-down) and the interaction of the reader and the text. Evidence suggests that good readers and listeners use two kinds of skills characteristic of interactive processing: (1) lower-level "identification" skills, through which they recognize words and structures necessary for decoding; and (2) higher-level "interpretive" skills, through which they reconstruct meaning of whole parts of the text (Eskey 1986). Both of these skill types are interactive in that they blend into one as the reader or listener attaches meaning to a text and makes it a part of what he or she knows (Eskey 1986).

what is noun, verb, adj.

Research on the Variables Involved in Comprehension

The research has documented a number of variables that affect comprehension of a text, be it oral or written. Chapter 2 discusses the first variable, the importance of context and background knowledge in understanding input. The degree to which the reader or listener is able to merge input with previously acquired knowledge structures, or *schemata,* determines how successful he or she will be in comprehending (Minsky 1982). This linking of new and existing knowledge helps the listener or reader make sense of the text more quickly. The key role of context has been verified by many studies in listening (Bransford and Johnson 1972) and in reading (Nunan 1985; Lee 1986a; Mueller 1980; Omaggio 1979). These experiments have shown that language users provided with prior contextual assistance, such as pictures or scripts, comprehend more accurately than they do in the absence of such support. The use of contextual and background information aids understanding by limiting the number of possible text interpretations.

A second variable is the degree to which the reader or listener uses strategies such as guessing in context. In both listening and reading, prediction of forthcoming input, or the "activation of correct expectancies," is one characteristic of native listener and reader processing (Oller 1983, p. 10). Many studies support the claim that learners who interact with the text through strategies such as predicting, skimming, scanning, and using background knowledge comprehend much better than learners who fail to use these strategies (Bacon 1992a; Barnett 1988; Carrell 1985; Palinscar and Brown 1984). Bacon (1992b) conducted a recent study examining how beginning-level Spanish students used strategies to comprehend authentic radio broadcasts. Among the findings were significant differences in strategy use between upper and lower achievers. Figure 1 summarizes the characteristics of successful versus less successful listeners, as reflected in Bacon's (1992b) study.

FIGURE 1 Summary of Characteristics of Successful Versus Less Successful Listeners

Successful Listeners	Less Successful Listeners
1. Showed greater flexibility: Greater number and range.	1. Showed less flexibility: Tended to stick with one or two strategies.
2. Not reluctant to rely on English when other strategies failed.	2. Unlikely to mention using English as a comprehension strategy.
3. Could verbalize their strategies for controlling input.	3. Expressed frustration with input.
4. Showed interest in understanding and learning.	4. Seemed to lose interest easily.
5. Able to summarize and add detail.	5. Unable to summarize, or seemed satisfied with little information.
6. Effectively used personal, world, or discourse knowledge.	6. Overdependent on previous knowledge.
7. Controlled comprehension process.	7. Distracted by unknown vocabulary or extraneous factors.
8. Used monitor *marginally* more successfully to help revise a hypothesis or choose between alternative interpretations. More realistic in evaluation of comprehension.	8. Used monitor, but not particularly successfully. Easily discouraged or overconfident of comprehension.
9. Were conscious of losing attention to meaning and could refocus.	9. When they lost their attention to meaning, had trouble refocussing.

Source: Bacon 1992.

A third variable that affects comprehension is the purpose for listening/reading or the nature of the task. The type of task determines the kind of strategy required. For example, a person listening to today's weather report might choose to attend only to the temperature and disregard other details (Wolvin and Coakley 1985). In reading, Munby (1979) has identified two kinds of reading that involve different objectives and skills. Extensive reading, usually for pleasure, requires the ability to understand main ideas, find specific information, and read quickly. Intensive reading, most often for information, requires the ability to read for details, understand implications, and follow relationships of thought throughout a text (Munby 1979).

A fourth variable relates to the length of text presented for comprehension. In beginning-level classes, students are typically given shorter, edited texts to listen to or read. Students who process shorter texts are more likely to use word-for-word processing strategies since the demands on memory permit greater attention to detail (Swaffar, Arens, and Byrnes 1991; Kintsch and van Dijk 1978). Some evidence suggests that longer texts may actually be easier for students to comprehend because they are more cohesive and interesting to students, though requiring more top-down processing (Allen, Bernhardt, Berry, and Demel 1988). More research is clearly needed in this area to verify the relationship between text length and comprehension ease.

A fifth variable in the comprehension process pertains to the type of oral or written text presented. Traditionally, the difficulty of texts has been judged on the basis of the simplicity of grammatical structures and the familiarity of the vocabulary. According to Lee (1987), this may be due to the fact that we have often tested comprehension itself on the basis of grammar and vocabulary recognition rather than on interaction with the text's message. However, empirical studies have shown that exposure to texts with unfamiliar grammar and vocabulary does not significantly affect comprehension (Lee 1987). Other factors, such as the quality of the text itself in terms of factual consistency and coherence, as well as the background knowledge and motivation of learners, may be more important considerations for teachers when selecting texts (Zabrucky 1986; Swaffar, Arens, and Byrnes 1991). These findings lend support to the claim that second language learners may comprehend more easily by relying on top-down strategies. In addition, as you learned in Chapter 2, the degree to which a text is motivated and episodically structured also affects the extent to which students are able to understand and recall it (Oller 1983).

A sixth variable involves the treatment of new vocabulary. The use of vocabulary lists with definitions does little to help the reader build vocabulary or comprehend more effectively while reading (Bensoussan, Sim, and Weiss 1984). More effective teacher strategies present new words in terms of their thematic and discourse relationship to the text instead of in terms of dictionary definitions, and use pre- and post-reading discussion to link text information to the readers' background knowledge (Grellet 1981; Nuttall 1982). According to Swaffar, Arens, and Byrnes (1991), readers should be encouraged to build their own vocabulary banks, since not all students need to learn the same words. They also suggest in-class vocabulary practice that provides opportunities for students to "… find additional words that relate to the same semantic category … identify how the same words are redefined by different contexts … increase awareness of pronounceability, and identify affixes, suffixes, or parts of speech" (1991, p. 68).

According to the research presented above, we should take into consideration the following variables when we provide opportunities for students to comprehend oral and written texts: (1) background knowledge of the learner; (2) strategies that learners use in the comprehension task; (3) purpose for listening/reading or the nature of the task; (4) length of text; (5) type of text; and (6) treatment of new vocabulary.

■ Use of Authentic Materials

Chapter 2 introduced the concept of using authentic materials. Empirical studies have confirmed the positive results gained by listeners and readers who are given opportunities to interact with authentic oral or written texts. In listening comprehension, for example, Herron and Seay (1991) conducted an experiment with intermediate-level French students to test the effect of using tapes of authentic radio segments as a substitute for other types of communicative oral activities and grammar practice. They concluded that students who listened to the tapes demonstrated significantly greater listening comprehension than did students who did not interact with the authentic segments. In a similar vein, Bacon's (1992b) recent study with beginning-level Spanish students who were exposed to authentic radio broadcasts showed that beginning-level students can successfully comprehend authentic, unedited discourse. Bacon's results also led her to conclude that students do not automatically transfer comprehension strategies from L1 to L2, and that students in beginning and intermediate levels of instruction benefit greatly from pre-listening preparation and guidance in strategy use: "When listeners are aware of the variety of strategies that are available to them, they can better choose, use, evaluate, and modify those that work best for them as individuals" (1992b, p. 331).

In reading, Vigil (1987) found significant differences in comprehension with beginning language students who read unedited authentic texts. Not only did their comprehension skills increase, but there were also improvements in oral and written language performance. The results of these and other studies indicate that we may be underestimating the positive effects of authentic texts on both listening and reading comprehension (see, for example, Bacon 1989 and Weissenrieder 1987).

While authentic materials are often thought to refer primarily to newspaper and magazine articles or news broadcasts, many other types of oral and written texts appropriate to specific age groups can be used effectively, including literary texts. Chapter 12 discusses in detail the use of videotexts, which provide the opportunity to bring the living culture right into the classroom. Earlier chapters of this *Handbook* have explored various possibilities for using folktales, stories, and legends. Christensen (1990) suggests the use of authentic teenage adventure novels because of their potential for sustaining interest by means of suspense, intrigue, fast action, and cliff-hanging chapter endings.[1] In addition to serving as a source of cultural context, literature provides opportunities for students to use their cognitive skills, develop their language abilities, and interact with one another through sharing of ideas.

Rice (1991) has suggested three ways for the profession to more successfully combine the teaching of language and literature:

1. define what we want students *to do* with literature and identify the skills they need: for example, trace a plot, describe characters, generate a poem that has similar sounds to the one they read;
2. introduce literature from the beginning levels of language instruction, designing the reading task according to the abilities of students: for example, beginning classes might figure out sound patterns of a poem, associate actions with emotions or responses, set up opposition between male and female characters in a story;
3. interrelate the proficiency concepts of *function, context,* and *accuracy* in developing an approach to teaching literature: for example, the literary equivalent of *context* might be the *genre* or type of text, *function* might be *the operations the reader must perform* in order to read or critique a particular type of text, and *accuracy* might include the

---

[1]Teachers of Spanish may be particularly interested in Christensen's (1990) ideas about using "Las adventuras de Hector," a new teenage adventure-novel series from Spain.

vocabulary, grammar, and cognitive skills necessary for carrying out the functions.

■ Implications for Teaching Listening and Reading

If we adopt the definition of reading as proposed by Swaffar, Arens, and Byrnes and extend it to listening, then L2 reading and listening comprehension are functions of "... cognitive development, the ability to think within the framework of the second language" (1991, p. 63). According to their framework and the results of the studies described above, research points to the following implications for teaching the receptive skills:

1. students' comprehension may increase if they are trained to use strategies such as activation of background knowledge and guessing;
2. students need pre-reading and pre-listening activities that prepare them for the comprehension task;
3. text appropriateness should be judged on the basis of text quality, interest level, and learners' needs;
4. authentic materials provide an effective means for presenting real language, integrating culture, and heightening comprehension;
5. vocabulary must be connected to text structure, student interest, and background knowledge in order to aid retention and recall;
6. students should be taught to interact with the text through the use of both bottom-up and top-down processes;
7. comprehension assessment should engage the learner in a hierarchy of procedures through which he or she interacts with the text.

■ The Role of Listening and Reading Across Instructional Levels

In Chapters 4 and 5, you learned about the key role that the listening skill plays in teaching foreign language to elementary and middle school students. Listening is used as the vehicle for language acquisition and serves as a springboard for integrating other skills and content. Elementary and middle school teachers use many techniques for improving listening comprehension, such as gestures, TPR, visuals, realia, and hands-on student participation.

For elementary school children, the transition from listening and speaking to reading is made through the use of the language experience chart approach, as described in Chapter 4. At both the elementary and middle school levels, culturally appropriate stories, myths, folktales, science fiction, and adventure stories can be presented to combine cultural understanding and the teaching of reading. Chapter 5 presented an approach for using an oral or a written text as the context for a thematic unit while integrating the practice of all skills and culture.

At the middle/junior high school and high school levels and beyond, listening should also play a prominent role if students are to acquire language. Learners need to attend to large amounts of comprehensible input in the target language, and they benefit from training in strategy development. Authentic input provides the context and meaning stage for the whole-language approach to grammar instruction (PACE model) presented in Chapter 6. The various types of authentic oral or written texts, as described in earlier chapters, can be presented to students at all levels of instruction. Beginning language learners benefit from experience in top-down processing or listening/reading for the gist, since this activity discourages the word-for-word decoding that often occurs in early language learning. However, the research discussed earlier in this chapter refutes the notion of consistently matching text length and text type to particular levels of instruction or to students' proficiency levels. For example, beginning-level students should not just be given short texts dealing with concrete information, such as menus and advertisements. Instead, students should be given the opportunity to use the information in the text, i.e., grammar, vocabulary, discourse markers that connect ideas, as a tool for achieving comprehension. In addition, by listening/reading from various perspectives, students can also gain additional insights about the text and the author's intent. Thus, this type of interactive listening and reading not only develops comprehension skills but can also enable students to learn new ideas and improve global language ability.

◼ A Model for Teaching Interactive Listening and Reading

A model for teaching listening and reading is presented here as a strategy for guiding students through oral and written texts, engaging them in interaction with the text, helping them to build strategies, and improving their comprehension. This framework is based on the Interactive Model for Reading suggested by Eskey (1986) and on the Procedural Model for Integrative Reading recently proposed by Swaffar, Arens, and Byrnes (1991). Several aspects of it also reflect certain stages of Phillips' (1984) Classroom Plan for Developing Reading Comprehension. The model presented here is interactive and procedural in nature, guiding the learner as he or she interacts with the text by using both bottom-up and top-down processes. It is also integrative, since it provides opportunities for students to combine listening, speaking, reading, and writing as they use their cognitive skills to derive meaning from the text, recreate the text, and react to the text in a personal way.

The interactive model outlined in Figure 2 can be implemented with any type of oral or written text. The extent to which each stage is completed in its entirety will undoubtedly depend on the length and nature of the text as well as on the instructional objectives. This model can also be used successfully with videotexts, as will be described in Chapter 12. Additionally, it can serve as an effective avenue for teaching literary texts such as short stories, plays, and poems. In fact, the interactive opportunities presented in this model are similar

FIGURE 2 **A Model for Teaching Interactive Listening and Reading**

Stages	Listener/Reader Use of Text Meaning
I. Pre-listening/Pre-reading	Students preview the text, establish a purpose for listening to/reading the text, predict meaning.
II. Identify main elements	Students identify main ideas, characters, settings, and events.
III. Identify details	Students listen and read intensively and connect main concepts to details.
IV. Organize/ revise main ideas/details	Students revise their charts of main ideas and supporting details.
V. Recreate text	Students reconstruct textual information.
VI. React to text/explore intertextuality	Students give opinions and reactions to text and relate other texts to it.

to Harper's (1988) plan for teaching literature, which guides students through a text by means of preinterpretation, interpretation, and synthesis activities. Appendix A12 presents an example of how an authentic reading can be explored by using this interactive model.

One issue that teachers continue to confront when teaching listening and reading is how much of the native versus target language to use when exploring oral or written texts with their students. There is some evidence to suggest that occasional use of the native language to check for comprehension and recall may be useful, since in this way comprehension skill is not confused with productive use of the target language (Swaffar, Arens, and Byrnes 1991; Lee 1986b; Tan and Ling 1979). It might be beneficial to conduct the pre-listening and pre-reading activities in the native language, particularly if students require new background information prior to the listening or reading task. Clearly, the decision to use either the native or target language for each phase

Listener/Reader Use of Text Language	Class Activities
Students use words and phrases as clues to meaning.	Students skim for the gist, scan for specific information, identify a purpose for listening to/reading the text, use their own background knowledge to explore the topic, and predict what they might learn in the text.
Students recognize discourse markers (adverbs, conjunctions, word order, clauses, phrases) that connect ideas and signal a shift in topic, setting, or event.	Students (in pairs or groups) discuss main ideas (perhaps following out-of-class preparation) by identifying the text topic and characters as well as the changes in events and settings of the story or text. Other activities: students match main ideas to specific sections of the text or select main ideas from a list of alternatives.
Students identify examples of text details that support main concepts.	Using the main ideas identified in Stage II, students create a chart of main ideas and supporting details. Other activity: students select details from a list of alternatives.
Students use vocabulary from text to make changes in summary.	Students (in pairs or groups) compare charts developed in Stage III, and verify that their organization of main ideas and details is consistent with the organization of the text and ideas presented in the text.
Students expand text phrases created earlier into sentences and paragraphs.	Following out-of-class preparation, students (in small groups) summarize or recreate the text.
Students use text as a reference to support their opinions.	Students discuss the text from their own points of view and share their opinions.

of the interactive model presented here must be made by each teacher after considering the level of students' proficiency and the task to be done. It would seem advantageous to use the target language to the maximum extent possible, while realizing that occasional use of the native language may be both necessary and helpful in guiding students in strategy use and in checking their comprehension.

TEACH AND REFLECT

The following activities will enable you to use the interactive model to present authentic reading and listening selections.

EPISODE ONE
Using an Interactive Reading Model to Teach an Authentic Written Text

For this activity, you will need to select a targeted level of instruction: elementary school, middle/junior high school, high school, or beyond.

Option 1: Select an authentic magazine or newspaper article of at least 750 words.
Option 2: Select an authentic literary text (folktale, story, novel excerpt, poem, etc.)

Check the text for the characteristics of good episodic organization. First, decide how this text might be used in a particular thematic unit in order to address short- and long-range objectives. Second, design a plan for teaching the text by using the interactive model presented in this chapter. Remember that you may need to devote a portion of several class periods in order to complete your work on the text. For each day you plan to spend on the reading, describe what students will do in all stages of the procedure. Your instructor may ask you to present an element of your plan to the class.

EPISODE TWO
Using an Interactive Listening Model to Teach an Authentic Taped Segment

For this activity, you will also need to select a targeted level of instruction: elementary school, middle/junior high school, high school, or beyond.

Option 1: Select an authentic taped segment (conversation, commercial, news report, song, etc.).
Option 2: Semi-script your own taped conversation: give two native speakers a particular situation or subject to discuss (for example, ask them to pretend that they are two students who meet for the first time while standing in the registration line); ask the speakers to talk spontaneously for 2-3 minutes. Do not prepare a written script, since the conversation should be as natural as possible.

Next, decide how this segment might be used in a particular thematic unit in order to address short- and long-range objectives. Then design a plan for teaching the taped segment by using the interactive approach presented in this chapter. Describe what students will do in each stage of the procedure. Your instructor may ask you to present to the class your taped segment and an element of your lesson.

DISCUSS AND REFLECT

The first case study for this chapter highlights the process of change in teaching listening and reading. In the second case study you will see how two teachers use different techniques with the same name, and how their results vary.

CASE STUDY 1
But the Students Don't Understand What I'm Saying

Mr. Cosgrove and Mrs. Sturgeon teach German at Warrington High School, an urban, multicultural school district in the eastern section of a large city. They both began their teaching careers 25 years ago when they accepted their present positions at the high school. Although they are good friends and work together cordially on school committees, Mr. Cosgrove and Mrs. Sturgeon do not employ similar approaches to teaching. Mr. Cosgrove believes in a teacher-centered classroom in order to maintain effective control of his classes. His instructional plans are grammar-oriented, for he feels that knowing a language means understanding the rules and English equivalents of target-language vocabulary. Although his command of German is very good, Mr. Cosgrove uses the language only during his presentation of dialogues and during the practice of grammar exercises. Since he feels that beginning-level students have great difficulty understanding spoken German, he translates everything he says into English. Mr. Cosgrove's daily plans follow the textbook organization fairly closely. Students do some communicative practice as provided in the textbook, although rarely in pairs or groups. Mr. Cosgrove has attended a few workshops over the years, but he doesn't agree with teaching strategies that propose that level one students should be given the opportunity to communicate extensively. He feels that level one students need to learn the grammar first and then in later levels apply the rules to meaningful communication. The school administration has given Mr. Cosgrove primarily level one and some level two classes to teach, for they feel that the upper levels should be given to teachers who have kept abreast of innovations in teaching.

On the other hand, Mrs. Sturgeon uses a communicative approach to teaching and provides ample opportunities for students to hear the target language and interact with one another. She organizes her units around contexts and functions, and makes sure that meaning is at the center of every activity. She has changed many elements of her teaching over the years as a result of attending numerous workshops and conferences. Her teaching load consists of levels three, four, and five.

The difference in teaching philosophy has resulted in high levels of frustration for Mr. Cosgrove's level one and two students when they initially enter Mrs. Sturgeon's level three classes. They want Mrs. Sturgeon to translate everything the way that Mr. Cosgrove did, and they resent the amount of time spent having to listen to the target language. Mrs. Sturgeon also experiences frustration as she feels that she can never really introduce upper-level kinds of activities, since these students have not acquired basic-level listening and speaking skills. For many years now, she has been dealing with this problem and has on occasion discussed it with Mr. Cosgrove, who has steadfastly refused to change his approach, feeling justified that the students *liked* German and *felt confident* in their understanding when they finished his class.

However, at the start of this academic year, Mr. Cosgrove was convinced that he needed to make some changes in his teaching. Over the summer he had gone to Germany for several weeks to visit his son, who was spending two years there engaged in business. Although his son knew virtually no conversational German when he went to Germany, he told his father that he learned how to speak German by hearing the real language spoken and by reading it in newspapers and magazines. His son was so convincing in his argument that Mr. Cosgrove resolved to ask Mrs. Sturgeon to help him make some changes in his teaching. He also acknowledged that his teaching had not reflected recent approaches to language instruction because he was afraid the new strategies wouldn't work and he would lose enrollments. Mrs. Sturgeon was thrilled with Mr. Cosgrove's new position, and, recognizing his professional and emotional vulnerability, she sought ways that they could both improve their teaching.

Ask yourself these questions:

1. What do you think the listening process is like for students in Mr. Cosgrove's classes?
2. What do you think the listening process is like for students in Mrs. Sturgeon's classes?
3. What are some ways Mrs. Sturgeon and Mr. Cosgrove might seek change in neutral and nonthreatening ways?

To prepare the case:

- Read Bacon (1989) for ideas about listening strategies.
- Read Herron and Seay (1991) for information about the effectiveness of authentic listening texts.
- Interview an experienced high school foreign language teacher to find out what he or she does when students fail to understand what has been said.

In thinking about a solution to her dilemma, Mrs. Sturgeon spoke with her friend, Mr. Kraft, who teaches English as a Second Language at Centerville Community College. Since English is the language under study as well as the language of instruction, Mr. Kraft never translates what he says because his students are all from a variety of linguistic and cultural backgrounds. The only language they share in common is English. Mrs. Sturgeon asked Mr. Kraft how he helps students with listening comprehension. He described how he uses the model for interactive listening presented in this chapter. Then he showed her, among other things, the pages of the textbook that follow. Using the interactive model presented in the CONCEPTUAL ORIENTATION section of this chapter, describe how each step is presented, what students do with the meaning of the listening text, and what students do with the language of the listening text.

SECTION A

Before You Listen

Getting Set

These people are getting ready to eat dinner.
What are they going to eat?
Did people eat the same kind of food thousands of years ago?
Which food was more popular then?

Talking It Over

You will hear a mini-lecture about diet. Look at the following list of words. Practice saying them. Which words do you think you will hear? Why? Discuss your answers.

animals	flesh-eater	meat
beans	food(s)	nutrition
bones	fruit	nuts
calories	gnawing	plant(s)
carnivorous	grains	roots
chewing	hungry	seeds
consuming	leaves	teeth
dinner	meals	vegetarian
eating		

80

Spelling It Out

Read the following definitions of some words from the mini-lecture. Listen to the words that match the definitions. Write down the spelling for each word.

1. __ __ __ __ __ __ : give the meaning for

2. __ __ __ __ __ __ __

   __ __ __ __   __ __: reducing the amount

3. __ __ __ __ __ __ __ : plan or set of rules

4. __ __ __ __ __ __ __ __ : rich

5. __ __ __ __ __ __ __ : throw away or get rid of

Now practice saying the words.

As You Listen

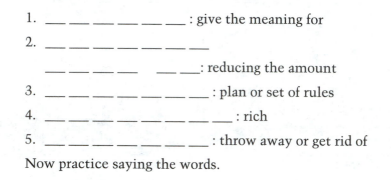 Checking It Off

Look at the vocabulary list on page 80. Listen to the mini-lecture. <u>Underline</u> the words that you hear. Discuss your choices.

Zeroing In: Main Idea

This mini-lecture has one main idea. Read the following sentences. Put an X in front of the most important point. Discuss your choice.

___ 1. One definition of diet is controlling the amount of food one eats.

___ 2. Americans eat more meat than any other group.

___ 3. To make our lives better and longer, we need to eat what pre-historic people ate.

___ 4. People started to eat meat about one and a half million years ago.

81

Look at the following phrases. They tell you that main ideas or important points will follow. Listen to the mini-lecture again. <u>Underline</u> the phrase that you hear. Discuss your answers.

1. The important thing to remember is . . .

2. The key point is . . .

3. One could conclude that . . .

Listen to this phrase from the mini-lecture. Answer the following questions. Discuss your answers.

1. What is the most important word? _____

2. Listen to the mini-lecture again. Does the main idea come at the beginning, the middle, or the end?

After You Listen

Practicing New Words

■ The words on the left are from the mini-lecture. Practice saying them. Match the words with their definitions on the right. Discuss your answers.

____ 1. to that effect
____ 2. maintaining
____ 3. consists of
____ 4. voracious
____ 5. ancestors
____ 6. mastodons
____ 7. conventional wisdom
____ 8. anthropologist
____ 9. take for granted
____ 10. fossilized

a. accept as fact without questioning
b. animal/plant of long ago preserved in rock
c. animals looking like elephants that are no longer living
d. belief most people think is true
e. is made up of
f. keeping
g. meaning something similar
h. person who studies human culture
i. relatives who lived long ago
j. wanting large amounts

82

■ Practice saying these words from the lecture. Some are nouns and some are adjectives.

Nouns	Adjectives
1. diet	dietary
2. definition	definitive
3. variety	various
4. purpose	purposeful
5. nutrition	nutritional
6. affluence	affluent
7. sophistication	sophisticated
8. tradition	traditional
9. ancestor	ancestral
10. convention	conventional
11. wisdom	wise
12. truth	truthful
13. technology	technological
14. access	accessible
15. fossil	fossilized

■ Read the following sentences. Write the correct form of the word in the blank. Words from number one on the list go in sentence number one, words from number two on the list go in sentence number two, and so forth. Circle whether the word is a noun or an adjective.

1. a. Americans have a _____ tradition of eating meat.

   noun   adjective

   b. Professor Matthews needs to go on a _____ .

   noun   adjective

2. a. Please give me the _____ for the word "archaeologist."

   noun   adjective

   b. This book contains the _____ study of the American diet.

   noun   adjective

3. a. It is wise to eat a _____ of food.

   noun   adjective

   b. One should have _____ things to eat in one's diet.

   noun   adjective

83

4. a. One _____ way to review for the test is to look at the lecture notes.   noun   adjective

    b. What is the _____ for making such a difficult assignment?   noun   adjective

5. a. It is important to maintain a balance in the body's_____ .
       noun   adjective

    b. What is the _____ value of a hamburger?
       noun   adjective

6. a. People who live in _____ countries eat a lot of meat.
       noun   adjective

    b. What people eat is determined by a country's_____ .
       noun   adjective

7. a. How _____ are these language-learning students?
       noun   adjective

    b. The _____ of the ancient culture surprised the anthropologist.   noun   adjective

8. a. Do you have a dietary _____ in your family?
       noun   adjective

    b. It is _____ to eat turkey on Thanksgiving.
       noun   adjective

9. a. Our _____ home was located in the north.
       noun   adjective

    b. Which _____ came from the Philippines?
       noun   adjective

10. a. The student followed _____ by typing the homework assignment.   noun   adjective

    b. The teacher follows a _____ method of instruction.
       noun   adjective

84

11. a. Does _____ always come with age?

    noun   adjective

    b. Many students feel their instructor is a _____ person.

    noun   adjective.

12. a. Be _____ when answering the question.

    noun   adjective

    b. Please tell me the _____ .

    noun   adjective

13. a. A teacher must keep up with all the latest _____ .

    noun   adjective

    b. There have been great _____ advances in the twentieth

    century.   noun   adjective

14. a. Computers have given us _____ to more information.

    noun   adjective

    b. Teachers should make themselves _____ to their students.

    noun   adjective

15. a. Animal bones became _____ .   noun   adjective

    b. Show me an example of a _____ .   noun   adjective

■ Read and discuss the following questions with your classmates.

1. You can add -ist to some English words to make them mean "a person who studies, plays or operates something." Some examples are:

    archaeology ⟶ archaeologist (a person who studies archaeology)

    anthropology ⟶ anthropologist (a person who studies anthropology)

    piano ⟶ pianist (a person who plays the piano)

    Can you think of some others?

2. The lecturer said that as countries become more wealthy, their people throw off their vegetarian traditions and begin to eat more meat. What other **traditions** do people **discard**?

3. The lecturer mentioned **technological advances** today. Can you think of some examples?

85

Writing It Down

Taking notes is a quick way to write down information. It is important because it helps us to remember the main ideas in a lecture. Read the summary of the mini-lecture. Decide which words are the most important. (The sentence has eight important words.) Cross out the words that are not important. Discuss your answers.

It is necessary to eat the same things that our ancestors did in order for health to improve and to live longer. (8)

There are many different ways to take notes. Here is one way. One blank means one word. Write the important words in the blanks. USE ABBREVIATIONS AND/OR SYMBOLS IF YOU CAN.

_____ _____ _____ _____ ⟶ _____ _____ /

⟶ _____ _____

 Listen to the mini-lecture one more time. Look at the notes while listening.

Source: James 1992.

Presentation of each step:

I. Pre-listening/Pre-reading _____

_____

_____

II. Identify main elements _____

_____

_____

III. Identify details _____

_____

_____

IV. Organize/revise main ideas/details _____

_____

_____

V. Recreate text _____

_____

_____

VI. React to text/explore intertextuality _____

_____

_____

What do students do with the meaning of the text at each stage?

I. _____

_____

II. _____

_____

III. _____

_____

IV. _____

_____

V. _____

_____

VI. _____

What do students do with the language of the text at each stage?

I. _____

_____

II. _____

_____

III. _____

_____

IV. _____

_____

V. _____

_____

VI. _____

For each of the above stages, identify some classroom activities you would like to try for a similar chapter on foods in the language that you teach. Describe how you would implement the steps described in this chapter.

_____

_____

_____

_____

_____

_____

_____

_____

_____

_____

_____

CASE STUDY 2
Reading Aloud

For 12 years, Mrs. Boone has been teaching French at Big Sky High School in a rural Midwestern town. One of the first things she noticed about her students when she began teaching was the transference of students' regional English accent to their French pronunciation. She began to ask her students to read aloud in French to help them practice their pronunciation. Generally, her procedure is to introduce the activity by telling students that it's time to practice pronunciation. Sometimes she puts them through some practice exercises, repeating words that have a particularly troublesome sound. Then she models for the students a short sentence she has selected that embodies the sound, and asks for whole class repetition. Then she asks for individuals to read aloud subsequent sentences that also contain the troublesome sound.

Ms. Ariel has taught in the same school as Mrs. Boone and has roughly the same number of years of teaching experience, but Ms. Ariel teaches Spanish. Mrs. Boone and Ms. Ariel belong to the same walking group, which meets after school for a mile walk around the track. One day as they walked, Mrs. Boone asked Ms. Ariel how she used reading aloud for pronunciation practice. Ms. Ariel replied that she did not use it at all for pronunciation practice, and wondered how one could use such a strategy for pronunciation. Of course, she said, the main purpose of reading aloud was so that students could comprehend the language and then discuss what it meant. Why, even the students listening to the oral reader could use the reading to figure out meaning. Today, in fact, the students read aloud a passage from _Mosén Millán,_ and their understanding of the novel was enhanced by having done so.

Both Mrs. Boone and Ms. Ariel were so surprised that they had used a technique by the same name for entirely different purposes that they decided to ask their students what they did in their minds as they read aloud in class.

Ask yourself these questions:

1. What are some possible metacognitive strategies that Mrs. Boone's students are using during oral reading? How about Ms. Ariel's students?
2. In each teacher's classroom, describe how these skills are being practiced: reading, listening, pronunciation.
3. How do the activities in the classes of Mrs. Boone and Ms. Ariel fit the descriptions of reading provided in this chapter?
4. Do you agree with Ms. Ariel's statement that her students' comprehension was enhanced by listening to their classmates read aloud? Explain.

To prepare the case:

■ Read Bacon (1992b) for information about the metacognitive strategies learners use while listening.
■ Interview a beginning and an advanced language student to find out what they think about while they are reading aloud.
■ Interview a beginning and an advanced language student to find out what they think about while someone else is reading aloud.

Conduct your own mini-experiment. Ask a student to read a paragraph aloud, and ask two other students to listen and then to answer the following questions:

1. What was the first thing that you did in order to make sense of this paragraph?
2. Did you do anything else to help you understand at any point during the listening?
3. At any point during the listening, did you change your mind regarding what this passage was about or what to listen for?
4. What can you remember hearing?
5. Can you remember anything else that you heard? Any new information?
6. Did you learn anything new? Any new information?
7. Do you remember anything else?
8. Do you remember any new words?
9. On a scale of 1–10, how confident are you that you understood this passage?
10. On a scale of 1–10, how much did you already know about this topic?

(Adapted from Bacon 1992a)

Summarize your findings below.

_____

_____

_____

_____

_____

_____

_____

_____

_____

_____

Write a description of the effectiveness of using reading aloud as a strategy in your foreign language classroom.

_____

_____

_____

_____

_____

_____

_____

_____

_____

REFERENCES

Allen, E. D., E. B. Bernhardt, M. T. Berry, and M. Demel. "Comprehension and Text Genre: An Analysis of Secondary School Foreign Language Readers." *Modern Language Journal* 72 (1988): 163–187.

Bacon, S. M. "Listening for Real in the Foreign-Language Classroom." *Foreign Language Annals* 22 (1989): 543–551.

Bacon, S. M. "The Relationship Between Gender, Comprehension, Processing Strategies, and Cognitive and Affective Response in Foreign Language Listening." *Modern Language Journal* 76 (1992a): 160–178.

Bacon, S. M. "Phases of Listening to Authentic Input in Spanish: A Descriptive Study." *Foreign Language Annals* 25 (1992b): 317–334.

Barnett, M. "Reading Through Context." *Modern Language Journal* 72 (1988): 150–159.

Bensoussan, M., D. Sim, and R. Weiss. "The Effect of Dictionary Usage on EFL Test Performance Compared with Student and Teacher Attitudes and Expectations." *Reading in a Foreign Language* 2 (1984): 262–276.

Bransford, J. D., and M. K. Johnson. "Contextual Prerequisites for Understanding: Some Investigations of Comprehension and Recall." *Journal of Verbal Learning and Verbal Behavior* 11 (1972): 717–726.

Byrnes, H. "The Role of Listening Comprehension: A Theoretical Base." *Foreign Language Annals* 17 (1984): 317–329.

Canale, M., and M. Swain. "Theoretical Bases of Communicative Approaches to Second Language Teaching and Testing." *Applied Linguistics* 1 (1980): 1–47.

Carrell, P. "Facilitating ESL Reading by Teaching Text Structure." *TESOL Quarterly* 19 (1985): 727–752.

Carrell, P., J. Devine, and D. Eskey (Eds.). *Interactive Approaches to Second Language Reading*. Cambridge: Cambridge University Press, 1988.

Chastain, K. *Developing Second Language Skills—Theory and Practice*. 3rd ed. San Diego, CA: Harcourt Brace Jovanovich, 1988.

Christensen, B. "Teenage Novels of Adventure as a Source of Authentic Material." *Foreign Language Annals* 23 (1990): 531–537.

Dunkel, P. A. "Developing Listening Fluency in L2: Theoretical Principles and Pedagogical Considerations." *Modern Language Journal* 70 (1986): 99–106.

Eskey, D. E. "Theoretical Foundations." Eds. F. Dubin, D. E. Eskey, and W. Grabe. *Teaching Second Language Reading for Academic Purposes*. Reading, MA: Addison-Wesley, 1986.

Feyten, C. "The Power of Listening Ability: An Overlooked Dimension in Language Acquisition." *Modern Language Journal* 75 (1991): 173–180.

Glisan, E. W. "A Plan for Teaching Listening Comprehension: Adaptation of an Instructional Reading Model." *Foreign Language Annals* 31 (1988): 9–16.

Goodman, K. S. "Reading: A Psycholinguistic Guessing Game." *Journal of the Reading Specialist* 6 (1967): 126–135.

Grellet, F. *Developing Reading Skills. A Practical Guide to Reading Comprehension Exercises.* Cambridge: Cambridge University Press, 1981.

Harper, S. N. "Strategies for Teaching Literature at the Undergraduate Level." *Modern Language Journal* 72 (1988): 402–408.

Herron, C. A., and I. Seay. "The Effect of Authentic Oral Texts on Student Listening Comprehension in the Foreign Language Classroom." *Foreign Language Annals* 24 (1991): 487–495.

James, G. *Interactive Listening on Campus.* Boston: Heinle & Heinle, 1992.

Joiner, E. G. "Listening in the Foreign Language." Ed. H. S. Lepke. *Listening, Reading, Writing: Analysis and Application.* Middlebury, VT: Northeast Conference on the Teaching of Foreign Languages, 1986: 43–70.

Kintsch, W., and T. A. van Dijk. "Towards a Model of Discourse Comprehension and Production." *Psychological Review* 85 (1978): 363–394.

Krashen, S. D. *Writing: Research, Theory and Application.* New York: Pergamon Press, 1984.

Lee, J. F. "Background Knowledge and L2 Reading." *Modern Language Journal* 70 (1986a): 350–354.

Lee, J. F. "On the Use of the Recall Task to Measure L2 Reading Comprehension." *Studies in Second Language Acquisition* 8 (1986b): 83–93.

Lee, J. F. "Comprehending the Spanish Subjunctive: An Information Processing Perspective." *Modern Language Journal* 71 (1987): 51–57.

Lepke, H. S. (Ed.). *Listening, Reading, Writing: Analysis and Application.* Middlebury, VT: Northeast Conference on the Teaching of Foreign Languages, 1986.

Minsky, M. "A Framework for Representing Knowledge." Ed. J. Haugeland. *Mind Design.* Cambridge, MA: MIT Press, 1982.

Mueller, G. A. "Visual Contextual Cues and Listening Comprehension: An Experiment." *Modern Language Journal* 64 (1980): 335–340.

Munby, J. "Teaching Intensive Reading Skills." Eds. R. Mackay, B. Barkenson, and R. R. Jordan. *Reading in a Second Language.* Rowley, MA: Newbury House, 1979.

Nunan, D. "Content Familiarity and the Perception of Textual Relationships in Second Language Reading." *RELC Journal* 16 (1985): 43–51.

Nuttal, C. *Teaching Reading Skills in a Foreign Language. Practical Language Series No. 9.* London: Heinemann, 1982.

Oller, J. W. "Some Working Ideas for Language Teaching." Eds. J. W. Oller and P. A. Richard-Amato. *Methods That Work.* Rowley, MA: Newbury House, 1983.

Omaggio, A. C. "Pictures and Second Language Comprehension: Do They Help?" *Foreign Language Annals* 12 (1979): 107–116.

Palinscar, A., and A. Brown. "Reciprocal Teaching of Comprehension Fostering and Comprehension-Monitoring Activities." *Cognition and Instruction* 1 (1984): 117–175.

Phillips, J. K. "Practical Implications of Recent Research in Reading." *Foreign Language Annals* 17 (1984): 285–296.

Rice, D. B. "Language Proficiency and Textual Theory: How the Twain Might Meet." *Association of Departments of Foreign Languages Bulletin* 22 (Spring 1991): 12–15.

Scarcella, R. C., and R. L. Oxford. *The Tapestry of Language Learning.* Boston, MA: Heinle & Heinle, 1992.

Stotsky, S. "Research on Reading/Writing Relationships: A Synthesis and Suggested Directions." *Language Arts* 60 (1983): 627–642.

Swaffar, J., K. Arens, and H. Byrnes. *Reading for Meaning.* Englewood Cliffs, NJ: Prentice Hall, 1991.

Tan, S., and C. Ling. "The Performance of a Group of Malay-Medium Students in an English Reading Comprehension Test." *RELC* 19 (1979): 81–89.

Vigil, V. D. "Authentic Text in the College-Level Spanish I Class as the Primary Vehicle of Instruction." Ph.D. Dissertation. University of Texas at Austin, 1987.

Villegas Rogers, C., and F. W. Medley, Jr. "Language With a Purpose: Using Authentic Materials in the Foreign Language Classroom." *Foreign Language Annals* 21 (1988): 467–478.

Weissenrieder, M. "Listening to the News in Spanish." *Foreign Language Annals* 71 (1987): 18–27.

Wolvin, A. D., and C. G. Coakley. *Listening.* 2nd ed. Dubuque, IA: William C. Brown Company, 1985.

Zabrucky, K. "The Role of Factual Coherence in Discourse Comprehension." *Discourse Processes* 9 (1986): 197–220.

Teaching Interactive Speaking

In this chapter, you will explore ways to develop students' speaking skills by engaging students in a variety of meaningful, interactive tasks and by integrating speaking with the other skills. A brief historical account of the role of speaking in foreign language teaching is presented. The teaching of speaking is examined in view of proficiency-based outcomes. You will explore many ways to develop activities that involve cooperative learning, various types of classroom interaction, and the use of imagination. Approaches to integrating speaking into the teaching of literature and culture are discussed. The effect of feedback on oral performance is examined, and several ideas are offered for providing students with helpful feedback. You will have the opportunity to design information-gap activities for two levels of instruction and a series of interactive speaking activities that are integrated with work done on an oral or written text. The first case study explains how a teacher, faced with teaching two levels of students in one class, tries to group students for cooperative learning tasks. The second case study describes the disappointing results a teacher gets when presenting a culture lesson.

CONCEPTUAL ORIENTATION

Although the speaking skill has received a great deal of attention since the onset of audiolingualism in the 1950s, the profession has struggled to understand how students learn to speak a foreign language, what they should be taught to say, and which classroom strategies are most effective in teaching speaking.

■ A Historical View of Speaking in Foreign Language Instruction

terrible method !!

The Audiolingual Method, which brought a new emphasis to listening and speaking, advocated teaching the oral skills by means of stimulus-response learning: repetition, dialogue memorization, and manipulation of grammatical pattern drills (Lado 1964). Speaking in the ALM mode usually meant repeating after the teacher, reciting a memorized dialogue, or responding to a mechanical drill. Unfortunately, students were seldom exposed to meaningful, contextualized input and were unable to transfer the memorized material into spontaneous communication. The cognitive approaches, first proposed in the 1960s, promoted more meaningful language use and creativity (Ausubel 1968). This cognitive methodology was based largely on Chomsky's (1965) claims that an individual's linguistic knowledge does not reflect conditioned behavior but rather the ability to create an infinite number of novel responses. Chomsky distinguished between "competence," the intuitive knowledge of rules of grammar and syntax and of how the linguistic system of a language operates, and "performance," the individual's ability to produce language. According to this theoretical framework, students must understand the rules of the language before they can be expected to perform, or use the language. Although the cognitive methods advocate creative language practice, extensive discussion about grammar rules (in either a deductive or an inductive mode) and mechanical practice often leave little time for communicative language use.

In the 1970s, greater attention began to be given to developing a more communicative approach to teaching language, focusing on the needs of the students and the nature of communication. Chomsky's definition of competence was expanded by theorists such as Canale and Swain (1980) to include (1) grammatical competence: use of appropriate grammar, vocabulary, and pronunciation; (2) sociolinguistic competence: use of elements such as style, register, and intonation in appropriate contexts and settings; (3) discourse competence: ability to combine language elements to show cohesion in form and coherence of thought; and (4) strategic competence: use of verbal and nonverbal communication strategies, such as gestures and circumlocution, to compensate for unknown language. In her support of a more communicative approach, Savignon stated that "The development of the learner's communicative abilities is seen to depend not so much on the time they [sic] spend rehearsing grammatical patterns as on the opportunities they are given to interpret, to express, and to negotiate meaning in real-life situations" (1983, p. vi). She further suggested the development of a communicative approach that includes appealing topics, a functional treatment of grammar, and emphasis on communication rather than on formal accuracy in the beginning stages.

Several methods for teaching language that have been developed since the late 1970s reflect many of Savignon's ideas for a communicative approach. Methods such as the Natural Approach (Terrell 1982), a modern-day version of the Direct Method, involve students in self-expression early on and minimize the need for grammatical perfection in beginning language learning. Students learn the foreign language in many respects as a child learns his or her native language, exposed to authentic language input and encouraged to create. However, the Natural Approach has been criticized for its lack of focus on accurate use of the foreign language, which may result in fossilization of incorrect forms later on (Higgs and Clifford 1982). Various humanistic or affective approaches to language instruction have been developed, such as Silent Way (Gattegno 1976), Community Language Learning (Curran 1976), and

Suggestopedia (Lozanov 1978), all of which place a top priority on the emotions or affect of the learner. In many affective approaches, learners determine the content of what they are learning and are encouraged to express themselves from the start. In Appendix A13, you will find a chart that illustrates the chronological development of language teaching in terms of the key eras when particular approaches to and/or methods were being used. You may find it helpful to review the chart and explore the role of speaking in each method.

Speaking in a Proficiency Mode

The concept of proficiency as developed and explored over the past decade has evidenced even more discussion concerning the role of speaking in the curriculum. What can we expect students at each level to be able to say in the foreign language? What classroom strategies might enable students to develop skill in speaking? The current concept of "proficiency" describes the competencies that enable us to define in more specific terms what it means to know a language. Liskin-Gasparro's statement, "If you can't use a language, you don't know a language" (1987, p. 26), reflects the basic idea underlying proficiency. Appendix A2 of this *Handbook* contains a brief historical summary of how the proficiency concept came about; you will find it helpful to review this chart in order to understand more fully the development of the proficiency concept.

In Chapters 2 and 3, you were introduced to the framework of proficiency, which defines language ability according to functions, contexts/contents, and accuracy. The ACTFL Guidelines in Appendix A1 provide detailed information about the performance characterized for listening, speaking, reading, and writing at each major border and sublevel of the scale. These criterion-referenced descriptions are experientially based, describing how speakers typically function at various levels of ability. Figure 1 illustrates the four major borders or levels of the rating scale in the form of an inverted pyramid, showing that language facility increases exponentially, rather than arithmetically; in other words, it takes increasingly longer to climb from one level to the next. Figure 2 illustrates the assessment criteria for each major level in terms of functions, context, content, accuracy, and text type. At this point, you will find it beneficial to familiarize yourself with the major borders of the rating scale. However, familiarity with the scale does not imply an ability to accurately rate speech samples. ACTFL conducts a rigorous training and practice program for those who wish to qualify as oral proficiency testers and be certified to conduct interviews and accurately rate the speaking skill (Buck, Byrnes, and Thompson 1989). Chapter 11 discusses the interview procedure itself and its significance to classroom testing.

What implications for teaching can we glean from this concept? The proficiency concept does not propose a single method, but rather offers an organizing principle that can help teachers establish course objectives, organize course content, and determine what students should be able to do upon completion of a course or program of study. As Bragger states, proficiency "... has provided educators with a framework into which methodology, curriculum, classroom

FIGURE 1 Inverted Pyramid Showing Major Levels of ACTFL Rating Scale

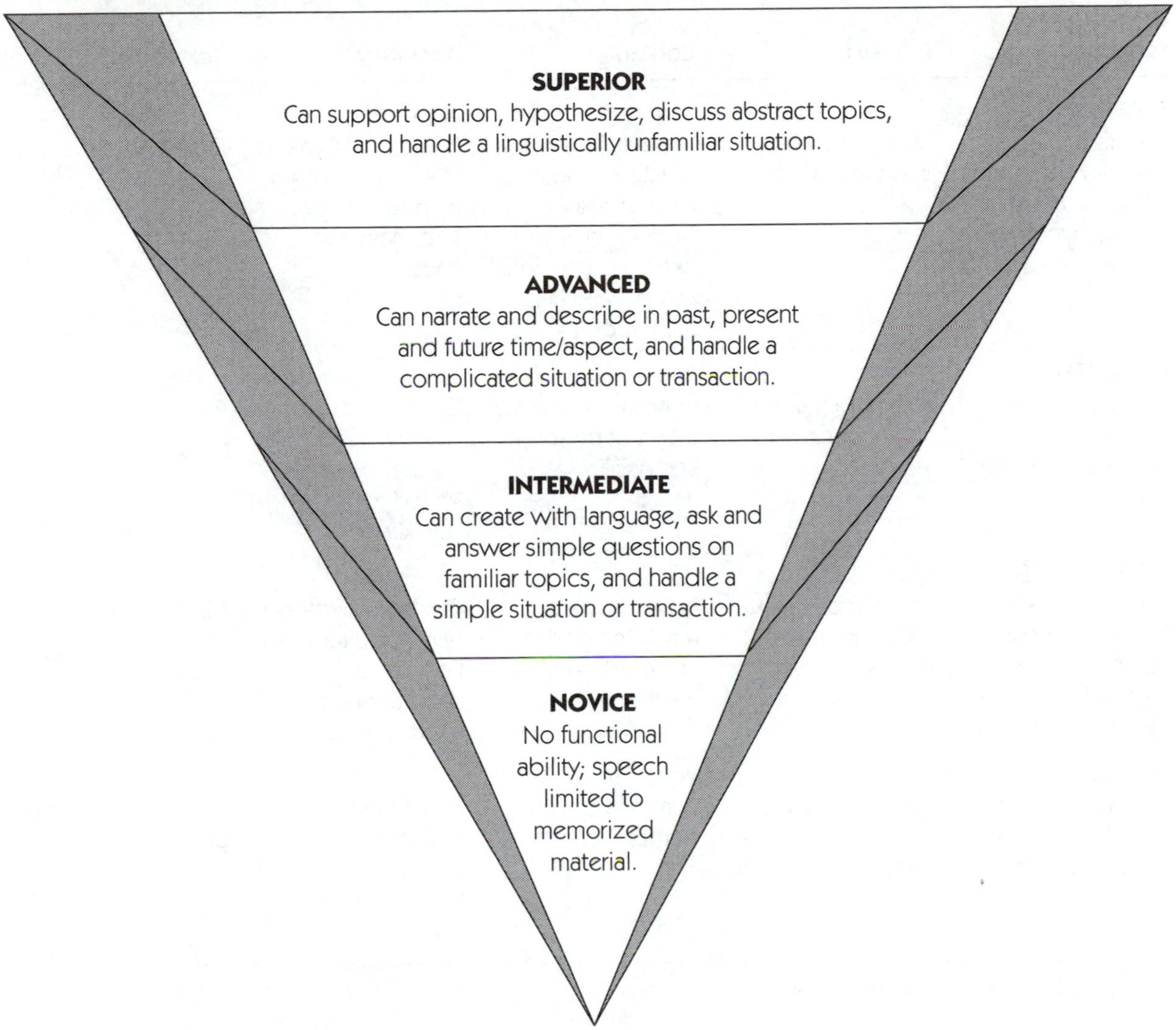

SUPERIOR
Can support opinion, hypothesize, discuss abstract topics,
and handle a linguistically unfamiliar situation.

ADVANCED
Can narrate and describe in past, present
and future time/aspect, and handle a
complicated situation or transaction.

INTERMEDIATE
Can create with language, ask and
answer simple questions on
familiar topics, and handle a
simple situation or transaction.

NOVICE
No functional
ability; speech
limited to
memorized
material.

Source: Buck, Byrnes, and Thompson 1989.

techniques and testing can fit with relative ease, and which allows for flexibility, teacher and student individuality, and variety" (1985, p. 43).

What are the characteristics of a proficiency-oriented classroom in which students learn how to speak a foreign language? Omaggio proposes the following hypotheses about how classroom instruction might best be organized:

Hypothesis 1: Opportunities must be provided for students to practice using the language in a range of contexts likely to be encountered in the target culture.

Corollary 1: Students should be encouraged to express their own meaning as early as possible in the course of instruction.

FIGURE 2 Assessment Criteria: Speaking Proficiency

Global Tasks/ Functions	Context	Content	Accuracy	Text Type
SUPERIOR Can discuss extensively by supporting opinions, abstracting and hypothesizing	Most formal and informal settings	Wide range of general interest topics and some special fields of interest and expertise; concrete, abstract and unfamiliar topics	Errors virtually never interfere with communication or disturb the native speaker	Extended discourse
ADVANCED Can describe and narrate in major time/aspect frames	Most informal and some formal settings	Concrete and factual topics of personal and public interest	Can be understood without difficulty by speakers unaccustomed to non-native speakers	Paragraph discourse
INTERMEDIATE Can maintain simple face-to-face conversation by asking and responding to simple questions	Some informal settings and a limited number of transactional situations	Topics related primarily to self and immediate environment	Can be understood, with some repetition, by speakers accustomed to non-native speakers	Discrete sentences and strings of sentences
NOVICE Can produce only formulaic utterances, lists and enumerations	Highly predictable common daily settings	Common discrete elements of daily life	May be difficult to understand, even for those accustomed to non-native speakers	Discrete words and phrases

Source: Buck, Byrnes, and Thompson 1989.

Corollary 2: A proficiency-oriented approach promotes active communicative interaction among students.

Corollary 3: Creative language practice (as opposed to exclusively manipulative or convergent practice) must be encouraged.

Corollary 4: Authentic language should be used in instruction wherever and whenever possible.

Hypothesis 2: Opportunities should be provided for students to carry out a range of functions (task universals) likely to be necessary for interacting in the target language and culture.

Hypothesis 3: There should be concern for the development of linguistic accuracy from the beginning of instruction.

Hypothesis 4: Proficiency-oriented approaches respond to the affective as well as the cognitive needs of students.

Hypothesis 5: Cultural understanding must be promoted in various ways so that students are prepared to understand, accept, and live harmoniously in the target-language community (1984, p. 51).

These hypotheses support the research presented in Chapter 1 of this *Handbook* concerning the language learning process. As discussed earlier, current research points to the need to provide opportunities for students to hear a great deal of authentic language, to use the language in meaningful interaction with others, to negotiate meaning in cooperation with others, and to participate in an environment that encourages and motivates self-expression in a non-threatening way (Long 1983; Krashen 1982; Vygotsky 1978). Taylor (1983) has identified five basic characteristics of communication in real-language situations:

1. Participants must be able to comprehend meaning conveyed beyond the sentence level.
2. The purpose of the exchange is to bridge some information gap; that is, to enable one speaker to acquire new information from another speaker.
3. Participants have the choice of what to say and how to say it.
4. Participants have an objective in mind while they are speaking.
5. Participants have to attend to many factors at the same time, such as remembering what was said, following shifts in topic, and knowing when to take turns speaking.

Bragger (1985) describes typical teacher behaviors that should be modified as we attempt to provide the type of classroom described above. She bases her suggestions on the behaviors of trained testers in oral proficiency interview situations and on their awareness of their own classroom behaviors as teachers. According to Bragger (1985), teachers should

- attempt to take part in real conversation with students, without interrupting while they are speaking and without correcting while they are trying to communicate; rather, teachers might keep track of repeated errors made by students and, at the conclusion of the conversation or communicative activity, comment on the general patterns of errors made;
- listen to the content of what students are saying rather than exclusively to the structural accuracy;
- use a normal rate of speech when talking to students, use authentic language, and speak to students as naturally as they would to native speakers of the language.

Classroom Strategies for Teaching Speaking

In Chapters 6 and 7, you explored ways to integrate the teaching of grammar, listening, and reading with the speaking skill. In Chapter 9, you will learn strategies for integrating writing with speaking and the other skills. Below are sample techniques for interactive speaking that are based on the research findings presented in Chapter 1, as well as on the implications of proficiency introduced in this chapter. These activities may be adapted for use with elementary school, middle school, secondary, and post-secondary classes.

■ Cooperative Learning

In cooperative learning, students work in pairs or in small groups of four or five to help one another complete a given task, attain a goal, or learn subject matter. Each person in the group has a responsibility, and students depend on one another as they work to complete their task. Students learn to work together and respect their classmates. They are also encouraged to develop their own abilities and identities. The teacher may give points or some form of credit to the entire group for achieving the objectives and may also give individual students credit for their contributions. Extensive research on cooperative learning by Johnson and Johnson (1987) suggests that this technique often produces higher achievement, increases retention, and develops interpersonal skills. Cooperative learning has also been shown to promote higher self-esteem and acceptance of differences, as well as to foster responsibility. Further, it encourages creativity by giving students opportunities to observe the problem-solving approaches and cognitive processing strategies of others (Kohn 1987). According to Johnson, Johnson, and Holubec (1988), cooperative learning provides the vehicle for teaching students to process skills that are needed to work effectively within a group. By using process observers and peer feedback on group processing skills, students begin to analyze and improve the group interaction. Figure 3 is an example of a questionnaire designed to encourage students to think about the group process and their own participation (Scarcella and Oxford 1992). Of particular benefit to foreign language study, cooperative learning activities teach students how to ask questions and negotiate meaning, skills that have traditionally been neglected in the classroom (Honeycutt and Vernon 1985).

Conducting Cooperative Learning Activities

Grouping Students

Research in cooperative learning has shown that the most effective way to configure small groups is to put together four students who represent a cross-section of the class in terms of level of past performance in the subject area, race or ethnicity, and sex (Slavin 1986). Slavin suggests "... a four-person team in a class that is one-half male, one-half female, and three-quarters white, one quarter minority might have two boys and two girls and three white students and one minority student. The team would also have a high performer, a low performer, and two average performers" (1986, p. 16). Students are assigned to groups or teams by the teacher, since they tend to choose partners who are like themselves.

FIGURE 3 Questionnaire: Conversational Skills

In today's activity	Often	Sometimes	Never
1. I checked to make sure that everyone understood what I said.			
2. I gave explanations whenever I could.			
3. I asked specific questions about what I didn't understand.			
4. I paraphrased what others said to make sure that I understood.			
5. I encouraged others to speak by making such remarks as "I'd like to know what _____ thinks about that" and "I haven't heard from _____ yet" and "What do you think, _____ ?"			

Source: Scarcella and Oxford 1992.

When a class does not evenly divide up into groups, a student can be assigned a role as a "floater." Floaters can have several functions, such as collecting information from each group (for example, during paired interviews), eavesdropping and reporting back to the class what he or she discovered, or serving as an observer of group processing. In this way, the extra student can contribute to the class at the end of the activity or during group reporting (Donato 1992).

Teaching Group Interaction Skills

In conducting cooperative learning tasks, the teacher often must teach the interaction skills that are lacking or in need of improvement, such as taking turns at talking. Kramsch suggests that teachers use the following features of natural discourse as they encourage students to take control of turn-taking:

- Tolerate silences; refrain from filling the gaps between turns. This will put pressure on students to initiate turns.
- Direct your gaze to any potential addressee of a student's utterance; do not assume that you are the next speaker and the student's exclusive addressee.
- Teach the students floor-taking gambits; do not grant the floor.
- Encourage students to sustain their speech beyond one or two sentences and to take longer turns; do not use a student's short utterance as a springboard for your own lengthy turn.
- Extend your exchanges with individual students to include clarification of the speaker's intentions and your understanding of them; do not cut off an exchange too soon to pass on to another student (1987, p. 22).

The teacher usually finds it necessary to teach "gambits," or strategies for opening and closing conversations (e.g., Hi! Nice to see you!) and conversational routines used in managing turn-taking and topics (e.g., I understand what you're saying, but I think that ...) (Keller and Warner 1979).

Structuring Group Tasks

The following are helpful guidelines for structuring cooperative learning and interactive activities:

1. Limit the size of the group; groups are most effective when they are no larger than five.
2. Motivate the activity with drama, actions, or visuals.
3. Set clear goals and describe outcomes clearly for the students.
4. Prime the students with the target language they need to accomplish the activity so they will know exactly how to say what they need to say.
5. Give directions and a model.
6. Set a time limit to help students feel accountable and to make the best use of the time available. Use a kitchen timer with a loud bell or buzzer to provide a neutral timekeeper and a clear signal for the end of the activity.
7. Circulate among the students throughout the activity to offer assistance and check progress.
8. Elicit feedback at the end of the activity (Knop 1986).

Detailed attention must be given to providing clear directions and examples before the task is begun (Johnson, Johnson, and Holubec 1988). Modeling the task with another student in front of the class (and talking about the task while it is performed) is another good way to provide support for the activity. While students are engaged in group activities, the teacher acts as both a process observer and a resource person. At the conclusion of the group activity, the groups report back to the whole class on their progress and on the process, thus helping the teacher to plan for future activities. Circulating around the room to monitor progress and making students responsible for reporting back to the class after the activity will encourage students to use the target language and may prevent them from reverting to the use of the native language. See Appendix A14 for a description of Donato's (1992) "Talk Scores," a technique for monitoring and evaluating group speaking activities.

Curtain and Pesola suggest that the elementary school foreign language teacher ask questions similar to the following when designing pair activities and cooperative learning tasks. These questions are also applicable to tasks done at higher levels of instruction.

1. What is the source of the message to be exchanged? Is there an information or opinion gap?
2. What language will be required to complete the activity? How much of it will need to be practiced or reviewed?
3. How is the language to be used guided or controlled?
4. What provision is made for clearly defined turn-taking? Does each partner have an opportunity to participate approximately equally?

5. Is the activity self-correcting? Can the partners find out immediately if they have been successful? Is there a way for the partners to monitor their own accuracy?

6. How can the teacher follow up on the activity in a communicative way? (1988, pp. 176–177)

Examples of Cooperative Learning Activities

Cooperative learning activities can range from the simple think-pair-share task described below (Kagan 1989) to a more complex simulation activity, as described later. The following are only a few of the many types of cooperative learning activities:[1]

■ peer tutoring (Fotos and Ellis 1991; Kagan 1989; Gaier 1985): teammates teach each other simple concepts in content areas such as math, science, or language arts. Richard-Amato (1988) suggests using this for a content-area class that includes ESL students.

■ think-pair-share (Kagan 1989): students use the following response cycle in answering questions: (1) they listen while the teacher poses a question; (2) they are given time to think of a response; (3) they are told to pair with a classmate and discuss their responses; and (4) they share their responses with the whole group.

■ jigsaw (Kagan 1989): each member of the group assumes responsibility for a given portion of the lesson; these members work with the members from the other groups who have the same assignment, thus forming "expert groups"; eventually, each member must learn the entire lesson by sharing information with others in the group. Figure 4 depicts the formation of teams and expert groups in a jigsaw activity. Slavin (1987) describes a form of Student Team Learning, called Student Teams-Achievement Division (STAD), in which students assemble in teams of four or five to learn the material covered in a lesson presented by the teacher and later take a quiz on the learned material; the team's overall score is determined by the extent to which each student improved over his or her past performance.

■ information gaps (Johnson 1979): one student has information that another one does not have but needs. For example, pairs of students might be given the task of finding an hour that they both have free this week to play a game of tennis. Each student might have a copy of his or her schedule of activities for the week, and they each have to ask questions in order to find out when the other person is free. As they share the information, they eventually find the time slot that is available for both of them. Figures 5 (Dreke and Lind 1986), 6 (Freed and Bauer 1989), and 7 (Freed and Knutson 1989) are sample information-gap activities in German, Spanish, and French, respectively.

Brooks describes another type of information-gap activity: "There are two parts to a whole diagram or picture, Part A and Part B.

[1]For a review of many research-based activities that use cooperative learning in the college classroom, refer to Cook (1991).

FIGURE 4A Sample Jigsaw Activity

The teacher will cut out the four sections of the house. Give each group only *one* of four sections.

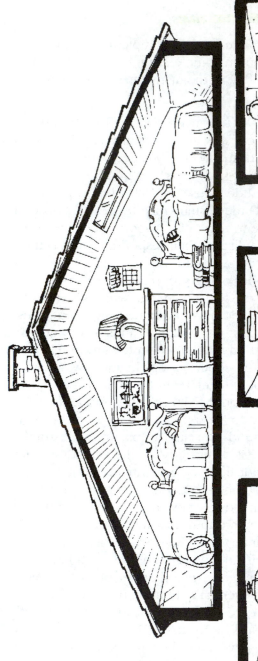
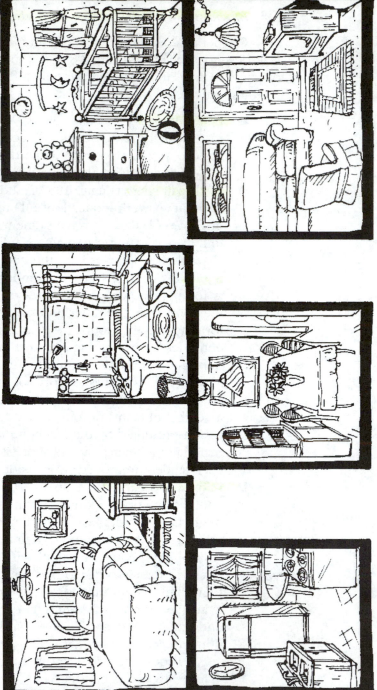

Figure 4B Jigsaw Activity for Four Groups of Students

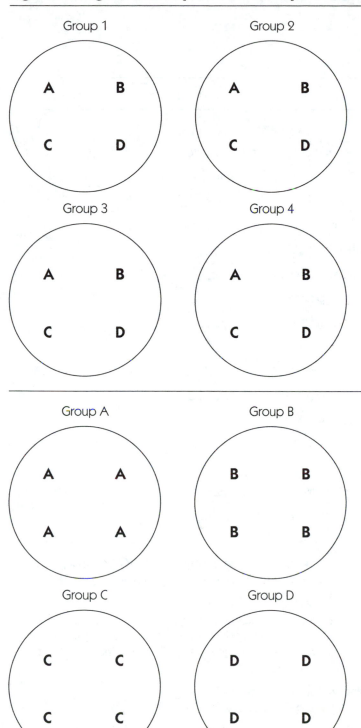

Group 1

Group 2

Group 3

Group 4

EXPERT GROUPS

STEP 1

- Divide the class heterogeneously into four groups.
- Give each group *one* section of the four picture segments in Figure 4A.
- Direct students to work cooperatively with their group so that each member can name the room(s) and the objects within the room(s). Each student should become an "expert."
- Label students within each group A, B, C, and D. (If there are more students in the class, double up on the letters — a different one for each group.)
- The four picture segments are returned to the teacher.

Group A

Group B

Group C

Group D

HOME GROUPS

STEP 2

- Students regroup according to the letter assigned to them.
- Students must pool their knowledge to answer questions provided by the teacher (see sample worksheet).
- Designate one student in each group as recorder.

Source: Fall 1991.

FIGURE 4C Jigsaw Activity Worksheet

Group _____

Names _____   _____

_____   _____

Each member of your group has seen one part of a house. You will need to work together to answer the following questions.

1. How many rooms are in the house ?   _____

2. How many bathrooms are there?   _____

3. How many bedrooms are there?   _____

4. How many of the following did you see?   _____

beds	_____	pictures	_____
tables	_____	sinks	_____
clocks	_____	doors	_____
chairs	_____	toys	_____
dressers	_____	pillows	_____
lamps	_____	bookshelves	_____
rugs	_____	waste baskets	_____
windows	_____		

5. How many children might live in this house?   _____

6. Do you think the children are older or younger?   _____

Variations: Selected readings may be given, or research assignments may be made, including biographies (each group studies one facet of the person's life) or cultural studies (each group studies one facet of a particular country or culture).

Target Language Use: To encourage use of the target language, give each student 5–10 bingo chips. Each time a student uses English, he or she must place a chip in a pile. Students receive bonus points depending on the number of chips they still have at the end of the activity.

Process Objectives: Students will work cooperatively.
Students will engage in peer teaching.

Content Objectives: Students will communicate in the target language.
Students will recall and/or name vocabulary items or basic facts and information.

Source: Fall 1991.

FIGURE 5A

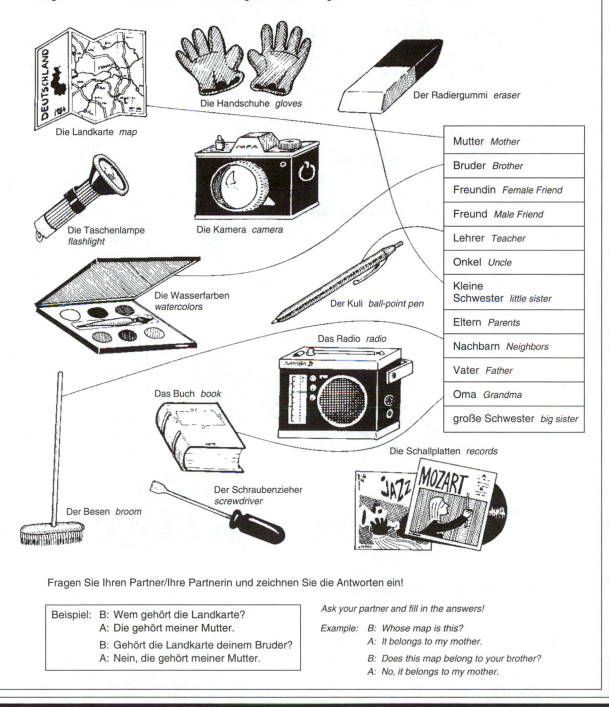

Besitzverhältnisse erfragen und bestimmen

Sie haben sich von Ihren Bekannten und Verwandten viele Sachen ausgeliehen. Jetzt wissen Sie nicht mehr so genau, wem was gehört.

Asking about and determining ownership*

You have borrowed a lot of items from your friends and relatives. Now you are not quite sure who owns what.

Die Landkarte *map*

Die Handschuhe *gloves*

Der Radiergummi *eraser*

Die Taschenlampe *flashlight*

Die Kamera *camera*

Die Wasserfarben *watercolors*

Der Kuli *ball-point pen*

Das Radio *radio*

Das Buch *book*

Der Schraubenzieher *screwdriver*

Der Besen *broom*

Die Schallplatten *records*

| Mutter *Mother* |
| Bruder *Brother* |
| Freundin *Female Friend* |
| Freund *Male Friend* |
| Lehrer *Teacher* |
| Onkel *Uncle* |
| Kleine Schwester *little sister* |
| Eltern *Parents* |
| Nachbarn *Neighbors* |
| Vater *Father* |
| Oma *Grandma* |
| große Schwester *big sister* |

Fragen Sie Ihren Partner/Ihre Partnerin und zeichnen Sie die Antworten ein!

Beispiel: B: Wem gehört die Landkarte?
A: Die gehört meiner Mutter.

B: Gehört die Landkarte deinem Bruder?
A: Nein, die gehört meiner Mutter.

Ask your partner and fill in the answers!

Example: B: Whose map is this?
A: It belongs to my mother.

B: Does this map belong to your brother?
A: No, it belongs to my mother.

Source: Dreke and Lind 1986, translations added.

FIGURE 5B

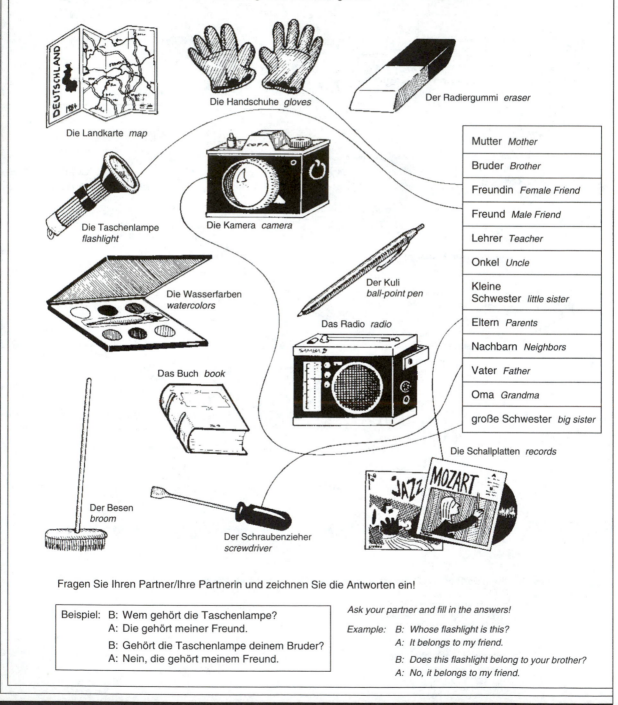

Besitzverhältnisse erfragen und bestimmen

Sie haben sich von Ihren Bekannten und Verwandten viele Sachen
ausgeliehen. Jetzt wissen Sie nicht mehr so genau, wem was gehört.

Asking about and determining ownership*

*You have borrowed a lot of items from your
friends and relatives. Now you are not quite
sure who owns what.*

Die Landkarte *map*

Die Handschuhe *gloves*

Der Radiergummi *eraser*

Die Taschenlampe *flashlight*

Die Kamera *camera*

Die Wasserfarben *watercolors*

Der Kuli *ball-point pen*

Das Radio *radio*

Das Buch *book*

Der Besen *broom*

Der Schraubenzieher *screwdriver*

Die Schallplatten *records*

Mutter	*Mother*
Bruder	*Brother*
Freundin	*Female Friend*
Freund	*Male Friend*
Lehrer	*Teacher*
Onkel	*Uncle*
Kleine Schwester	*little sister*
Eltern	*Parents*
Nachbarn	*Neighbors*
Vater	*Father*
Oma	*Grandma*
große Schwester	*big sister*

Fragen Sie Ihren Partner/Ihre Partnerin und zeichnen Sie die Antworten ein!

Beispiel: B: Wem gehört die Taschenlampe?
A: Die gehört meiner Freund.

B: Gehört die Taschenlampe deinem Bruder?
A: Nein, die gehört meinem Freund.

Ask your partner and fill in the answers!

Example: B: Whose flashlight is this?
A: It belongs to my friend.

B: Does this flashlight belong to your brother?
A: No, it belongs to my friend.

Source: Dreke and Lind 1986, translations added.

14. La sala de estar

Context

In this activity you will work with another student to describe the location of furniture in a room. You will carry out a telephone conversation between an interior designer and a client. One of you will work with a completed floor plan and the other will work with the blank plan. Both of you may consult the *Lista de Muebles* (List of Furniture).

First Student

You are the interior designer. You must call your client and indicate what furniture you have chosen and where it should be placed. Since this is a phone conversation, you must give instructions with words alone. Do not look at or point to your partner's diagram.

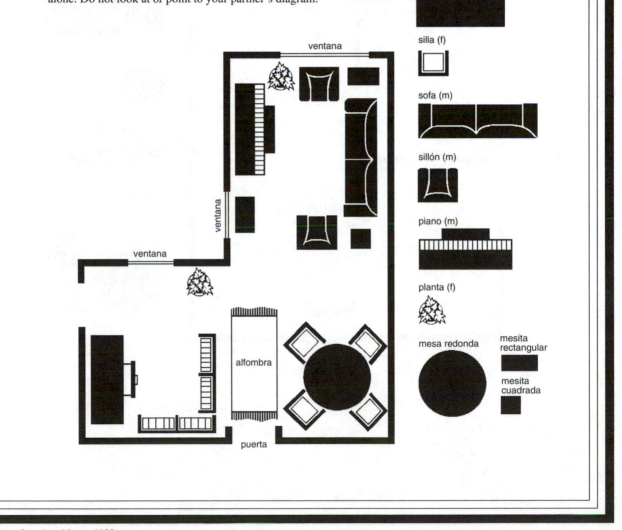

Source: Freed and Bauer 1989.

Second Student

You are the client. You call your decorator for instructions on completing the floor plan for your living room. Using only the *Lista de Muebles* and verbal cues from the decorator, fill in the blank floor plan. You can ask for repetition or clarifications as often as you like, but you cannot see the designer's floor plan. When you have finished, compare your diagrams to see if they are the same.

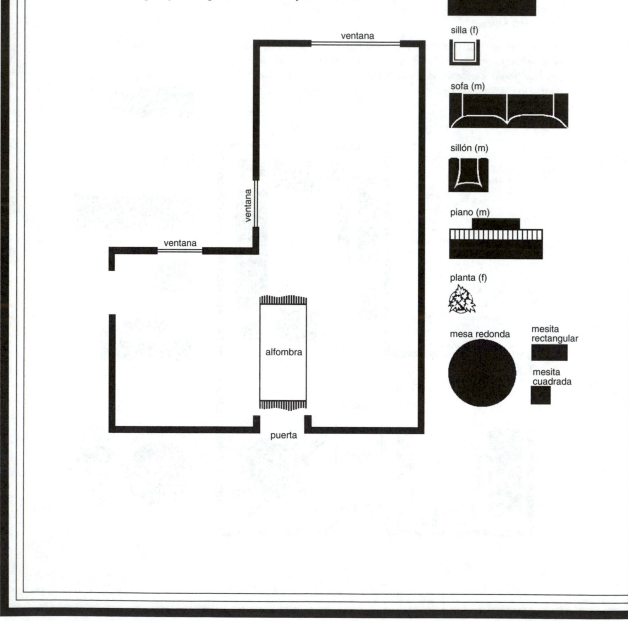

Source: Freed and Bauer 1989.

14. Géographie de l'Afrique francophone

Context

You will work with a partner on this activity to practice learning the geography of French-speaking sub-Saharan Africa. One of you will have a map of Africa with names of Francophone countries filled in. The other will receive a blank map.

First Student

You have the completed map. Your task is to give instructions to your partner on where each country is located. The only country on your partner's map is Niger, so that must be your point of departure.

VOCABULAIRE UTILE

à l'est de *to the east of*
à l'ouest de *to the west of*
au nord de *to the north of*
au sud de *to the south of*
côte, f. *coast*
golfe, m. *gulf*
océan, f. *ocean*

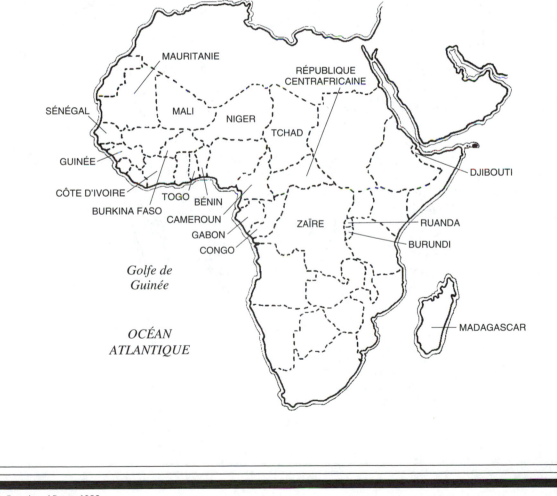

Source: Freed and Bauer 1989.

Second Student

You have a blank map. Your partner will tell you where to write in each country name. He or she will begin using Niger as a point of reference. You can ask for repetition or clarification as often as you like, but you can't look at his or her map.

When you have finished, compare maps to check for accuracy.

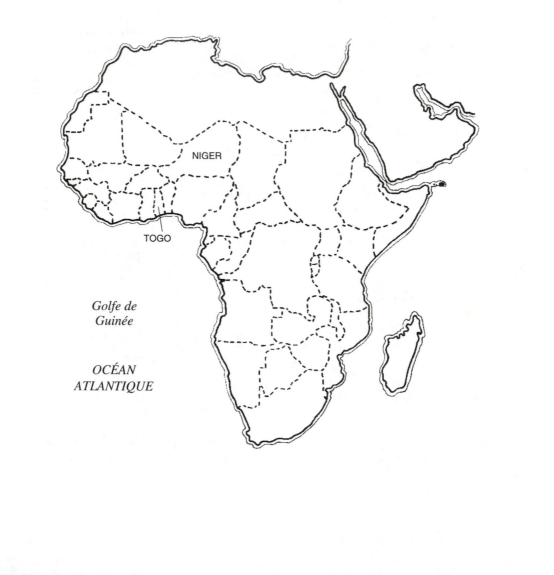

Source: Freed and Bauer 1989.

When both parts are superimposed, they form a complete diagram. One student receives Part A, the other Part B. The teacher then asks the students to talk to one another in the foreign language to find out how their part of the diagram is both different from and similar to that of the partner and to draw in or add the missing information so that, by the end of their conversation, they both have replicas of the same master diagram" (1992, p. 67).

Figure 8 illustrates how the same jigsaw activity used in Figure 4 can be adapted for use as an information-gap activity of the kind described above. This type of information-gap task can be created by drawing a picture, diagram, or arrangement of items on a sheet of paper. After the master is drawn, the two parts (or three parts for three-way jigsaws) can then be drawn so that when superimposed, they form the complete picture or diagram (Brooks 1992). Information-gap activities provide a good opportunity for students to learn how to ask for clarification, how to request information, and how to negotiate when faced with misunderstandings.[2]

- problem solving (Long and Crookes 1986): group members must share information in order to solve a problem, such as how to find lost luggage at an airport.
- storytelling: students recreate a familiar story, add more details, change the ending, or create a story with visuals.
- cooperative projects (Kagan 1989): group members work together to complete a group project such as a presentation, composition, or art project. Oxford (1992) describes the "Heritage Project," a successful cooperative model for teaching culture in language classes, in which students design a culture-related project and have a large degree of freedom in topic choice, grouping, implementation, and time management.[3]

Other Types of Interactive Activities

Various types of activities provide opportunities for students to interact with one another and use the language for communication. Snyder and DeSelms (1983) note that interaction enables students to develop self-worth and to understand one another. Among the many possible activities are

- movement activities (Bassano and Christison 1987): students get up from their seats and walk around the room in order to obtain information from classmates. For example, students might have a list of ten activities in present tense and would ask classmates whether or not they do each activity (wake up at 6:00 a.m., eat breakfast every morning, etc.); students share the information with the class afterwards.

---

[2]Recent high school and college textbooks include numerous pair and small-group tasks, including information-gap activities (Freed and Bauer 1989; Freed and Knutson 1989; Dreke and Lind 1986) and strategic interaction (DiPietro 1987).

[3]For many ideas on long-term task-oriented projects, see Fried-Booth (1986).

- Your partner has a picture that is identical to yours except that it is missing the seven objects numbered on your picture. Tell your partner (or describe) what is missing and where he or she should draw it.
- Draw the objects that are missing from your picture as your partner tells you what to draw and where to draw it.
- When completed, both pictures should be identical.

Source: Fall 1991.

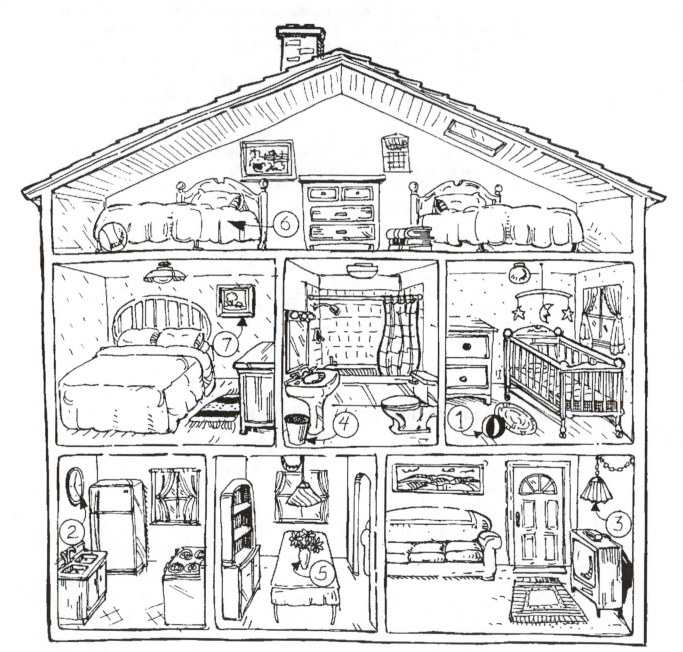

FIGURE 8B What's Missing?

- Your partner has a picture that is identical to yours except that it is missing the seven objects numbered on your picture. Tell your partner (or describe) what is missing and where he or she should draw it.
- Draw the objects that are missing from your picture as your partner tells you what to draw and where to draw it.
- When completed, both pictures should be identical.

Source: Fall 1991.

- **paired activities and interviews**: students interview each other for specific information and share their findings with the class.[4]
- **conversation cards** (Bonin and Birckbichler 1975): working in groups of three, two students ask each other questions according to cues on their cards while the third student checks for accuracy, helps the other two students, and might also report back to the class. Fleak (1992) suggests that the third student use a monitor sheet that contains suggested correct linguistic forms and possible answers; the sheet can also be given to all students as they check their responses in class or at home.
- **role plays:** students act out situations such as a restaurant scene or a visit to a doctor. Beginning students can be given role-play cards with vocabulary/grammar hints provided, intermediate-level students can practice role plays around survival situations, and advanced-level learners can present role plays around a problematic situation in which someone must solve a conflict or persuade someone else to do something (Di Pietro 1987; Omaggio 1986). It is advantageous to present the situation card in the native language so that students completely understand the task and so that they are not given the target language words and expressions that they are being asked to generate in the role play. However, when preparing role plays, students benefit from well-organized instructions and guidance, such as a model situation and hints concerning vocabulary and grammar use. The extent to which the teacher offers specific suggestions will depend on the cognitive and linguistic levels of the students. Younger learners, for example, require more structured role play directions in order to help them focus their ideas.

  Richards describes the following procedure for using role play with intermediate-level learners:
  1. Learners participate in a preliminary activity in which the topic and situation are introduced.
  2. They then work through a model dialogue on a related topic that provides examples of the type of language that will be required.
  3. Assisted by role cards, learners perform the role play.
  4. Learners listen to recordings of native speakers performing the role play with the role cards.
  5. Follow-up activities exploit the native speaker performance.
  6. The entire sequence is then repeated with a second transaction on the same topic. (1985, pp. 85–88)
- **sharing opinions, debating, narrating, describing, explaining**: these activities are particularly useful as students move into the advanced level of study, since they provide the impetus for self-expression, use

---

[4]An earlier section in this chapter describes ways to configure small groups by placing students together who represent a cross-section of the class in terms of level of performance, race/ethnicity, and sex. This same procedure could be used in configuring heterogeneous pairs of students.

of paragraph-length and extended discourse, and manipulation of more sophisticated vocabulary and grammatical structures.

Imaginative Activities

Sadow has developed a number of imaginative activities for the language classroom, in which students are asked to "... solve a problem they would not normally have to face, concoct a plan they would never have dreamt of on their own, reconstruct the missing parts of stories, and act in outlandish ways" (1987, p. 33). According to Sadow, imaginative activities have the following characteristics:

1. Students work from the known to the unknown.
2. The problem is deliberately ambiguous.
3. Any logical response to the problem is acceptable.
4. Role play is commonly used.
5. Listening skills are crucial at several points in the activity.
6. The teacher sets up the activity and then withdraws.
7. There is a summing up or debriefing following student discussion. (1987, pp. 33–34)

When students first begin to do imaginative work, Sadow (1987) suggests that they work with structured paired activities such as rewriting conversations or dialogues to change the characters, perhaps by switching male and female or altering age and status. Beginning-level students might be engaged in activities such as designing a mask with unusual facial features, designing half-built houses, or inventing a job interviewer they would like to encounter (Sadow 1987). At the intermediate and advanced levels, challenging problem-solving activities can be presented that promote interaction and critical thinking. Students are presented with an unusual problem to solve, such as the following, suggested by Ur (1981): *You all are extraterrestrials who, for the first time, are coming into contact with earthly objects, such as toothbrushes, watches, lightbulbs, and keys. Without reference to human civilization, figure out the possible functions of the objects.* Many kinds of imaginative activities can be based on stories that students have heard or read, and they can recreate and adapt these stories or create their own versions.[5]

Simulations and Gaming

Other types of activities in which students combine language use and imagination include simulations and gaming. Role playing, games, and dramatic techniques can help the teacher overcome the limitations of the classroom by simulating real-life scenarios. Simulations and gaming strategies have been

---

[5]For a wealth of activities designed to promote divergent thinking and language production, consult Sadow (1982).

designed in order to (1) increase motivation and interest; (2) convey and reinforce information; (3) develop language skills; (4) change attitudes; and (5) teach and evaluate language and cultural awareness (Greenblat 1988). Simulation reduces students' level of anxiety by allowing students to make mistakes that might be less acceptable in real-world communication, and helps to build a positive self-image (Gardner and Lalonde 1990; Harper 1985). Through simulations and gaming activities, students can also experience the culture of the target language as they interact in the simulation culture (Saunders and Crookall 1985).

The tasks involved in conducting classroom simulations and games include presenting new language, preparing students for the task, setting up the task, giving instructions, organizing and managing groups, establishing the teacher's role, and evaluating the task after it is completed. An example of a simulation/game is the "island game," which Crookall and Oxford describe as follows: "The scene is an island upon which you, the participants, have been marooned. In order to escape from the island you must make decisions on what information to reveal, what destination you wish to go to, whom you wish to go with, and the like. This involves weighing complex sets of data on the above questions as well as on your own and others' personal profiles. There is no single correct solution to the problem" (1990b, p. 253). Other types of games include (1) nonverbal games such as relays or musical chairs; (2) board-advancing games in which students perform certain tasks, such as responding to commands, describing pictures, doing simple math problems, after which they advance small game pieces (dice or buttons) forward on the game board; (3) word-focus games, such as class SCRABBLE®, in which students are given words and must make other words from them; (4) treasure hunts, in which students look for specific things (the task may involve an abstract characteristic, such as finding things that represent liberty or beauty); and (5) guessing games, such as "Guess What I Am, Who I Am, or What I'm Doing" (Richard-Amato 1988). The use of computerized language learning simulation is discussed in Chapter 12.

Sadow (1987) suggests the use of simulations or reenactment of scenes from a literary passage or historical event as a strategy for integrating speaking with the study of literature and history. According to Cazden (1992), reenactments or performance activities stimulate discussion as the groups plan and decide upon an interpretation of the text, and then later, in the post-performance discussion when the small groups' interpretive decisions are explained and compared.[6]

▉ Speaking and the Study of Literature

In Chapter 7, you explored strategies for guiding students through oral and written texts and using these texts as springboards for discussion and creative extension activities. One of the advantages to the interactive model for teaching

---

[6]For an extensive treatment of simulation/gaming activities, consult Crookall and Oxford (1990a).

listening and reading is that it helps students understand the text and feel comfortable with it before being plunged into creative speaking. The difficulty students often experience in trying to discuss readings, particularly literary texts, is that their reading level is usually higher than their speaking level. Therefore, they cannot communicate orally in the same style or at the same level as the text. The interactive model compensates for this difference in skill level by encouraging students to express their thoughts in their own words or at their own speaking level, while using parts of the text prose for additional support. Breiner-Sanders (1991) suggests that, when beginning to use reading as a basis for conversation, teachers select reading materials that are targeted more closely to students' speaking level, in order to help them gain confidence in discussing texts. Iandoli describes an approach to teaching oral communication with literature study that includes the following activities:

1. extensive pre-reading discussion in groups to enable students to make predictions about the text;
2. group discussion of the text and development of text interpretations;
3. brief oral synopses or interpretations of the reading without notes;
4. personalized questions and answers;
5. text-specific questions and answers;
6. dramatic reenactment of the text (1991, pp. 481–484).

As mentioned earlier, another strategy for integrating speaking and the reading of literary texts is to engage students in reenacting or simulating scenes from a literary passage (Sadow 1987). These activities provide opportunities for students to use the target language in preparing their reenactments while interacting with the text and assimilating text language into their linguistic repertoire.

■ Speaking and Culture

Undoubtedly, students cannot be taught to communicate effectively without an understanding of the target culture. This *Handbook* advocates the close integration of culture and contextualized language use. Chapter 3 presents ways to integrate culture in the curriculum planning and lesson design processes. In Chapters 6 and 7, you explored ways in which culture can be integrated in an initial authentic context—story, conversation, written text—and used as the basis for communication. Chapters 9 and 11 will present additional ideas for integrating culture with writing and testing, respectively.

Loew (1981) has proposed that culture be the central part of the second language curriculum. She offers the following rationale:

■ The knowledge of the cultural context of words is essential to accurate communication.
■ The knowledge of the target language culture is essential to a capability for positive interaction with native speakers of that language.
■ The skills and knowledge acquired while developing a deep understanding of the target language culture can be expanded to be applied

by students in their contacts with members of other culture groups from other countries and of the varied groups that compose American society. This capability will enrich their own cultural identity while improving the prospects for harmonious human relations (Loew 1981; cf. Allen 1985, p. 145).

Allen (1985) has suggested a framework that describes cultural proficiency in terms of (1) information about the culture; (2) experience, or how the learner approaches and becomes familiar with the culture; and (3) authenticity, or the attitude of the learner or the effect on the learner in terms of socioeconomic

FIGURE 9 Proposed Trisection for Culture

	INFORMATION	EXPERIENCE	AUTHENTICITY
N	Isolated concrete facts.	Ability to *list* memorized concrete facts concerning the culture.	Ability to function limited to neutral or tourist environment. Limited interaction.
I	Isolated concrete facts. Simple, conventional survival situations.	Ability to *recognize* and *identify* simple social phenomena. Ability to *answer* and *ask* simple questions concerning basic social phenomena.	Survival competence. *Awareness* of limited number of social patterns of behavior.
A	Simple, conventional patterns of social behavior. The beginnings of more complicated, less conventional patterns of social behavior.	Ability to *describe* basic, concrete social phenomena. Limited ability to *hypothesize, interpret, draw conclusions* concerning basic, social phenomena.	Limited social competence. *Awareness* of additional social patterns of behavior.
S	Virtually all the patterns of conventional social behavior. Patterns of cultural thought. Values and other *abstract* cultural patterns. Current events, national policies.	Ability to *describe abstract* cultural phenomena. Ability to *explain, predict, analyze* both concrete and abstract cultural phenomena.	Working social and professional competence.
NNC	Entire range of social and professional behavior. Topics typically within the competence of the culture-bearer, both concrete & abstract, including geography, history, literature, etc.	Ability to *evaluate* (make value judgments about) both concrete and abstract cultural phenomena. Ability to *synthesize* the various phenomena of the culture into a coherent whole.	Full social & professional competence. *Understanding.* *Empathy.*

(**N** *Novice;* **I** *Intermediate;* **A** *Advanced;* **S** *Superior;* **NNC** *Near Native Culture*)

Source: Allen 1985

behavior. Figure 9 illustrates Allen's (1985) proposed schema for assessing cultural proficiency. The Sample Culture-Based Syllabus for an Introductory-level French Course in Appendix A3 and referred to in Chapter 3, illustrates how cultural topics can be easily integrated into the curriculum.

The following are sample techniques for focusing on culture while integrating speaking and other skills:

- culture capsule, developed by Taylor, a foreign language teacher, and Sorenson, an anthropologist, (Taylor and Sorenson 1961): students hear a brief description of an aspect of difference between the American culture and the target culture, discuss the difference, perform role plays based on the ideas, and integrate this information into activities that incorporate the other skills.

- culture assimilator (Fiedler, Mitchell, and Triandis 1971): students listen to a description of or watch an incident of cross-cultural interaction in which miscommunication occurs between an American and a member of the target culture, they choose from a list of alternatives an explanation of the episode, and finally they read feedback paragraphs that explain whether each alternative is likely and why.

- cultural mini-drama (Gordon 1974): students listen to, watch, or read a series of episodes in which miscommunication is taking place; each successive episode reveals additional information, with the exact problem in understanding revealed in the last part. Students are led in discussion in order to understand how misunderstandings arise when wrong conclusions are reached about the target culture on the basis of one's own cultural conditioning.

◾ Providing Useful Feedback in Speaking Activities

The type of feedback that language teachers have traditionally given students has been in response to the correctness of language use. A "very good" awarded by the teacher undoubtedly means that the student used accurate grammar, vocabulary, and/or pronunciation, or used the designated linguistic pattern being practiced. Oral feedback given by the teacher in the classroom can generally be of two types: (1) error correction and (2) response to the content of the student's message, much as in natural conversation.

Clearly, a great deal of research is still needed in order to more fully understand the role of oral error correction in the classroom. According to Terrell (1985), correcting students' errors directly does not help them correct their mistakes in the future, may frustrate students, and may cause them to focus on language use rather than on meaning. Other researchers, such as Vigil and Oller (1976), maintain that lack of error correction may lead to fossilization, or aspects of the interlanguage that are never eliminated. Until further findings are revealed, it seems safe to assume that, as with correction of written work, students benefit most when (1) the feedback they receive focuses on understanding of the message itself, not just on accuracy of form; (2) they receive a great deal of natural feedback on their message, as in real conversation; and (3) they are made increasingly more responsible for their language accuracy so that their oral proficiency can improve.

What kind of feedback focuses on the message while signaling to the student that there is a problem, most likely due to form or vocabulary error? The following is an example of such an exchange between a Spanish teacher and a student:

Teacher: Estoy cansada hoy, clase. Trabajé hasta muy tarde anoche. ¿Qué hicieron Uds. anoche? Sí, Susana, ¿qué hiciste tú? [I'm very tired today, class. I worked until very late last night. What did all of you do last night? Yes, Susana, what did you do?]

Student: Pues, tú no hiciste nada. [Well, you didn't do anything.]

Teacher: ¿Quién? ¿Yo? Sí, yo hice mucho anoche. [Who? Me? Yes, I did a lot last night.]

Student: ¡Oh! Yo no hice nada. [Oh! I didn't do anything.]

In this exchange, the error is identified indirectly while focusing on the misunderstanding that results from the incorrect person of the verb. When errors are treated in this way, students must think about what went wrong in communication while they are developing strategies for negotiating meaning. Another technique, particularly in beginning language instruction, is to acknowledge the student's response by rephrasing it in a correct manner. Either type of error correction suggested here should be employed cautiously, in a very positive, helpful manner. In highly communicative or group activities, the teacher might do best to keep a mental note of patterns of errors and use them as the focus for subsequent language activities.

Kramsch (1987) suggests extensive use of natural feedback rather than overpraising everything students say. Statements such as "Yes, that's interesting," "I can certainly understand that!" "That's incredible!" and "Hmm, that's right" show students that you are listening to what they're saying, and this strategy encourages students to focus more on meaning. When conversing with the class as a follow-up to group interaction, Kramsch (1987) also proposes that teachers give students explicit credit for their contributions by quoting them ("As X just said,..."). In this way, teachers are not taking credit for what students have said by using it to suggest their own ideas.

At more advanced levels of study, where one of the goals is to refine language use, students can be given increasingly greater responsibility for their accuracy. The following are a few ideas that merit further research:

- peer editing of oral language samples: the teacher records role plays or situations that students enact in the classroom, after which pairs of students listen to the tapes in order to correct linguistic errors and identify ways to improve their message's content.
- teacher feedback: at certain designated times throughout the year or semester, perhaps following speaking exams, the teacher might give helpful feedback to each student concerning progress made in speak-

ing; this feedback would include patterns of errors that merit attention, with specific suggestions on how to improve accuracy.

■ error tracking system: students keep track of errors made in speech as determined by peer editing and feedback from the teacher; an error awareness sheet might be used that is similar to the one presented in Chapter 9 for writing.

TEACH AND REFLECT

The following activities will enable you to use the information presented in this chapter for the purpose of designing information-gap activities and integrating speaking tasks within the study of an oral or written text.

EPISODE ONE
Creating Information-Gap Activities for Various Levels of Instruction

Create the following information-gap activities in the language you teach, according to the instructions below:

1. Elementary school level: Design an information-gap activity that would be appropriate for elementary school children. You might create this for the content-based lesson you designed in the TEACH AND REFLECT section of Chapter 4, or you could create it for practice within another context. Decide what the purpose of the activity is and how it relates to your unit objectives. Include specific directions for students and your procedure for grouping students; what will you do if you don't have an even number? Your instructor may ask you to present your activity to the class.

2. Secondary school level: Using a chapter from a textbook suggested by your instructor, create an information-gap activity to provide speaking interaction among your students. Decide what the purpose of the activity is and how it relates to your chapter or unit objectives. What functions/contexts will students practice? What grammar and vocabulary are integrated? Include specific directions for students and your procedure for grouping students; what will you do if you don't have an even number? Your instructor may ask you to present your activity to the class.

EPISODE TWO
Integrating Speaking with Oral or Written Texts

For this activity, you will need to work from the authentic reading or taped segment that you prepared in the TEACH AND REFLECT section of Chapter 7. Another option is to work with a literary reading, such as a short story. Design three activities for integrating speaking as a follow-up to exploration of the oral or written text:

1. an interactive activity, such as a movement activity, paired interview, or role play;
2. an imaginative activity, such as changing the text or reenacting a part of the text;
3. a culture-based activity, such as a culture mini-drama or culture capsule.

Identify the objective of each activity. Include instructions to the students and your procedure for grouping students, if applicable. Your instructor may ask you to present one or more of these activities to the class.

DISCUSS AND REFLECT

The first case study presents the challenge of teaching two levels of instruction within the same class and examines how grouping for cooperative learning tasks might be done. The second case study prompts you to think about why a slide presentation given in a certain manner was unsuccessful and asks you to explore other possible alternatives that might be more effective.

CASE STUDY 1
Defining Groups for Cooperative Learning Activities

Today is the first of four teacher work/in-service days for Hans Klaus in the new school year. His principal, Mark Henry, called him in July to tell him that he would have a combined class of German II (15 students) and German III (5 students). Although he tried to convince him to establish two separate classes, using every pedagogically sound argument he could think of, the principal could not change the situation, except by not offering German III at all. Mr. Klaus rejected that choice, of course.

Now, as he ponders the class list, he is thinking about how he will handle the two ability levels of the class, especially in speaking tasks. Mr. Klaus regularly assigns his students short speaking tasks that can be completed in pairs or small groups—sometimes as many as four tasks during a class period. How, he asks himself, will a German III student be able to talk with a German II student? Then, as he recalls the performance of the students on the class list in last year's German classes, he realizes that more than two levels are represented in the class anyway. For speaking tasks, he decides to organize the students into groups of four or five for role playing and other activities. Here is the class list, with students' proficiency level, German class level, and German grade.

Student Name	Proficiency level in speaking	German class level	German grade last year	Group
John	novice low	German II	D+	Group A
Marie	novice low	German II	B-	Group B
Kayla	novice low	German II	A	Group C
Jihae	novice low	German II	C+	Group D
Sabrina	novice high	German II	B+	Group E

Sally	novice high	German II	A-	Group E
Carola	novice high	German II	A+	Group D
Roy	intrmd. low	German II	A+	Group C
Becky	intrmd. low	German II	B+	Group B
Darrin	intrmd. low	German II	C+	Group A
Gary	intrmd. mid.	German II	C-	Group A
Constanza	intrmd. mid.	German II	C+	Group B
Betty Jo	intrmd. mid.	German II	B	Group C
Kim	intrmd. mid.	German II	A-	Group D
Diego	intrmd. high	German II	B+	Group E
Yvonne	intrmd. low	German III	A-	Group E
Colette	intrmd. mid.	German III	C+	Group D
Fred	intrmd. mid	German III	B	Group C
Chiang	intrmd. high	German III	A-	Group B
Elisabeth	intrmd. high	German III	A	Group A

Ask yourself these questions:

1. What reasons do you think the principal might have had for setting up the schedule this way?
2. What are some of the pedagogically sound arguments Mr. Klaus might have used to convince Mr. Henry that the two German classes should not have been combined?
3. How did Mr. Klaus define his groups?
4. What are some likely student reactions?
5. What reasons can you give for organizing groups in this fashion?

To prepare the case:

■ Consult Slavin (1986) and Slavin (1987) for additional details about grouping students for cooperative learning tasks.
■ Interview an experienced teacher in any discipline who regularly conducts cooperative learning activities. Find out how he or she groups students.
■ Interview an experienced foreign language teacher who has a combined class with two different levels. Find out how he or she approaches language instruction in this situation.

Mr. Klaus grouped his students on the basis of their previous grades in German and on their oral proficiency levels. Describe other variables you would take into consideration as you are placing your students into groups.

_____

_____

_____

_____

_____

_____

_____

Now describe how you might deal with two different language levels in the same class (levels III and IV, for example). What types of oral activities might be particularly beneficial in this situation?

_____

_____

_____

_____

_____

_____

CASE STUDY 2
Friday Is Culture Day

Mrs. Beecher has been teaching Spanish and Social Studies at Pelican High School for eight years. Her approach to teaching Spanish is essentially communicative in nature, as she involves her students in meaningful interaction with one another. She occasionally uses cooperative learning in her classes, although she is still experimenting with various techniques. Mrs. Beecher travels to Hispanic countries frequently and brings back materials she can use in her classes, such as slides, posters, magazines, and realia.

Today is Friday and a rather chaotic day, because students are having their individual and club pictures taken for the yearbook. Because Mrs. Beecher realizes that she can accomplish very little today in terms of serious work, she decides to pull out her slides from Peru and show them to her classes. Since she visited the country, she has much that she can tell students about the scenes depicted on the slides.

After her first-period Spanish II class entered her classroom, Mrs. Beecher explained that she would be showing slides from Peru while describing them in Spanish. She asked students to take notes on the presentation, because afterwards she would ask them questions. After her 25-minute slide presentation, Mrs. Beecher began asking questions. She was amazed and a little upset when she discovered that students had not taken notes as she had instructed and could not answer most of her questions.

Ask yourself these questions:

1. What was Mrs. Beecher's objective in presenting the slide demonstration?
2. What might this lesson indicate about Mrs. Beecher's approach to teaching culture?
3. Mrs. Beecher thought that no serious work could be done today. What do you think she meant by *serious?* Was she justified in thinking this?
4. Why do you think the students failed to take notes during the slide presentation?
5. What are some possible students' reactions to Mrs. Beecher's activity?

To prepare the case:

■ Read Allen (1985) and Chapters 1 and 5 in Seelye (1984) for detailed information on approaches to integrating culture into language teaching.
■ Read Chapter 9 of Curtain and Pesola (1988), which deals with experiencing culture in the classroom.
■ Interview an experienced social studies teacher to learn about strategies he or she uses for teaching students about other cultures.

If you were Mrs. Beecher, how might you (1) integrate this slide presentation into classroom work on a given unit; and (2) use cooperative learning as a strategy for helping students understand and discuss the information given in the presentation?

_____

_____

_____

_____

_____

_____

_____

Now describe three strategies for integrating the study of culture into the language curriculum.

_____

_____

_____

_____

_____

_____

What are some ways that Mrs. Beecher might use her skill in teaching Social Studies as a vehicle for integrating culture into her Spanish curriculum?

_____

_____

_____

_____

_____

_____

_____

What might you do with your classes on a day similar to Mrs. Beecher's chaotic Friday?

_____

_____

_____

_____

_____

_____

_____

REFERENCES

Allen, W. W. "Toward Cultural Proficiency." Ed. A. Omaggio. *Proficiency, Curriculum, Articulation: The Ties That Bind*. Middlebury, VT: Northeast Conference on the Teaching of Foreign Languages, 1985: 137–166.

Ausubel, D. *Educational Psychology: A Cognitive View*. New York: Holt, Rinehart and Winston, 1968.

Bassano, S., and M. A. Christison. "Developing Successful Conversation Groups." Eds. M. H. Long and J. C. Richards. *Methodology in TESOL: A Book of Readings*. New York: Newbury House/Harper, 1987.

Bonin, T., and D. Birckbichler. "Real Communication Through Conversation Cards." *Modern Language Journal* 59 (1975): 22–25.

Bragger, J. "The Development of Oral Proficiency." Ed. A. Omaggio. *Proficiency, Curriculum, Articulation: The Ties That Bind*. Middlebury, VT: Northeast Conference on the Teaching of Foreign Languages, 1985: 41–75.

Breiner-Sanders, K. E. "Higher-Level Language Abilities: The Skills Connection." Ed. J. K. Phillips. *Building Bridges and Making Connections*. Northeast Conference on the Teaching of Foreign Languages, 1991: 57–88.

Brooks, F. B. "Can We Talk?" *Foreign Language Annals* 25 (1992): 59–71.

Buck, K., H. Byrnes, and I. Thompson. *The ACTFL Oral Proficiency Interview Tester Training Manual*. Hastings-on-Hudson, NY: ACTFL, 1989.

Canale, M., and M. Swain. "Theoretical Bases of Communicative Approaches to Second Language Teaching and Testing." *Applied Linguistics* 1 (1980): 1–47.

Cazden, C. B. "Performing Expository Texts in the Foreign Language Class-room." Eds. C. Kramsch and S. McConnell-Ginet. *Text and Context—Cross Disciplinary Perspectives on Language Study*. Lexington, MA: Heath, 1992.

Chastain, K. *Developing Second Language Skills*. San Diego, CA: Harcourt Brace Jovanovich, 1988.

Chomsky, N. *Aspects of the Theory of Syntax*. Cambridge, MA: M.I.T. Press, 1965.

Cook, L. "Cooperative Learning: A Successful College Teaching Strategy." *Innovative Higher Education* 16 (1991): 27–38.

Crookall, D., and R. L. Oxford. *Simulation, Gaming, and Language Learning*. New York: Newbury House Publishers, 1990a.

Crookall, D., and R. L. Oxford. "The Island Game." Eds. D. Crookall and R. L. Oxford. *Simulation, Gaming, and Language Learning*. New York: Newbury House, 1990b: 251–259.

Curran, C. *Counseling-Learning in Second Languages*. Apple River, IL: Apple River Press, 1976.

Curtain, H. A., and C. A. Pesola. *Languages and Children—Making the Match*. Reading, MA: Addison-Wesley, 1988.

DiPietro, R. J. *Strategic Interaction: Learning Languages Through Scenarios*. New York: Cambridge University Press, 1987.

Donato, R. Personal communication, 1992.

Dreke, M. and W. Lind. *Wechselspiel*. New York: Langenscheidt, 1986.

Fall, T. Personal communication, 1991.

Fiedler, F. E., T. Mitchell, and H. Triandis. "The Culture Assimilator: An Approach to Cross-Cultural Training." *Journal of Applied Psychology* 55 (1971): 95–102.

Fleak, K. "Moving Toward Accuracy: Using the Student Monitor Sheet with Communicative Activities." *Foreign Language Annals* 25 (1992): 173–178.

Fotos, S., and R. Ellis. "Communicating About Grammar: A Task-Based Approach." *TESOL Quarterly* 25 (1991): 605–628.

Freed, B., and B. W. Bauer. *Contextos: Spanish for Communication*. New York: Newbury House, 1989.

Freed, B., and E. Knutson. *Contextes: French for Communication*. New York: Newbury House, 1989.

Fried-Booth, D. L. *Project Work*. New York: Oxford University Press, 1986.

Gaier, S. J. *Peer Involvement in Language Learning*. Orlando: Harcourt Brace Jovanovich, 1985.

Gardner, R. C., and R. Lalonde. "Social Psychological Considerations." Eds. D. Crookall and R. L. Oxford. *Simulation, Gaming, and Language Learning*. New York: Newbury House Publishers, 1990: 215–221.

Gattegno, C. *The Common Sense of Foreign Language Teaching*. New York: Educational Solutions, 1976.

Gordon, R. L. *Living in Latin America: A Case Study in Cross-Cultural Communication*. Skokie, IL: National Textbook Company, 1974.

Greenblat, C. S. *Designing Games and Simulations: An Illustrated Handbook*. Newbury Park, CA: Sage, 1988.

Harper, S. N. "Social Psychological Effects of Simulation in Foreign Language Learning." Ed. D. Crookall. *Simulation Appplications in L2 Education and Research*. Oxford,: Pergamon Press, 1985. Special issue of System, 13 (3).

Higgs, T. V., and R. T. Clifford. "The Push Toward Communication." Ed. T. V. Higgs. *Curriculum, Competence, and the Foreign Language Teacher*.

ACTFL Foreign Language Education Series, vol. 13. Lincolnwood, IL: National Textbook, 1982: 57–79.

Honeycutt, C. A., and N. D. Vernon. "Who Should Be Asking the Questions in the Second Language Classroom?" Ed. P. Westphal. *Meeting the Call for Excellence in the Foreign Language Classroom*. Lincolnwood, IL: National Textbook Company, 1985.

Iandoli, L. J. "Improving Oral Communications in an Interactive Literature Course." *Foreign Language Annals* 24 (1991): 479– 486.

Johnson, D. D., and R. T. Johnson. *Learning Together and Alone: Cooperation, Competition, and Individualization*. Englewood Cliffs, NJ: Prentice Hall, 1987.

Johnson, D. D., R. T. Johnson, and E. J. Holubec. *Cooperation in the Classroom*. Edina, MN: Interaction Book Company, 1988.

Johnson, K. "Communicative Approaches and Communicative Processes." Eds. C. J. Brumfit and K. Johnson. *The Communicative Approach to Language Teaching*. Oxford: Oxford University Press, 1979.

Kagan, S. *Cooperative Learning: Resources for Teachers*. San Juan Capistrano, CA: Resources for Teachers, 1989.

Keller, E., and S. T. Warner. *Gambits 1: Openers; Gambits 2: Links; Gambits 3: Responders, Closers and Inventory*. Hull, Canada: Public Service Commission of Canada, 1979.

Knop, C. K. Workshop handout. Concordia College, Moorhead, MN, 1986.

Kohn, A. "It's Hard to Get Out of a Pair—Profile: David and Roger Johnson." *Psychology Today* (October 1987): 53–57.

Kramsch, C. "Interactive Discourse in Small and Large Groups." Ed. W. Rivers. *Interactive Language Teaching*. Cambridge: Cambridge University Press, 1987: 17–30.

Krashen, S. *Principles and Practice in Second Language Acquisition*. New York: Pergamon Press, 1982.

Lado, R. *Language Teaching*. New York: McGraw-Hill, 1964.

Liskin-Gasparro, J. E. "If You Can't Use a Language, You Don't Know a Language." *Middlebury Magazine* (Winter 1987): 26–27.

Loew, H. Z. "A Global Orientation to Culture Content." Eds. D. L. Lange and C. Linder. *Proceedings of the National Conference on Professional Priorities*. Hastings-on-Hudson, NY: ACTFL Materials Center, 1981.

Long, M. H. "Native Speaker/Non-Native Speaker Conversation in the Second Language Classroom." Eds. M. A. Clarke and J. Handscomb. *On TESOL '82: Pacific Perspectives on Language Learning and Teaching*. Washington, DC: TESOL, 1983.

Long, M. H., and G. Crookes. "Intervention Points in Second Language Classroom Processes." Paper presented at RELC Seminar, Singapore, 1986.

Lozanov, G. *Suggestology and Outlines of Suggestopedy*. New York: Gordon and Breach, 1978.

Omaggio, A. "The Proficiency-Oriented Classroom." Ed. T. Higgs. *Teaching for Proficiency, the Organizing Principle*. Lincolnwood, IL: National Textbook Company, 1984: 43–84.

Omaggio, A. *Teaching Language in Context*. Boston, MA: Heinle and Heinle, 1986.

Oxford, R. L. "Encouraging Initiative and Interest Through the Cooperative 'Heritage Project.'" *Northeast Conference on the Teaching of Foreign Languages Newsletter* 32 (Fall 1992): 13–16.

Richard-Amato, P. A. *Making It Happen—Interaction in the Second Language Classroom*. New York: Longman, 1988.

Richards, J. *The Context of Language Teaching*. Cambridge: Cambridge University Press, 1985.

Sadow, S. A. *Idea Bank: Creative Activities for the Language Class*. Rowley, MA: Newbury House, 1982.

Sadow, S. A. "Speaking and Listening: Imaginative Activities for the Language Class." Ed. W. Rivers. *Interactive Language Teaching*. Cambridge: Cambridge University Press, 1987.

Saunders, D., and D. Crookall. "Playing with a Second Language." *Simulation/ Games for Learning* 15, 1985.

Savignon, S. *Communicative Competence: Theory and Practice*. Reading, MA: Addison-Wesley, 1983.

Scarcella, R. C., and R. L. Oxford. *The Tapestry of Language Learning*. Boston, MA: Heinle & Heinle, 1992.

SCRABBLE®. Registered trademark of Milton Bradley Company. Springfield, MA. Copyright 1989.

Seelye, N. N. *Teaching Culture—Strategies for Intercultural Communication*. Lincolnwood, IL: National Textbook Company, 1984.

Slavin, R. E. *Using Student Team Learning*. 3rd edition. Baltimore, MD: Johns Hopkins University Press, 1986.

Slavin, R. E. "Cooperative Learning and the Cooperative School." *Educational Leadership* (November 1987): 6–13.

Snyder, B., and C. DeSelms. "Personal Growth Through Student-Centered Activities." Ed. A. Garfinkel. *The Foreign Language Classroom: New Techniques*. Lincolnwood, IL: National Textbook Company, 1983.

Taylor, B. P. "Teaching ESL: Incorporating a Communicative, Student-Centered Component." *TESOL Quarterly* 17 (1983): 69–88.

Taylor, H. D., and J. Sorenson. "Culture Capsules." *Modern Language Journal* 45 (1961): 350–354.

Terrell, T. "The Natural Approach to Language Teaching: An Update." *Modern Language Journal* 66 (1982): 121–132.

Terrell, T. "The Natural Approach to Language Teaching: An Update." *The Canadian Modern Language Review* 41 (1985): 461–479.

Ur, P. *Discussions That Work: Task-Centred Fluency Practice*. Cambridge: Cambridge University Press, 1981.

Vigil, N., and J. W. Oller. "Rule Fossilization: A Tentative Model." *Language Learning* 26 (1976): 281–295.

Vygotsky, L. *Mind in Society: The Development of Higher Psychological Processes*. Cambridge, MA: Harvard University Press, 1978.

CHAPTER 9

Teaching Meaningful Writing as Process and Product

This chapter presents ideas for helping students use writing as a tool for learning. The nature of the writing process is examined, as is the relationship between writing and learning. You will explore the role of writing in foreign language instruction for the elementary school, middle school, high school, and beyond. The developmental nature of writing will be used as the framework for learning to teach writing as a process. The written product will be discussed in terms of various techniques for scoring and grading compositions. You will have the opportunity to design your own writing assignments appropriate for students at all developmental levels. In addition, you will create your own procedure for grading compositions. In the first case study, you will see how one teacher does not get the results she expects on a writing assignment. In the second case study, you will explore ways in which a teacher might implement peer editing in the writing process.

CONCEPTUAL ORIENTATION

Despite students' best efforts to put their ideas into a foreign language and despite teachers' attentive efforts to provide corrective and supportive response, writing in another language remains a challenge for many students and teachers. Dvorak points out that the writing skill has historically been defined "... in terms of *language* development" (1986, p. 147). In the audiolingual era, writing took a backseat in comparison to other skills, and exposure to the written language was delayed until students had a good foundation in listening and speaking. Even with more current communicative approaches to language instruction, the impact on the teaching of writing has been a surprisingly slow process. Foreign language teachers still search for ways to ease students into the writing process, motivate them to want to write, and provide ways to improve their writing skills.

■ The Writing Process

A number of theorists have made the claim that learning to write is a developmentally natural process (Emig 1981; Kroll 1981; Kantor and Rubin 1981). That is, the writing skill develops in predictable stages as children learn to separate and then join their speaking and writing competencies (Dvorak 1986). Children first express their oral ideas in written form, then learn to write while keeping in mind the responses of the reader, and some finally reach the stage of using written language in order to create a certain focus or effect, as in poetic writing (Kroll 1981; Bereiter 1980).

Thus, writing develops in stages. Studies show that as early as the age of eight, children can distinguish between spoken and written prose, and, further, that they are aware of the beginning, middle, and end of a text (Bereiter 1980; Gundlach 1981). Written narratives at different grade levels indicate that children become increasingly able to write more descriptive details about characters' reactions and motives as well as about the story's main actions (Bartlett 1981). Research indicates that until they reach high-school age, children are not able to revise their writing successfully (Scardamalia 1981) and cannot tailor their writing for the reader (Crowhurst and Piche 1979).

Scarcella and Oxford (1992) maintain that writers draw on four types of competencies:

1. grammatical competence: use of grammar rules, morphology, syntax, spelling, and punctuation;
2. sociolinguistic competence: rules that enable writers to vary their writing according to their purpose, topic, and audience;
3. discourse competence: ability to organize texts cohesively and coherently through the use of devices such as pronoun reference and ellipsis or deletion of repetitive words;
4. strategic competence: use of strategies such as brainstorming writing ideas, writing drafts, and revising.

According to Scarcella and Oxford (1992), effective writers are proficient in the four components of communicative competence outlined above. Many studies have examined the competencies of both skilled and unskilled writers and the types of strategies they use in the writing process: Zamel (1982), Lapp (1984), Richards (1990), and Magnan (1985). This research has led to a comparison between the two types of writers, as depicted in Figure 1.

FIGURE 1 Comparison of Skilled and Unskilled Writers

Skilled Writers	Unskilled Writers
Spend time planning for writing	Spend little time planning
Use a recursive, nonlinear approach	Use a linear approach
Are reader-centered	Are writer-centered
Review what they write	Spend little time reviewing
Focus more on the message itself	Focus on mechanics
Use revisions to clarify meaning	Use revisions to correct form errors

As is apparent in this comparison in Figure 1, for skilled writers writing is a continuous attempt to find out what one wants to convey (Zamel 1982). This process involves pre-writing planning; jotting down thoughts in abbreviated form; writing drafts; making ongoing decisions about word choice, syntax, and style; reviewing and revising multiple times; re-reading from the reader's perspective; putting the text aside for a while; and then contemplating the final written text, which expresses the author's intended meaning (Cooper 1975). The order of these steps may differ in L1 and L2. According to Scott (1992), familiar words and phrases help L2 students generate ideas they are capable of writing about, while L1 students think of ideas they wish to express and choose words as they write.

Krashen's theory, as discussed in Chapter 1, offers some additional insights into the writing process. His research (1984) suggests that good writers do extensive reading and thereby develop an understanding of how language and text structure are used to convey an author's message. Krashen's theory parallels the idea that speaking skill requires a great deal of exposure to hearing the language spoken. In addition, in Krashen's (1984) Monitor Model, writers who monitor or attend to form excessively may experience interference in the composing process.

The Relationship Between Writing and Learning

Research in writing and cognitive psychology underscores the value of writing as a learning mode. That students *write to learn* fits well with the Vygotskian (1978) framework presented in Chapter 1, in which the learner acquires knowledge and skills by interacting with language in social contexts. In order to think and learn, we manipulate language by conversing to ourselves in what Vygotsky calls "private speech" (self-talk)—the mediator between thought and language (1962, p. 149). According to Vygotsky, "Thought is born through words" (1962, p. 153). In other words, language is a tool for building and shaping our thoughts rather than simply a means for conveying them. The writing process can help push students to the next developmental level. A similar claim is made in a study done by Emig (1983), who proposes that writing and learning are parallel processes since they both (1) are multifaceted; (2) benefit from self-provided feedback; (3) serve analytical and connective functions in organizing individual facts and images into whole ideas and essays; (4) are engaged and self-rhythmed (cf. Walvoord 1986). Other research has illustrated the usefulness of writing in order to do abstract thinking. For example, studies have shown that when an object is shown to children and then removed, the children can describe the object more accurately if they had talked or written about it while it was present (Anglin 1973; Bruner, Oliver, and Greenfield 1966). Such findings indicate that writing is a vehicle that leads students to rely less on physical reality and more on abstraction and conceptualization (Walvoord 1986).

The Role of Writing in the Foreign Language Classroom

Elementary School Instruction

In Chapter 4, you learned about how elementary school instruction makes the transition from oral to written skills through the use of the language experience chart approach. Students learn to read and write based on their experiences and oral communication. This strategy is based upon the developmental approach to writing described earlier in the chapter. For young children, meaningful writing activities focus on their concrete worlds. Curtain and Pesola (1988) suggest a variety of copying/labeling activities: labeling items in a picture; completing graphs, charts, and maps; copying a language-experience story; making lists. Activities that integrate reading and writing while emphasizing meaning and students' experiences include reading and writing simple stories; reading and writing songs, rhymes, and poems that have been learned orally; writing weather reports with accompanying pictures; and writing dialogue journals to be answered by the teacher (Curtain and Pesola 1988). Writing can also be used successfully in activities that integrate culture, such as those described in Chapter 4.

Middle School Instruction

Nerenz (1990) stresses the need for functional writing activities that engage the learner in real language use and self-expression: taking down or preparing short messages; writing postcards, notes, and letters; keeping dialogue journals; and preparing a monthly target language newsletter. In Chapter 5, you saw how writing can be used to integrate units of instruction. Laidlaw (1989) suggests the use of fixed-form poetry to tap the creative processes of young learners while enabling them to synthesize information. A sample integrative activity, perhaps from a social studies lesson and resulting writing assignment, is the following fixed-form poem:

> **Monument Poem**
> Line 1: Name of the monument
> Line 2: Four adjectives describing the monument
> Line 3: Constructed in (date, century)
> Line 4: Constructed by _____
> Line 5: Which is (on the right bank, left bank, in Paris,...)
> Line 6: Which is near (another monument or landmark)
> Line 7: Don't miss (the monument name) because _____
> (cf. Nerenz 1990, pp. 120–121)

Another example of fixed-form poetry that can be used effectively for learners at any developmental stage is the *cinquain* poem. One version (Allen and Valette) follows:

Line 1: State the subject in one word (usually a noun).
Line 2: Describe the subject in two words (often a noun and adjective or two adjectives).
Line 3: Describe an action about the subject in three words (often three verbs).
Line 4: Express an emotion about the subject in four words.
Line 5: Restate the subject in another single word, reflecting what you have already said (usually a noun). (1977, pp. 321–322)

Adaptations of the form can be consistent with what students are studying—for example, requiring the use of past tenses in line three or gerunds in line two when appropriate.

Secondary-Level Instruction and Beyond

Foreign language teachers at the secondary and post-secondary levels have traditionally used writing for two purposes: as a support skill and as a communicative skill (Magnan 1985). Students often use writing as a support skill when they try to learn a linguistic system. For example, they copy down learned material, paying attention to grammatical features, vocabulary, and spelling, and they complete grammar practice exercises to reinforce their knowledge of structures (Omaggio 1986). In traditional writing activities of this nature, teachers tend to emphasize linguistic accuracy and provide models for students to follow in order to avoid making errors (Scarcella and Oxford 1992). Richards identifies the following examples of traditional writing activities:

- providing models to which learners make minor changes and substitutions
- expanding an outline or summary
- constructing paragraphs from frames, tables, and other guides
- producing a text through answering a set of questions
- sentence combining: developing complex sentences following different rules of combination (1990, p. 107).

Although these types of activities tend to be grammar-focused, they might be more effectively used if presented in context within a purposeful task and with communication of the message as the primary goal.

The second way in which writing is used in the foreign language classroom is as a communicative skill through which students can express their ideas and opinions. Greater emphasis on communication in the classroom has brought a realization that students may benefit from earlier exposure to personal and creative writing. According to Dvorak, "It is difficult for student and teacher to think of writing as a purposeful or communicative exercise if the goal of writing activity, whether stated or unstated, is grammatical accuracy" (1986, p. 157). Students benefit from being given purposes for writing; for example, instead of assigning students the task of asking a classmate three questions about him- or herself, we might ask them to construct a class newspaper using reporters who write brief articles about their fellow students. In this case, they have a more authentic task and real reasons to ask questions. According to the developmental view of the writing process, early writing assignments should be those that build upon students' oral skills (Dvorak 1986). In such tasks, the purpose of writing reflects speech: notes, letters, diaries/journals, short stories. Various studies have shown the effectiveness of using journal writing in developing students' writing fluency and in increasing their motivation to write (Semke 1980; Peyton 1990). Figure 2 depicts a three-stage developmental approach to teaching writing in the language classroom (Dvorak 1986).

Teaching Writing as a Process

The following statement by Chastain provides a rationale for teaching writing as a process:

> Learning that the composing process is one in which writers make continuing efforts to produce the desired outcome enables students and teachers to shift their attention from the product to the process, from the pressure of trying to produce a perfect paper the first time to the reality of finding the most reliable way to express what one wants to say as the culmination of a process (1988, p. 252).

As early as 1965, Rohman proposed three stages in the writing process: pre-writing, writing, and re-writing. Flower and Hayes (1981) added to this theory the idea that writing is recursive and not linear; that is, writers use the various

FIGURE 2 Three-Stage Developmental Approach to Teaching Writing as a Process

Stage	Example
1. Through guided compositions and contextualized writing tasks, students focus on language form and their own ability to communicate.	Students take a phone message for a parent who is to meet a colleague arriving at the airport. Students write descriptive adjectives, possibly of clothing items, to help the parent identify the person.
2. Students begin to differentiate oral and written language by writing for a wider variety of purposes and learn how a text's purpose guides the content and form; they practice strategies for editing and improving grammatical and lexical choices.	Students write two descriptions of themselves: one for the new student files in their school and one as part of a letter of application for a home-stay study-abroad program (Scott 1992).
3. Students fine-tune their written language to suit the purpose, audience, and context by learning to use elements such as tone and voice (Dvorak 1986, pp. 158–159).	Working in pairs, students compare their two compositions, noting differences in the selection of vocabulary and structures depending on the audience.

stages interactively and repeatedly, as necessary. The writing process, which is created each time the writer composes, depends upon the nature of the task; the writer's long-term memory, which stores the knowledge of the topic, audience, and writing plans; and the writing processes available to the writer, such as planning and revising (Flower and Hayes 1981). Much of the literature over the past decade has suggested various types of process-oriented approaches to teaching writing (Barnett 1989; Chastain 1988; Hewins 1986; Gaudiani 1981).

Barnett (1989) has suggested a plan for incorporating the writing-process approach into a typical four-skills foreign language course. Her model features the following stages:

1. **Pre-writing stage**: students brainstorm and organize ideas. According to Barnett, "Prewriting activities help students start their papers: they involve students with a composition topic, let them realize what might be included in their papers, help them work out rhetorical problems, or review or provide useful vocabulary" (1989, p. 36). For example, students brainstorm a list of all possible ideas, perhaps in small groups as well as individually. Then they organize those ideas into meaningful sequences or groups of ideas. Staton (1983) suggests the use of journals for dialogue between students and teachers as a way to respond to tentative organization patterns.

2. **Writing stage:** students write their first drafts on the basis of their ideas from the pre-writing stage. Barnett (1989) suggests that instructors give students a direction sheet that guides them through the writing of the first draft. Helpful ideas such as how to organize the composition, how to use punctuation, and what to look for in reviewing the text can be included on the sheet.

3. **Re-writing stage:** after the teacher reads the first drafts and makes comments, students write the final draft, or next draft if there are more than two drafts. In making comments on the first drafts, Barnett (1989) concentrates on what the student is trying to say, responds positively wherever possible, points out grammatical problems and confusing sections, and suggests improvements. According to Barnett, "This method of checking the first draft takes from five to eight minutes per paper; for 25 one-page compositions, between two and three hours, less than the time needed to mark all grammar errors" (1989, p. 38). Gaudiani (1981) has proposed the use of peer editing as a part of the revision process. Students help one another to improve their writing by reading another student's draft and responding to elements such as clarity of the message, structural accuracy, vocabulary appropriateness, effectiveness of the organization, and mechanics. Many studies support the benefits of peer evaluation of writing in improving writing ability (Ford 1973; Lagana 1972).

This process-oriented approach to writing gives students the guidance and encouragement they need in order to become good writers. Teachers benefit also as they spend less time grading errors, respond more to meaning, and receive a better written product in the end. Barnett (1989) gives her students a direction sheet titled "Comment ècrire une composition" (see Appendix A18) that summarizes the thinking and writing process and suggests how to organize ideas and prepare the final draft of the composition. The categories on this direction sheet can also be used by the teacher for assessment purposes (see Appendix A19 for scoring guide).

Scarcella and Oxford (1992) have proposed a "tapestry approach" to teaching writing that differs from the process-oriented approach in several ways: (1) it does not teach students to revise all types of writing because certain types of writing (such as taking telephone messages) do not lend themselves to multiple revisions (Jenkins and Hinds 1987); (2) it focuses on all aspects of the learner's writing proficiency, including grammatical competence, by illustrating necessary grammatical structures and reminding students of typical errors to look for and correct as they edit; (3) it provides for peer revision and involves teachers as helpers in the revision process; and 4) it does not view the stages of writing as mutually exclusive and happening in a set order, but sees writing as a uniquely individual process.

In an integrative, process-oriented approach, opportunities for writing are presented in realistic contexts. Contexts such as authentic oral and written texts, as described in Chapter 7, can be integrated effectively with writing. Scarcella and Oxford (1992) suggest integrating writing and the reading of literary texts so that writing can help students learn about literature. Stern (1985) proposes the use of literature-based simulation activities that work well with writing. For example, in the "dramatic monologue," each student selects a character from a literary work and writes about a particular situation or issue while assuming the role of the character and considering the character's feelings, ideas, and style of speech. In the "dramatic dialogue," students write conversations involving the characters of a story, play, or poem. Authentic texts can also be presented to students as models that they analyze and emulate, adopting the same style or organization when creating their own written samples, or "pastiches" (Gaudiani 1981). In this way, students develop writing skill by imitating the style of texts they read and by focusing on the organization, grammar, and lexicon characteristic of individual texts.

Teaching Writing as a Product: Correcting and Grading Writing Samples

Much of the literature on correcting and grading writing assignments supports the claim that students' writing skills may improve with teacher response that focuses on content rather than on grammatical errors (Kepner 1991; Semke 1984; Zamel 1983; Donovan and McClelland 1980). Semke's (1984) study indicates that students who received comments on their writing content spent more time composing, made greater progress, and developed a higher level of writing skill than those who did not receive such response. Alternatives to written response include providing taped comments or having individual conferences with students when possible (Walvoord 1986).

The research generally indicates that overt error correction by the teacher is ineffective and may actually impede student progress (Omaggio 1986; Hendrickson 1978). Some studies suggest that students can improve their writing by being made responsible for correcting their own grammatical errors (Lalande 1984; Walz 1982). For example, teachers might use indirect correction by locating errors and giving hints about how to correct them and then asking students to self-correct. Lalande found that students were able to reduce the number of errors in their writing when the teacher marked all errors using the "Essay Correction Code" (ECCO) and tracked error frequency with the "Error Awareness Sheet" (EASE) (1984, pp. 116–117). (See Appendices A15 and A16 for examples of the ECCO and EASE.) In a recent study, Chastain (1990) found that there may be some relationship between the quality of student compositions and whether or not a grade is being given by the teacher. His study showed that (1) periodic grades on compositions may motivate students to work harder to increase the length of the written text and complexity of its sentences and (2) including ungraded written work in language classes enables students to work on developing their writing skills without constant preoccupation with grades. Recently, the portfolio approach has been suggested as an alternative to grading every individual writing assignment. In this approach, a representative sample of the student's best written work is assembled, and the entire portfolio is evaluated for a grade (Leki 1991; Tierney, Carter, and Desai 1991). The portfolio concept, which has been used in language arts, may provide many interesting alternatives for language instruction as future research is done.

Perkins (1983) suggests three types of rating systems for compositions:

1. holistic (also called integrative or global): the rater gives one grade as an overall impression of the entire text; criteria may include clarity, effectiveness of message, support of main idea, etc. (Omaggio 1986);
2. analytical: the rater scores various components of the composition separately and gives specific responses to the student; components may include content, organization, vocabulary, language use, and mechanics. (Two examples of analytical scoring sheets are provided in Appendices A17 and A19: the ESL Composition Profile Scale [Jacobs et al. 1981] and a scoring chart that might be used in conjunction with Barnett's direction sheet for how to write a composition);
3. primary trait: the rater assigns a holistic score to one particular feature of writing, such as organization or vocabulary usage, that has been identified in the writing assignment.

Foreign language teachers may find it beneficial to use the three types of scoring systems with different writing assignments, depending on the nature and purpose of the task.

TEACH AND REFLECT

The following activities will give you practice in designing writing tasks that are appropriate for various levels of instruction.

EPISODE ONE
Designing a Writing Activity for Elementary or Middle School Learners

In the TEACH AND REFLECT sections of Chapters 4 and 5, you designed storytelling lessons appropriate for elementary and middle school students, respectively. Now design a writing activity suitable for either an elementary school or a middle school lesson. Describe how the writing activity will be integrated with the lesson content, culture, and other skills.

EPISODE TWO
Designing a Writing Activity for Secondary Levels or Beyond

For this activity, select a chapter in a textbook for the target language you teach, as approved by your instructor. Develop a creative writing composition task that you might assign as a part of your work on the chapter. Keep in mind Chastain's objectives to be accomplished prior to making written assignments:

1. students should be interested in the topic;
2. students should have some reason for writing about that topic;
3. students should have several ideas and some information needed to write about the topic; and
4. students should be aware of the system the teacher will use to evaluate their compositions (1988, p. 254).

Use a process approach as you guide students in writing their compositions. Develop a grading scale for assigning a grade to the final drafts.

DISCUSS AND REFLECT

The first case study in this chapter prompts you to think about why a teacher doesn't get the results she expects on a writing task. The second case study offers the opportunity for you to help a language teacher incorporate peer editing into her teaching of writing.

CASE STUDY 1
A Writing Assignment That Doesn't Work

Dr. Marie Flayer teaches French full-time at Flagston High School and part-time at Ardamore Community College. She has been teaching at the high school for eight years and recently started teaching a class each semester at the college after completing her Ph.D. Dr. Flayer is well respected in the school district and community as an instructor who knows her subject area and how to relate it to her students. She brings the language to life in the classroom and involves students in meaningful language use.

This year, Dr. Flayer was given a French IV class to teach at the high school for the first time. She was quite enthusiastic about the assignment because she wanted to try more advanced-level activities such as composition writing. In levels one through three at Flagston, the focus is on developing listening and speaking skills, and the creative writing skill is introduced in level four.

During the second week of classes, Dr. Flayer assigned her first composition. She asked students to write three paragraphs about their summer vacations, and she gave them three days to complete the task. She reminded them about using the past tenses in French as they wrote. She was rather surprised to hear the many complaints by the students, and wondered why they thought this assignment was so difficult, given their extensive knowledge of French. The students seemed not to be pleased with their work as they handed in their compositions to Dr. Flayer. Some of the best students said that they had spent more than four hours writing their three paragraphs. Dr. Flayer collected the compositions on Friday and went home in a good mood, satisfied that she had made her students create with the language and certain that the students' complaints were exaggerated.

Dr. Flayer's happy mood soon changed to despair on Sunday as she painstakingly plowed through the stack of compositions that no native speaker of French would ever understand. It was quite apparent that students had done their assignments with their dictionaries in hand, for there were French words used that even Dr. Flayer had never before seen. There were so many grammatical errors that the message was practically incomprehensible. It was clear, Dr. Flayer thought, that her students had not spent sufficient time on this task, or they would have been able to use the language more accurately. She spent four hours correcting all the errors with her red pen, in the hope that students would at least learn from their mistakes when she returned their compositions.

Ask yourself these questions:

1. What was Dr. Flayer's approach to integrating writing into her teaching?
2. How did she prepare students to write the composition?
3. Did she use a process-oriented approach? Explain.
4. What was her rationale for correcting the errors found in the compositions?

To prepare the case:

■ Consult the following sources for more information about process-oriented approaches to teaching writing: Barnett (1989), Chastain (1988), Dvorak (1986), and Hewins (1986).

■ Consult Chapter 7 of Rivers (1987) for ideas on teaching writing by using an interactive approach and involving students in pair and group writing activities.

■ Consult the following sources for more information about error correction: Kepner (1991), Chastain (1990), Lalande (1984), and Semke (1984).

- Talk with high school or college students about how they feel when a teacher returns their writing assignments covered with red ink.
- Ask other language teachers what color pens they use to correct papers. Think about the effect of using red to make corrections.

Appendix A20 contains a Checklist for Preparing the Writing Task (Jacobs, et al. 1981). Evaluate Dr. Flayer's writing task according to the criteria presented in the list.

_____

_____

_____

_____

_____

_____

If you were Dr. Flayer, what would you have done differently in making this assignment? Describe the various steps or processes through which you might have guided your students.

_____

_____

_____

_____

_____

_____

_____

How would you have corrected and graded these compositions?

_____

_____

_____

_____

_____

Give three alternatives for what Dr. Flayer might now do with these compositions. Consider how each alternative will help students learn to write.

_____

_____

_____

_____

_____

_____

_____

CASE STUDY 2
Integrating Peer Editing into the Writing Process

Miss Reynolds has been teaching Spanish and German at Yuristown High School for three years. She has a heavy teaching schedule of seven classes, with one of the Spanish classes having levels three and four together. Miss Reynolds believes in teaching language for proficiency, and she provides many opportunities for her students to use the language in meaningful contexts. Because of time constraints, and her own training and teaching experience, she tends to focus more on listening and speaking in her classroom.

Recently she has spoken to Mrs. Savage, who has been teaching English at Yuristown for seven years, about the issue of doing more writing activities in her language classes. Miss Reynolds has assigned periodic compositions and even used a process-oriented approach to some degree as she guided students' writing. However, she has been frustrated that students did not seem to care much about correcting their errors, and she ended up practically rewriting their compositions for them. Mrs. Savage suggested that Miss Reynolds try peer editing, a technique that English teachers have been using for some time. She explained that students work in pairs (usually with one weaker student and one stronger) to help each other correct their mistakes. Mrs. Savage also suggested the use of some type of correction code and the use of the Error Awareness Sheet to help students keep track of their errors.

Ask yourself these questions:

1. At what stage of the writing process would the peer editing be done?
2. What difficulties could Miss Reynolds anticipate when introducing the peer editing technique to her classes?
3. What type of guidance will Miss Reynolds need to give her students so that they can use peer editing successfully?

To prepare the case:

■ Consult the Appendix for an example of how to teach students to evaluate others' writing (Koch and Brazil 1978).
■ Read Chapter 4 in Walvoord (1986) on using student peer groups.
■ Consult Chapter 8 of Scarcella and Oxford (1992) for sample peer review and writer response sheets.
■ Interview an experienced English teacher to find out how he or she does peer editing in the classroom.

Imagine that you are Miss Reynolds. Develop your own instruction sheet similar to the one found in Appendix A21 to help students use peer editing.

_____

_____

_____

_____

_____

_____

_____

_____

_____

Now adapt the Essay Correction Code (ECCO) in Appendix A15 for use with the foreign language you teach. Change the code as necessary for your language (include examples in the foreign language) and to make the code easy for students to understand.

_____

_____

_____

_____

_____

_____

_____

Remember that you have one class of level three and four Spanish students together. How might you use this situation to your advantage for the purposes of peer editing?

_____

_____

_____

_____

_____

_____

_____

_____

_____

REFERENCES

Allen, E. D., and R. M. Valette. *Classroom Techniques: Foreign Languages and English as a Second Language*. New York: Harcourt Brace Jovanovich, 1977.

Anglin, J. M. (Ed.). *Beyond the Information Given: Studies in the Psychology of Knowing*. New York: Norton, 1973.

Barnett, M. A. "Writing as a Process." *The French Review* 63 (1989): 39–41.

Bartlett, E. *Learning to Write: Some Cognitive and Linguistic Components*. Papers in Applied Linguistics: Linguistics and Literary Series: 2. Washington, DC: Center for Applied Linguistics, 1981.

Bereiter, C. "Development in Writing." Eds. L. Gregg and E. Steinberg. *Cognitive Processes in Writing*. Hillsdale, NJ: Erlbaum, 1980.

Bruner, J., R. P. Oliver, and P. M. Greenfield. *Studies in Cognitive Growth*. New York: Wiley, 1966.

Chastain, K. *Developing Second-Language Skills—Theory and Practice*. San Diego, CA: Harcourt Brace Jovanovich, 1988.

Chastain, K. "Characteristics of Graded and Ungraded Compositions." *Modern Language Journal* 74 (1990): 10–14.

Cooper, C. R. "Measuring Growth in Writing." *English Journal* 64 (1975): 111–120.

Crowhurst, M., and G. G. Piche. "Audience and Mode of Discourse Effects on Syntactic Complexity in Writing at Two Grade Levels." *Research in the Teaching of English* 13 (1979): 101–109.

Curtain, H., and C. Pesola. *Languages and Children—Making the Match*. Reading, MA: Addison-Wesley, 1988.

Donovan, T. R., and B. W. McClelland. *Eight Approaches to Teaching Composition*. Urbana, IL: NCTE, 1980.

Dvorak, T. "Writing in the Foreign Language." Ed. B. H. Wing. *Listening, Reading, Writing: Analysis and Application*. Middlebury, VT: Northeast Conference on the Teaching of Foreign Languages, 1986: 145–167.

Emig, J. "Non-Magical Thinking: Presenting Writing Developmentally in Schools." Eds. C. Frederiksen and J. Dominic. *Writing: The Nature, Development and Teaching of Written Communication*. Vol. 2. Hillsdale, NJ: Erlbaum, 1981.

Emig, J. *The Web of Meaning: Essays on Writing, Teaching, Learning, and Thinking*. Ed. D. Goswami and M. Butler. Upper Montclair, NJ: Boynton, 1983.

Flower, L., and J. R. Hayes. "A Cognitive Process Theory of Writing." *College Composition and Communication* 32 (1981): 365–387.

Ford, B. W. *The Effects of Peer Editing Grading on the Grammar-Usage and Theme-Composition Ability of College Freshmen*. Ed.D. Dissertation, University of Oklahoma, 1973. Dissertation Abstracts International 73, 15321.

Gaudiani, C. *Teaching Writing in the Foreign Language Curriculum*. Vol. 43 in *Language in Education: Theory and Practice*. Washington, DC: Center for Applied Linguistics, 1981.

Gundlach, R. "On the Nature and Development of Children's Writing." Eds. C. Frederiksen and J. Dominic. *Writing: The Nature, Development, and Teaching of Written Communication*. Vol. 2. Hillsdale, NJ: Erlbaum, 1981.

Hendrickson, J. M. "Error Correction in Foreign Language Teaching: Recent Theory, Research, and Practice." *Modern Language Journal* 62 (1978): 387–398.

Hewins, C. P. "Writing in a Foreign Language: Motivation and the Process Approach." *Foreign Language Annals* 19 (1986): 219-223.

Jacobs, H. L., S. Zingraf, D. Wormuth, V. Hartfield, and J. Hughey. *Testing ESL Composition: A Practical Approach*. Rowley, MA: Newbury House, 1981.

Jenkins, S., and J. Hinds. "Business Letter Writing: English, French and Japanese." *TESOL Quarterly* 21 (1987): 327–343.

Kantor, K., and D. Rubin. "Between Speaking and Writing: Processes of Differentiation." Eds. B. Kroll and R. Vann. *Exploring Speaking-Writing Relationships: Connections and Contrasts*. Urbana, IL: NCTE, 1981.

Kepner, C. G. "An Experiment in the Relationship of Types of Written Feedback to the Development of Second-Language Writing Skills." *Modern Language Journal* 75 (1991): 305–313.

Koch, C., and J. Brazil. *Strategies for Teaching the Composition Process*. Urbana, IL: NCTE, 1978.

Krashen, S. *Writing: Research, Theory and Applications*. Oxford: Pergamon Press, 1984.

Kroll, B. "Developmental Relationships Between Speaking and Writing." Eds. B. Kroll and R. Vann. *Exploring Speaking-Writing Relationships: Connections and Contrasts*. Urbana, IL: NCTE, 1981.

Lagana, J. R. *The Development, Implementation, and Evaluation of a Model for Teaching Composition Which Utilizes Individualized Learning and Peer Grouping*. Ph.D. Dissertation, University of Pittsburgh, 1972. *Dissertation Abstracts International* 73, 04127.

Laidlaw, A. "Formula Poetry Fun." A Presentation to the Washtenaw/Livingston Academic Alliance of Foreign Language Teachers. Ypsilanti, MI. February, 1989.

Lalande, J. F., II. "Reducing Composition Errors: An Experiment." *Foreign Language Annals* 17 (1984): 109–117.

Lapp, R. *The Process Approach to Writing: Towards a Curriculum for International Students.* MA Thesis, University of Hawaii, 1984.

Leki, I. "Coaching from the Margins: Issues in Written Response." Ed. B. Kroll. *Second Language Writing—Research Insights for the Classroom.* Cambridge: Cambridge University Press, 1991: 57–68.

Magnan, S. "Teaching and Testing Proficiency in Writing: Skills to Transcend the Second-Language Classroom." Ed. A. Omaggio. *Proficiency, Curriculum, Articulation: The Ties That Bind.* Middlebury, VT: Northeast Conference on the Teaching of Foreign Languages, 1985: 109–136.

Nerenz, A. G. "The Exploratory Years: Foreign Languages in the Middle-Level Curriculum." Ed. S. Magnan. *Shifting the Instructional Focus to the Learner.* Middlebury, VT: Northeast Conference on the Teaching of Foreign Languages, 1990: 93–126.

Omaggio, A. C. *Teaching Language in Context.* Boston, MA: Heinle & Heinle, 1986.

Perkins, K. "On the Use of Composition Scoring Techniques, Objective Measures, and Objective Tests to Evaluate ESL Writing Ability." *TESOL Quarterly* 17 (1983): 651–671.

Peyton, J. K. *Students and Teachers Writing Together: Perspectives on Journal Writing.* Alexandria, VA: TESOL, 1990.

Richards, J. *The Language Teaching Matrix.* Cambridge: Cambridge University Press, 1990.

Rivers, W. M. *Interactive Language Teaching.* Cambridge: Cambridge University Press, 1987.

Rohman, G. "Pre-Writing: The Stage of Discovery in the Writing Process." *College Composition and Communication* 16 (1965): 106–112.

Scarcella, R., and R. Oxford. *The Tapestry of Language Learning.* Boston, MA: Heinle & Heinle, 1992.

Scardamalia, M. "How Children Cope with the Cognitive Demands of Writing." Eds. C. Frederiksen and J. Dominic. *Writing: The Nature, Development, and Teaching of Written Communication.* Vol. 2. Hillsdale, NJ: Erlbaum, 1981.

Scott, V. "Write from the Start: A Task-Oriented Developmental Writing Program for Foreign Language Students." Ed. R. Terry. *Dimension: Language '91* (Southern Conference on Language Teaching), 1992: 1–15.

Semke, H. D. *The Comparative Effects of Four Methods of Treating Free-Writing Assignments on the Second Language Skills and Attitudes of Students in*

College Level First Year German. Unpublished Ph.D. Dissertation, University of Minnesota, 1980. *Dissertation Abstracts* 41, 4629-A.

Semke, H. D. "Effects of the Red Pen." *Foreign Language Annals* 17 (1984): 195–202.

Staton, J. "Dialogue Journals: A New Tool for Teaching." *ERIC CLL News Bulletin* 6, 2 (1983).

Stern, S. *Teaching Literature in ESL/EFL: An Integrated Approach.* Unpublished doctoral dissertation. University of California at Los Angeles, 1985.

Tierney, R. J., M. A. Carter, and L. E. Desai. *Portfolio Assessment in the Reading-Writing Classroom.* Norwood, MA: Christopher-Gordon, 1991.

Vygotsky, L. S. *Thought and Language.* Cambridge: MIT Press, 1962.

Vygotsky, L. S. *Mind in Society: The Development of Higher Psychological Processes.* Cambridge, MA: Harvard University Press, 1978.

Walvoord, B. *Helping Students Write Well.* 2nd ed. New York: The Modern Language Association of America, 1986.

Walz, J. C. *Error Correction Techniques for the FL Classroom.* Washington: CAL, 1982.

Zamel, V. "Writing: The Process of Discovering Meaning." *TESOL Quarterly* 16 (1982): 195–209.

Zamel, V. "The Composing Processes of Advanced ESL Students: Six Case Studies." *TESOL Quarterly* 17 (1983): 165–187.

10 Handling Student Diversity in the Language Classroom

In this chapter, you will explore the various types of student diversity that may be present in your classroom. First, you will learn about key learning styles that students bring to the language learning task and how you can deal with potential teacher-student style clashes. Second, the chapter presents information about strategies that students tend to use to aid their learning, and it offers a plan for integrating strategy training into your teaching. Third, a profile of learning disabled and handicapped students is given, with suggestions for ways to help these students succeed in the language classroom. Fourth, a profile of "at-risk" students is offered, along with implications for teaching language. This section includes strategies for conducting effective learning experiences for students of diverse cultural, ethnic, and racial backgrounds. Fifth, the chapter highlights some of the characteristics of and learning approaches used by gifted learners. In the TEACH AND REFLECT section, you will design a lesson geared to various learning styles, and you will compile culturally appropriate visuals for use in your teaching. In the case studies, you will explore ways through which language teachers can provide effective learning experiences for students of diverse abilities and backgrounds.

CONCEPTUAL ORIENTATION

Understanding Students' Learning Styles

You already know that students bring with them differences in background knowledge that can influence their learning. Likewise, students use a variety of learning styles, approaches, and ways of interacting when learning a new language. Of importance here are five key elements described by Scarcella and Oxford (1992) and Oxford (1990a):

1. **analytic-global:** the difference between a detail-oriented individual and a holistic one. Analytic students concentrate on grammatical details and often do not participate well in communicative activities; they would rather find the meanings of words in a dictionary than guess in context. Global students like interactive tasks in which they

use main ideas. They have difficulty dealing with grammatical details and are content to use guessing strategies.

2. **sensory preferences:** the physical, perceptual avenues for learning, such as visual, auditory, and hands-on (kinesthetic or movement-oriented and tactile or touch-oriented). Visual students prefer to read and visualize information; they usually dislike having to process oral input in the absence of visual support. Auditory students enjoy conversations and other types of verbal interaction and often have difficulty with written work. Hands-on students do well with movement around the classroom and work easily with objects and realia.

3. **intuitive/random and sensory/sequential learning:** the type of organization students prefer in the presentation of material. Intuitive students think in an abstract, and nonsequential or random manner, making sense of the global picture. Sensory/sequential students prefer to learn new information by means of a step-by-step, ordered presentation; they perform task by task and often have difficulty seeing the bigger picture.

4. **orientation to closure:** the degree to which students need to reach conclusions and can tolerate ambiguity. Students oriented toward closure want all rules spelled out for them and are skillful in using metacognitive skills such as planning, organizing, and self-evaluating; however, they often tend to analyze things prematurely and experience difficulty dealing with abstract or more subtle issues. A study done by Ehrman and Oxford (1989) shows that the desire for closure might have a negative effect on a student's ability to participate in open-ended communication. "Open learners," or those who have less need for closure, learn by osmosis rather than by conscientious effort and appear to use more effective language learning strategies than students who require quick closure (Scarcella and Oxford 1992, p. 62).

5. **competition-cooperation:** the degree to which learners benefit from competing against or cooperating with others. Competitive learners are motivated by competition in which winning is of utmost importance. Cooperative individuals prefer working with others in a helpful, supportive situation. Studies have shown that the high degree of competitiveness in education may account for the fact that learners seldom report using cooperative, social strategies (Kohn 1987; Reid 1987). According to Bailey (1983), competition in language learning may result in feelings of anxiety, inadequacy, hostility, fear of failure, guilt, and too strong a desire for approval. As you learned in Chapter 8, cooperative learning provides an avenue for student interaction while increasing self-esteem, achievement, motivation, and the use of cognitive strategies (Kohn 1987).

What implications do these learning styles have for teaching language in a classroom situation? In a recent study, Oxford and Lavine (1992) examine the mismatch that often exists between instructors' teaching styles and the learning styles of their students. They claim that "students whose learning processes resemble the teacher's are more likely to achieve good grades (and want to continue studying the language) than are students with opposing styles, who may drop the course or even discontinue studying the language" (Oxford and Lavine 1992, p. 38). They further assert that style wars between teachers and students are often disguised as "poor language aptitudes," "personality clashes," and "bad learner attitudes" (p. 42). Oxford and Lavine (1992) suggest six ways in which these teacher-student style conflicts can be dealt with realistically:

1. **Assess students' and teachers' styles and use this information in understanding classroom dynamics.** As teachers and students become aware of their major learning style preferences, they may be able to help one another understand diverse views and make an effort to compensate for any style mismatches. Instruments for assessing learning styles can be used, such as the Learning Styles Inventory (Kolb 1982) and the Myers-Briggs Type Indicator (Myers and McCaulley 1985), among others.[1]

2. **Change your teaching behavior.** Teachers can orient their teaching styles to meet their students' needs by providing a variety of multisensory, abstract, and concrete learning activities that appeal to different learning styles. Learners who are analytic, sequential, or closure-oriented usually like questions and exercises requiring unambiguous information such as completions, definitions, true-false, slash sentences, cloze passages, and guided writing. Learners who are global, intuitive, or open often prefer open-ended activities, personalized questions, simulations and games, interviews, reading for the gist, and social conversation. Visual learners need visual stimuli such as transparencies, slides, video, charts, maps, magnetic or felt boards, posters, board games, and puppets. They benefit from written directions and from being shown, not told, what to do. Auditory learners prefer auditory input from radio, television, video, songs, interviews, oral reports, discussions, telephone conversations, and recordings. They need oral instructions and must be told, not shown, what to do. Hands-on learners require hands-on experiences such as making things, manipulating real cultural items, taking notes, doing TPR activities, and following directions. If these learners "... do not receive enough sensory stimuli, they might create their own movement activities unrelated to the learning task (such as tapping pencils, drawing, doodling, wiggling, or bouncing)" (Oxford and Lavine 1992, p. 43).[2]

3. **Change students' behavior.** Language learners use their style preferences to their own advantage. Learners can benefit when teachers realize this and when teachers provide opportunities for students to move beyond their "stylistic comfort zone" through the use of strategies with

---

[1]For information about obtaining these and other style assessment instruments, consult Lavine and Oxford (1990).

[2]For additional information concerning the types of language activities that appeal to learners with different learning styles, consult Oxford and Lavine (1992).

which they might not initially feel comfortable (Scarcella and Oxford 1992). For example, an analytic learner can benefit from an activity that involves understanding global meaning, while a global student similarly can benefit from doing some linguistic analysis in order to improve accuracy.

4. **Change the way group work is done in the classroom.** Teachers can use the principles of cooperative learning in grouping students for interactive work. In certain tasks, students with similar learning styles might be grouped together, while in other activities, students might be grouped in a heterogenous fashion so that members might practice stretching beyond their comfort zones.

5. **Change the curriculum.** Teachers might organize lessons as a series of activities or episodes, each with a different objective and style. New materials might be developed in learning-style modules. Multimedia materials could be integrated into the curriculum for classroom and individual use in order to guarantee the tapping of different sensory styles.

6. **Change the way style conflicts are viewed.** Teachers who encourage students to become aware of learning style preferences help promote flexibility and openness to the use of many styles.

As illustrated above, a communicative teaching approach that provides for a variety of activities, individual guidance, and an emphasis on meaning can enable students to experience many learning styles.

Teaching Effective Language Learning Strategies

Scarcella and Oxford define *language learning strategies* as "... specific actions, behaviors, steps, or techniques—such as seeking out conversation partners, or giving oneself encouragement to tackle a difficult language task—used by students to enhance their own learning" (1992, p. 63). Oxford (1990b) has developed a system for categorizing the following six general types of language learning strategies, which are depicted in more detail in Figure 1:

1. **planning/evaluating (metacognitive) strategies,** such as paying attention, consciously searching for practice opportunities, planning for language tasks, self-evaluating one's progress, and monitoring errors;

2. **emotional/motivational (affective) strategies,** such as anxiety reduction, self-encouragement, and self-reward;

3. **social strategies,** such as asking questions, cooperating with native speakers of the language, and becoming culturally aware;

4. **memory strategies,** such as grouping, imagery, rhyming, and structured reviewing;

5. **cognitive strategies,** such as reasoning, analyzing, summarizing, and general practicing;

FIGURE 1 Oxford's Strategy Classification System

Direct Strategies: Memory, Cognitive, and Compensation Strategies

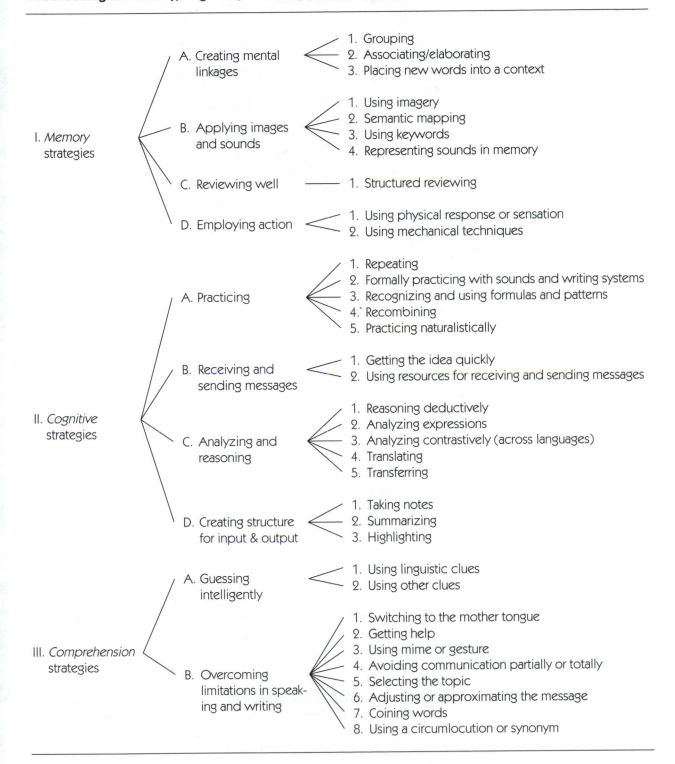

I. *Memory* strategies

A. Creating mental linkages
1. Grouping
2. Associating/elaborating
3. Placing new words into a context

B. Applying images and sounds
1. Using imagery
2. Semantic mapping
3. Using keywords
4. Representing sounds in memory

C. Reviewing well
1. Structured reviewing

D. Employing action
1. Using physical response or sensation
2. Using mechanical techniques

II. *Cognitive* strategies

A. Practicing
1. Repeating
2. Formally practicing with sounds and writing systems
3. Recognizing and using formulas and patterns
4. Recombining
5. Practicing naturalistically

B. Receiving and sending messages
1. Getting the idea quickly
2. Using resources for receiving and sending messages

C. Analyzing and reasoning
1. Reasoning deductively
2. Analyzing expressions
3. Analyzing contrastively (across languages)
4. Translating
5. Transferring

D. Creating structure for input & output
1. Taking notes
2. Summarizing
3. Highlighting

III. *Comprehension* strategies

A. Guessing intelligently
1. Using linguistic clues
2. Using other clues

B. Overcoming limitations in speaking and writing
1. Switching to the mother tongue
2. Getting help
3. Using mime or gesture
4. Avoiding communication partially or totally
5. Selecting the topic
6. Adjusting or approximating the message
7. Coining words
8. Using a circumlocution or synonym

FIGURE 1 *(continued)*

Indirect Strategies: Metacognitive, Affective, and Social Strategies

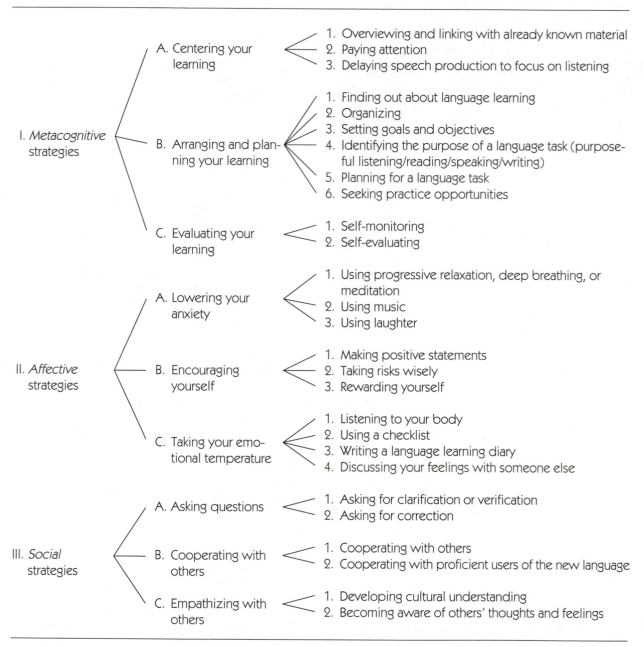

I. *Metacognitive* strategies

A. Centering your learning
1. Overviewing and linking with already known material
2. Paying attention
3. Delaying speech production to focus on listening

B. Arranging and planning your learning
1. Finding out about language learning
2. Organizing
3. Setting goals and objectives
4. Identifying the purpose of a language task (purposeful listening/reading/speaking/writing)
5. Planning for a language task
6. Seeking practice opportunities

C. Evaluating your learning
1. Self-monitoring
2. Self-evaluating

II. *Affective* strategies

A. Lowering your anxiety
1. Using progressive relaxation, deep breathing, or meditation
2. Using music
3. Using laughter

B. Encouraging yourself
1. Making positive statements
2. Taking risks wisely
3. Rewarding yourself

C. Taking your emotional temperature
1. Listening to your body
2. Using a checklist
3. Writing a language learning diary
4. Discussing your feelings with someone else

III. *Social* strategies

A. Asking questions
1. Asking for clarification or verification
2. Asking for correction

B. Cooperating with others
1. Cooperating with others
2. Cooperating with proficient users of the new language

C. Empathizing with others
1. Developing cultural understanding
2. Becoming aware of others' thoughts and feelings

Source: Ehrman and Oxford 1990.

6. **compensation strategies (to compensate for limited knowledge),** such as guessing meanings from the context in reading and listening and using synonyms and gestures to convey meaning when the precise expression is not known (cf. Scarcella and Oxford 1992, p. 63).

The use of appropriate learning strategies often results in increased language proficiency and greater self-confidence (Cohen 1990; Oxford and Crookall 1989). Research supports the idea that many learners are relatively unaware of the strategies they use and do not take advantage of the full range of available strategies (Oxford and Crookall 1989). Oxford (1990a) suggests that instructors teach students how to use strategies in order to help them in the language learning process. Earlier chapters of this *Handbook* presented ways to teach students effective strategies for comprehending oral and written input and communicating in oral and written form. Strategy training can be integrated with language learning activities and conducted through simulations, games, and other interactive tasks. Oxford has developed the following eight-step model for integrating strategy training into classroom activities:

1. **Identify students' needs** to determine what strategies they are currently using, how effective the strategies are, and how they can be improved.
2. **Choose relevant strategies** to be taught.
3. **Determine how best to integrate strategy training** into regular classroom activities.
4. **Consider students' motivations and attitudes** about themselves as learners and about learning new ways to learn.
5. **Prepare materials and activities.**
6. **Conduct "completely informed training,"** in which students learn and practice new strategies, learn why the strategies are important, learn to evaluate their use of the strategies, and learn how to apply them in new situations.
7. **Evaluate the strategy training.**
8. **Revise the strategy training procedure** for the next set of strategies to be taught (1990a, pp. 48-49).[3]

Teaching Foreign Language to Learning-Disabled and Handicapped Students

At times in the academic history of the United States, the study of foreign languages has been thought of as most appropriate for the academically or socially elite. Today, however, most foreign language teachers "have no quarrel with including a large range of talents in their classes to be sure that no one is denied a chance" (Garfinkel and Prentice 1985, p. 3). Prior to 1977, students with physical, emotional, or intellectual problems were placed together in classes often categorized as "special education." However, the research soon showed that this type of grouping is an ineffective means of addressing individ-

---

[3]For detailed examples of strategy training conducted with groups of language learners, along with the results, consult Ehrman and Oxford (1990) and Oxford et al. (1990). For studies examining the relationship between personality and its impact on language study, refer to Ely (1988) and Moody (1988).

ual differences and often denies certain students the opportunity to study certain subjects (Goodlad and Oakes 1988). With Public Law 94-142 placed into effect in 1977, public schools are directed "… to search out and enroll all handicapped children and to educate these children in the *least restrictive environment* in which they are able to function and still have their special needs met" (Good and Brophy 1991, p. 389). Schools are now mainstreaming students who have physical, intellectual, or emotional impairments, or removing them from special, segregated environments and returning them to the regular classrooms (Good and Brophy 1991).

Dr. Melvin Levine of Boston Children's Hospital has developed the following concise description of a learning disability, based on the official definition formulated by the National Advisory Committee on Handicapped Children in 1968 and later incorporated into Public Law 94-142:

> Learning disability is the term currently used to describe a handicap that interferes with someone's ability to store, process, or produce information. Such disabilities can affect both children and adults. The impairment can be quite subtle and may go undetected throughout life. But learning disabilities create a gap between a person's true capacity and his day-to-day productivity and performance (1984, p. 3).

According to Levine (1984), individuals with learning disabilities often exhibit certain deficiencies:

- difficulty in keeping attention focused: tuning in and out, inconsistent performance, impulsive behavior, and a negative self-image;
- language difficulties: oral, aural, and written;
- spatial orientation problems: words look different, and reversals in letters and in placement of letters and words are common;
- poor memory;
- fine motor control problems: a breakdown between head and paper, handwriting difficulties;
- sequencing problems: difficulty in putting a series of items in correct order, difficulty in following instructions, difficulty in organizing work (cf. Spinelli 1989, p. 142).

How can the foreign language teacher address the needs of mainstreamed special education students? Research suggests that the instructional methods that are effective with special education students tend to be the same ones that are effective with other students, except that special education students may need closer supervision (Larrivee 1985). Students with learning disabilities or handicaps may need more individualized instruction and more one-to-one instruction from the teacher (Madden and Slavin 1983), while students with behavior disorders may require closer supervision (Thompson, White, and Morgan 1982).

Many studies point to the possibility that learning disabled students have difficulties with a foreign language because of problems in phonology and syntax in the native language (Sparks, Ganschow, and Pohlman 1989; Javorsky, Sparks, and Ganschow 1992; Sparks et al. 1992). Additionally, the research has shown a high correlation between difficulties in listening comprehension and difficulties in reading comprehension (Sinatra 1990; Townsend 1987). According to Liberman (1989), both the reader and listener comprehend by means of phonology, so limitations in phonological processing may affect both skills. In their recent study, Sparks et al. (1992) have found that students' native language skills may affect their abilities to learn a foreign language in a traditional classroom setting at both the secondary and post-secondary levels.

However, further research is clearly needed to examine the relationship between communicative methods and the progress of learners labeled as special education students. Students are often categorized as learning disabled as a result of the type of instruction they receive and not necessarily because of verified learning problems or deficiencies. For example, Bruck (1978) has discovered that students with learning disabilities who learned French by means of a traditional approach actually acquired little knowledge of the language, because the method exploited the areas in which they had the most difficulties: memory work, learning language out of context, understanding abstract rules. Learning disabilities, particularly in cases of students labeled "mildly disabled," may be exacerbated by traditional classrooms that emphasize rules and bottom-up processing. Spinelli (1989) and Curtain (1986) have suggested that immersion programs may provide the best environment in which special education students can learn a foreign language, since students are involved in meaningful interaction and hands-on experiences. When immersion experiences are unavailable, content-based and whole-language approaches (see Chapter 6) can provide the same type of instructional support.

Although much more research is needed in teaching languages to students with special needs, current findings point to the following implications for the language teacher:

1. Use a well-organized daily classroom routine, with frequent praise and repetition of ideas (McCabe 1985).
2. Emphasize meaning rather than the analysis of language structures (McCabe 1985).
3. Use frequent review and repetition, and presentation of small amounts of material at one time (Sparks et al. 1992).
4. When conducting listening and reading activities, give fewer instructions at one time, provide pre-listening/pre-reading discussion, and give comprehension questions prior to and again after the reading selection, focusing on a literal rather than a figurative level (Barnett 1985).
5. Provide opportunities for students to learn through more than one modality, particularly through the tactile (touching, manipulating objects) or kinesthetic (use of movement, gestures) modalities (Spinelli 1989). The Orton-Gillingham approach emphasizes the use of the tactile and kinesthetic modalities in teaching reading to dyslexic/learning disabled students (Gillingham and Stillman 1960; Sparks, Ganschow, Kenneweg, and Miller 1991). Kennewig (1986) uses an adaptation of this method in her Spanish class for learning disabled students.
6. Have realistic expectations of what special education students can do, and measure their progress in terms of their own abilities rather than in terms of what the entire class can attain.

7. Provide ample opportunities for learning disabled students to interact with other students in the class by means of cooperative learning activities. Emphasize how important it is for all students to understand, respect, and help one another in the learning process.
8. Allow extra time, if needed, for learning disabled students to complete assignments and tests.
9. For students with severe reading problems, provide alternate methods of evaluation, such as oral testing.
10. Provide time for more individualized work with special education students and offer continued feedback on their progress. During this time, work with them on developing effective learning strategies.[4]

Language teachers who work with handicapped students must make arrangements to ensure that these students have access to various areas in the classroom and that their special physical needs are met. The teacher needs to be aware of how students' physical limitations will affect participation in certain types of hands-on activities, such as TPR, and how he or she will need to provide alternative activities.[5]

Spinelli (1989) suggests many ways for teachers to accommodate hearing impaired and visually impaired students in the language classroom. Clearly, the teacher must make special allowances for these students' special needs while at the same time giving them the chance to succeed in their language learning. In the case of hearing impaired students, for example, the visual and written modalities might be stressed in combination with study of the culture. Spinelli (1989) describes an approach to language instruction for deaf students in which they are taught to use sign language in the foreign language through the use of videotapes showing target-culture signing. Students might also be given the scripts that often accompany audiocassette programs, and they should be permitted to refer to their textbooks or other written material during oral presentations such as vocabulary and grammar practice. The teacher may need to prepare written scripts of the oral activities to assist students with comprehension. Hearing impaired students can often tell the teacher how they learn most effectively and can suggest ways for the teacher to aid their learning.

In the case of visually impaired students, teachers can help students compensate for the absence of visual support by capitalizing on oral skills and the use of discussion. In addition, visually impaired students need extra class time to process material that they read in braille. Partnerships between class members can be arranged for TPR activities that involve manipulatives, and may result in greater use of the target language. For example, in practicing vocabulary dealing with clothing, a visually impaired student tells a sighted student where to place specific items of clothing on a laminated paper doll (Kraft 1992). In exam situations, special considerations can be made, such as giving

---

[4]For information on addressing the needs of learning disabled students in language classes at the post-secondary level, consult Freed (1987), Gajar (1987), and Demuth and Smith (1987).

[5]For more detailed suggestions about teaching handicapped students, consult Gearheart and Weishahn (1984), Good and Brophy (1991), and Reynolds and Birch (1988).

only oral exams for these students or having each student dictate his or her answers to another student, who writes them down (Phillips de Herrera 1984).

Providing Effective Learning Experiences for At-Risk Students

As foreign language teachers face the challenge of teaching special needs students who have been mainstreamed into the regular classes, they are also encountering more and more children labeled "at-risk" or "high risk." Phi Delta Kappa conducted a study that began with the assumption that students "are at risk if they are likely to fail—either in school or in life" (Frymeier and Gansneder 1989, p. 142). These students have a high likelihood of dropping out of school, being low achievers, or even committing suicide. They are at risk because of a wide variety of circumstances they face outside of school: poverty, dysfunctional family life, neglect, abuse, or cultural/ethnic/racial background. According to Barry Garfinkel, M.D. and Director of the Division of Child and Adolescent Psychiatry at the University of Minnesota Hospital and Clinic, the "three strongest social correlates of suicidal behavior in youth are family breakdown, a youth's unemployment, and decreasing religious observance among the young" (interviewed by Frymier 1989, p. 290). "At-riskness" has been described as "a function of what bad things happen to a child, how severe they are, how often they happen, and what else happens in the child's immediate environment" (Frymier and Gansneder 1989, p. 142). At-risk students often display emotional and/or psychological symptoms such as depression, anxiety, difficulty in concentrating, and excessive anger, as well as physical symptoms such as respiratory problems, headaches, and muscle tension (Vanucci 1991).

A majority of at-risk students are minority students, such as Hispanics and blacks, who often are also from low socio-economic environments. They frequently experience problems in school because of their loss of identity or ethnic roots, difficulty in integrating themselves into the majority culture, and other students' incorrect perceptions of them. In many cases, the difficulties that minority students face seem insurmountable when the students are placed in classrooms that stress total conformity to the majority culture. Among the findings described above, Sparks et al. (1992) found that learning disabled and high-risk students may be similar with respect to their difficulties in the language classroom. Clearly, more research is needed to verify this claim.

Although educators have come a long way in the past 20 years in learning to address the needs of at-risk and minority students, subtle biases still persist in today's classrooms. It seems surprising that in 1992 the following results of studies examining the treatment of girls and boys in schools were revealed:

- Girls receive significantly less attention from classroom teachers than do boys.
- African American girls have fewer interactions with teachers than do white girls, despite evidence that they attempt to initiate interactions more frequently.

■ Sexual harassment of girls by boys—from innuendo to actual assault—in our nation's schools is increasing ("The AAUW Report" 1992).

The Gender/Ethnic Expectations and Student Achievement (GESA) Program was developed in Los Angeles in 1970 for the purpose of helping teachers confront and overcome their own gender and ethnic biases within the classroom. Grayson and Martin (1988) identified five areas in which teachers tend not to treat all students equally: (1) instructional contact: opportunities for students to respond and acknowledgement or feedback from the teacher; (2) grouping/organization: includes wait time for responses and physical closeness of teacher and students; (3) discipline: touching and reproof; (4) developing students' self-esteem: includes listening and probing, and guiding students through the thought process; and (5) evaluation: high-level questioning and analytical feedback.

Much of the research in multicultural education and teaching at-risk students has clear implications for classroom instruction.[6] The following list illustrates possible strategies that foreign language teachers might use as they attempt to provide successful language learning for *all* students:

1. Engage students in activities that encourage social interaction and promote the use of higher order thinking skills to challenge students' creativity (Kuykendall 1989); see Appendix A22 for a chart of strategies to extend student thinking.
2. Relate learning about another language and culture to students' own life experiences (Kuykendall 1989).
3. Offer descriptive instead of evaluative feedback, in an effort to encourage progress rather than cause frustration. Also, display each student's work at some time during the academic year (Kuykendall 1989).
4. Maintain direct, sincere eye contact when communicating with individual students (Kuykendall 1989).
5. Make every effort to give all students equal opportunities to participate (Grayson and Martin 1988).
6. Use heterogenous and cooperative groupings for interactive tasks, as described in Chapter 8 (Kuykendall 1989).
7. Make the language curriculum reflect the individual cultures of the students by including study of key historical/political figures from various cultures, inviting guest speakers from various cultures, engaging students in discussion in the target language about their own cultures, and discussing in the target language current events that involve the students' own cultures (Kuykendall 1989).
8. If there are native speakers of the target language who are students in the language class, encourage their ethnic pride by engaging them in activities such as providing oral input in the target language, helping other students undertake culture projects, offering classmates additional cultural information, and sharing family photographs.

_____

[6]See "A Multicultural Curriculum Worthy of Our Multicultural Society" 1991.

9. When presenting the cultures of the people who speak the target language, include people of different age groups, both male and female, and from as many geographical regions as possible.

10. When sharing opinions or discussing abstract topics, encourage students to express their own ideas concerning values, morals, and religious views, as shaped by their own cultures and religious convictions.

11. Use visuals that portray males and females of diverse racial and ethnic origins.

12. Hold the same achievement expectations for all students in the class, except in cases of physical or intellectual disabilities (Kuykendall 1989).

13. Provide opportunities for students to help one another. Sullivan and McDonald (1990) found that cross-age peer tutoring is an effective strategy that enables students to exercise autonomy, gain self-esteem, achieve at a higher level than normal, and learn more about students who are different from themselves. In Sullivan and McDonald's study, high school Spanish III students in an urban school district taught Spanish to elementary school children. According to Hartup, "cross-age contacts . . . may be particularly useful as a means of intervening in inadequate socialization [while] deliberately designed cross-age interactions may facilitate socialization for children who have encountered certain kinds of developmental difficulties" (1976, p. 54).[7]

14. Maintain positive teacher-parent relationships by inviting parents to see students' work in the foreign language, such as special projects, exhibits, or drama presentations. Talk to parents about their children's individual talents and progress (Kuykendall 1989).[8]

Teaching Gifted Learners

Johnson and Johnson point out that a "concern of all educators is how to challenge the academic capabilities of all students and maximize their intellectual development" (1991, p. 24). Challenging the academic capabilities of gifted learners is neither more nor less important a charge than challenging the academic capabilities of slow learners. A specific definition of the term *gifted* was provided by Congress in P.L. 97-35 (1981), the Omnibus Education Reconciliation Act:

> Children who give evidence of high performance capability in areas such as intellectual, creative, artistic, leadership capacity, or specific academic fields, and who require services or activities not ordinarily provided by the school in order to fully develop such capabilities (Sec. 582[3][A]).

---

[7]For in-depth information about culturally diverse classrooms, see *Children of Promise* (Heath et al 1991).

[8]Thanks to Valerie Sullivan from Woodland Hills High School, Pittsburgh, Pennsylvania, for helpful feedback on this section.

In their presentation of the work of 29 researchers, Sternberg and Davidson (1986) conclude that giftedness is viewed most often in terms of cognitive processing capacities. Although identification of gifted learners has been a major focus of much of the literature in the area of gifted education, most measures have proven unsatisfactory. Researchers agree that multiple measures are preferred over any single achievement test and that efforts should be made to specify alternate types of giftedness (Feldhusen 1989). The National Council of State Supervisors of Foreign Languages describes linguistically gifted students as those who have an IQ, based on a standardized intelligence test, in the top 3–5% of the student population and scores of 500–600 on the SAT exam (Bartz 1982). Although functional definitions generally refer to the upper 2% of the population as the highly gifted and the top 5% of the population as the gifted, to date there is no data to show what portion of the general population and what portion of the gifted population are linguistically gifted. Nor is there conclusive evidence to explain why certain students are gifted learners.

The research in giftedness as it relates specifically to foreign and second language learning is scant at best. Shrum (1989) has suggested that linguistically gifted students may be able to process language more rapidly. Rubin (1975) hypothesizes that *good* language learners (1) are willing and accurate guessers; (2) have a strong, persevering drive to communicate; (3) are often uninhibited and willing to make mistakes in order to learn or communicate; (4) focus on form by looking for patterns, classifying, and analyzing; (5) take advantage of all practice opportunities; (6) monitor their own speech and the speech of others; and (7) pay attention to meaning (cf. Oxford, Lavine, and Crookall 1989, p. 30).

Program models for gifted learners have traditionally involved *acceleration,* which is instruction provided at a level and pace appropriate to the student's level of achievement or readiness (Feldhusen 1989), and *enrichment,* which is in-depth study on broad topics involving higher level thinking processes. *Differentiated* instruction for gifted learners allows for modification of instruction according to the learner's needs and abilities, often within, but not limited to, the regular classroom setting.

The language teacher's task is to organize instruction so that the linguistically gifted can benefit while the other learners also benefit (Fenstermacher 1982). Gifted learners need opportunities to use all of their abilities and to acquire new knowledge and skills. The following are strategies that might be used by the language teacher to teach gifted learners:

1. Provide opportunities for students to study and research certain cultural topics in greater depth, for example, through projects in which they investigate the living patterns of the target language group.
2. Present taped segments and readings that are appropriately challenging.
3. Provide opportunities for students to use their critical thinking skills through debate of controversial societal issues and interpretation of literary works.[9]

---

[9]Gifted language students at Woodland Hills High School, Pittsburgh, Pennsylvania, have the opportunity to work with one another in a special program in which they read key literary works and share possible interpretations of particular aspects or issues (Sullivan 1992).

4. Allow gifted students to choose the topic of their taped segments or readings from time to time, thereby encouraging work in areas of interest.

5. Build in some time for gifted students to work with one another on assignments or projects, with the teacher serving as facilitator.

6. Allow some opportunities for gifted students to assume leadership roles through activities such as serving as group leaders/facilitators and providing peer help to students who have missed class or need extra assistance.

7. Involve gifted learners in interaction with other students in the class through cooperative learning tasks, such as those presented in Chapter 8. The research has shown that cooperative learning for gifted students may result in (1) higher mastery and retention of material than that achieved in competitive or individual learning (Johnson and Johnson 1991); (2) increased opportunities to use critical thinking and higher-level reasoning strategies (Johnson and Johnson 1991); (3) acquisition of cognitive restructuring, along with practice gained by explaining tasks and solutions to peers—in other words, learning through teaching (Fulghum 1992); and (4) enhancement of social interaction and self-esteem (Johnson and Johnson 1991).

Differentiated instruction for gifted learners will require that teachers deepen and widen fields of study, allow for accelerated progress through assigned material, minimize the extent of drill and practice activities, provide for in-depth study and use of critical thinking skills, and employ every possible strategy to ensure that instruction and practice are contextualized and meaningful.

TEACH AND REFLECT

In the following activities, you will have the opportunity to use the information presented in this chapter to help you design activities that appeal to various learning style preferences and to help you compile culturally appropriate pictures.

EPISODE ONE
Designing a Language Lesson Appropriate for Diverse Learning Styles

For this activity, you can either use a lesson you have created during earlier chapters of this *Handbook* or design a new one. Your lesson could focus on any of the elements previously discussed: for example, a presentation of grammar with a whole language approach, or work with an authentic listening or reading as appropriate for students at the elementary school, middle school, or high school level and beyond. Within your lesson, design at least three activities that appeal to different learning styles. Refer to the elements of learning styles described earlier in this chapter (Scarcella and Oxford 1992; Oxford 1990a).

Compiling Culturally Appropriate Visuals

Select a chapter from a textbook for the target language you teach, as approved by your instructor. Compile a minimum of 20 pictures that you might use to present material from the chapter. Your pictures should depict males and females of various ages and diverse ethnic and racial backgrounds. Situations should also be portrayed in contrasting scenes involving urban, rural, and suburban life-styles. Include people and scenes from the target culture as well. Explain how the pictures could be used to accomplish specific objectives within the chapter. Make a list of the sources where you found the pictures. Your instructor might ask you to share the pictures and sources with the class.

DISCUSS AND REFLECT

In the first case study, you will explore the kinds of learning style diversity a beginning teacher discovers as she prepares to teach a special education Spanish class. In the second case study, you will help an experienced teacher review some of the kinds of social, economic, ethnic, and academic diversity in his French II class.

CASE STUDY 1
Preparing to Teach a Special Education Spanish I and II Class

Miss Vella is a first-year Spanish teacher at Westtown High School, part of a small rural district in a farming community. She has been taught the latest research in language learning and teaching and is thoroughly prepared to teach Spanish for real communication. Miss Vella has developed a repertoire of strategies for involving students in active language use, and she has successfully used whole language tasks and cooperative learning in her student teaching. She believes in using the target language as much as possible, integrating culture with her teaching, and providing opportunities for students to succeed with the language.

Upon accepting her first teaching position at Westtown, Miss Vella was told by the principal that one of the classes she would be teaching in the fall is "conversational Spanish." The class consists of twelve special education students: eight in Spanish level I and four in Spanish level II. The principal told her that "the goal for the class is to make students aware of different cultures through the use of Spanish."

Miss Vella was a little perplexed by this assignment, since the class would be made up of special education students, rather than having them mainstreamed, and since levels I and II were combined. She realized that she would need to do some research because she had received little preparation in college for this type of situation.[10]

---

[10]Many thanks to Alison Conklin for the inspiration for this case study.

Ask yourself these questions:

1. What expectations should Miss Vella have for these students?
2. What difficulties might these students have in a language class?
3. What additional information will Miss Vella need to know about these students as she plans for the class?
4. According to the principal, the goal for this class is "to make students aware of different cultures through the use of Spanish." How does this goal reflect a philosophy or an attitude concerning what special education students are able to do? What is your opinion of this goal?
5. What techniques might work well in teaching these students Spanish?

To prepare the case:

■ Read Spinelli (1989) and McCabe (1985) for more information on how to teach the slower student.
■ Interview an experienced special education teacher to discuss potential difficulties students might experience as well as how a language teacher might plan for these difficulties.
■ Talk to an experienced language teacher who has worked with mainstreamed and/or special education students to gain additional insights about implications for language teaching.

How would you approach Miss Vella's "conversational Spanish" class? Describe your expectations and the types of classroom activities you would provide.

_____

_____

_____

_____

_____

_____

_____

_____

_____

Special education students need a good deal of individualized instruction and attention. How would you include opportunities for you to work with students on an individual basis?

_____

_____

_____

_____

_____

_____

_____

CASE STUDY 2
Cultural Diversity in a Small Rural Community

Mr. Davensmith was excited about starting his second teaching job, which was in Johnson County, a small, rural school system in the southeastern United States. Mr. Davensmith moved to Johnson County because his wife had secured a position at a state university in a neighboring county. During his interview, Mr. Davensmith had learned from the principal that the primary source of income in the community was raising beef cattle, growing cabbage and other vegetables, and doing piecework in the local textile factory. Many of the citizens had grown up in the county and shared similar religious and social values. Mr. Davensmith expected that the students in his French class would be mostly farmers' children. In actuality, however, he found that these were some of the students in his French II class:

Betty, whose parents cooperatively owned and operated a dairy farm having 100 milk cows. Betty spent extra time after school helping her French I teacher last year, and she also completed an in-depth study of French culture. She hopes to earn enough money to go to France next summer to improve her oral and listening skills. She prefers to read and write French, but her former French teacher told her she would have to improve her listening and speaking abilities if she wanted to continue to study the language.

Calvin, who is Betty's neighbor. He works on his parents' farm, helping to raise alfalfa hay for local horse farms. Calvin has been in enrolled in learning disability classes since the fifth grade and knows he is dyslexic, but he compensates for it by watching for the letters _d, b,_ and _c._ His parents note that he tracks grain and hay prices in three local marketplaces and keeps track of his father's financial records.

Bentley, who spends his summers, part of the spring, and most of the fall helping trim and harvest white pines for landscaping companies and Christmas tree distributors. He is in the eleventh grade, but he is two years younger than his grade-level peers because he had been promoted through two grade levels, one in elementary school and one in middle school. He wears a hearing aid in each ear, sits near the center of the semicircle Mr. Davensmith has arranged for the class, but sometimes does not hear what other students say. Bentley likes to check frequently with Mr. Davensmith to be sure he "has it right." He does best if he can write his work. Bentley likes Mr. Davensmith and has confided in him that he is worried about the stability of his home life since his parents argue all the time. Bentley is a small fellow who is often the target of jokes. He is on the wrestling team and has grown in stoutness if not in height since he began to work on the Christmas tree farms.

Susan, whose mother, a single parent, had moved from a large urban area so that she could raise horses and write a book about her experiences as an investigative reporter. Susan had been enrolled in a gifted student program that focused on creative writing. She feels somewhat isolated in this community because she was used to going to a major national museum for her Saturday entertainment. In her new home, there is an ample library, but most people just take advantage of the Bookmobile. Susan seldom feels challenged in her French class.

Miguel, who is from Mexico. His parents were hired on a local cabbage farm to help with the harvest. Miguel prefers not to speak Spanish at school, is enrolled in an advanced ESL program, and earned A's in French I. He would like to play football on the school team, but he cannot stay after school for practice because he often helps his family on the cabbage farm. Miguel is a kinesthetic learner, and in his spare time he likes to play the guitar and carve wood. He especially likes to be with long-term residents of the mountains when they are playing banjos and fiddles or whittling.

Carlos, who is from Colombia. His father had recently purchased a large cabbage farm and hired Miguel's family. Carlos speaks English without a trace of accent, although he often has difficulty understanding regional expressions that some of his school friends use. For example, one of his friends gave him directions to his home, saying "cross the branch, and turn left." Carlos thought the branch referred to the road, not the creek.

Navid, an Iranian girl whose father is a professor of electrical engineering at the nearby university. Navid likes details and is always straightening up the stacks of papers on Mr. Davensmith's desk. She is shy and interacts with her peers very little. She earns very good grades in French and hopes to major in that language in college.

Bela and Aggrey, the twin sons of Akinseye Sindabu, who is attending the university as a doctoral student in agricultural economics. Mr. Sindabu will return to his native Kenya next year as Director of Agricultural Development. Bela and Aggrey had learned three languages before leaving Kenya, and they have earned all A's in their French I class. Their pronunciation is perfect, and their written work is sufficiently accurate to keep Mr. Davensmith very happy.

Ask yourself these questions:

1. In what ways do these students differ?
2. What do they have in common?
3. What learning strategies from those outlined by Scarcella and Oxford (1992) do you think each student might use most frequently?
4. Make a list of the various ways in which these students represent a multi-cultural group. Be sure to include those aspects that are as obvious as national origin, but do not neglect more subtle cultural differences and similarities such as "hometown youngster" versus "transplant."
5. A colleague was overheard stating "teach through the strengths to turn the weaknesses into strengths." Discuss this statement and its relationship to the benefits and disadvantages in matching learning styles.

To prepare the case:

- Read Chapter 5 of Richard-Amato (1988) to identify three classroom activities that relate to the affective environment of a foreign language classroom. Determine which of the activities would best engage Mr. Davensmith's students.
- Read McCarthy (1987) for an explanation of the 4-MAT system for teaching to student learning styles.
- Interview an experienced foreign language teacher to find out what he or she does to encourage cooperative attitudes among students who differ and are similar along the lines you identified.

Imagine that you are Mr. Davensmith and are planning to teach a segment about French bread. You want to be sure that students understand that the bread is purchased daily, has a hard outer shell and chewy white center, is not wrapped in plastic, and is shaped like a long, thin torpedo, ranging from 12" to about 24" long. You also want them to understand that, in France, bread is the staple food, often served with cheese and a beverage as a full meal, especially for people working in fields or traveling. How will you make this lesson relevant?

_____

_____

_____

_____

_____

_____

_____

_____

Imagine that you are Mr. Davensmith's principal. How could you help him work with this group of students so that each student can realize his or her greatest potential?

_____

_____

_____

_____

_____

_____

_____

_____

REFERENCES

"The AAUW Report: How Schools Shortchange Girls." *American Association of University Women Outlook* 86 (1992): 15–23.

Bailey, K. M. "Competitiveness and Anxiety in Adult Second Language Learning: Looking at and Through the Diary Studies." Eds. H. W. Seliger and M. H. Long. *Classroom-Oriented Research in Second Language Acquisition.* Rowley, MA: Newbury House, 1983: 67–103.

Barnett, H. "Foreign Languages for the Learning Disabled: A Reading Teacher's Perspective." *New York State Association of Foreign Language Teachers Bulletin* 36 (1985): 7–9.

Bartz, W. "The Role of Foreign Language Education for Gifted and Talented Students." *Foreign Language Annals* 15 (1982): 329–334.

Bruck, M. "The Suitability of Early French Immersion Programs for the Language Disabled Child." *Canadian Modern Language Review* 34 (1978): 884–887.

Clark, B. *Growing Up Gifted.* Columbus, OH: Charles E. Merrill, 1983.

Cohen, A. D. *Language Learning: Insights for Learners, Teachers, and Researchers.* New York: Newbury House/Harper, 1990.

Curtain, H. A. "The Immersion Approach: Principle and Practice." Ed. B. Snyder. *Second Language Acquisition: Preparing for Tomorrow.* Central States Conference Proceedings. Lincolnwood, IL: National Textbook Company, 1986.

Demuth, K. A., and N. B. Smith. "The Foreign Language Requirement: An Alternative Program." *Foreign Language Annals* 20 (1987): 67–77.

Ehrman, M. E., and R. L. Oxford. "Effects of Sex Differences, Career Choice, and Psychological Type on Adults' Language Learning Strategies." *Modern Language Journal* 73 (1989): 1–13.

Ehrman, M. E., and R. L. Oxford. "Adult Language Learning Styles and Strategies in an Intensive Training Setting." *Modern Language Journal* 74 (1990): 311–327.

Ely, C. M. "Personality: Its Impact on Attitudes Toward Classroom Activities." *Foreign Language Annals* 21 (1988): 25–32.

Feldhusen, J. F. "Synthesis of Research on Gifted Youth." *Educational Leadership* (March 1989): 6–11.

Fenstermacher, G. "To Be or Not to Be Gifted: What Is the Question?" *Elementary School Journal* 82 (1982): 299–303.

Freed, B. "Exemptions from the Foreign Language Requirement: A Review of Recent Literature, Problems, and Policy." *American Departments of Foreign Languages Bulletin* 18 (1987): 13–17.

Frymier, J. "Understanding and Preventing Teen Suicide." *Phi Delta Kappan* 70 (1989): 290–293.

Frymier, J., and Gansneder, B. "The Phi Delta Kappa Study of Students at Risk." *Phi Delta Kappan* 70 (1989): 142–146

Fulghum, R. "A Bag of Possibles and Other Matters of the Mind." *Newsweek* Special Issue Fall/Winter (1992): 88, 90, 92.

Gajar, A. H. "Foreign Language Learning Disabilities: The Identification of Predictive and Diagnostic Variables." *Journal of Learning Disabilities* 20 (1987): 327–330.

Garfinkel, A., and M. Prentice. *Foreign Language for the Gifted: Extending Cognitive Dimensions.* Lincolnwood, IL: National Textbook Company, 1985.

Gearheart, B., and M. Weishahn. *The Exceptional Student in the Regular Classroom.* 3rd ed. St. Louis: Mosby, 1984.

Gillingham, A., and B. W. Stillman. *Remedial Training for Children with Specific Disability in Reading, Spelling, and Penmanship.* Cambridge, MA: Educators Publishing Service, 1960.

Good, T., and J. Brophy. *Educational Psychology: A Realistic Approach.* 4th ed. New York: Longman, 1990.

Good, T., and J. Brophy. *Looking in Classrooms.* 5th ed. New York: HarperCollins, 1991.

Goodlad, J. I., and J. Oakes. "We Must Offer Equal Access to Knowledge." *Educational Leadership* 45 (1988): 16–22.

Grayson, D. A., and M. D. Martin. *Gender/Ethnic Expectations and Student Achievement—The GESA Facilitator.* Earlham, IA: Gray Mill Foundation, 1988.

Hartup, W. W. "Cross-Age Versus Same-Age Peer Interaction: Ethological and Cross-Cultural Perspectives." *Children as Teachers.* New York: Academic Press, 1976.

Heath, S. B., L. Mangiola, S. R. Schecter, and G. A. Hull, Eds. *Children of Promise.* Washington, D.C.: National Education Association, 1991.

Herron, C. "Who Should Study Foreign Languages? The Myth of Elitism." *Foreign Language Annals* 15 (1982): 441–449.

Javorsky, J., R. L. Sparks, and L. Ganschow. "Perceptions of College Students With and Without Learning Disabilities About Foreign Language Courses." *Learning Disabilities: Research and Practice* 7 (1992): 31–44.

Johnson, D. W., and R. T. Johnson. "What Cooperative Learning Has to Offer the Gifted." *Cooperative Learning* 11 (1991): 24–27.

Kennewig, S. "Language Disability Students: Spanish Is for You." Paper presented at the Fifth Conference on the Teaching of Spanish. Miami University, OH, October 1986.

Kohn, A. "It's Hard to Get Out of a Pair—Profile: David and Roger Johnson." *Psychology Today* (October 1987): 53–57.

Kolb, D. *Experiential Learning: Experience as the Source of Learning and Development*. Englewood Cliffs, NJ: Prentice Hall, 1982.

Kraft, B. Personal communication, 1992.

Kuykendall, C. *Improving Black Student Achievement by Enhancing Students' Self-Image*. Washington, DC: Mid-Atlantic Equity Center, 1989.

Larrivee, B. *Effective Teaching for Successful Mainstreaming*. New York: Longman, 1985.

Lavine, R. Z., and R. L. Oxford. "Teacher-Student Conflict in the Classroom: It's a Matter of Style." American Departments of Foreign Languages Presentation. MLA Convention, Chicago, December 1990.

Levine, M. "Learning Abilities and Disabilities." *The Harvard Medical School Health Letter: Medical Forum* 9 (1984): 1–3.

Liberman, A. "Reading Is Hard Just Because Listening Is Easy." Eds. C. Von Euler, I. Lundberg, and G. Lennerstrand. *Brain and Reading*. Hampshire, England: MacMillan, 1989: LIV, 197–205.

Madden, N., and R. Slavin. "Mainstreaming Students with Mild Handicaps: Academic and Social Outcomes." *Review of Educational Research* 53 (1983): 519–569.

McCabe, L. "Teaching the Slower Student." *New York State Association of Foreign Language Teachers Bulletin* 36 (1985): 5–6.

McCarthy, B. *The 4 MAT System*. Barrington, IL: Excel, Inc., 1987.

Moody, R. "Personality Preferences and Foreign Language Learning." *Modern Language Journal* 72 (1988): 389–401.

"A Multicultural Curriculum Worthy of Our Multicultural Society." *The Professional Journal of the American Federation of Teachers* 15 (Winter 1991): 12–33.

Myers, I. B., and M. H. McCaulley. *A Guide to the Development and Use of the Myers-Briggs Type Indicator*. Palo Alto: Consulting Psychologists Press, 1985.

Oxford, R. L. "Language Learning Strategies and Beyond: A Look at Strategies in the Context of Styles." Ed. S. Magnan. *Shifting the Instructional Focus to the Learner*. Northeast Conference on the Teaching of Foreign Languages, 1990a: 35–55.

Oxford, R. L. *Language Learning Strategies: What Every Teacher Should Know*. New York: Newbury House/Harper, 1990b.

Oxford, R. L., and D. Crookall. "Research on Language Learning Strategies: Methods, Findings, and Instructional Issues." *Modern Language Journal* 73 (1989): 404–419.

Oxford, R. L., D. Crookall, A. Cohen, R. Lavine, M. Nyikos, and W. Sutter. "Strategy Training for Language Learners: Six Situational Case Studies and a Training Model." *Foreign Language Annals* 22 (1990): 197–216.

Oxford, R. L., and M. E. Ehrman. "Psychological Type and Adult Language Learning Strategies: A Pilot Study." *Journal of Psychological Type* 16 (1989): 22–32.

Oxford, R. L., and R. Z. Lavine. "Teacher-Student Style Wars in the Language Classroom: Research Insights and Suggestions." *Association of Departments of Foreign Languages Bulletin* 23 (Winter 1992): 38–45.

Oxford, R. L., R. Z. Lavine, and D. Crookall. "Language Learning Strategies, the Communicative Approach, and Their Classroom Implications." *Foreign Language Annals* 22 (1989): 29–39.

Phillips de Herrera, B. "Teaching English as a Foreign Language to the Visually Handicapped." Paper presented at the Annual Convention of Teachers of English to Speakers of Other Languages. Houston, TX, March 6–11, 1984.

Reid, J. M. "The Learning Style Preferences of ESL Students." *TESOL Quarterly* 21 (1987): 87–111.

Reynolds, M., and J. Birch. *Adaptive Mainstreaming: A Primer for Teachers and Principals*. 3rd ed. While Plains, NY: Longman, 1988.

Richard-Amato, P. A. *Making It Happen—Interaction in the Second Language Classroom*. New York: Longman, 1988.

Rubin, J. "What the 'Good Language Learner' Can Teach Us." *TESOL Quarterly* 9 (1975): 41–51.

Scarcella, R. C., and R. L. Oxford. *The Tapestry of Language Learning*. Boston, MA: Heinle and Heinle, 1992.

Shrum, J. "Challenging Linguistically Gifted Students in the Regular Foreign Language Classroom." Ed. R. M. Milgram. *Teaching Gifted and Talented Learners in the Regular Classroom*. New York: Charles R. Thomas, 1989.

Sinatra, G. "Convergence of Listening and Reading Processing." *Reading Research Quarterly* 25 (1990): 115–130.

Skon, L., D. W. Johnson, and R. T. Johnson. "Cooperative Peer Interaction Versus Individual Competition and Individualistic Efforts: Effects on the Acquisition of Cognitive Reasoning Strategies." *Journal of Educational Psychology* 73 (1981): 83–92.

Sparks, R. L., L. Ganschow, J. Javorsky, J. Pohlman, and J. Patton. "Test Comparisons Among Students Identified as High-Risk, Low-Risk, and Learning Disabled in High School Foreign Language Courses." *Modern Language Journal* 76 (1992): 142–159.

Sparks, R. L., L. Ganschow, S. Kenneweg, and K. Miller. "Use of an Orton-Gillingham Approach to Teach a Foreign Language to Dyslexic/Learning Disabled Students: Explicit Teaching of Phonology in a Second Language." *Annals of Dyslexia* 41 (1991): 96–118.

Sparks, R. L., L. Ganschow, and J. Pohlman. "Linguistic Coding Deficits in Foreign Language Learners." *Annals of Dyslexia* 39 (1989): 179–195.

Spinelli, E. L. "Beyond the Traditional Classroom." Ed. H. S. Lepke. *Shaping the Future: Challenges and Opportunities*. Northeast Conference on the Teaching of Foreign Languages, 1989: 139–158.

Sternberg, R., and J. Davidson, Eds. *Conceptions of Giftedness*. New York: Cambridge University Press, 1986.

Sullivan, V. J. Personal communication, 1992.

Sullivan, V. J., and W. E. McDonald. "Cross-Age Tutoring in Spanish: One Motivating Method." *The Pennsylvania State Modern Language Assoc. Bulletin* (Fall 1990): 13–17.

Thompson, R. H., K. R. White, and D. P. Morgan. "Teacher-Student Interaction Patterns in Classrooms with Mainstreamed Mildly Handicapped Students." *American Educational Research Journal* 19 (1982): 220–236.

Townsend, D., C. Carrithers, and T. Bever. "Listening and Reading Processes in College and Middle-Age Readers." Eds. R. Horowitz and S. J. Samuels. *Comprehending Oral and Written Language*. New York: Academic Press, 1987: 217–242.

U.S. Congress Omnibus Education Reconciliation Act of 1981. Title V, Education Programs. Subtitle D, Elementary and Secondary Education Block Grant. Chapter 2, Consolidation of Federal Programs for Elementary and Secondary Education. Subchapter C, Special Projects, Section 582 (3)(A). 97th Congress. Washington, DC: GPO, August 13, 1981.

Vanucci, S. R. "Understanding Dysfunctional Systems." Unpublished Manuscript, 1991.

11 Classroom Testing in Context

This chapter presents strategies for designing tests that are contextualized, integrative, and interactive. A summary of test types according to purpose and format is provided. The chapter features suggestions for planning testing and creating contextualized tests. You will explore various alternatives to paper-and-pencil assessment, including ideas for testing and grading classroom speaking. You will have the opportunity to adapt a textbook test to make it more interactive and integrative, and you will also create your own test. In the case studies, you will see how one teacher implemented oral testing, and you will consider several options for evaluating production of the foreign language.

CONCEPTUAL ORIENTATION

If we accept the claim that foreign language teaching has historically separated form from context, then the notion that classroom testing has been anything but contextualized will most certainly not be disputed. Even in an era of communicative approaches and proficiency-oriented instruction, testing procedures often fall back upon grammar-translation principles of testing specific grammatical structures point by point (Bachman 1990). Oller (1991a) reminds us that language testing has also traditionally been linked to grading. As Oller points out, at least from the learner's perspective, "The function of testing ... sometimes reduces to the formula: TEST ➜ GRADE" (1991, p. 33).

■ Types of Tests

One of the key purposes for testing, and one that is unfortunately often disregarded, is to gather information that will enable teachers and learners to make a decision of some sort. Oller outlines five kinds of tests according to the kind of information they gather:

- *Instructional.* Good tests instruct students and enable them to improve their proficiency in the target language.

- *Managerial*. Such tests provide feedback to both teachers and students and help them manage instruction and study practices—for instance, by providing a sensible basis for grading.
- *Motivational*. The tests serve as rewards or as goals, urging students and teachers toward higher achievement relative to well-defined goals.
- *Diagnostic*. The tests help teachers and students identify specific instructional problems.
- *Curricular*. Good tests define the curriculum as a whole (1991a, p. 36).

Described in broad categories, testing can be classified as either summative or formative. Summative testing often occurs at the end of a course, and it is designed to evaluate the sum total of what has been taught and learned. There are usually no opportunities for further input or performance. The most common example of a summative test is a final exam. Formative tests, on the other hand, are designed to help "form" or shape the learners' ongoing understanding or skills while the teacher and learners still have opportunities to interact for the purposes of repair and improvement. Examples include quizzes (5–15 minutes), class interaction activities such as paired interviews, and chapter or unit tests. Unfortunately, however, even tests that are usually formative, such as quizzes, become summative instruments when they are used simply as opportunities to put grades in a gradebook to be averaged at the end of a given term. A sufficient amount of formative testing must be done in the classroom in order to enable students to revisit and review the material in a variety of ways.

Research on foreign language testing has distinguished between two different testing formats: (1) discrete point tests and (2) integrative or global tests (Carroll 1961). The contrast between these two formats often reflects different teaching philosophies. A discrete point test focuses on one linguistic component at a time: grammar, vocabulary, syntax, or phonology. Test items include a variety of formats, such as multiple-choice, true-false, matching, and completion, in which the language is segmented into parts for individual analysis. Discrete point tests have traditionally featured unconnected sentences lacking in meaningful or natural contexts. These tests have also tended to assess one skill at a time, such as listening, reading, or writing. Unlike discrete point tests, integrative or global tests assess the student's ability to use various components of the language at the same time, and often multiple skills as well. For example, an integrative test might ask students to listen to a taped segment, identify main ideas, and then use the information as the topic for discussion, as the theme of a composition, or to compare the segment to a reading on the same topic.

Test Design: Contextualized, Integrative, Interactive, Pragmatic

Two basic principles foreign language teachers follow in the development of tests is to test *what* was taught and to test it in a manner that reflects the *way* in which it was taught. For example, if students spend 50% of their class time developing oral skills, then nearly half of their test should evaluate their oral skills. Similarly, students who learn in class how to narrate in the past by writing paragraphs about events that occurred during their childhood should be tested on their learning by being asked to write paragraphs about past events in their lives. Since a large portion of classroom time is spent in learning language for communication in real-life contexts, testing should also reflect language used for communication within realistic contexts (Shrum 1991).

Current research in testing argues for a more direct connection between teaching and testing. The same kinds of activities designed for classroom interaction can serve as valid testing formats, with instruction and evaluation more closely integrated. As Oller points out, "Perhaps the essential insight of a quarter of a century of language testing (both research and practice) is that good teaching and good testing are, or ought to be, nearly indistinguishable" (1991a, p. 38). Oller (1991a) even claims that "teaching to the test," in the case of global, contextualized testing, does not present a problem since performance on these global tests is an indication of overall progress with the language. Shohamy (1990) suggests that language teachers make extensive use of formative testing that is integrated into the teaching and learning process.

Oller (1991b) suggests the use of *pragmatic* tests, in which the learner has the opportunity to process authentic language within normal contextual constraints and link that language to his or her own experience. Pragmatic tests involve the use of linguistic content, such as grammar, syntax, and vocabulary, and extralinguistic content, such as gestures and tone of voice in speaking, subtle, indirect implications in writing, and the learner's own background knowledge and experience. Shohamy (1990) also suggests that tests should reflect a broad view of language as it is used in numerous contexts and in various language modalities—that is, listening, speaking, reading, or writing. Thus, pragmatic tests draw on the student's extralinguistic or world knowledge. Pragmatic tests are integrative in nature as they require attention to many linguistic elements at once and often the use of more than one skill at a time. However, all integrative tests are not necessarily pragmatic in nature; only those tests that draw on students' extralinguistic or world knowledge are considered pragmatic. Formats of pragmatic tests have included cloze exercises,[1] essay writing, narration, oral interviews, and role plays. Bachman (1990) calls such tests "communicative language tests," based upon the theory that language ability is a complex and multifaceted construct. According to Bachman (1990), communicative tests have the following characteristics:

---

[1]The cloze test consists of a written passage with every "nth" word deleted. It is considered a global test of proficiency since it requires attention to longer stretches of linguistic context and often to inferences about extralinguistic context (Oller 1979). An example, deleting every seventh word, is: Confusion exists concerning the real purposes, aims, and goals of a college. What are these? What should a college be? Some believe the chief function 1. _____ even a liberal arts college is 2. _____ vocational one. I feel that the 3. _____ function of a college ... (Oller and Conrad 1971, p. 184).

- test items create an "information gap," requiring test takers to process complementary information through the use of multiple sources of input, such as a tape recording and a reading selection on the same topic;
- tasks are interdependent—that is, "tasks in one section of the test build ... upon the content of earlier sections" (p. 678);
- test tasks and content are integrated within a given domain of communicative interaction;
- tests attempt to measure a broader range of cohesion, function and sociolinguistic appropriateness than did earlier tests, which tended to focus on the formal aspects of language—grammar, vocabulary, and pronunciation (p. 678).

In Chapter 9, you learned of recent work that used a portfolio approach to assess students' writing samples. In the language arts field, portfolio assessment has been used as a way to describe and evaluate student performance across various language skills, particularly in reading and writing (Tierney, Carter, and Desai 1991). In the foreign or second language classroom, teachers might have students assemble samples of their work in the four skills and culture and evaluate these periodically: audiotapes and/or videotapes students have made of their speaking exchanges, written texts they've read and summarized in written form, compositions and letters, notes they've taken while listening to an oral text or presentation, projects they've created that integrate two or more skill areas and culture. Future research in portfolio assessment will undoubtedly reveal many exciting new alternatives to traditional modes of testing and the habit of grading every assignment.

An Interactive Model for Testing

Swaffar, Arens, and Byrnes propose an interactive model for testing reading that parallels their approach to teaching reading. Their test design, which can also be applied to the testing of other skills, features three components to verify whether the student can:

1. understand both linguistic and extralinguistic pragmatic aspects of the text;
2. connect comprehension of the text to production or self-expression;
3. express meaning in one's own words (1991, pp. 157-159).

The principles underlying this type of model might be used to design tests that are (1) interactive—student interacts with an assigned text; (2) pragmatic—student uses both linguistic and extralinguistic information; and (3) integrative—student uses more than one skill at a time. For example, earlier chapters presented ideas for contextualizing language teaching by using an initial oral or written text. In a testing format, students might be put through similar steps. Hence, the test would include a series of questions that enable the teacher to evaluate the students' ability to interact with a text, isolate significant details, use the target language to write about ideas in the text, and use the target language to express their opinions about the text. This is far different from the simple plot summaries or single factual questions that often appear on tests. The design illustrated below is an adaptation of a five-step model proposed by Swaffar, Byrnes, and Arens (1991). Sample items from their text are included to exemplify each step.

1. Students listen to or read an authentic segment;

2. Students identify main ideas by focusing on content or text schema;
    Instructions: Identify and write down key words from the text which provide the following information about the main idea of the text:
    who: _____   what: _____
    when: _____   where: _____
    Using these words, write a sentence expressing the main idea of the text.

3. Students identify details (vocabulary development);
    Instructions: Find synonyms or references from the text for the following words:

4. Students use the grammatical structures in the text to further explore text ideas;
    Instructions: In the story, events and their timing are of major importance. Write two sentences about major events in the story. Use past tenses.

5. Students develop their points of view.
    Instructions: What do you think would have happened if the story had continued? Write a 3–5 sentence description of another ending to the story. (This section could also engage students in attention to particular cultural points.)

    (Swaffar, Byrnes and Arens 1991).

This model tests students on their listening and/or reading skills; grammatical, lexical, and cultural knowledge; ability to interact with the text; and productive skills; all within the framework of a real context. See Appendix A23 for an example of a German reading used as a test within this framework.

▦ Planning for Classroom Testing

The following are general guidelines to help you design a chapter or unit test:

- ■ review your objectives for the chapter/unit;
- ■ think of the contexts in which the language was used in this unit or chapter;
- ■ think of the linguistic functions that students have learned to perform;
- ■ think of the ways in which students have learned to interact with one another;

As you design the test, keep in mind the following principles:

- prepare an integrative test that reflects the types of activities done in class—what students learned to do orally should be tested orally, not with paper and pencil;
- provide opportunities for students to use global language skills in a naturalistic context;
- provide a model whenever possible to illustrate what students are to do;
- provide instructions in the native language until you are certain that learners' ability to perform the task is not limited by a misunderstanding of the instructions;
- develop a grading system that rewards both linguistic accuracy and creativity;
- return graded tests promptly to show students their progress.

■ Alternatives to Paper-and-Pencil Testing

Although they may spend a large portion of their class time listening to and speaking the target language, students are most often formally tested on their knowledge by means of written tests and quizzes since these have traditionally offered a concrete and visual assessment. Often, teachers who are committed to oral testing find it a time-consuming activity. Throughout this chapter you will find efficient ways to conduct testing of oral and written skills. For instance, informal means of testing can complement information gained by formal assessment. The teacher might, for example, grade certain classroom activities that are representative of students' performance in any of the skill areas: a role play presented to the class, a written essay, comprehension of a reading.

More so than others, the listening and speaking skills lend themselves to testing without written means. Among the many possible formats for testing listening and speaking without paper and pencil are the following ideas that can be adapted for use with elementary school, middle school/junior high school, high school, and post-secondary students:

LISTENING FORMATS:
- Students respond to TPR commands.
- Students verify a description of a picture.
- Students listen to a narrative and number pictures or put them in order.

LISTENING AND SPEAKING FORMATS:
- Students respond to oral questions in an interview procedure.
- Students recreate an oral story with the teacher.
- Students discuss an audio or video segment.
- Students invent a different ending for a story.

SPEAKING FORMATS:
- Students describe a picture.
- Students invent a story about a picture.

- Students present a spontaneous conversation or role play.
- Students respond to a given situation in a culturally appropriate way.
- Students present a narration/description or monologue.
- Students conduct a debate.

The Oral Proficiency Interview and Its Implications for Classroom Testing

As you learned in earlier chapters, the ACTFL Oral Proficiency Interview (OPI) is a standardized procedure for the global assessment of oral proficiency. It measures language production holistically by identifying patterns of strengths and weaknesses within the assessment criteria of functions, contexts, and accuracy. An official OPI is a face-to-face, tape-recorded interview lasting from 5 to 30 minutes and conducted by a certified proficiency tester. Below is a brief description of how the interview is conducted. As pointed out in Chapter 8, an understanding of the scale and/or the interview procedure does not imply an ability to rate oral speech samples. Further, the OPI is not designed to be used as a classroom test. Appendix A24 describes the procedures for obtaining an ACTFL Oral Proficiency Interview.

> The interview begins with a brief **warm-up** in order to help the interviewee feel comfortable and confident. Next, the interviewer moves the conversation forward through one or more **level checks** in order to verify whether the tasks at a given level can be performed. This phase demonstrates the tasks/contexts that the interviewee can perform with confidence and accuracy. Once the interviewer has determined that the speaker can handle the tasks and topics of a particular level, he or she raises the interview to the next-highest major level by means of **probes**. The interaction in this phase illustrates the limitations of the interviewee's proficiency. The level check and probe phases may need to be repeated as each level is verified and the next level is examined. After the level checks and probes have been conducted and the interviewer believes that the evidence points to a particular level, the interviewee is asked to participate in a role play, which serves as a final level check or probe. The role play checks functions that cannot easily be elicited by means of the conversation itself. Finally, the interview is brought to a close in the **wind-down**, at which time the discussion returns to a comfortable linguistic level for the interviewee and ends on a positive note (Buck, Byrnes and Thompson 1989).

A modified version of the oral proficiency interview, using taped responses, has been developed as a cost-effective alternative to the face-to-face interview. Interviewees are given open-ended questions and linguistic tasks to complete with the aid of visuals such as drawings to describe places, a sequence of pictures to narrate events, and maps to give directions. Their oral responses are recorded individually and evaluated by a tester. A study by Stansfield and Kenyon (1992) revealed high correlations between the proficiency ratings given in the oral proficiency interview (OPI) and those given in the simulated oral proficiency interview (SOPI).

The design of the OPI has provided many ideas for classroom testing of oral skills:

- interviews between teacher and student;
- interviews between students;
- spontaneous role plays with 2–3 students;
- oral monologues;
- conversation cards with 3 students: Students 1 and 2 ask each other questions according to the instructions on their cards, while Student 3 checks accuracy and records responses (Bonin and Birckbichler 1975);
- situation cards: students respond in a culturally appropriate way to situations described on cards in English;
- narration/description: one or more students narrate and/or describe an event in present, past, or future time frame.

Conducting oral testing in the classroom poses two challenges: (1) how to manage the procedure with large classes and (2) how to grade speaking. In planning for testing, the teacher might consider the following alternatives: (1) test only part of the class orally on each chapter or unit, making sure that at the end of the grading period every student has the same number of oral test grades; (2) conduct oral testing over the course of several days so that part of the class is tested each day; (3) while a group of students is being tested orally, engage the rest of the class in an interesting reading or writing task.

The grade assigned to a speaking test should reflect various components of the speech sample. A scale like the following one can be used in a variety of settings to produce a fairly specific global assessment of the linguistic functions used to communicate. This format can be used to design a 25-point global assessment. The system presumes that teachers delineate for students the purpose of the testing situation, describe what the students are expected to do with the target language, and designate linguistic tasks that will be evaluated. A teacher may decide to limit the testing situation to only one linguistic task, such as describing a family member, or the task may include several more simple linguistic tasks, such as greeting or asking for information. In this scoring system, a student can earn one to five points for completion of linguistic tasks. Five of the points are allocated to the category of "effort to communicate," in which the teacher may reward better-than-usual performance for those students who have difficulty with oral communication. This category can also be used to indicate to the student that performance did not reflect adequate preparation or did not meet expectations described in the task. Finally, fifteen of the points are allocated to describe the way in which the student used the target language to complete the tasks: grammar, use of vocabulary, and pronunciation.

Learner task:	Points assigned:
Completion of linguistic tasks	1 (inadequate completion) through 5 (thorough completion)
Effort to communicate	1 (low effort) through 5 (high effort)

Grammatical correctness	1 (many errors, low use of designated structures) through 5 (few errors, use of designated structures)
Use of vocabulary	1 (inappropriate vocabulary) through 5 (appropriate, recently learned vocabulary)
Accurate pronunciation	1 (many inaccuracies) through 5 (pronunciation is accurate)

The scale may be applied to conversations among learners as they work in small groups or as they interact with the teacher in communicative tasks. Scoring may be done by the teacher as students speak, or from audiotapes prepared by the learners outside of class. One way to evaluate non-spontaneous speech is through the use of audiotapes made by the learner in a non-threatening environment, perhaps at home or in a learning center corner of the classroom. Audiotapes provide learners with the opportunity to replay, hear themselves, and refine their work. Thus, they can present their best work to the teacher. These tapes, combined with a global rating system like that shown above, also provide ease of evaluation.

TEACH AND REFLECT

In these activities, you will examine a sample chapter test to see how to construct a contextualized test, and then you will design your own test.

> **EPISODE ONE**
> **A Sample Contextualized Test**
>
> Figure 1 illustrates a chapter test that represents one type of contextualization. Answer the following questions about it:
>
> 1. Identify the principal statement of context. Why do you think it appears where it does. Is it specific or general?
> 2. Identify items that ask the learner to *know* discrete vocabulary, grammatical points, or skills. Identify the items that ask the learner to *synthesize* discrete vocabulary points, grammatical points, or skills. Identify the items that require that the learner *use the target language to communicate* information. How is the test structured?
> 3. Describe the relationship between the exercises and between the items within a given exercise. What implications are there for the learner?
> 4. Would you describe this test as pragmatic, according to Oller's (1991b) definition? Explain.
> 5. How might you change this test to make it more integrative and interactive? Your instructor may ask you to adapt other tests specific to your foreign language.

FIGURE 1 Sample Contextualized Test

FIGURE 1 Sample Contextualized Test

Examen: Capítulo 3

▶ **RESPONDA EN LA HOJA DE RESPUESTAS.**

Contexto Lupe, Memo y Jorge están en el centro estudiantil y hablan sobre la importancia de tener un buen trabajo y tiempo para divertirse.

I. ¡Escuchemos! (*20 puntos*) Antes de ir al centro estudiantil, Memo oye el siguiente anuncio de empleo. Escuche el anuncio y conteste las siguientes preguntas.

1. ¿Tienen puestos en qué especialidades? Nombre dos.
2. Según el anuncio es importante que la persona tenga ciertas capacidades. Nombre dos.
3. ¿Cuál es un beneficio de trabajar en esta compañía? Mencione una cosa.
4. ¿A qué número de teléfono hay que llamar?

II. El trabajo. (*10 puntos*) Lupe, Memo y Jorge hablan sobre el trabajo. Abajo está lo que dice Lupe. Escriba oraciones completas con las claves dadas.

1. A mí/gustar/llevarme bien con la gente
2. A Jorge/fascinar/las oportunidades de viajar
3. A Fausto y a Eliana/importar/recibir buenas prestaciones sociales
4. A Teresa y a mí/molestar/trabajar horas extras
5. Memo, ¿a ti/interesar/los incentivos del trabajo?

III. Las actividades preferidas. (*20 puntos*) Jorge, Lupe y Memo están hablando sobre la importancia de la diversión en la vida. ¿Cuáles son los deportes y las actividades que más les gustan? Complete las oraciones con los deportes o las actividades correspondientes. No repita palabras. ¡OJO! Hay más de una respuesta correcta en todas las situaciones.

Jorge: A mí me gustan los deportes acuáticos, sobre todo __1__ y __2__. ¡Me encanta estar en el agua!

Lupe: ¿De veras? Yo prefiero los deportes que se pueden hacer bajo techo, por ejemplo, __3__ y __4__.

Memo: ¡Esos son muy entretenidos! Pero de vez en cuando es lindo estar fuera de casa, ¿no? A mí me interesa mucho __5__ y __6__.

Jorge: Es cierto, es divertido. Sin embargo, a veces tengo ganas de quedarme en casa para relajarme. Entonces me interesa __7__ o __10__.

Memo: Tienes razón, Lupe. De todos modos, es importante tener un poco de diversión para relajarse y olvidarse del trabajo.

FIGURE 1 (continued)

IV. Los amigos. (*15 puntos*) Jorge, Memo y Lupe hablan nuevamente sobre sus amigos. Lea lo que dice Memo y escriba oraciones completas utilizando el presente del indicativo o el presente del subjuntivo según el caso.

1. Es cierto/Jorge y yo/hacer mucho trabajo
2. Es posible/Roberto/buscar trabajo a jornada parcial
3. Es necesario/Rosario/descansar más
4. No es posible/Eliana y Fausto/ir pronto de vacaciones
5. ¿Es verdad/Memo/conocer a Severiano Ballesteros?

V. Leamos: Entrevista de empleo. (*15 puntos*) Lea el artículo y luego conteste las siguientes preguntas.

1. ¿Qué debe preguntar Ud. en la entrevista?
2. ¿Es bueno o malo ser breve y conciso en sus respuestas?
3. Según la lectura, ¿al entrevistador le molesta que uno beba y fume durante la entrevista?

Ahora, complete las siguientes frases con la información del artículo.

4. Para aprovechar una entrevista, es importante que Ud. ... (*3 items*)
5. No es bueno que Ud. ... (*3 items*)

Entrevista de empleo: factor decisivo

Cómo aprovechar la entrevista

(1) Siempre debe estar preparado para reciprocar buenas contestaciones.

(2) Pregunte lo necesario; por ejemplo, oportunidades de progreso y beneficios marginales.

(3) Sea sincero en todo momento y comunique fortaleza en áreas de interés.

Algunos aspectos contraproducentes que pueden volverse en su contra durante una entrevista son:

Fumar, beber, masticar chicle o comerse las uñas, vanagloriarse, hacer chistes, comentarios personales, discutir con el entrevistador, poner al entrevistador a la defensiva, aparentar estar obsesionado con el aspecto salarial y beneficios marginales y finalmente el desconocimiento o ignorancia con relación a la empresa.

Algunos aspectos positivos durante una entrevista son:

Ser puntual, demostrar en todo momento cortesía y respeto, transmitir energía y entusiasmo, ser breve y conciso en sus respuestas.

VI. Escribamos: El trabajo. (*20 puntos*) Como Ud. sabe, además de tener una buena presencia, es necesario hacer otras cosas para conseguir un empleo. Escriba un párrafo de por lo menos ocho frases en el que Ud. incluye lo siguiente:

- el tipo de trabajo que a Ud. le interesa y por qué;
- lo que Ud. necesita estudiar para conseguir trabajo;
- lo que debe hacer Ud. si le interesa un anuncio de empleo.

Utilice los verbos como **gustar**, el presente del subjuntivo con expresiones impersonales y la nominalización con **lo que, lo de, eso de** y **esto de** cuando sea adecuado.

Source: Glisan and Shrum 1991.

FIGURE 1 Sample Contextualized Test (English Translation)

Test: Chapter 3

▶ **ANSWER ON THE ANSWER SHEET.**

Context: Lupe, Memo and Jorge are at the Student Center and are discussing how important it is to have a good job as well as time to have fun.

I. Let's Listen. *(20 points)* Before going to the Student Center, Memo hears the following employment ad. Listen to the ad and answer the following questions.

1. In what fields are jobs being offered? Name two.
2. According to the ad, it is important for the person to have certain skills. Name two.
3. What is an advantage of working for this company? Name one thing.
4. What is the phone number to call?

II. The Job. *(10 points)* Lupe, Memo and Jorge are talking about work. Below is what Lupe says. Write complete sentences using the clues provided.

1. I / to like / to get along with people.
2. Jorge / to enjoy / traveling opportunities.
3. Fausto and Eliana / to care about / getting good benefits.
4. Teresa and I / to be bothered / to work overtime.
5. Memo, are you / to be interested in / incentives offered at work?

III. Favorite Activities. *(20 points)* Jorge, Lupe and Memo are talking about how important it is to have fun in life. What sports and activities do they like best? Complete the sentences with the appropriate sports and activities. Do not repeat any words. REMEMBER: there is more than one correct answer in each case.

Jorge: I like water sports, especially __1__ and __2__ . I love to be in the water!
Lupe: Really? I prefer indoor sports; for example __3__ and __4__ .
Memo: Those are lots of fun! But every once in a while it's nice to go outside, isn't it? I really like __5__ and __6__ .
Jorge: That's true. It's fun. But sometimes I like to stay home and relax, That's when I like __7__ or __10__ .
Memo: You're right, Lupe. In any case, it's important to have a little fun so you can relax and forget about work.

FIGURE 1 (continued)

IV. Friends. *(15 points)* Jorge, Memo and Lupe are once again talking about their friends. Read what Memo says and write complete sentences (using present indicative or present subjunctive, as required).

1. It' s true that / Jorge and I / to do a lot of work
2. It's possible that / Roberto / to look for part time work
3. Rosario / to need / to rest more
4. It's not possible for / Eliana and Fausto / to go on vacation soon
5. Is it true that / Memo / to know Severiano Ballesteros?

V. Let's Read: Job Interview. *(15 points)* Read the article and answer the following questions.

1. What should you ask during the interview?
2. Is it good or bad to give concise answers?
3. According to the reading, does the interviewer mind if you drink and smoke during the interview?

Now, complete the following phrases with information from the article.

4. To take full advantage of an interview, it is important that you ... *(3 items)*
5. It is not good for you to ... *(3 items)*

Job Interview: Decisive Factor

How to take full advantage of the interview

(1) Always be prepared to give good answers.

(2) Ask what is necessary; for example, opportunities for advancement and fringe benefits.

(3) Always be honest and show your strength in fields of interest. Some counterproductive aspects that could turn against you during the interview are:

Smoking, drinking, chewing gum or biting your nails, boasting, joking, making personal comments, arguing with the interviewer, making the interviewer feel defensive, appearing to be obsessed with the salary and benefits, and finally, being unaware or ignorant of the company.

Some positive aspects during the interview are: Be on time, at all times be courteous and respectful, convey your energy and enthusiasm, be brief and concise in your answers.

VI. Let's Write: The Job. *(20 points)* As you know, in addition to looking good, you must do other things to get a job. Write a paragraph (at least 8 sentences) including the following:

- the type of job you are interested in and why;
- courses you need to take in order to get work;
- what you must do if an ad for a job is of interest to you.

Use verbs such as gustar, present subjunctive with impersonal expressions and nominalization with **lo que, lo de, eso de** and **esto de,** when appropriate.

Source: Glisan and Shrum 1991.

EPIDSODE TWO
Designing Your Own Test

Use the same textbook chapter for which you designed objectives in Episode One of the TEACH AND REFLECT for Chapter 3. Design a pragmatic, integrative, interactive test for the chapter. Refer to the objectives you wrote in Chapter 3 as you create the test. Describe how the test would be graded. Also, explain how you would assess speaking skill and what type of grading scale you would use.

DISCUSS AND REFLECT

In the first case study, you will see how a successful teacher helps a beginning teacher use the technique of oral testing. In the second case study, you will see how a teacher concerned with the fairness of grading examined several evaluation options.

CASE STUDY 1
Using Audiotapes for Global Communicative Assessment

Among her teaching duties, Ms. Zerkle has three classes of Spanish III at Riverside High School in Niagara City Schools. This year she has a student teacher, Mr. Rafferty, from Cedar State College. Mr. Rafferty had heard about Ms. Zerkle's success in using oral testing with her students and was very excited about learning how to use these techniques. Mr. Rafferty has been student teaching now for three months, and he has seen Ms. Zerkle give several oral tests. She told him yesterday that she would like his help in designing the oral tests for an exam on the first five chapters the students had studied. She gave him the following sample content and set of linguistic tasks for a speaking test in the students' textbook (Glisan and Shrum 1991). Ms. Zerkle also gave Mr. Rafferty a list of tips to ensure his successful implementation of this oral test.

SPEAKING TEST, CHAPTERS 1–5
(25 points per situation; select only one situation.)

Situation A: You and a friend are riding in your car along a country road, and your friend tosses an empty soft-drink can out the window. You are upset, because you have been campaigning for a cleaner environment for the last three years. With a classmate who plays the role of your friend, hold the following conversation:

Student A (the driver):
* ask why your friend tossed the can
* disagree with your friend about the freedom to litter

- explain the effects of littering
- offer some alternatives to tossing the can
- explain recycling

Student B: (the can tosser):
- explain why you tossed the can
- say that you're not worried about the effects of littering, it's a big (and free) country, so you should be allowed to do what you like
- ask about some alternatives to littering
- become persuaded by your friend's point of view

You will be evaluated on your performance of these linguistic tasks:
- asking for and giving explanations for past actions
- persuading someone or becoming persuaded by citing reasonable and logical arguments
- hypothesizing about possible effects of actions

Situation B: Imagine that you have escorted your 75-year-old aunt to a large trade show, a county agricultural fair, or a crafts exhibit at a city street fair. Unfortunately, the walking has tired her out, and she has stumbled and fallen. You ask one of the local exhibitors to make an emergency phone call for an ambulance. With a class-mate who plays the role of the local exhibitor, conduct the following conversation.

Student A (the nephew):
- explain that your aunt has fallen and ask if the exhibitor will make a call for you
- describe your aunt's age and her physical condition: she has had two heart attacks, and you think she has just broken her ankle
- describe what you and your aunt were doing when the accident happened
- use *if*-clauses to make hypotheses about what would or could have happened and what might still happen

Student B (the exhibitor):
- make the call, saying aloud what you are doing as you dial and speak with the operator
- give the location of the accident
- relate the story about the injury that Student A has told you, using expressions such as "he said that ..."
- tell the nephew what the operator said about the probable time of the ambu-lance's arrival

You will be evaluated on these linguistic tasks:
- asking someone to do something for you
- relating a past event
- conveying information
- hypothesizing about past and future possibilities

Tips for Mr. Rafferty for oral testing:

1. Working in pairs, students should prepare an audiotape of one of the conversations outlined on the situation sheet handout; use the native language on your handout so that you don't give away key vocabulary the students should know.

2. Allow the students at least 3 days to prepare their audiotapes outside of class.

3. Students should write the names of all participants on their tape and rewind the tape to the place where you (the instructor) will start to listen to their conversation.

4. When they get their graded tape back, students should listen to themselves again and read the instructor's written comments on the evaluation sheet; they should also listen to the spoken comments you left on the tape.

5. When you grade the tapes, be sure you have each student's evaluation sheet and a pen or pencil and a tape recorder. Grade the tapes in a quiet place so that you can listen carefully to the students' content. Let your spoken and written comments contain positive statements about what the students have done. In your comments, respond to content and linguistic accuracy. It should take you about 30 to 50 minutes to grade the tapes for one class of 25 students, if you don't waste time between tapes.

Ask yourself these questions:

1. Were opportunities provided for students to practice using language in a range of contexts likely to be encountered in the target culture? Explain.
2. Were opportunities provided for students to practice carrying out a range of tasks likely to be necessary in the target culture? Explain.
3. Was there concern for the development of linguistic accuracy? Explain.
4. What do you think about Ms. Zerkle's tips for Mr. Rafferty?

To prepare the case:

■ Read Nerenz and Knop (1982) for information about group size and language learning opportunities. Extrapolate these findings to foreign language testing.

- Read Hughes (1989) for additional ideas about classroom testing.
- Study Ms. Zerkle's tips, and prepare your thoughts on these questions for class discussion:
  1. What reasons would Ms. Zerkle have for asking students to perform this task in pairs?
  2. If this is an oral test, what reasons do you think Ms. Zerkle has for giving students so many days to prepare their tapes?
  3. What purpose will Mr. Rafferty's oral comments on the students' tapes serve?

Imagine that you are Mr. Rafferty. You have found that many students are having difficulty making the audiotapes outside of class: some do not have tape recorders at home and do not have time to complete the assignment at other times during the school day. Describe a way that you might have students complete the assignment in class. How will you deal with the problem of lost class time?

_____

_____

_____

_____

_____

_____

_____

_____

For the next speaking test, you have decided to try testing students' spontaneous oral skills instead of asking them to prepare a tape in advance. Describe two ways that you might accomplish this in a classroom setting. Explore the issues of test format, how many students will be tested at once, and the grading procedure.

_____

_____

_____

_____

_____

_____

_____

_____

_____

_____

_____

DISCUSS AND REFLECT

> **CASE STUDY 2**
> **Evaluating Student Production of L2**
>
> Mr. McCorkle teaches French at Mochick Middle School. He is a professionally active teacher, attending state and national conferences at least once a year. Recently, during the summer, he helped write the curriculum guide to be used in his school system for teaching foreign languages for the next five-year period. His classroom is student-centered, and the state supervisor of foreign languages frequently asks him to give demonstrations to other groups of foreign language teachers on ways to improve student use of the target language for real communication both in and out of class. Mr. McCorkle is well-informed and up-to-date professionally. However, he continues to struggle with ways to evaluate student performance, especially speaking and writing, on tests. He wants to be sure that he weights the evaluation elements in a manner consistent with the difficulty of the communication task for his students. Recently, he located the procedure for grading speaking shown in Figure 2.

Ask yourself these questions:

1. What is the main purpose of this scale?
2. How could the scale be used?
3. Which learner performance does this scale reward? What tasks does a learner need to be able to perform in order to score well on this scale?

FIGURE 2 Evaluation Sheet for Speaking Tests (25 points)

Instructor: Circle a numerical score (higher = better) for each student.

Student A: _____   Student B: _____

Coverage of tasks   Coverage of tasks
6 5 4 3 2 1^2 6 5 4 3 2 1

Effort to communicate   Effort to communicate
7 5 3 1   7 5 3 1

Comprehensibility to partner and instructor   Comprehensibility to partner and instructor
4 3 2 1   4 3 2 1

Accuracy of vocabulary   Accuracy of vocabulary
4 3 2 1   4 3 2 1

Grammatical accuracy   Grammatical accuracy
4 3 2 1   4 3 2 1

Source: Glisan and Shrum 1991.

Mr. McCorkle continued his search for ways to evaluate writing. He examined the ESL Composition Profile (Jacobs, Zingraf, Wormuth, Hartfield and Hughey 1981), which appears in Appendix A17.

Ask yourself these questions:

1. What is the main purpose of this profile?
2. How could the profile be used?
3. Which learner performance does this profile reward? What tasks does a learner need to be able to perform in order to score well on this profile?

To prepare the case:

- Read Phillips (1992) and Young (1990) for information about students' levels of anxiety on foreign language tests.
- Read Shohamy (1988) for additional examples of rating for production of oral language.
- Ask a foreign language teacher for permission to interview a high-achieving student and a low-achieving student in his or her class to find out their general view of foreign language tests, their view of speaking tests, their view of written tests, their feelings about quizzes, and their views about how they would like their knowledge to be tested.

---

[2]The number of points in these categories may be adjusted, depending on the linguistic tasks contained in a given communicative task. For instance, this sheet represents a conversational situation containing three linguistic tasks; a student earns two points for having completed each one. If there were two tasks, a student could earn a maximum of four points for completing both tasks in the category "Coverage of Tasks." In such a situational conversation, the number of points possible in the category "Effort to Communicate" might become nine, so that the total for the conversation remains at 25 for consistency in record keeping throughout a course.

Describe how each of these scales could be used in a contextualized test like the one given in the TEACH AND REFLECT section of this chapter.

_____

_____

_____

_____

_____

_____

Using these two scales, describe the difference between discrete point and global evaluation.

_____

_____

_____

_____

_____

_____

Create your own scale for use in global evaluation of speaking or writing.

_____

_____

_____

_____

_____

_____

_____

REFERENCES

Bachman, L. F. *Fundamental Considerations in Language Testing*. Oxford: Oxford University Press, 1990.

Bachman, L. F. "What Does Language Testing Have to Offer?" *TESOL Quarterly* 24 (1991): 671–704.

Bonin, T., and D. Birckbichler. "Real Communication Through Conversation Cards." *Modern Language Journal* 59 (1975): 22–25.

Buck, K., H. Byrnes, and I. Thompson. *The ACTFL Oral Proficiency Interview Tester Training Manual*. Hastings-on-Hudson, NY: ACTFL, 1989.

Carroll, J. "Fundamental Considerations in Testing for English Proficiency of Foreign Students." *Testing the English Proficiency of Foreign Students*. Washington, DC: Center for Applied Linguistics, 1961: 31–40.

Glisan, E. W., and J. L. Shrum. *Enlaces*. Boston: Heinle & Heinle, 1991.

Henning, G. "Priority: Testing. Priority Issues in Assessment of Communicative Language Abilities." *Foreign Language Annals* 23 (1990): 379–384.

Hughes, A. *Testing for Language Teachers*. Cambridge: Cambridge University Press, 1989.

Jacobs, H. L., S. Zingraf, D. Wormuth, V. Hartfield, and J. Hughey. *Testing ESL Composition: A Practical Approach*. Rowley, MA: Newbury House, 1981.

Nerenz, A. G., and C. K. Knop. "The Effect of Group Size on Students' Opportunity to Learn in the Second Language Classroom." Ed. A. Garfinkel. *ESL and the Foreign Language Teacher*. Report of Central States Conference on the Teaching of Foreign Languages, Lincolnwood, IL: National Textbook Company, 1982: 47–60.

Oller, J. *Language Tests at School*. London: Longman, 1979.

Oller, J. "Foreign Language Testing: Its Breadth (Part 1)." *Association of Departments of Foreign Languages Bulletin* 22 (1991a): 33–38.

Oller, J. "Foreign Language Testing: Its Depth (Part 2)." *American Departments of Foreign Languages Bulletin* 23 (1991b): 5–13.

Oller, J., and C. Conrad. "The Cloze Technique and ESL Proficiency." *Language Learning* 21 (1971): 183–194.

Phillips, E. M. "The Effects of Language Anxiety on Students' Oral Test Performance and Attitudes." *Modern Language Journal* 76 (1992): 14–26.

Savignon, S. *Communicative Competence: Theory and Classroom Practice— Texts and Contexts in Second Language Learning*. Reading, MA: Addison-Wesley, 1983.

Shohamy, E. "A Proposed Framework for Testing the Oral Language of Second/Foreign Language Learners." *Studies in Second Language Acquisition* 12 (1988): 165–179.

Shohamy, E. "Language Testing Priorities: A Different Perspective." *Foreign Language Annals* 23 (1990): 385–394.

Shohamy, E., C. M. Gordon, and R. Kraemer. "The Effect of Raters' Background and Training on the Reliability of Direct Writing Tests." *Modern Language Journal* 76 (1992): 27–33.

Shrum, J. L. "Testing in Context: A Lesson from Foreign Language Learning." *Vision* 1 (1991): 3, 7–8.

Stansfield, C. W., and D. M. Kenyon. "The Development and Validation of a Simulated Oral Proficiency Interview." *Modern Language Journal* 76 (1992): 129–41.

Swaffar, J., K. Arens, and H. Byrnes. *Reading for Meaning.* Englewood Cliffs, NJ: Prentice Hall, 1991.

Tierney, R. J., M. A. Carter, and L. E. Desai. *Portfolio Assessment in the Reading-Writing Classroom.* Norwood, MA: Christopher-Gordon, 1991.

Young, D. J. "An Investigation of Students' Perspectives on Anxiety and Speaking." *Foreign Language Annals* 23 (1990): 539–553.

CHAPTER 12

Using Technology to Support Contextualized Language Instruction

In this chapter, you will explore the ways in which technology can be used to support contextualized language instruction. The purpose of this chapter is to offer a definition of technology, briefly introduce you to the most commonly available technological tools, describe how foreign language teachers use these tools, offer some guidelines for the selection and use of technological tools in the foreign language classroom, and provide some guidance for you as you encounter future technological advances. In the TEACH AND REFLECT section of this chapter, you will apply some guidelines for the selection of videotexts and assess the instructional usefulness of an exercise contained in some computer-assisted software. In the first case study, you will assist a teacher as she attempts to use video segments in her teaching, and in the second case study you will see how a teacher and her students used a computer-assisted writing program. For an extensive summary of the state-of-the-art technology in service to the teaching and learning of foreign and second languages, you may wish to consult Garrett (1991).

CONCEPTUAL ORIENTATION

■ What Is Technology?

According to Gendron (1977, cf. Saettler 1990), *technology* is "any systematized practical knowledge, based on experimentation and/or scientific theory, which enhances the capacity of society to produce goods and services, and which is embodied in productive skills, organization, or machinery" (p. 23). In terms of educational technology, it refers to the uses teachers and learners make of machines to systematize practical knowledge. Educational technology is not the use of machines to organize knowledge or to function as fancy "add-ons" to instruction. In fact, the kind of learning that occurs with the use of technology may be different from traditional learning and should be measured on its own terms, rather than by standardized tests. For instance, Tierney reports the results of a long-term study in which, from ninth grade through twelfth grade, students' familiarity with computers moved from knowledge of how to edit and print out text to knowledge of how to use hypermedia and desktop publishing. Similarly, the students' views of technology's usefulness moved from (1) interest in learning about computers and willingness to help each other do so, to (2) ways technology could help them get jobs, to (3) ways to use their words that were "dynamic rather than static," pursuing multiple lines of thought and exploring different perspectives (1992, p. 10).

Technological devices can be useful for language teachers who wish to bring the sounds and sights of another language and culture into the classroom. Language labs, tape recorders, overhead projectors, and slide/filmstrip projectors have long been used in language teaching and learning. New ways to use video and computer-related technologies are rapidly becoming commonplace in language classrooms as teachers design instruction that appeals to the media-related interests of students. According to Lucie Fjeldstad, IBM President in charge of multimedia in education, "An average kid will have spent 20,000 hours in front of TV by the age 16. We need to take the entertaining aspects of television and add it [sic] to education" (cf. Rogers 1992, p. 50). Advances in technology are occurring so rapidly that it is difficult to develop instructional uses for them. As Garrett points out, "Technology that can be taken for granted today is already light-years ahead of the profession's ability to integrate a principled use of it into the classroom and the curriculum" (1991, p. 74).

■ Why Use Technology?

In classroom teaching and learning, students generally encounter a body of content and process knowledge that the teacher has organized in order to aid understanding and internalization. The decision regarding how to engage students with instructional processes rests with the teacher. Thus, in the case of technology, the teacher determines to what extent technological devices will be used to enhance language learning. Accordingly, Johnson (1991) points out that the uses students will make of computers ultimately depend on teachers.

Students who are familiar with television are used to rapid changes in scenes; entertaining and colorful visual stimuli; associated and synchronized auditory accompaniments, whether musical or voiced; story lines that are quickly resolved; and completely contextualized scenes and language. Add to this list the effect of blending visual and auditory presentations, occasionally enhanced with a splash of reading from the screen, and one can easily see the potential for using this technology to captivate student interest. Furthermore, a videotape, videodisc, or satellite transmission can enliven the target culture and language for students in classrooms.

A teacher's decision to use a tape recorder, overhead, video, or computer-related technology is similar to the decision to use a particular practice exercise or workbook handout. The technological device, like the practice exercise, is a tool that helps the learner interact with the body of content knowledge and processes. Teachers who have a philosophy of how students learn will opt to design instructional tasks that are consistent with that philosophy. The excitement of using a new technology is often accompanied by anxiety on the part of the teacher and the students. Certainly, an increased expenditure of time to design meaningful instruction will be needed. As you, the teacher, decide how to deliver instruction with the assistance of a technological tool, consider the following guidelines for selection:

- What can my students presently do with the language?
- What will this tool help them learn how to do?
- How will it help them learn how to do it?
- What will it cost in terms of time, planning, supplies, and equipment?
- Is there a high school, college, or university in my area that could help by providing services or resources?
- What are the alternatives?
- Is this the best way to accomplish the objectives of instruction and meet the needs of my students?

One of the challenges of teaching foreign languages is to present students with a living, vibrant people who use the target language for daily communication. Cultural elements, from daily table manners to world-famous paintings and literature, constitute the multidimensional environment in which the language is used. The textbook can offer authentic visual and print dimensions. Authentic audio can be delivered by means of the teacher, classroom guests who are native speakers, tape recordings, and video. Time and expertise are required to make successful use of any tool in the classroom. What constitutes successful use? If learning *on the part of the student* has been helped by the use of a tool, then the tool has been used successfully. The foreign language teaching profession has made considerable strides in producing video to be used for the development of reading skills, Computer-Assisted Language Learning (CALL) to enhance learners' writing skills, and textbooks to help learners improve their listening and speaking skills. The following sections offer a brief description of the primary forms of technology that foreign language teachers employ, along with some tips to guide you in their use.

Using the Overhead Projector to Provide Visual Support

The overhead projector is a tool language teachers use frequently because it can supplement or substitute for the chalkboard while still allowing the teacher to face the class. The teacher stands next to the projector, facing the class, and is freed from standing next to the projected image on a screen or wall. An additional benefit is that the teacher can prepare the transparency in advance, and through the use of masks (opaque paper) or overlays (additional transparencies with coordinated material) manipulate the order and arrangement of the presentation. The teacher can add information or student input directly onto the transparency, using a permanent or water-soluble transparency marker. For example, a set of interview questions can be printed onto the transparency in permanent ink, answers offered by the class in whole-class or small groups can be added during the lesson and washed off between class periods, and the original interview transparency is ready to be used again during the next class. Here are some tips for smooth use of the overhead:

- Use permanent as well as water-soluble pens.
- Use black, blue, purple, or green ink, because other colors are hard to see.
- Use a medium-grade transparency.
- Single transparency sheets offer more flexibility than a roll of transparencies.
- Use a liquid spray appliance cleaner to remove from the transparency any accumulated oil from your hands.
- Set the overhead up in advance, positioning it nearer to or farther from the screen to make the image a legible size and the entire page visible at once; from time to time during the presentation, turn and look at the projected image to make sure your viewers are seeing the entire page.
- Stand next to the projector and face the class, using a pen or your finger to point out salient information on the projected image; walking up to the screen to point out something is distracting to the viewers, and the projection light shines in your eyes.
- Use the overhead for brief periods of time (5–10 minutes) as you would any other activity; the drone of the machine's fan and the dimmed lights tend to limit student attentiveness.
- To minimize any tremor in your hand, rest your hand on the machine when you point to parts of the transparency.
- Don't use the overhead just to use the overhead; be sure that what you present suits that medium.
- Number your transparencies if you are using more than one so you can keep track of where you are.
- Involve students in writing on the transparency.
- Turn off the bulb; letting the fan run after you've finished using the projector will preserve the life of the bulb, particularly on older projectors.
- Plan the activity following the use of the overhead so you can leave the overhead visible for a few minutes to allow students time to copy it if necessary.

Using Language Labs to Strengthen Listening Comprehension Skills

In accepting the challenge of offering the target language in ways that were authentic and useful, language teachers took advantage of the emerging technology of the 1950s and began to use language labs as extensively as budgets would allow. The prevailing behaviorist view of how learning happens influenced the design of instructional materials that were implemented through language labs. Wearing earphones, students sat in three-sided booths and listened to a tape that was broadcast from a main console. Student tasks were limited to listening to and repeating after native speakers who modeled drill sentences. Some labs offered student recording and playback. Labs were interactive only in the sense that the teacher could monitor and speak with students from the main console and students could reply or record their responses on a separate recording track of an audiotape.

Generally, if a school purchased a lab, time in the lab was assigned to each group of students on a per-week or biweekly basis, and each teacher took his or her classes to the lab on a given day. In some schools, generally at the post-secondary level, students completed lab work as out-of-class assignments, sometimes helped by a teaching assistant.

As language labs became more sophisticated, requiring higher and higher levels of technical expertise to keep them in working order, teachers used them less and less, feeling that their time was better spent working with students and not with sensitive and often temperamental equipment that required extensive technical skill to repair. Further, three-sided booths did not encourage communication between people and even led to damage of the equipment. As some labs simply fell into disuse, developers of technology began to listen to the advice of teachers who had used labs and modified their product accordingly.

Modern labs have certainly come a long way since the 1950s, incorporating important changes in their physical appearance and in the instructional tasks that students and teachers can perform. Today, labs generally involve wireless transmission of taped sound and often make use of authentic materials that engage students in contextualized two- or three-way communication between student, teacher, and other students. Labs are mobile, and headsets can be incorporated into any lesson since they often drop from the ceiling or can be retrieved by students from a central console in the regular classroom. Sophisticated laboratory systems offer students the opportunity to view video programs and work on computerized language lessons.

As an alternative to a lab, many teachers use one or more small cassette tape recorders in their classrooms. One can be used for listening as a whole class, or several can be placed around the classroom as listening stations with individualized directions for singles, pairs, or triads of students. See Chapter 7 for ways to use authentic taped materials to enhance listening practice for students.

■ Using Video to Combine Visual and Auditory Learning

For most students, video and television are common modes of experiencing the world. Through video, nearly every aspect of language structure and usage can be explored, but video can most productively be used if the teacher actively manipulates the video and its presentation in order to help students develop comprehension. This means doing something more than just setting the video up and letting it run. Commercially available video materials, teacher- and student-made video of student interactions and performance, and off-air recordings of broadcast materials are ways teachers can enliven their students' classroom experiences. However, users of video have a responsibility to secure permission prior to recording published and broadcast materials.

Perhaps our understanding of video as an instructional medium can be enhanced if we think of a video, or a contextualized segment of video, as a *videotext*. It is a text in the sense that it presents an authentic piece of language that could be presented in written form as well. As we elect to use videotext, we should apply the same criteria and careful judgement in selection and use as we apply to reading or listening texts.

Video can be presented by using a videocassette or videodisc and its appropriate recorder/playback machine. The videodisc offers some advantages; it allows the user to locate specific frames rapidly and accurately, and can accommodate connection of a computer to the videodisc player, thus integrating the two technologies and their capabilities.

Selecting the Video Material

The teacher's first task is to select the video material. The best segments are those that are long enough to present a realistic context but short enough so as not to thwart students' ability to comprehend by using contextual cues and language knowledge. In Figure 1, Joiner (1990) offers guidelines to assist teachers as they select videotexts.

Altman points out the golden rule of video pedagogy: *"Don't expect—or even seek—full comprehension"* (1989, p. 42). As we become tolerant of incomplete comprehension, we begin to appreciate the greatest value of authentic materials in general and of video in particular. The use of video teaches students to "hear, to break down the spoken chain into appropriate chunks, and gives students practice in understanding. *At the same time, it does not ask them to understand what they are not yet prepared to understand"* (Altman 1989, p. 42). Since video is a familiar medium, students relate easily to it. When they find that they understand portions of the video, their confidence improves. As teachers, we need to remain aware of the level of our students' comprehension by checking it through recognition questions, discussion, or short in-class quizzes. Altman compares the strategies students use in comprehending a video to "finding hidden objects in drawings of trees" (1989, p. 43). Strategies such as asking students to make direct transcriptions of the video soundtrack are counterproductive to the type of strategy building this medium makes possible. Video provides the context for a wide variety of communicative and interactive activities in the classroom. As you select video materials, keep these points in mind:

- Remember the function you expect the program to perform.
- Select short segments.
- View the program repeatedly and completely before assigning it.
- Manipulate the video in order to make it more comprehensible (Altman 1989).

FIGURE 1 Choosing Videotexts

I. BASIC DATA

Title:
Subject:
Length (of broadcast or of sequence):

Circle the words below that apply.

Format/Standard: VHS   BETAMAX   UMATIC/PAL   SECAM   NTSC
Aids: Transcription   Study Guide   Suggested   Segmentation   Test
Other (specify) _____

II. GENERAL CHARACTERISTICS OF VIDEOTEXT

Circle the words/check the phrases that apply.

Category:
      Literature   Civilization   Oral communication   Contemporary culture
Purpose of text:
      To inform   To instruct   To entertain   To persuade
Audience for which text is intended:
      General
      Limited (specify) _____
Linguistic assumptions with respect to viewers/listeners:
      Assumes native/near-native ability to comprehend the language in question
      Assumes less than native ability to comprehend the language in question
Cultural assumptions with respect to viewers/listeners:
      Assumes familiarity with the culture portrayed
      Assumes lack of, or limited, familiarity with the culture portrayed
      Culture not an important consideration

III. TECHNICAL CHARACTERISTICS OF VIDEOTEXT

Check the point along the line that best represents your opinion.

Quality of Images
      fuzzy, blurred _____ : _____ : _____ : _____ : _____ very clear

Quality of Sound Track
      inaudible _____ : _____ : _____ : _____ : _____ very clear

Editing of Video
      amateurish _____ : _____ : _____ : _____ : _____ skillful

IV. LINGUISTIC/PARALINGUISTIC CHARACTERISTICS OF VIDEOTEXT

A. Image
In the space provided, note the following elements.

View of society represented in text (historical, outmoded, up-to-date)

Gestures/body language/dress (handshake, proximity of speakers, types of clothing)

Socio-cultural groups represented in text (levels of society, age groups, professions/occupations, rural/urban/small town)

Printed text/graphics

FIGURE 1 Choosing Videotexts (continued)

B. Soundtrack/Script
Check the point along the line that corresponds to your opinion.

Rate of delivery:

slow _____ :_____ : _____ :_____ :_____ very rapid

Quality of articulation:

incomprehensible _____ : _____ : _____ : _____ : _____ very clear

Voiceover (off-screen) narration:

none _____ : _____ : _____ : _____ : _____ extensive

Check all choices that apply.

On-screen speakers:	One(monologue)
	Two (dialogue, interview)
	More than two (conversation, discussion)
Accents of speakers:	Metropolitan, non-regional French
	Regionally accented European French
	Canadian French
	African French
	Caribbean French
Types of spoken language:	Spontaneous free speech (conversation)
	Deliberate free speech (interviews, discussions)
	Oral presentation of a written text (newscasts, lectures, commentaries)
	Oral presentation of a fixed, rehearsed script (films, plays)
Levels of language:	Familiar
	Informal conversational
	Formal conversational
	Formal non-conversational
	Archaic
Vocabulary:	Limited, primarily concrete, high-frequency words
	Extensive, but non-technical
	Technical
Music/sound effect:	Distracting (may hinder comprehension)
	Helpful (may aid comprehension)

C. Relationship of Image to Sound

Message received primarily through image
Message received primarily through sound
Verbal message and visual message redundant
Verbal message and visual message complementary

D. Language in Context
List below the functions and contexts illustrated in the text.

Content/context (making a telephone call from a phone booth, getting a hotel room, ordering a meal in a restaurant)

Functions (narrating, describing, giving commands, asking directions)

FIGURE 1 Choosing Videotexts (continued)

V. POTENTIAL USEFULNESS

For attaining course goals

Of little use _____ :_____ : _____ : _____ : _____ Very useful

For motivating students

Of little use _____ : _____ : _____ : _____ : _____ Very useful

Source: Joiner 1990.

Video Modalities

Since video so nicely combines image and sound in authentic language contexts, instruction that uses video can be accomplished by separating the modes in which video is perceived. The modes follow, along with a brief description of the use and benefits of each (Altman 1989):

Image and sound together. Play a short segment of sound and image together. Follow up with comprehension questions. Segments that use natural conversation to repeat objects that students see can effectively reinforce vocabulary. For instance, watching peers in France order pastries at a pastry shop creates a form of redundancy.

Image alone. Viewing the image alone allows students to identify the greatest number of cultural elements. Altman points out that weaker students—that is, those whose linguistic understanding is most limited—often benefit most from this modality because there is no language to interfere with the visual message.

Sound alone. Turning down the "brightness" or "contrast" of the monitor enables students to hear the soundtrack without the image.

a. Sound and image, then sound alone. Using this strategy requires playing the sound and image together, followed by comprehension questions, then playing only the sound without the image. This procedure enables students to listen without dependence on the visual image.

b. Sound alone first, then sound and image together. Advanced classes benefit most from this strategy, which requires students to understand through use of their listening skills. On the basis of that understanding, students can then guess the events that might be happening in the image and describe them.

c. Sound alone first, then image alone. Similar to the previous strategy, students can listen to the sound, predict what the image will contain, and then narrate it as they view the image. According to Altman, this strategy works best when information on the soundtrack that is not available in the image must be remembered and narrated by the student.

d. Neither sound nor image. Much of the preparatory and follow-up practice, and hence much of the learning that can be stimulated through video, happens before and after the video is viewed, without sound or image. The teacher prepares comprehension questions and practice exercises for use without the video, and student language production about the video occurs prior to or following the viewing.

Stempleski and Tomalin suggest the use of *pause/freeze frame control,* that is, pausing the video at the initial point of an interaction, asking students to predict the dialogue exchange, followed by immediate comparison with the actual words (1990, p. 15).

Interactive video. The term interactive has several meanings when used in discussions of technology and language teaching. It usually conjures up in a foreign language teacher's mind a conversation or some other kind of verbal exchange between people. When language teachers use the term to describe a lesson or program, they continue to think of human involvement and use the term to refer to the degree of interactiveness between the student and the computer (Garrett 1991). However, in the case of "interactive audio" and "interactive video," *interactive* refers to the interaction between the machine that delivers the sound or picture and the computer that controls the machine and that may deliver textual material through its screen, to accompany or alternate with the video presentation (Garrett 1991). The use of the videodisc is thus combined with the use of a computer program. For example, students might watch a particular scene on video and then be given synchronized computerized assistance with vocabulary, idioms, grammar, or cultural notes.

One of the concerns sometimes expressed about the use of video, especially if a feature-length film is the videotext, relates to the ability of learners to process captioned reading material, or subtexts, while listening to acoustically rich, authentic video segments. In his discussion of the benefits of captioning for advanced students, Garza (1991) found that captioning:

- allowed students to use already developed reading comprehension skills to develop aural comprehension;
- increased the accessibility of the salient language of authentic video materials;
- allowed students to use multiple language processing strategies to accommodate the various modalities of input;
- increased the memorability of the essential language;
- promoted the use of new lexicon and phrases in an appropriate context.

Integrating Video into Language Instruction

As is the case with other technological tools, video can be used to enhance language learning. Video can provide the authentic input, both visual and auditory, necessary for language acquisition and development of cultural awareness. Teachers can help students develop strategies for understanding linguistic and paralinguistic aspects of language while guiding students through video segments by using the interactive model for listening and reading presented in Chapter 7. This model is organized in a fashion similar to the list of activities in Figure 2 that can be used as students are guided through viewing of the videotext (Joiner 1990). The activities proceed from pre-viewing, to identifying important information, to using the information for real communication; tasks include attention to cultural elements and the language of the text itself; extension activities are suggested.

FIGURE 2 Using Videotexts

I. GENERAL POSSIBILITIES FOR EXPLOITING VIDEOTEXTS

Replay sequences (or entire video) for more detailed viewing
Use pause/still frame
Interrupt viewing to check comprehension
Cut off sound to focus on image
Replace soundtrack with own narration or ask students to narrate
Select certain sequences for intensive viewing, pass over others
Assign certain sequences for out-of-class viewing
View with or without script

II. PREPARATION OF STUDENTS FOR LISTENING/VIEWING

Supply essential cultural information
Review/introduce essential vocabulary/structures
Preview (overview of content, text characteristics)
Motivate, arouse interest
Provide listening/viewing tasks

III. LISTENING/VIEWING TASKS

A. Skills-oriented Tasks
Comprehension (listening, reading)
    yes-no questions, true-false, multiple choice, physical response, checklist, fill-ins
Comprehension plus production (listening, reading, speaking, writing)
    open-ended questions, role-play, brainstorming, debate, discussion, note-taking, summaries, continuations

B. Culture-oriented Tasks
Awareness: notice, identify
Understanding: compare, contrast with other cultures
Integration: imitate, role-play

C. Script-oriented Tasks
Find examples of redundancy
Underline certain structures/vocabulary items
Identify words/phrases used to express emotion, to persuade, etc.
Read aloud portions of the script
Rewrite portions of the script
Cross out extra words in "doctored" version of script
Fill-in words omitted from script

IV. EXPANSION ACTIVITIES

Play game, work puzzle
Build or make something
Read related material
Learn song or dance and perform
Create own audio or video broadcast

Source: Joiner 1990.

Samples of viewing guides for use prior to and following the viewing of the videotext offer students clues on how to benefit from the experience. Figure 3 is an example of a viewing guide that could be used prior to viewing as an advance organizer, in order to encourage students to visualize the spoken and performed messages they will see. Helping students watch the video and listen for verbal clues could also be conducted in groups of three. In Figure 4, learners are directed to watch and listen for language functions, paralinguistic information, and emotional states that are expressed with language. Figure 5 is an example of a pre- or post-viewing guide that uses pictures and drawings to maximize reliance on viewing and listening skills.

FIGURE 3 Viewing Guide

Where are the park, the post office, the police station?

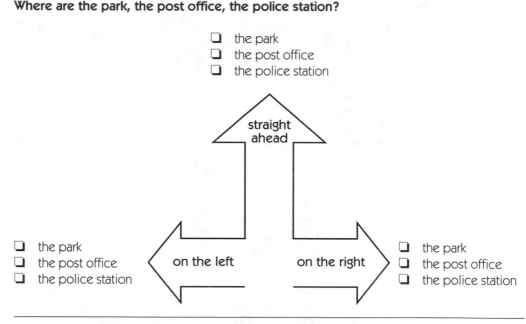

Source: Lonergan 1984.

FIGURE 4 Video Guide: Watching and Listening for Cues

Learner A	**Learner B**	**Learner C**
As you watch the sequence, note down examples of:	As you watch the sequence, note down examples of:	As you watch the sequence, note down examples of:
• displeasure • disappointment • optimism	• agreement • disagreement • pessimism	• direct commands • indirect commands • resignation

Source: Lonergan 1984.

FIGURE 5 Pre- or Post-Viewing Guide

Mettez, selon le cas, des croix dans les boîtes:

Françoise demande [room symbols] avec [shower/bathtub symbols]

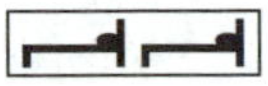

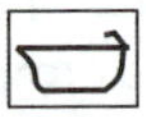

Françoise doit payer
- ❑ plus que 100Ff
- ❑ 100Ff
- ❑ moins que 100Ff

Elle prend la chambre
- ❑ 47
- ❑ 107
- ❑ 407

Elle part le demain
- ❑ vers 8 h.
- ❑ vers 7 h.
- ❑ vers 9 h.

Source: Lonergan 1984.

Information-gap activities can be created using a technique called *video split* (Lavery 1981), in which half of a class views, with the sound turned off, a videotext that has five or six speaking actors. The other half of the class hears only the sound and does not see the visual aspects of the videotext. The teacher then pairs the students, one viewer with one listener, and assigns each pair the task of recreating the conversation(s) in the videotext. Students verify the accuracy of their recreation by watching the videotext with sound.

Using CALL to Enhance Language Learning

In nearly every foreign language class, most of the students will be somewhat computer literate, and some will be computer experts. Many of their skills have been acquired through countless hours spent before a monitor, teaching themselves. The research indicates that students have positive attitudes about computers (Kulik and Kulik 1986, 1987). The individualization possibilities presented by computers also make this medium an attractive one for teachers. They imagine a bank of questions that can be purposefully or randomly accessed to create reliable and valid class tests, individualized tests, and make-up tests, with weighting of certain parts to suit the learner's needs. Teachers also dream of practice exercises that can be accessed to offer students additional individualized practice on troublesome points, especially if only one or two students require the extra work. Teachers wish for feedback systems that offer students meaningful comments on their input in response to computerized stimuli, and limitless branching possibilities, depending on their interests, needs, and abilities, including dictionary and thesaurus support and other reference materials.

Here, as always, the learner and the language learning process are of central importance. Accordingly, the acronym CALL (Computer-Assisted Language Learning) has replaced the more generic terms, CAI (Computer-Assisted Instruction) and CALI (Computer-Assisted Language Instruction). It is generally assumed that CALL serves as a supplement or enrichment rather than a substitute for regular classroom learning. However, the question that most foreign language teachers have as they consider using CALL is "Does it enhance language learning?" Research examining CALL has suggested that the design of the CALL program can encourage the development of language learning skills and result in more learning (Johansen and Tennyson 1983; Robinson 1989). Other studies have claimed that learner differences can affect learner strategies and attitudes as well as the benefits gained from using CALL programs (Chapelle and Jamieson 1986; Pederson 1986).[1]

There is much investigation that remains to be done into the use of CALL. Garrett cautions that the research currently available cannot answer the question "Does it work?" on a broad scale because of the many uncontrolled variables that occur in the experiments. She suggests that research is needed to investigate specific issues such as "What kind of software, integrated how into what kind of syllabus, at what level of language learning, for what kind of language learners, is likely to be effective for what specific learning purposes?" (1991, p. 75) Further, we do not know conclusively whether CALL helps the learning of L2 subskills of reading, writing and grammar, reading comprehension and vocabulary acquisition, or listening comprehension. We also do not know whether students at certain levels of proficiency benefit from using computers more than do students at other levels. We do not know what kind of immediate feedback or tutorial help is most beneficial for learners, nor do we know whether the program, the learner, or a combination of both best facilitates learning.

Although the basic questions of what and how much and when to implement CALL have yet to be answered, at some time in your career, you are likely to have to select computer hardware or software. Since computer software is generally designed by technicians who are not foreign language teachers, you may find the guidelines offered by Underwood (cf. Beauvois 1992, p. 457) in Figure 6 very helpful. For a description of the types of computerized programs, see Figure 7.

Of these program types, tutorials, drill and practice, holistic practice, and many games programs can be considered instructional in that learners are instructed by the computer. In such programs, the students respond, not initiate, along predetermined learning paths. There is generally a set of high- and low-level learning objectives (Wyatt 1987). In modeling, discovery, and simula-

---

[1]For further information regarding CALL research, consult Dunkel (1991) and Pederson (1986).

FIGURE 6 Criteria for Communicative CALL

1. Communicative CALL will aim at acquisition practice rather than learning practice .... There will be no drill.
2. In a Communicative CALL lesson or activity, grammar will always be implicit rather than explicit. Grammar will be built into the lesson ....
3. Communicative CALL will allow and encourage the student to generate original utterances ....
4. Communicative CALL will not try to judge and evaluate everything the student does ....
5. Communicative CALL will avoid telling students they are "wrong."
6. Communicative CALL will not try to "reward" students with congratulatory messages, lights, bells, whistles, or other such nonsense ....
7. Communicative CALL will not try to be "cute."
8. Communicative CALL will use the target language exclusively ....
9. Communicative CALL will be flexible ....
10. Communicative CALL will allow the student to explore the subject matter .... Exploratory CALL can offer the student an environment in which to play with language or manipulate it to see how things go together ....
11. Communicative CALL will create an environment in which using the target language feels natural, both on screen and off. An important source of comprehensive input that is often overlooked in the discussion of computer materials is the communication that usually takes place, not between computer and user, but between users ....
12. Communicative CALL will never try to do anything that a book could do just as well. (This rule should apply to any use of the computer.)
13. Above all, Communicative CALL will be fun ....

Source: Underwood (1984), c.f. Beauvois 1992.

tion programs, students are initiators, work *with* the computer, and take more responsibility for their learning. There are no predetermined learning paths, and it may only be possible to specify learning objectives in high-level terms (Wyatt 1987). Word and idea processing programs, spell checkers, on-line thesauruses, and text analysis programs are considered helpful for students who are completely responsible for their own learning. Students are initiators and use the computer as a tool to reduce labor. Learning objectives or paths are not specified or embodied in the computer program (Wyatt 1987).

In early research efforts, it was shown that the type of software influences the kinds of responses students can produce. Piper's (1986) study found that EFL students working in groups with one computer using early text-based CALL programs produced holophrastic utterances and repetitions largely without lexical or syntactic variety. There was little evidence of negotiation of meaning and no self-correction of error. By contrast, other researchers found that grouping of this sort enhances the social and language-use interaction patterns of the students as they communicate in the group using the target language (Johnson, Johnson, and Stanne 1986). However, it must be noted that the tasks presented to the learners through the software used in these settings are cooperative learning tasks, designed primarily to promote interaction. As CALL programming has developed, Abraham and Liou (1991) have shown improved results in kinds and numbers of language functions used, and in topics discussed in CALL groups. Recent research has shown no negative effects on learning when students are paired around a computer that uses cooperative learning tasks to introduce new material or practice newly learned material (Chang and Smith 1991).

Figure 7 Some Types of Programs Used in CALL

Program Type	Examples of Functions and Contents
1. *Tutorial*	introducing new material—e.g., the Cyrillic alphabet in beginning Russian
2. *Drill and practice*	allowing mastery of material already presented—e.g., grammatical forms, culturally appropriate behavior
3. *Game*	adding elements of peer competition, scoring, and timing to a wide variety of practice activities
4. *Holistic practice*	providing higher-level, contextualized practice activities—e.g., cloze passages
5. *Modeling*	demonstrating how to perform a language task—e.g., how a good reader handles difficult sections of a reading passage
6. *Discovery*	providing situations in which linguistic generalizations can be made—e.g., inferring rules for generating comparative forms
7. *Simulation*	allowing students to experiment with language use—e.g., levels of formality in a conversational simulator
8. *Adventure reading (interactive fiction)*	offering "participatory" reading materials—e.g., student as detective explores murder location, gathers clues
9. *Annotation*	providing a wide range of language "notes" (vocabulary, syntax, plot, etc.) available on demand during reading or listening activities
10. *Idea processor*	planning and editing outlines—e.g., before writing activities, after listening to lectures
11. *Word processor*	creating and editing written assignments
12. *On-line thesaurus*	expanding vocabulary, improving writing style
13. *Spelling checker*	guarding against errors during or after writing activities
14. *Textual analysis*	revealing structural and stylistic aspects of written work—e.g., complexity and variety of sentence types, subject/verb agreement errors

Source: Wyatt 1987.

Johnson (1991) cautions that the computer is merely the medium of delivery and that the design of the task is still of primary importance. Further, Chun and Brandl (1992) point out that much software tends to be restricted to language forms rather than being open ended to encourage meaningful communication, as illustrated in Figure 8. Chun and Brandl describe software currently under development that includes numerous communicative-gap exercises in which participants in the conversational arrangement have certain pieces of information but are required to talk with each other to find the pieces they do not have. One of their exercises is presented in the TEACH AND REFLECT section of this chapter for your practice and study.

An exciting use of the computer's capacity for electronic communication is through local area networks (LANs). Researchers have begun to examine the

FIGURE 8 Continuum of Learning Activities

Form Restricted	Meaning Enhancing	Meaningful Communication
grammar-based	*guided communication*	*free (human) communication*
not contextualized; single, isolated words or sentences	contextualized, interrelated sentences; but somewhat restricted grammatically, semantically, pragmatically	fully contextualized grammatically, semantically, pragmatically; interrelated sentences
CALL exercises: fill-in-the-blank; multiple choice; cloze	CALL exercises: communicative-gap exercises	CALL exercises: artificial intelligence with parsing, speech recognition
User's input: single words, single letters	User's input: whole sentences, but limited syntax and semantics	User's input: unrestricted, complete, original sentences

Source: Chun and Brandl 1992.

theoretical rationale and possible outcomes for use of LANs for L2 writing (Kreeft Peyton 1986; Kreeft Peyton and Mackinson-Smyth 1989; Esling 1992). Beauvois (1992) reports successful conversations between students and teachers using a synchronous, real-time network in which users view each other's comments on their computer screens and thus are able to "chat" with each other in, as it were, a kind of "slow motion" conversation.

Finally, experts highlight the importance of the role of the teacher in the use of CALL. Johnson encourages teachers to "never assume that computer-based curricula are 'teacher-proof' or that they are even adequate. Computers can be a way to bring students together to interact, to negotiate meaning, to think and to negotiate strategies related to the social and academic tasks at hand. The teacher's role is still essential" (1991, p. 79).

■ Using Software to Assist with Language Learning Processes

Computer software is now being developed to assist language students with the global process of language learning. Such software goes beyond the mechanical drill formats typical of early programs and provides opportunities for students to practice meaningful language use and self-expression. An example of such software is the unique **système-D** package developed by Noblitt, Pet, and Solá (1991), which enables students to develop their creative writing skills in French. It differs from other CALL programs in that it offers students the opportunity to express themselves by accessing a 4,400-word dictionary, a verb conjugator, a grammar index, a vocabulary index, and a phrase index.

Students can use the English/French dictionary, the French/English dictionary, and the verb conjugator for reference aids as they compose written texts. The dictionary includes most verbs used by elementary, intermediate, and advanced students. The program features a complete conjugation screen for each verb in all tenses in the affirmative, negative, and reflexive forms. In addition, the grammar index provides a complete list of grammatical structures with brief but clear explanations. In the vocabulary index, many commonly used words are arranged in 65 categories by context/theme. Finally, the phrase index includes a wealth of idiomatic expressions, organized by language functions.

The challenging nature of creative writing opportunities offered by **système-D** was confirmed in Scott's study (1990). However, her study points out that the feature of this program students use most is the dictionary. She suggests that teachers create a series of interesting real-life situations with tasks that students need to do in order to respond to each situation in writing. The tasks direct students to consult the grammar, vocabulary, and phrase indexes in **système-D**. According to Scott, "...students who are encouraged to access the unique linguistic features of the software should, over time, increase their general competence in preparation for autonomous written expression without depending upon the software" (1990, p. 64). Although further research is needed to confirm the long-term benefits of using **système-D**, the program provides an exciting and challenging tool for teaching creative writing in French. Scott (1990) includes a detailed description of **système-D** and her proposed framework for including task-oriented writing activities that engage students in the use of various writing strategies.

Another new type of software, **Hypertext**, consists of text materials that students explore in a variety of ways by using a complex system of cross-referencing. These programs are often integrated with audio, video, and graphic materials. Garrett (1991) gives an example of a reading comprehension presentation via **Hypertext**, in which the student can select certain words with a mouse or cursor and be directly referenced to a synonym, paraphrase, translation, grammatical analysis, map, picture, audio rendition, or cultural note. Students reading literary texts can call up the author's biographical information or explanations of historical or political background, interpretations of the works, etc.

Yet another recent application of computer technology is in computerized language learning simulation. Jones (1982) identifies the necessary elements of a simulation as (1) a simulated environment or a representation of the real world; (2) structure, created by rules of conversational interaction; and (3) reality of function or the learner's "reality" perspective of the event. A simulated environment is provided by the computer, which presents an image on the display screen. The structure of a simulation is created by rules concerning the student task. For example, the purpose of a conversational simulation may be to practice a particular set of grammatical structures. In simulations, the computer appears to understand language and produce it meaningfully, thus supporting the learner's "reality" perspective of the exchange (Crookall and Oxford

1990). An example of a simulation program is **Terri** (Coleman 1985), which presents an animated image on the screen of a room containing several objects; in response to student commands, **Terri** moves the objects around the room. At perhaps a higher level of instruction is the **Escape From Utopia** program (Cook and Fass 1986), an adventure scenario. When the students enter any of the buildings, such as the hotel and the police station, they conduct conversations, being careful not to make any mistakes that might raise their "suspicion index" (Crookall and Oxford 1990, p. 186). (Refer to Crookall and Oxford [1990] for a detailed description of computerized language learning simulations.)

What the Future of Technology Holds for Language Learning

The future of technology in language learning is becoming the present more rapidly than the profession can assimilate the currently available materials. Video offers the opportunity to present language in its cultural context, underscoring the most important contribution technology can make in language teaching, which is the integration of teaching language and culture. The addition of computer-mediated technology allows for further integration of language, literature, and culture (Garrett 1991). As Garrett points out, there is good news and bad news about the use of technology in foreign and second language education. The good news is the enormous potential that technological applications have for enhancing language learning. The bad news is that the potential is realized at high cost in dollars and professional expertise.

TEACH AND REFLECT

The following activities will give you practice in selecting videotexts and instructional software.

EPISODE ONE
Selecting Video Materials

Randomly select three videos from a collection in a school's library or media center. Rentals from a private company or purchases from video or computer catalogues may also be used. Apply to them the guidelines presented in this chapter for the selection of videotexts (Joiner 1990). View and critique the videos by using the criteria listed in the guidelines, and select a two-minute segment of the video to use in your class. Outline a step-by-step process you will follow that incorporates the video modalities described in this chapter. Be sure to include a justification using this particular segment. Your instructor may ask you to present your segment to the class.

EPISODE TWO
Examining the Potential Use of a CALL Exercise

Figure 9 is an example of a CALL meaning-enhancing communicative-gap exercise presented by Chun and Brandl (1992, pp. 260-262). Using what you learned about information-gap activities in earlier chapters, analyze this activity for its communicative potential. Then answer the following questions:

1. How do you think students will communicate with the computer in this exercise?
2. What do you think students will be able to do, as a result of using this exercise, when they communicate with peers?
3. What kind of grouping circumstances do you envision when using this kind of exercise with a class?
4. At what point in a lesson would this exercise be used?
5. How would you revise this activity for your language? Consult Figure 6 (Underwood 1984, cf. Beauvois 1992, p. 457).

FIGURE 9 "Room": Example of a Meaning-Enhancing Communicative Gap Exercise

The exercise called "Room" is designed to simulate a typical conversation between, for example, room-mates or housemates. The functional goal of this situation is to locate objects in a room and to differentiate between stationary physical location vs. the action or motion involved in placing an object somewhere. In German this entails comprehending the grammatical difference between the accusative and the dative cases when using the so-called "two-way" prepositions. In addition, the use of pronouns can be practiced once their referents have been established. Consider, for example, typical everyday questions and answers:

A: "Honey, where did you put the keys?"
B: "I put them on the table." or
A: "Where are my glasses?"
B: "They're next to the lamp."

In order to simulate an authentic situation the program displays the picture of a messy room including many different objects which are located in various places (see illustration). In the program, the user is asked to imagine the following situation:

"You are living in the year 2101 with a robot for a roommate. Unfortunately you are not a very orderly person, but you usually know where all your things in your living room are. Your roommate, who is programmed to be very orderly, wants to clean up your room, but it/he/she cannot find anything. You know where all the objects are and help your room-

mate find these things when it/he/she asks you."

As stated above, the goal of this exercise is to establish a brief-meaningful dialogue between the user and the computer. At the student's command, the computer in its function as a robot asks a question aurally about the location of an object in the room. The user responds to the question by typing in the location of the particular object. In response to correct grammatical input from the user, the object that was sought flashes on the screen and the computer concludes each mini-conference conversation by telling the user that it found the object.

For each question generated by the computer, an object on the screen is chosen at random, and a question is asked using one of two different syntactic structures, e.g.:

A: *Wo ist mein Füller?* (Where is my fountain pen?) or

B: *Wohin hast du meinen Füller gelegt?* (Where did you put my fountain pen?)

Accordingly the student answers:

A: *Er liegt auf dem Fernseher.* (It is on [top of] the TV.) or

B: *Ich habe ihn auf den Fernseher gelegt.* (I put it on [top of] the TV.)

The computer concludes the mini dialogue by reinforcing the student's answer:

A: *Ich habe ihn gefunden. Er liegt auf dem Fernseher.* (I found it. It's on top of the TV.) or

B: *Ich habe ihn gefunden. Du hast ihn auf den Fernseher gelegt.* (I found it. You put it on top of the TV.)

Note that this concluding response from the computer reinforces not only the two-way prepositions but also the pragmatically necessary shifts in pronominal reference, which make the discourse natural and coherent.

The program incorporates a number of built-in features to help learners during the communication process. For example, students can retrieve any of the oral questions or statements of the computer in written format by simply clicking on a button on the screen. They can listen to the computer's questions or responses as many times as they want to, also at the touch of a button. An on-line dictionary allows users to look up any of the vocabulary words used in the program. Furthermore, the software also provides a detailed grammatical review of the two-way prepositions in German, so that students are reminded about the formal requirements of the situation.

Unlike most programs which require users to input single words and thus need only to check single words, this program has an error-checking device which checks the grammaticality of entire sentences. The error-checking program goes through students' answers word by words from left to right and highlights the first words which either is in the wrong place or contains a spelling or morphological mistake. When users see a word highlighted, they then have several options: they may choose to get feedback with grammatical information, hints, or see the correct answer.

If they choose grammatical feedback, the program anticipates many of the most common students' mistakes and provides, based on the mistakes, either a general feedback message, e.g., "A pronoun should be in this position of the sentence," or, in a case where the student used a pronoun with the wrong case or gender, more detailed grammatical information, "The gender of your pronoun is wrong." While many other programs provide these same options, e.g., to get hints, grammatical explanations, or the correct answer, most do so only for single words rather than entire sentences.

Source: Chun and Brandl 1992.

DISCUSS AND REFLECT

In the first case study in this chapter, you will assist a teacher as she plans to use video in her classroom. The second case study illustrates how teachers and students used software designed to help with the writing process.

CASE STUDY 1
Incorporating Video in Language Instruction

Mrs. Silver has taught German at Ridge Runner High School in Beaverton for three years. She began her teaching career in Austria, teaching elementary school, but she changed to teaching high school German when her children grew up and left for college. She is a dynamic, energetic, and enthusiastic teacher who expects as much from her students as she gives in preparation and presentation. In class, Mrs. Silver speaks German almost entirely and uses a wide variety of communicative activities. She spends several hours each day planning her lessons.

Over the past several months, Mrs. Silver has been reading about the use of video in language teaching, and she has attended a workshop on listening comprehension that offered some ideas about integrating video. She soon became interested in experimenting with video in her German classes. She used her many connections in her Austrian hometown to her advantage and asked a relative who was working in a television station to seek permission for her to obtain a videotape of various television segments. The station sent Mrs. Silver a video containing several segments from a television drama, some news broadcasts, a variety of commercials, and a talk show segment. The station granted her permission to use the video for educational purposes. Mrs. Silver received the video in the mail today and set about planning how to integrate it into her teaching.

Ask yourself these questions:

1. What will Mrs. Silver have to consider as she decides how to integrate the video segments into her teaching?
2. What functions and contexts might be addressed with the types of segments included in her video?
3. How might she use Joiner's (1990) guide to using videotexts as she plans her lessons?
4. How might she address the fact that the video contains authentic speech and has not been produced for use in teaching?

To prepare the case:

- Read the article by Joiner (1990) on how to select and use videotexts.
- Read the section of Garrett's (1991) article that deals with using video in the classroom.
- Interview an experienced language teacher who has had some experience with video in language teaching. Obtain some practical suggestions.

Now describe the steps you would go through to implement some of these video segments into your teaching, if you were Mrs. Silver.

_____

_____

_____

_____

_____

Describe specific activities in which you would engage students as they watch the talk show segment. Use the interactive model for teaching listening and reading that is presented in Chapter 7.

_____

_____

_____

_____

_____

_____

_____

What are some other avenues for obtaining videotapes other than purchasing those that are commercially prepared for instructional use?

_____

_____

_____

_____

_____

_____

CASE STUDY 2
A Student's Perspective and a Teacher's Perspective on the Use of système-D for Writing Processes, by Virginia M. Scott, Vanderbilt University

Lauren Yann has been assigned to write a composition on **système-D**, the word processing program for writing in French. She has been told that the bilingual dictionary; the verb conjugation screens; and the grammar, vocabulary, and phrase index in **système-D** will make the writing task much easier. Her composition task is to write a description of herself for the new-student files.

Lauren's French teacher, Mrs. Bulles, purchased **système-D** because she heard that it could help students learn how to write from the earliest stages of their language study. After having spent time working with the software and showing her students how the program works, she is confident that her French II students will not only write better compositions but will also enjoy their writing assignments. Furthermore, she is interested in the **système-D** tracking device, which logs all the inquiries that students make during the writing process. Mrs. Bulles looks forward to seeing how much time her students spend on their assignment and what kinds of information they access in **système-D** in order to express their ideas.

When Lauren hands in her composition, she tells Mrs. Bulles that she had a difficult time. She says that she didn't really know what to say and that most of the words that she looked up were not in the **système-D** dictionary. In looking over the composition, Mrs. Bulles sees that it is filled with grammatical and lexical errors. In fact, the composition done with **système-D** is no different than something that Lauren could have written without the software. Mrs. Bulles read the log created by the tracking device of the program documenting the inquiries that Lauren made as she wrote in **système-D**, and noted that Lauren spent one hour and forty-six minutes working on a text that is barely two paragraphs long, with most of the time being spent on English dictionary inquiries. Mrs. Bulles concludes that, while **système-D** appears to be a good program, intermediate-level French students are unable to benefit from the information in the software. She decides to postpone using **système-D** until her students are more advanced in French.

Ask yourself these questions:

1. Why do you think Lauren had difficulty with the assignment?
2. Why do you think there were so many errors in her composition?
3. Do you think Mrs. Bulles could have provided more adequate instruction about how to access information in **système-D** in addition to that provided in the software?
4. Do you think Mrs. Bulles is correct in assuming that the problem was due to Lauren's lack of proficiency in French?

To prepare the case:

- Read Scott and Terry's (1992) *Teacher's Guide* for **système-D**.
- Read Scott (1990) for information about using this software program.

- For additional information about task-based writing, read Scott (1992).
- Consult Figure 6 for guidelines for effective CALL programs.

What do you think of the following suggestions for Mrs. Bulles?

1. Students should be made to understand that French and English words do not exactly match and that being dependent on the dictionary can be counterproductive.

2. The first writing assignment on **système-D** should be informal. A treasure hunt through "**système-D** land," designed to guide students to use the important features of the software, will increase their understanding of how the software can function as a support system during the writing process. The following is a brief example of a **système-D** treasure hunt:
   - Look up the verb *to do* and type the definition in French.
   - Look up the Note, and type a sentence using the verb.
   - Look up the Conjugate screen for the verb, and type the *vous* form of the verb in the present tense.
   - Look up *faire expressions* in the Grammar Index, and type one of your choosing.
   - Look up *sports* in the Vocabulary Index, and type two sports that you enjoy.
   - Look up *linking* ideas in the Phrase Index.
   - Type three sentences that use the information you have gotten from **système-D**.

3. All writing assignments for elementary and intermediate-level students should be explicitly directive and task-oriented. When giving a composition topic, teachers should tell students where to find the necessary information in **système-D**. The following is a brief example of a **système-D** task-oriented writing guideline:

SITUATION: You are writing a description of yourself for the new- student files. Information screens in **système-D** are indicated by a *.

TASKS:
1. Describe yourself physically.
   * PHRASES: Describing people.
   * VOCABULARY: Body, Face, Hair colors
   * GRAMMAR: Adjective agreement, Adjective position
2. Describe your personality.
   * PHRASES: Linking ideas
   * VOCABULARY: Personality
3. Use the log of inquiries to analyze how individual students are going about the writing process. Discuss the log with students to help them understand how they can use **système-D** more productively.
4. From the earliest stages of their language study, encourage students to express themselves autonomously by experimenting with the words and phrases that they find in **système-D**.

Here is a sample composition from a student after 20 weeks of French study:

Je suis un petit garçon parce que mes parents sont des petits gens. Ma figure est ovale et mes oreilles sont petites. J'ai des courts cheveux et j'ai des grands sourcils. J'ai des larges pieds.

Je suis intéressant parce que suis très étrange. Je suis indépendant. Je suis drôle et je dis des choses étranges. J'ai ét frivole, mais maintenant en 1992 je ne suis pas frivole! Je suis très paresseux.

[I am a small young man because my parents are small people. My face is oval, and my ears are small. I have short hair, and I have large eyebrows. I have big feet.

I am interesting because I am very strange. I am independent. I am funny, and I say some strange things. I have been frivolous, but now in 1992 I am not frivolous. I am very lazy.]

Characterize the composition in terms of linguistic functions used, variety of vocabulary, and diversity of content. Ask a French teacher to help you identify the grammatical errors, then characterize the composition in terms of frequency and seriousness of errors. Finally, what do you think of the quality of this composition, keeping in mind that it was written by a beginning French student?

_____

_____

_____

_____

_____

_____

_____

_____

_____

_____

_____

_____

REFERENCES

Abraham, R. G. and H.-C. Liou. "Interaction Generated by Three Computer Programs." Ed. P. Dunkel. *Computer-Assisted Language Learning and Testing*. New York: Newbury House, 1991, pp. 85–109.

Altman, R. *The Video Connection*. Boston: Houghton Mifflin, 1989.

Beauvois, M. H. "Computer-Assisted Classroom Discussion in the Foreign Language Classroom: Conversation in Slow Motion." *Foreign Language Annals* 25 (1992): 455–464.

Chang, K. R., and W. F. Smith. "Cooperative Learning and CALL/IVD in Beginning Spanish: An Experiment." *Modern Language Journal* 75 (1991): 205–211.

Chapelle, C., and J. Jamieson. "Computer-Assisted Language Learning as a Predictor of Success in Acquiring English as a Second Language." *TESOL Quarterly* 20 (1986): 27–46.

Chun, D. M., and K. K. Brandl. "Beyond Form-Based Drill and Practice: Meaning-Enhanced CALL on the Macintosh." *Foreign Language Annals* 25 (1992): 255–267.

Coleman, D. W. "*Terri:* A CALL Lesson Simulating Conversational Interaction." Ed. D. Crookall. *Simulation Applications in L2 Education and Research*. Oxford: Pergamon Press, 1985.

Cook, V. J., and D. Fass. "Natural Language Processing in EFL." Ed. J. Higgins. "How Real is a Computer Simulation?" *ELT Documents* 113 (1982). London: British Council, 1986.

Crookall, D., and R. L. Oxford. *Simulation, Gaming, and Language Learning*. New York: Newbury House, 1990.

Dunkel, P. *Computer-Assisted Language Learning and Testing: Research Issues and Practice*. New York: Newbury House, 1991.

Esling, J. H. "Researching the Effects of Networking." Ed. P. Dunkel. *Computer-Assisted Language Learning and Testing*. New York: Newbury House, 1991, pp. 111–131.

Garrett, N. "Technology in the Service of Language Learning: Trends and Issues." *Modern Language Journal* 75 (1991): 74–101.

Garza, T. J. "Evaluating the Use of Captioned Video Material in Advanced Foreign Language Learning." *Foreign Language Annals* 24 (1991): 239–258.

Gendron, B. *Technology and the Human Condition*. New York: St. Martin's, 1977.

Jamieson, J. *Cognitive Styles, Working Styles on Computers and Second Language Learning*. Unpublished doctoral dissertation. Urbana: University of Illinois, 1986.

Johansen, K., and R. Tennyson. "Effects of Adaptive Advisement Perception in Learner-Controlled, Computer-Based Instruction Using a Rule-Learning Task." *Educational Communication and Technology* 31 (1983): 226–236.

Johnson, D. M. "Second Language and Content Learning with Computers: Research in the Role of Social Factors." Ed. P. Dunkel. *Computer-Assisted Language Learning and Testing: Research Issues and Practice*. New York: Newbury House, 1991: 61–83.

Johnson, D. W., and R. T. Johnson. "Computer-Assisted Cooperative Learning." *Educational Technology* 26 (1986): 12–18.

Johnson, R. T., D. W. Johnson, and M. B. Stanne. "Comparison of Computer-Assisted Cooperative, Competitive and Individualistic Learning." *American Educational Research Journal* 23 (1986): 382–392.

Joiner, E. G. "Choosing and Using Videotext." *Foreign Language Annals* 23 (1990): 53–64.

Jones, K. *Simulations in Language Teaching*. Cambridge: Cambridge University Press, 1982.

Kreeft Peyton, J. K. "Computer Networking: Making Connections Between Speech and Writing." *ERIC/CLL News Bulletin* 10 (1986): 5–7.

Kreeft Peyton, J. K., and J. Mackinson-Smyth. "Writing and Talking About Writing: Computer Networking With Elementary Students." Ed. D. M. Johnson. *Richness in Writing: Empowering ESL Students*. New York: Longman, 1989.

Kulik, C. C., and J. A. Kulik. "Effectiveness of Computer-Based Education in Colleges." *AEDS Journal* 2 (1986): 267–276.

Kulik, J. A., and C. C. Kulik. "Review of Recent Research Literature on Computer-Based Instruction." *Contemporary Educational Psychology* 12 (1987): 222–230.

Lavery, M. *Active Viewing*. Canterbury: Pilgrim's Publications, 1981.

Lonergan, J. *Using Video in Language Teaching*. Cambridge: Cambridge University Press, 1984.

Noblitt, J. S., W. J. A. Pet, and D. Solá. *système-D 2.0*. Boston, MA: Heinle & Heinle, 1991.

Pederson, K. M. "An Experiment in Computer-Assisted Second-Language Reading." *Modern Language Journal* 70 (1986): 36–41.

Pederson, K. M. "Research on CALL." Ed. W. F. Smith. *Modern Media in Foreign Language Education: Theory and Implementation*. Lincolnwood, IL: National Textbook Company, 1987: 99–131.

Piper, A. "Conversation and the Computer: A Study of Conversational Spin-Off Generated Among Learners of English as a Foreign Language Working in Groups." *System* 14 (1986): 187–198.

Robinson, G. "The CLCCS CALL Study: Methods, Error Feedback, Attitudes, and Achievement." Ed. W. F. Smith. *Modern Technology in Foreign Language Education: Applications and Projects*. Lincolnwood, IL: National Textbook Company, 1989: 119–134.

Rogers, M. "MTV, IBM, Tennyson and You." *Newsweek* (Fall/Winter 1992): 50, 52.

Saettler, P. *The Evolution of American Educational Technology*. Englewood, CO: Libraries Unlimited, 1990.

Schaeffer, R. *Computer-Supplemented Structural Drill Practice Versus Computer-Supplemented Semantic Practice by Beginning College German Students: A Comparative Experiment*. Unpublished doctoral dissertation. Columbus, OH: Ohio State University, 1979.

Schaeffer, R. "Meaningful Practice on the Computer: Is It Possible?" *Foreign Language Annals* 14 (1981): 133–137.

Scott, V. "Task-Oriented Creative Writing with *système-D*." *CALICO Journal* 7, iii (1990): 58–67.

Scott, V. "Write from the Start: A Task-oriented Developmental Writing Program for Foreign Language Students." *Dimension: Language '91, Making a World of Difference*. Valdosta, GA: Southern Conference on Language Teaching, 1992: 1–15.

Scott, V., and R. Terry. *Teacher's Guide to système-D*. Boston: Heinle & Heinle, 1992.

Stempleski, S., and B. Tomalin. *Video in Action*. New York: Prentice-Hall, 1990.

Tierney, R. J. "Shortchanging Technology." *Electronic Learning*. Special Edition, May/June (1992): 10.

Underwood, J. *Linguistics, Computers and the Language Teacher: A Communicative Approach*. Rowley, MA: Newbury House, 1984.

Wyatt, D. H. "Applying Pedagogical Principles to CALL Software Development." Ed. W. F. Smith. *Modern Media in Foreign Language Education: Theory and Implementation*. Lincolnwood, IL: National Textbook Company, 1987: 85–89.

Appendix

The "B" Appendices consist of supporting materials that contain information pertinent to the professional development of language teachers.

APPENDIX AA

Foreign Language Pedagogy: Performance Standards for Foreign Language Teachers

Appendix AA presents a list of performance standards, or content-specific skills, that today's language teachers should possess in order to **contextualize language instruction** effectively. Most of the pedagogical practices outlined in this document have been discussed in detail in this *Handbook* and have been integrated in an approach to teaching language for real communication. This list, which supports the *Handbook's* approach to language acquisition and instruction, should be beneficial to both beginning and experienced language teachers as they continue their professional development.

INTRODUCTION

Content specific pedagogy, indispensable to teaching, is not only qualitatively different from the knowledge that is contained in the subject matter, but cannot exist in education without prior study of the academic discipline. As an example, high school foreign language teachers may have experienced, in the course of their own college language classes, a half dozen different techniques for language learning (drills, translations, deductive grammar teaching, inductive approaches, role play, scenarios, information-gap tasks, paired interviews, simulations, etc.)—How then does the teacher decide which approach to take and for what skill? The discipline of the subject gives no guidance on this question.

Discussions of content specific pedagogy concern the reformulation of the subject (in this case, language) into another entity, the subject matter as it is explained, taught, and learned. Content specific pedagogy implies, therefore, the ability to select and perform instructional activities that are anchored in our best knowledge of how individuals develop language abilities.

The foreign language content specific skills listed on the following pages are to provide direction for all individuals involved in foreign language teaching: instructors of methods courses, foreign language professors, clinical instructors, interns, teachers, student teachers, and foreign language supervisors. The list should be used as a guide for the continual professional development of both preservice and inservice teachers. Furthermore, although the skills are listed under separate topic headings, it is expected that they will be implemented by the teacher in an integrated manner.

This list or guide codifies our best knowledge of how people learn a foreign language. As such, it should be subject to periodic review and revision as further research dictates.

The following performance standards were developed as part of the School/University Collaborative to provide consistency in the professional development of pre-service and in-service of foreign language teachers.

Committee:

Richard Donato, University of Pittsburgh
Thekla Fall, Pittsburgh Public Schools
Roxane Gaal, Pittsburgh Public Schools
Eileen Glisan, Indiana University of Pennsylvania
Gregorio Martin, Duquesne University
Mary Shields, Pittsburgh Public Schools

LINGUISTIC AND CULTURAL FOUNDATION

Since content specific pedagogy can only be useful to the teacher who is well grounded in the language, it is recommended that teachers demonstrate a speaking proficiency of Advanced or better according to the ACTFL/ETS Scale.

In addition to this minimal level of speaking proficiency, teachers and interns should also demonstrate a basic understanding of the cultures reflected in the target language. Important cultural aspects include:

- a familiarity with one or more countries where the language is spoken in terms of historical movements, daily life styles, the arts, and key historical and contemporary figures.
- an understanding of the relationships between the target culture and that of the United States.

AFFECTIVE DOMAIN

The teacher will:

- create a positive foreign language learning experience by offering praise and encouragement in the target language.
- build success in the target language experience by focusing objectives on students' needs and abilities.
- demonstrate enthusiasm for and an interest in what he/she is teaching.
- motivate students by personalizing activities and incorporating students' interests and talents.
- earnestly try to understand students' communicative efforts.
- use body language to show acceptance of students' ideas and messages (smiles, head-nodding, interested facial expression, etc.).
- enable students to gain confidence in speaking by providing opportunities for them to practice new material through choral repetition, small group, or pair work before requiring individual responses.
- increase student motivation to use the target language by providing practice in highly functional language that students will want to use with one another in personal communications.

LISTENING COMPREHENSION

The teacher will:

- establish a target language environment through oral commands to handle classroom routines (opening books, lining up, etc.).

- provide students with pre-listening activities (e.g. visuals, graphic organizers, brainstorming) to build in success.
- include authentic materials and language input (audio cassettes, video tapes, native music, and guest speakers) in listening activities, taking care to correlate the task with the level of student proficiency.
- devise pure listening comprehension activities by employing a variety of non-verbal comprehension checks such as signaling, Total Physical Response (TPR) commands.
- use listening activities as a basis for developing speaking, reading, and writing skills.

DEVELOPING VOCABULARY SKILLS

The teacher will:

- introduce new vocabulary in a context using familiar vocabulary and grammar.
- make and effectively use visuals for introducing new vocabulary.
- provide the opportunity for students to mentally bind vocabulary and meaning by using Total Physical Response (TPR) techniques at the elementary and advanced levels in introducing a wide range of concrete vocabulary.
- design contextualized practice of new vocabulary.
- check for comprehension of new vocabulary using yes/no either/or, and identification questions and techniques.

ACTIVE PARTICIPATION OF ALL STUDENTS

The teacher will:

- demonstrate effective use of choral repetition, pair-work, and small group work utilizing cooperative learning techniques.
- incorporate instruction on group process skills into small group activities.
- develop and implement activities that promote cooperation such as: information-gap activities, role plays, scenarios, paired interviews, jigsaw activities, simulations, and group problem-solving activities.
- demonstrate the effective use of a variety of

instructional games and sponge activities in the target language that are appropriate for the language level and age level of the students.
- utilize audio-visual equipment in a manner that engages all students in the task (pre- and post-activities, defining the task, holding students accountable).
- design a variety of activities, incorporating students various learning styles, to provide practice for each objective.

CULTURE

The teacher will:

- embed culture into language activities such as structure practice, communicative interactions, and visuals used in various exercises.
- integrate the teaching of language and culture by incorporating listening, speaking, reading, writing, and grammar practice.
- use the target language whenever possible to present cultural topics.
- use a multi-modal approach whenever possible to introduce new cultural concepts.
- emphasize cultural similarities as well as differences (compare and contrast cultures).
- present vocabulary in a cultural context. Provide connotative meanings as well as denotative.
- teach cultural topics ranging from customs related to daily life to the literature, history, art, and music of at least one county where the language is spoken.
- use small-group techniques such as role-play, discussions, and brainstorming for cultural instruction.
- present culture without promoting cultural stereotypes and biases.
- use cultural discussions to enable students to recognize cultural stereotyping and biases.

SPEAKING

The teacher will:

- utilize novice, intermediate and advanced level speaking activities (e.g., personalized questions, sentence builders, story telling, sur-

veys/polls, paired interviews, information-gap tasks, group problem-solving, situations with complications).
- provide regular opportunities for students to express personal meanings in interaction with each other and in a variety of contexts, including those encountered in the target culture.
- distinguish between manipulative drills and exercises and authentic, creative, and personalized speaking activities.
- create speaking activities appropriate to student level and interest.
- provide opportunities for students to participate in speaking activities that are *not* structured around a specific grammatical topic.
- provide opportunities for students to proceed from word to sentence level or from sentence to paragraph level, as appropriate.
- provide frequent opportunities for verbal interaction that is independent of any printed materials (i.e. books, worksheets).

THE NEGOTIATION OF MEANING

Rationale:

The Negotiation of Meaning is the process by which participants in an interaction arrive at mutual comprehension and understanding. Negotiation of Meaning has been shown to be critical in developing second language skills, since it is how foreign language input is made accessible to the learners and provides the opportunity for the learner to test out their growing knowledge of the language. Unfortunately, many teachers do not know how to talk to their classes in the target language and, as a consequence, either conduct classes primarily in English (using the target language only in the context of textbook exercises, repetitions, or exercises on cassettes), or maintain audio-lingual notions that the target language must be spoken at native speed without verbal adjustments common in natural talk. The concept of NM emphasizes that communication in the classroom cannot be reduced to the display of language facts (e.g., in the completion of textbook exercises) but must provide opportunities for the learners' creative construction and expression of their own thoughts. *In short, repetitions after the teacher, verbalizations based on rote learning, and students' verbal answers to textbook exercises do not constitute speaking activity nor do they play a major role in foreign language development.*

The teacher will:

- conduct the class in the target language at least 80% of the class period.
- give foreign language definitions of unknown words and expressions by means of para-phrase, relevant examples, or gesture.
- maintain conversations with students using either/or questions, verbal prompts, clarification requests, and comprehension checks.
- expand and/or remodel student one-word utterances.
- add information to a student's utterance.
- increase understanding of the target language using strategies such as facial expressions, gestures, adjustments in speed of speech, simplified vocabulary and syntax, use of visuals, and paraphrase.

READING

The teacher will:

- guide students through the reading process by using Phillip's five-stage reading plan (preteaching/preparation stage, skimming/scanning stage, decoding/intensive reading stage, comprehension stage, transferable/integrating skills stage).
- teach students strategies for understanding reading material, such as using the SQ3R technique (survey, question, read, recite, review), utilizing the context to figure out meaning, and previewing material.
- guide students through authentic readings (those prepared for native speakers: newspaper/magazine articles, literary pieces, etc.) by creating tasks appropriate for the given linguistic level of students.
- provide opportunities for students to read for various purposes, such as to find specific information, to glean main ideas, and to understand details.
- use reading as a basis for writing by providing opportunities for students to express their own thoughts or think critically in written form.

- build upon the reading skill by integrating listening and speaking practice.
- check reading comprehension by utilizing the five types of comprehension questions: 1) answerable with yes/no, true/ false, or multiple choice; 2) answers are quotable directly from text; 3) answers are found in text but cannot be quoted directly; 4) answers require inference; 5) answers require evaluation or judgment to be made.

GRAMMAR EXPLANATIONS

The teacher will:

- present a clear, logical, and correct explanation of target language grammatical principles. (deductive explanation)
- help and guide students to construct an understanding of a grammatical principle through the use of coaching and questioning strategies. (assisted performance)
- provide target language input which exemplifies a specific grammatical principle so that students can clearly understand the concept. (inductive explanation)
- select the most appropriate of the three strategies (deductive, inductive, and assisted performance) based on the complexity of the grammatical concept and the ability level of students.
- demonstrate and make clear how a grammatical principle is used (function) in the everyday world.
- respond to students' questions about the target language without needless elaboration, complication, or extraneous detail.
- recognize that even the most well-conceived grammar explanation may not be immediately received and applied by students.

STUDENT EVALUATION

The teacher will:

- design a variety of test items to test listening comprehension, speaking, reading, writing, and culture individually and in combination.
- evaluate student performance using global as

well as discrete-point assessments.

- utilize holistic contextualized assessment procedures such as TPR, oral interviews, role play, cloze, presentations, and portfolio assessment in addition to traditional test devices such as multiple choice, dictation, etc.
- develop questions in the target language at various levels according to Bloom's Taxonomy and the ACTFL/ETS Proficiency Scale.
- utilize evaluation for formative as well as summative purposes by using a variety of correction strategies and developing future lessons based on the students' performance.

WRITING

The teacher will:

- provide opportunities for students to proceed from word to sentence level or from sentence to paragraph level, as appropriate.
- use writing for purposes of both skill-getting (as a support skill—writing emphasizes the understanding of the way the language oper-ates) and skill-using (use of the language for expressive writing and purposeful communication).
- guide students through the various iterative processes involved in writing, such as prewriting, composing the draft, revising, etc.
- provide opportunities for peer editing in the writing process.
- utilize a variety of correction strategies, such as primary trait, analytical, holistic, as appropriate to the given writing task.
- provide constructive feedback concerning both language use and content/ideas of the written piece.
- hold students responsible for their written errors by having them correct their own errors and make revisions.
- provide ample opportunities for students to use writing as a vehicle for creative expression.
- utilize writing as an important tool for synthesizing grammar/vocabulary and for building on the other skills.

Source: School/University Collaborative, Pittsburgh, PA 1992.

APPENDIX A1

ACTFL Proficiency Guidelines

The 1986 proficiency guidelines represent a hierarchy of global characterizations of integrated performance in speaking, listening, reading and writing. Each description is a representative, not an exhaustive, sample of a particular range of ability, and each level subsumes all previous levels, moving from simple to complex in an "all-before-and-more" fashion.

Because these guidelines identify stages of proficiency, as opposed to achievement, they are not intended to measure what an individual has achieved through specific classroom instruction but rather to allow assessment of what an individual can and cannot do, regardless of where, when, or how the language has been learned or acquired; thus, the words "learned" and "acquired" are used in the broadest sense. These guidelines are not based on a particular linguistic theory or pedagogical method, since the guidelines are proficiency-based, as opposed to achievement-based, and are intended to be used for global assessment.

The 1986 guidelines should not be considered the definitive version, since the construction and utilization of language proficiency guidelines is a dynamic, interactive process. The academic sector, like the government sector, will continue to refine and update the criteria periodically to reflect the needs of the users and the advances of the profession. In this vein, ACTFL owes a continuing debt to the creators of the 1982 provisional proficiency guidelines and, of course, to the members of the Interagency Language Roundtable Testing Committee, the creators of the government's Language Skill Level Descriptions.

ACTFL would like to thank the following individuals for their contributions on this current guidelines project:

Heidi Byrnes   Seiichi Makino
James Child   Irene Thompson
Nina Levinson   A. Ronald Walton
Pardee Lowe, Jr.

These proficiency guidelines are the product of grants from the U.S. Department of Education.

GENERIC DESCRIPTIONS—SPEAKING

Novice

The Novice level is characterized by the ability to communicate minimally with learned material.

Novice-Low

Oral production consists of isolated words and perhaps a few high-frequency phrases. Essentially no functional communicative ability.

Novice-Mid

Oral production continues to consist of isolated words and learned phrases within very predictable areas of need, although quantity is increased. Vocabulary is sufficient only for handling simple, elementary needs and expressing basic courtesies. Utterances rarely consist of more than two or three words and show frequent long pauses and repetition of interlocutor's words. Speaker may have some difficulty producing even the simplest utterances. Some Novice-Mid speakers will be understood only with great difficulty.

Novice-High

Able to satisfy partially the requirements of basic communicative exchanges by relying heavily on learned utterances but occasionally expanding these through simple recombinations of their elements. Can ask questions or make statements involving learned material. Shows signs of spontaneity although this falls short of real autonomy of expression. Speech continues to consist of learned utterances rather than of personalized, situationally adapted ones. Vocabulary centers on areas such as basic objects, places, and most common kinship terms. Pronunciation may still be strongly influenced by first language. Errors are frequent and, in spite of repetition, some Novice-High speakers will have difficulty being understood even by sympathetic interlocutors.

Intermediate

The Intermediate level is characterized by the speaker's ability to:
— create with the language by combining and recombining learned elements, though primarily in a reactive mode;
— initiate, minimally sustain, and close in a simple way basic communicative tasks; and
— ask and answer questions.

Intermediate-Low

Able to handle successfully a limited number of interactive, task-oriented and social situations. Can ask and answer questions, initiate and respond to simple statements and maintain face-to-face conversation, although in a highly restricted manner and with much linguistic inaccuracy. Within these limitations, can perform such tasks as introducing self, ordering a meal, asking directions, and making purchases. Vocabulary is adequate to express only the most elementary needs. Strong interference from native language may occur. Misunderstandings frequently arise, but with repetition, the Intermediate-Low speaker can generally be understood by sympathetic interlocutors.

Intermediate-Mid

Able to handle successfully a variety of uncomplicated, basic and communicative tasks and social situations. Can talk simply about self and family members. Can ask and answer questions and participate in simple conversations on topics beyond the most immediate needs; e.g., personal history and leisure time activities. Utterance length increases slightly, but speech may continue to be characterized by frequent long pauses, since the smooth incorporation of even basic conversational strategies is often hindered as the speaker struggles to create appropriate language forms. Pronunciation may continue to be strongly influenced by first language and fluency may still be strained. Although misunderstandings still arise, the Intermediate-Mid speaker can generally be understood by sympathetic interlocutors.

Intermediate-High

Able to handle successfully most uncomplicated communicative tasks and social situations. Can initiate, sustain, and close a general conversation with a number of strategies appropriate to a range of circumstances and topics, but errors are evident. Limited vocabulary still necessitates hesitation and may bring about slightly unexpected circumlocution. There is emerging evidence of connected discourse, particularly for simple narration and/or description. The Intermediate-High speaker can generally be understood even by interlocutors not accustomed to dealing with speakers at this level, but repetition may still be required.

Advanced

The Advanced level is characterized by the speaker's ability to:
— converse in a clearly participatory fashion;
— initiate, sustain, and bring to closure a wide variety of communicative tasks, including those that require an increased ability to convey meaning with diverse language strategies due to a complication or an unforeseen turn of events;
— satisfy the requirements of school and work situations; and
— narrate and describe with paragraph-length connected discourse.

Advanced

Able to satisfy the requirements of everyday situations and routine school and work requirements. Can handle with confidence but not with facility complicated tasks and social situations, such as elaborating, complaining, and apologizing. Can narrate and describe with some details, linking sentences together smoothly. Can communicate facts and talk casually about topics of current public and personal interest, using general vocabulary. Shortcomings can often be smoothed over by communicative strategies, such as pause fillers, stalling devices, and different rates of speech. Circumlocution which arises from vocabulary or syntactic limitations very often is quite successful, though some groping for words may still be evident. The Advanced-level speaker can be understood without difficulty by native interlocutors.

Advanced-Plus

Able to satisfy the requirements of a broad variety of everyday, school, and work situations. Can discuss concrete topics relating to particular interests and special fields of competence. There is emerging evidence of ability to support opinions, explain in detail, and hypothesize. The Advanced-Plus speaker often shows a well developed ability to compensate for an imperfect grasp of some forms with confident use of communicative strategies, such as paraphrasing and circumlocution. Differentiated vocabulary and intonation are effectively used to communicate fine shades of meaning. The Advanced-Plus speaker often shows remarkable fluency and ease of speech but under the demands of Superior-level, complex tasks, language may break down or prove inadequate.

Superior

The Superior level is characterized by the speaker's ability to:
— participate effectively in most formal and informal conversations on practical, social, professional, and abstract topics; and
— support opinions and hypothesize using native-like discourse strategies.

Superior

Able to speak the language with sufficient accuracy to participate effectively in most formal and informal conversations on practical, social, professional, and abstract topics. Can discuss special fields of competence and interest with ease. Can support opinions and hypothesize, but may not be able to tailor language to audience or discuss in depth highly abstract or unfamiliar topics. Usually the Superior level speaker is only partially familiar with regional or other dialectical variants. The Superior-level speaker commands a wide variety of interactive strategies and shows good awareness of discourse strategies. The latter involves the ability to distinguish main ideas from supporting information through syntactic, lexical and suprasegmental features (pitch, stress, intonation). Sporadic errors may occur, particularly in low-frequency structures and some complex high-frequency structures more common to formal writing, but no patterns of error are evident. Errors do not disturb the native speaker or interfere with communication.

GENERIC DESCRIPTIONS—LISTENING

These guidelines assume that all listening tasks take place in an authentic environment at a normal rate of speech using standard or near-standard norms.

Novice-Low

Understanding is limited to occasional isolated works, such as cognates, borrowed words, and high-frequency social conventions. Essentially no ability to comprehend even short utterances.

Novice-Mid

Able to understand some short, learned utterances, particularly where context strongly supports understanding and speech is clearly audible. Comprehends some words and phrases from simple questions, statements, high-frequency commands and courtesy formulae about topics that refer to basic personal information or the immediate physical setting. The listener requires long pauses for assimilation and periodically requests repetition and/or a slower rate of speech.

Novice-High

Able to understand short, learned utterances and some sentence-length utterances, particularly where context strongly supports understanding and speech is clearly audible. Comprehends words and phrases from simple questions, statements, high-frequency commands and courtesy formulae. May require repetition, rephrasing and/or a slowed rate of speech for comprehension.

Intermediate-Low

Able to understand sentence-length utterances which consist of recombinations of learned elements in a limited number of content areas, particularly if strongly supported by the situational context. Content refers to basic personal background and needs, social conventions and routine tasks, such as getting meals and receiving simple instructions and directions. Listening tasks pertain primarily to spontaneous face-to-face conversations. Understanding is often uneven; repetition and rewording may be necessary. Misunderstandings in both main ideas and details arise frequently.

Intermediate-Mid

Able to understand sentence-length utterances which consist of recombinations of learned utterances on a variety of topics. Content continues to refer primarily to basic personal background and needs, social conventions and somewhat more complex tasks, such as lodging, transportation, and shopping. Additional content areas include some personal interests and activities, and a greater diversity of instructions and directions. Listening tasks not only pertain to spontaneous face-to-face conversations but also to short routine telephone conversations and some deliberate speech, such as simple announcements and reports over the media. Understanding continues to be uneven.

Intermediate-High

Able to sustain understanding over longer stretches of connected discourse on a number of topics pertaining to different times and places; however, understanding is inconsistent due to failure to grasp main ideas and/or details. Thus, while topics do not differ significantly from those of an Advanced level listener, comprehension is less in quantity and poorer in quality.

Advanced

Able to understand main ideas and most details of connected discourse on a variety of topics beyond the immediacy of the situation. Comprehension may be uneven due to a variety of linguistic and extralinguistic factors, among which topic familiarity is very prominent. These texts frequently involve description and narration in different time frames or aspects, such as present, nonpast, habitual, or imperfective. Texts may include interviews, short lectures on familiar topics, and news items and reports primarily dealing with factual information. Listener is aware of cohesive devices but may not be able to use them to follow the sequence of thought in an oral text.

Advanced-Plus

Able to understand the main ideas of most speech in a standard dialect; however, the listener may not be able to sustain comprehension in extended discourse which is propositionally and linguistically complex. Listener shows an emerging awareness of culturally implied meanings beyond the surface meanings of the text but may fail to grasp sociocultural nuances of the message.

Superior

Able to understand the main ideas of all speech in a standard dialect, including technical discussion in a field of specialization. Can follow the essentials of extended discourse which is propositionally and linguistically complex, as in academic/professional settings, in lectures, speeches, and reports. Listener shows some appreciation of aesthetic norms of target language, of idioms, colloquialisms, and register shifting. Able to make inferences within the cultural framework of the target language. Understanding is aided by an awareness of the underlying organizational structure of the oral text and includes sensitivity for its social and cultural references and its affective overtones. Rarely misunderstands but may not understand excessively rapid, highly colloquial speech or speech that has strong cultural references.

Distinguished

Able to understand all forms and styles of speech pertinent to personal, social and professional needs tailored to different audiences. Shows strong sensitivity to social and cultural references and aesthetic norms by processing language from within the cultural framework. Texts include theater plays, screen productions, editorials, symposia, academic debates, public policy statements, literary readings, and most jokes and puns. May have some difficulty with some dialects and slang.

GENERIC DESCRIPTIONS—READING

These guidelines assume all reading texts to be authentic and legible.

Novice-Low

Able occasionally to identify isolated words and/or major phrases when strongly supported by context.

Novice-Mid

Able to recognize the symbols of an alphabetic and/or syllabic writing system and/or a limited number of characters in a system that uses characters. The reader can identify an increasing number of highly contextualized words and/or phrases including cognates and borrowed words, where appropriate. Material understood rarely exceeds a single phrase at a time, and rereading may be required.

Novice-High

Has sufficient control of the writing system to interpret written language in areas of practical need. Where vocabulary has been learned, can read for instructional and directional purposes standardized messages, phrases or expressions, such as some items on menus, schedules, timetables, maps, and signs. At times, but not on a consistent basis, the Novice-High level reader may be able to derive meaning from material at a slightly higher level where context and/or extralinguistic background knowledge are supportive.

Intermediate-Low

Able to understand main ideas and/or facts from the simplest connected texts dealing with basic personal and social needs. Such texts are linguistically noncomplex and have a clear underlying internal structure, for example chronological sequencing. They impart basic information about which the reader has to make only minimal suppositions or to which the reader brings personal interest and/or knowledge. Examples include messages with social purposes or information for the widest possible audience, such as public announcements and short, straightforward instructions dealing with public life. Some misunderstandings will occur.

Intermediate-Mid

Able to read consistently with increased understanding simple connected texts dealing with a variety of basic and social needs. Such texts are still linguistically noncomplex and have a clear underlying internal structure. They impart basic information about which the reader has to make minimal suppositions and to which the reader brings personal interest and/or knowledge. Examples may include short, straightforward descriptions of persons, places, and things written for a wide audience.

Intermediate-High

Able to read consistently with full understanding simple connected texts dealing with basic personal and social needs about which the reader has personal interest and/or knowledge. Can get some main ideas and information from texts at the next higher level featuring description and narration. Structural complexity may interfere with comprehension; for example, basic grammatical relations may be misinterpreted and temporal references may rely primarily on lexical items. Has some difficulty with the cohesive factors in discourse, such as matching pronouns with referents. While texts do not differ significantly from those at the Advanced level, comprehension is less consistent. May have to read material several times for understanding.

Advanced

Able to read somewhat longer prose of several paragraphs in length, particularly if presented with a clear underlying structure. The prose is predominantly in familiar sentence patterns. Reader gets the main ideas and facts and misses some details. Comprehension derives not only from situational and subject matter knowledge but from increasing control of the language. Texts at the Advanced level include descriptions and narrations such as simple short stories, news items, bibliographical information, social notices, personal correspondence, routinized business letters and simple technical material written for the general reader.

Advanced-Plus

Able to follow essential points of written discourse at the Superior level in areas of special interest or knowledge. Able to understand parts of texts which are conceptually abstract and linguistically complex, and/or texts which treat unfamiliar topics and situations, as well as some texts which involve aspects of target-language culture. Able to comprehend the facts to make appropriate inferences. An emerging awareness of the aesthetic properties of language and of its literary styles permits comprehension of a wider variety of texts, including literary. Misunderstandings may occur.

Superior

Able to read with almost complete comprehension and at normal speed expository prose on unfamiliar subjects and a variety of literary texts. Reading ability is not dependent on subject matter knowledge, although the reader is not expected to comprehend thoroughly texts which are highly dependent on knowledge of the target culture. Reads easily for pleasure. Superior-level texts feature hypotheses, argumentation and supported opinions and include grammatical patterns and vocabulary ordinarily encountered in academic/professional reading. At this level, due to the control of general vocabulary and structure, the reader is almost always able to match the meanings derived from extralinguistic knowledge with meanings derived from knowledge of the language, allowing for smooth and efficient reading of diverse texts. Occasional misunderstandings may still occur; for example, the reader may experience some difficulty with unusually complex structures and low-frequency idioms. At the Superior level the reader can match strategies, top-down or bottom-up, which are most appropriate to the text. (Top-down strategies rely on real-world knowledge and prediction based on genre and organizational scheme of the text. Bottom-up strategies rely on actual linguistic knowledge.) Material at this level will include a variety of literary texts, editorials, correspondence, general reports and technical material in professional fields. Rereading is rarely necessary, and misreading is rare.

Distinguished

Able to read fluently and accurately most styles and forms of the language pertinent to academic and professional needs. Able to relate inferences in the text to real-world knowledge and understand almost all sociolinguistic and cultural references by processing language from within the cultural framework. Able to understand a writer's use of nuance and subtlety. Can readily follow unpredictable turns of thought and author

intent in such materials as sophisticated editorials, specialized journal articles, and literary texts such as novels, plays, poems, as well as in any subject matter area directed to the general reader.

GENERIC DESCRIPTIONS—WRITING

Novice-Low

Able to form some letters in an alphabetic system. In languages whose writing systems use syllabaries or characters, writer is able to both copy and produce the basic strokes. Can produce romanization of isolated characters, where applicable.

Novice-Mid

Able to copy or transcribe familiar words or phrases and reproduce some from memory. No practical communicative writing skills.

Novice-High

Able to write simple fixed expressions and limited memorized material and some recombinations thereof. Can supply information on simple forms and documents. Can write names, numbers, dates, own nationality, and other simple autobiographical information as well as some short phrases and simple lists. Can write all the symbols in an alphabetic or syllabic system or 50-100 characters or compounds in a character writing system. Spelling and representation of symbols (letters, syllables, characters) may be partially correct.

Intermediate-Low

Able to meet limited practical writing needs. Can write short messages, postcards, and take down simple notes, such as telephone messages. Can create statements or questions within the scope of limited language experience. Material produced consists of recombinations of learned vocabulary and structures into simple sentences on very familiar topics. Language is inadequate to express in writing anything but elementary needs. Frequent errors in grammar, vocabulary, punctuation, spelling and in formation of nonalphabetic symbols, but writing can be understood by natives used to the writing of nonnatives.

Intermediate-Mid

Able to meet a number of practical writing needs. Can write short, simple letters. Content involves personal preferences, daily routine, everyday events, and other topics grounded in personal experience. Can express present time or at least one other time frame or aspect consistently, e.g., nonpast, habitual, imperfective. Evidence of control of the syntax of noncomplex sentences and basic inflectional morphology, such as declensions and conjugation. Writing tends to be a loose collection of sentences or sentence fragments on a given topic and provides little evidence of conscious organization. Can be understood by natives used to the writing of nonnatives.

Intermediate-High

Able to meet most practical writing needs and limited social demands. Can take notes in some detail on familiar topics and respond in writing to personal questions. Can write simple letters, brief synopses and paraphrases, summaries of biographical data, work and school experience. In those languages relying primarily on content words and time expressions to express time, tense or aspect, some precision is displayed; where tense and/or aspect is expressed through verbal inflection, forms are produced rather consistently, but not always accurately. An ability to describe and narrate in paragraphs is emerging. Rarely uses basic cohesive elements, such as pronominal substitutions or synonyms in written discourse. Writing, though faulty, is generally comprehensible to natives used to the writing of nonnatives.

Advanced

Able to write routine social correspondence and join sentences in simple discourse of at least several paragraphs in length on familiar topics. Can write simple social correspondence, take notes, write cohesive summaries and resumes, as well as narratives and descriptions of a factual nature. Has sufficient writing vocabulary to express self simply with some circumlocution. May still make errors in punctuation, spelling, or the formation of nonalphabetic symbols. Good control of the morphology and the most frequently used syntactic structures, e.g., common word order patterns, coordination, subordination, but

makes frequent errors in producing complex sentences. Uses a limited number of cohesive devices, such as pronouns, accurately. Writing may resemble literal translations from the native language, but a sense of organization (rhetorical structure) is emerging. Writing is understandable to natives not used to the writing of nonnatives.

Advanced-Plus

Able to write about a variety of topics with significant precision and in detail. Can write most social and informal business correspondence. Can describe and narrate personal experiences fully but has difficulty supporting points of view in written discourse. Can write about the concrete aspects of topics relating to particular interests and special fields of competence. Often shows remarkable fluency and ease of expression, but under time constraints and pressure writing may be inaccurate. Generally strong in either grammar or vocabulary, but not in both. Weakness and unevenness is one of the foregoing or in spelling or character writing formation may result in occasional miscommunication. Some misuse of vocabulary may still be evident. Style may still be obviously foreign.

Superior

Able to express self effectively in most formal and informal writing on practical, social and professional topics. Can write most types of correspondence, such as memos as well as social and business letters, and short research papers and statements of position in areas of special interest or in special fields. Good control of a full range of structures, spelling or nonalphabetic symbol production, and a wide general vocabulary allow the writer to hypothesize and present arguments or points of view accurately and effectively. An underlying organization, such as chronological ordering, logical ordering, cause and effect, comparison, and thematic development is strongly evident, although not thoroughly executed and/or not totally reflecting target language patterns. Although sensitive to differences in formal and informal style, still may not tailor writing precisely to a variety of purposes and/or readers. Errors in writing rarely disturb natives or cause miscommunication.

Source: Buck, K., A. Byrnes, and I. Thompson. *The ACTFL Oral Proficiency Tester Training Manual.* Yonkers, NY: ACTFL, Inc., February 1989.

The Proficiency Concept: A Historical Summary

Prior to World War II   Foreign language instruction centered on the development of literacy skills—reading and writing.

World War II   Realization that Americans had difficulty communicating with foreigners. Army Language School (later to become the Defense Language Institute) in Monterey, California, began teaching for oral communication.

1950s   Foreign Service Institute (FSI) Language School began to rate speaking ability of students and personnel, using an interview-based evaluation procedure linked to a rating scale.

1960s   Educational Testing Service (ETS) staff members were trained in the Oral Proficiency Interview (OPI) procedure and began to test Peace Corps personnel.

1970s   Application of OPI to educational setting (as part of certification procedure for bilingual and ESL teachers, evaluating students and personnel). "Common Yardstick project" began, bringing together ETS with the English Speaking Union of Great Britain, the British Council, the Deutscher Volkschoch-schulerband, representatives of the U.S. government, and various business and academic groups, for the purpose of refining the FSI (currently called Inter Language Roundtable [ILR] scale and interview procedure for academic use.

1978–1979   President's Commission on Foreign Language and International Studies formed to assess need for language specialists, recommend types of language programs needed, recommend how to call public attention to the importance of foreign language and international studies, and identify legislative changes. Report of the Commission, "Strength Through Wisdom," recommended that foreign language proficiency test be developed to assess foreign language teaching in the United States. MLA-ACLS (Modern Language Association-American Council on Language Studies) Language Task Force for the President's Commission made similar recommendations.

1980   ILR scale was expanded at Levels 0 and 1, and levels were renamed.

1981   Under the sponsorship of two grants, ACTFL continued development of longer verbal descriptions of each level in the form of "guidelines" for the four skills and culture.

1982–present   ACTFL conducts training workshops for foreign language professionals.

Sample Culture-based Syllabus for Introductory-level French Course

CONTEXT	GRAMMAR	FUNCTIONS	CULTURE TOPICS
1 Meeting each other; departure for France			
Greetings		Extend greetings	Notions of register, body language
Introductions	*To be*	Make introductions	Notions of register, body language
Simple conversation	Interrogative form	Carry out simple conversation	
Leave-taking	*To go*	Say good-bye	Notions of register, body language
	Definite article		Tie to basic concrete objects related to travel
2 Arrival in France			
Customs & other formalities	*To have*		Formalities of travel abroad
Baggage retrieval	Negation	Expressing negation	
Local transportation	Indefinite article		Role of public transportation; importance of train
Time	Cardinal numbers	Determining time	
Telephone	Cardinal numbers	Placing phone call	How to telephone; use of phone book; system governing phone numbers.
3 At train station			
Finding way around			Train station as microcosm of culture: notion of class structure of society
Buying ticket	Official time; Immediate future	Interpreting train schedule	Different kinds of tickets
Days, months, seasons			Calendar: Catholic country, saint's days
Date and year			Key dates in country's history (14 July 1789)
4 On the train			
Activities during trip			Basic facts about country: population, geography, different regions
Weather	*To do, to make*		Weather pattern typical for each region across seasons; daily forecast
	Imperative		
5 Arrival at destination; meet hosts			
Account of trip	*To come*	Recounting trip	
Tell about self		Telling about self	
Family members		Describing family	
Ordinal numbers			
	To take, to eat		Typical schedule of meals (time, content, etiquette)
6 Arrival at hosts' home			
The house	Adjectives; Plural of nouns	Describe (simply) house	Housing typical of various socio-economic strata
Daily schedule of family activities			Typical pattern of conventional, social life
	Direct object pronoun		

Source: Allen, W.W. "Toward Cultural Proficiency." Ed. A. Omaggio. *Proficiency, Curriculum, Articulation: The Ties That Bind.* Middlebury, VT: Northeast Conference on Teaching Foreign Languages, 1985, pp. 162–165.

Excerpt from Course-Level Curriculum Plan

PROGRAM GOALS

Language: **French**   *Level:* **I**

Composite Proficiency Goal: Novice High (60% of time they operate at intermediate low—starting to create)

PERFORMANCE GOALS:

I. LISTENING: Proficiency Goal—Novice High

The student will be able to:

A. understand familiar and memorized material—word, phrase length and short sentence length.
B. identify type of context heard.
C. extract specific information and main ideas in spoken material.
D. react to classroom commands.

II. SPEAKING: Proficiency Goal—Novice High

The student will be able to:

A. begin to create simple statements using familiar, memorized material.
B. name and identify basic objects, people, and places.
C. give autobiographical information: name, age, place of origin, address.
D. describe family, people and things.
E. describe daily routine and leisure-time activities.
F. utilize learned words, phrases, and sentences in basic face-to-face conversations.
G. handle simple survival tasks.

III. READING: Proficiency Goal—Novice High

The student will be able to:

A. comprehend some visual material needed for survival.
B. identify main idea in recombined familiar material: letters, ads, articles, short stories.
C. scan authentic material for specific information.

IV. WRITING: Proficiency Goal—Novice High

The student will be able to:

A. copy basic material.
B. list basic material.
C. create simple sentences and letters using familiar material.
D. fill in forms such as magazine subscriptions, passport applications.
E. write exercises for grammatical practice.

V. CULTURE: Proficiency Goal—

The student will be able to:

A. demonstrate knowledge of geography of francophone countries, location of some capital cities, some rivers, lakes, seas, and some mountain ranges.
B. use basic phrases of courtesy in social situations (i.e., at the table, in introductions, interruptions, greetings, and farewells).
C. give street address, phone number, time of day, and dates in culturally established forms.
D. understand differences in customs in reference to holidays.

COURSE OBJECTIVES: Indicators of Achievement
Language: French   *Level:* 1 (Novice High)

	Functions	Control (Full, Partial, Emerging)	Contexts
LISTENING	1. understand familiar & memorized material.	1. full	self
	2. identity type of context.	2. partial	family
	3. extract specific information and main ideas in spoken material.	3. partial	school
	4. react to classroom commands.	4. full	weather
SPEAKING	1. create simple statements with familiar material.	1. full	dates/times
	2. name & identify basic objects, people, places.	2. full	numbers
	3. give autobiography information.	3. full	colors
	4. describe people, things, family.	4. partial	
	5. describe daily routine and leisure activities.	5. partial	clothing (shopping)
	6. utilize learned words and phrases in basic fact-to-face conversation.	6. partial	sports/ leisure
	7. give basic commands.	7. partial	food
	8. use survival language.	8. emerging	
	9. spell name.	9. full	
READING	1. comprehend visual survival material.	1. partial	transportation
	2. extract main ideas in recombined material.	2. partial	occupations
	3. scan authentic material for specific information	3. full	geography
	4. derive meaning of simple unfamiliar material using context.	4. emerging	
WRITING	1. copy basic material.	1. full	holidays
	2. list basic material.	2. full	
	3. create simple sentences and letters using familiar material.	3. partial	
	4. fill in forms.	4. full	
	5. write exercises for grammar practice.	5. partial	

EVALUATION

Grading Period: 1st 9 Weeks   *Language:* French   *Level:* I

Functions/Items to be Tested

Listening (30%)	Speaking (25%)	Reading (15%)	Writing (20%)	Culture (10%)
Extract specific information from recombined material i.e.: gender, appropriate responses, fill-in missing words or letters	1. Introduce people 2. Greet and say goodbye to people 3. Identify objects in classroom 4. Ask who, where, and what someone is 5. Express preferences and dislikes 6. Count to 30 7. Give basic command using -er verbs	Extract specific information from authentic things, i.e.: schedule/calendar Questions to answer based on recombined familiar material	List: Identify basic vocabulary Fill in blanks: grammar items—gender, definite & indefinite articles, verb forms, commands, numbers Answer questions using given elements of sentence structure Create very simple dialogue using familiar material	1. Greetings 2. Farewells 3. Use of titles (Monsieur, Madame, Mademoiselle) 4. Educational systems comparison between French and American

Source: Shaler Area School District, Pittsburgh, PA, 1992.

Unit Plan: Grade 4

Topic: **Self**   *Suggested Time:* **4 weeks**   *Mastery Level:* **80%**

Theme: **My Community and Me**

Skill	Functions	Content	Structures
LISTENING	• responding physically to commands (TPR) • pantomiming • role playing • hearing an unfamiliar story, making no attempt to translate; to be taped and read by the teacher • writing dictated sentences based on material heard in language experience • illustrating material covered in language experience	• description of human needs and wants and the way in which the community provides for these needs and wants • descriptions of typical school day and a typical weekend day	*Verbs* • present indicative and infinitives of the following (1st, 2nd, 3rd persons singular): - regular action verbs - radical changing verbs (*tener, poder, querer*) - reflexives (*llamarse, ponerse, quitarse*) - irregulars (*poner, ir, haber [hay], hacer, saber, ser, estar*) • progressive tense (*estar* + gerund) • preterite: 1st and 2nd persons of above verbs
SPEAKING	• understanding and answering questions which solicit information (name, age, etc.) • using basic greetings and culturally appropriate expressions • asking simple questions • expressing ideas in simple sentences without reliance on memorized material • using vocabulary related to a broad range of categories (dates, numbers, weather, food, rooms of the house, etc.)	• description of human needs and wants and the way in which the community provides for these needs and wants • description of a typical school day and a typical weekend day	• near future (*ir* + *a* + infinitive) • commands: singular familiar affirmative *Basic Word Order* • ability to circumlocute and paraphrase *Nouns, Adjectives, and Idioms* • possessive adjectives (1st person) • common qualifying adjectives (position and agreement) • demonstrative adjectives • all *tener* idioms • interrogatives (*cuàl, còmo, dònde, adònde, cuàndo*, etc.) • negative words • agreement: subject/verb; adjective/noun

Skill	Functions	Content	Structures
READING	• reproducing (orally) any written symbol • reading established sets of sight words • reading an unfamiliar story and answering questions in the foreign language by finding the correct answers in the text • reading familiar material based on language experience with good intonation and pronunciation	• selected areas from listening and speaking content areas for reading reinforcement	• correct pronunciation • good intonation • fluency • comprehension
WRITING	• copying with correct spelling, accents, and punctuation • writing dictated material based on language experience situations • completing sentences by following a model • answering direct questions using single words or simple phrases • constructing a sentence using subject, verb, object	• selected areas from listening and speaking content areas for writing reinforcement	• copying • spelling • punctuation • following sentence patterns
CULTURE	• understanding and appreciating the foreign culture	• comparison of the local community with a community in a Spanish-speaking country	• participation in class discussions and activities

Source: Pittsburgh Public Schools, Pittsburgh, PA, 1992.

Unit Plan: Grade 10

APPENDIX A6

SPANISH 1 Unit 2

Main purposes: To enable students to describe their worlds (self, family, friends, interests, etc.), to share this information with others, and to understand the personal worlds of people from various Hispanic countries.

Content

I. Describing possession
   Vocabulary: school supplies, household possessions
   Grammar: definite articles, possession with *de, hay* + noun, numbers 0–20, possessive adjectives
   Pronunciation: consonants *p, t;* sound [k]
   *Culture: typical possessions of Hispanic student

II. Discussing likes and dislikes
   Vocabulary: words related to student life and activities, leisure-time activities
   Grammar: *gustar, ser + de* for possession, *-er/-ir* verbs
   Pronunciation: consonant *d*
   *Culture: typical leisure-time activities of young Hispanics

III. Describing one's family
   Vocabulary: kinship terms (nuclear family), descriptive adjectives
   Grammar: *tener, tener + que* + infinitive, information words, *ser* + adjective
   Pronunciation: sound [b]
   Culture: Hispanic last names; Hispanic families

   * = content not included in text

Learning Outcomes

Students will be able to:

Listening:
1. Identify main ideas of conversations pertaining to possessions, likes and dislikes, and family.
2. *Identify numbers 0-20 in taped segments heard.
3. Identify main ideas in taped advertisements.
4. *Identify names of people heard in conversations.

Speaking:
1. Describe their possessions.
2. Express their likes and dislikes.
3. Describe their families.

4. Ask other classmates about their possessions, likes and dislikes, and families.

Reading:
1. *Identify main ideas in society page article dealing with a family event.
2. *Demonstrate understanding of letter from a friend in which he/she discusses personal likes/dislikes and family.

Writing:
1. *Write a letter to a friend, describing your personal likes/dislikes and family.
2. *Complete a passport application form.

Culture:
1. Describe the typical Hispanic family.
2. Describe Hispanic last names.
3. *Describe typical possessions and likes/dislikes of Hispanic youngsters.

   * = outcomes not included in the text

Teaching Strategies and Activities:

Vocabulary: Total Physical Response activities for school supplies and possessions, using realia. TPR-adapted activities for likes and dislikes using pictures. Recycle indefinite articles and colors.

Grammar: Inductive presentations of all grammar points. Divide *-er/-ir* verbs into (1) singular forms and (2) plural forms for presentation. Recycle infinitives from Unit 1.

Listening: Authentic taped segments; video.

Reading: Readings in text and article from society pages.

Speaking: Interviews in pairs, describing family and likes/dislikes. Situations in groups of three. Recycle introductions of people.

Writing: Filling in forms. Writing friendly letters.

Culture: Reading and discussion. Native speaker visits the class.

Source: Original material from Glisan 1991.

Bloom's Taxonomy of Thinking Processes

Level of Taxonomy	Definition	What the Student Does	Verbs to Help You Design Activities
Knowledge	Recall or location of specific bits of information	responds absorbs remembers recognizes	tell - list - define - name - recall - identify - state - know - remember - repeat - recognize
Comprehension (understanding)	Understanding of communicated material or information	explains translates demonstrates interprets	transform - change - restate - describe - explain - review - paraphrase - relate - generalize - summarize - interpret - infer - give main idea
Application (using)	Use of rules, concepts, principles, and theories in new situations	solves novel problems demonstrates uses knowledge constructs	apply - practice - employ - use - demonstrate - illustrate - show - report
Analysis (taking apart)	Breaking down information into its parts	discusses uncovers lists dissects	analyze - dissect - distinguish - examine - compare - contrast - survey - investigate - separate -categorize - classify - organize
Synthesis (creating new)	Putting together of ideas into a new or unique product or plan	discusses generalizes relates contrasts	create - invent - compose - construct - design - modify - imagine - produce - propose - what if . . .
Evaluation (judging)	Judging the value of materials or ideas on the basis of set standards or criteria	judges disputes forms opinions debates	judge - decide/select/justify - evaluate - critique - debate - verify - recommend - assess

Source: from Curtain, H.A., and C.A. Pesola. *Languages and Children—Making the Match*. Reading, MA. Addison-Wesley, 1988, p. 113

Elementary School Foreign Language Teacher Observation Guide

___ 1. Teacher uses target language for all classroom purposes.
     ___ uses natural speed and intonation
     ___ uses gestures, facial expressions, and body language
     ___ uses concrete referents such as props, realia, manipulatives, and visuals (especially with entry-level students)

___ 2. Teacher uses linguistic modifications when necessary to make the target language more comprehensible for the students.
     ___ uses controlled, standardized vocabulary
     ___ uses controlled sentence length and complexity
     ___ uses restatements, expansions, and repetitions

___ 3. Teacher keeps use of the native language clearly separated from use of the target language.

___ 4. Teacher provides students with opportunities for extended listening.

___ 5. Teacher uses authentic communication to motivate all language use.

___ 6. Teacher maintains a pace with momentum and a sense of direction.

___ 7. Teacher changes activities frequently and logically.

___ 8. Students are active throughout the class period.
     ___ individually
     ___ as part of groups

___ 9. Teacher introduces and tests structures and vocabulary in meaningful contexts.

___ 10. Teachers and students use visuals and realia effectively.

___ 11. There is evidence of detailed planning.

___ 12. Discipline is positive, prompt, nondisruptive.

___ 13. Environment is attractive and reflects the target culture.

___ 14. There is evidence of cultural content in activities.
     ___ stereotypes are not reinforced
     ___ global and multicultural awareness is encouraged

___ 15. Classroom routines provide students with clear clues to meaning.

___ 16. Lessons contain elements of subject-content instruction.

___ 17. Teacher practices sensitive error correction with primary focus on errors of meaning rather than on errors of form.

___ 18. Teacher provides hands-on experiences for students, accompanied by oral and written language use.

___ 19. Teacher accelerates student communication by teaching functional chunks of language.

___ 20. Teacher constantly monitors student comprehension through interactive means such as
     ___ comprehension checks
     ___ clarification requests personalization
     ___ using a variety of questioning types

___ 21. There are varied groupings of students and varied interaction patterns.
    ___ teacher/student
    ___ student/teacher
    ___ student/student

___ 22. There is careful introduction to second language literacy.

___ 23. Reading is based on student-centered, previously mastered oral language.

___ 24. Teacher shows patience with student attempts to communicate.

___ 25. Teacher plans activities that provide students with successful learning experiences.

___ 26. Teacher appears enthusiastic and motivated.

___ 27. Questions and activities provide for a real exchange of information and opinions.

___ 28. Teacher incorporates activities from a variety of cognitive levels.

___ 29. Students ask as well as answer questions.

___ 30. Teacher uses a variety of classroom techniques.

___ 31. Lessons incorporate both new and familiar material.

___ 32. Teacher includes several skills in each lesson.

___ 33. Teacher gives clear directions and examples.

___ 34. Teacher uses varied and appropriate rewards.

___ 35. Teacher allows ample wait-time after asking questions.

Source: Curtain, H. A., and C. A. Pesola. *Language and Children—Making the Match*.
Reading, MA: Addison-Wesley, 1988, pp. 194-195.

Identifying Immersion Language Objectives

Content-obligatory and content-compatible language objectives include the following kinds of language skills:

- Functions, such as: requesting/giving information, comparing, and describing
- Vocabulary
- Grammar, such as: question formation, adjective agreement, and comparatives.

Let's examine a Grade 1 mathematics lesson. The objective is for students to learn to construct and interpret information from simple pictographs. Because you know students will need food vocabulary for an upcoming social studies unit,

People Need Food, you have selected a variety of fruits for the introductory lesson on graphing. You have selected red, green, and yellow apples, green and yellow pears, bananas and oranges. As you demonstrate to students how to graph the number of each type of fruit, you will find that you must use certain language so that students understand how to construct and interpret graphs (content-obligatory language objectives). Other language objectives, such as the names of the fruits selected, may be varied at your discretion (content-compatible language objectives). Review the content-obligatory and content-compatible language objectives below that were identified by a veteran immersion teacher.

CONTENT-OBLIGATORY LANGUAGE OBJECTIVES

Functions	Vocabulary	Grammar
Understanding directions	Ordinal numbers 1–10 Horizontal axis	Singular and plural nouns
Understanding requests for information— How many red apples are there?	Vertical axis	Definite and indefinite articles
Describing—There are 3 green apples.		

CONTENT-COMPATIBLE LANGUAGE OBJECTIVES

Functions	Vocabulary	Grammar
Expressing preferences— I like red apples. Expressing dislikes— I don't like green apples.	apples pears bananas oranges	Noun/adjective agreement

Source: Lorenz, E., and M. Met. *Planning for Instruction in the Immersion Classroom*. Rockville, MD: Montgomery County Public Schools, 1989, pp. 28-29.

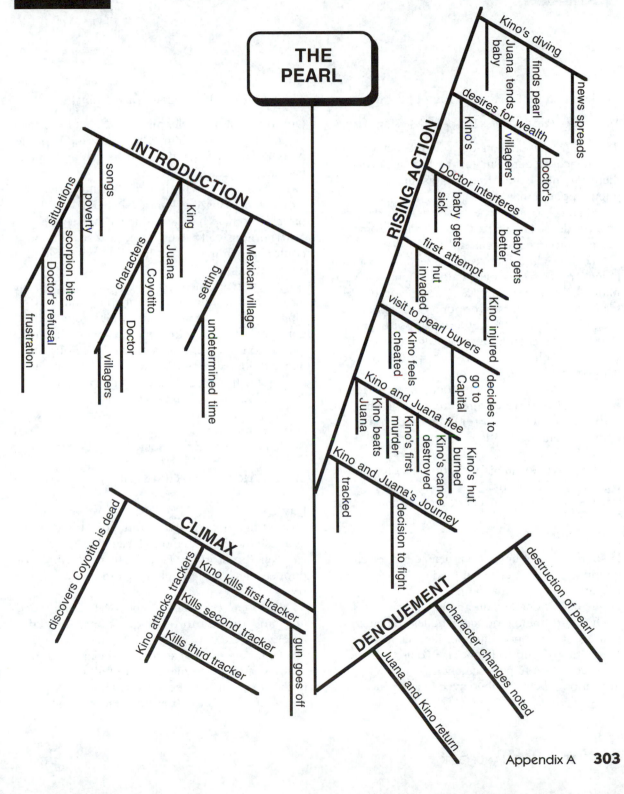

Completed Classroom Map for *The Pearl* by John Steinbeck

THE PEARL

INTRODUCTION

- Mexican village
  - undetermined time
- King
  - Juana
  - Coyotito
    - Doctor
    - villagers
  - characters
- songs
  - poverty
  - situations
    - scorpion bite
      - Doctor's refusal
      - frustration

RISING ACTION

- Kino's diving
  - finds pearl
  - news spreads
- Juana tends for baby
  - villagers'
    - Doctor's
  - desires for wealth
- Kino's
  - sick
  - baby gets better
- Doctor interferes
  - baby gets
  - Kino injured
- first attempt
  - hut invaded
- visit to pearl buyers
  - Kino feels cheated
  - decides to go to Capital
  - Kino's hut burned
- Kino and Juana flee
  - Juana
  - Kino beats
  - Kino's first murder
  - Kino's canoe destroyed
- Kino and Juana's Journey
  - tracked
  - decision to fight

CLIMAX

- discovers Coyotito is dead
- Kino attacks trackers
  - Kino kills first tracker
  - Kills second tracker
  - Kills third tracker
- gun goes off

DENOUEMENT

- Juana and Kino return
- character changes noted
- destruction of pearl

Sample Lesson in Whole Language Learning

Type of context: Story—**Le Lion et la souris**

Structure: *Passé composé* of *er* verbs using *"avoir"*

Text: Un jour un lion dort et une petite souris commence à courir sur lui. Le lion se réveille. Il met sa grande patte sur la petite souris et ouvre la gueule pour la manger.

"Pardon, ô Roi," crie la souris. Elle demande au lion de la laisser partir et elle lui promet de l'aider exactement comme il l'a aide.

Le lion aime bien cette idée de la souris—l'idée que la souris peut l'aider. Donc il lève la patte et la souris s'en va. Quelques jours plus tard, des chasseurs prennent le lion dans un piège. Les chasseurs veulent l'apporter au roi. Donc ils l'attachent à un arbre avec une corde et vont chercher un chariot pour pouvoir l'apporter.

A ce moment, la petite souris passe et remarque la situation dangereuse du lion. Elle s'approche du lion, prend la corde dans ses dents, et commence à la couper.

"Oh, merci, petite souris!"

"Vous voyez que je vous dis la vérité, n'est-ce pas?" répond la souris.

Les petits amis peuvent devenir de grands amis.

Vocabulaire:

la souris:	petit animal qui n'aime pas les chats
courir:	aller très vite à pied
la patte:	main d'un animal
la gueule:	bouche d'un animal
le chasseur:	homme qui cherche les animaux
le piège:	truc pour attraper les animaux
le roi:	Henri II, Louis XIV, Louis XVII, etc.
la corde:	un fil pour attacher
le chariot:	petit et rouge avec quatre roues

The Lion and the Mouse *(Translation)*

One day a lion is sleeping, and a little mouse begins to crawl on him. The lion wakes up. He puts his big paw on the little mouse and opens his mouth to eat it.

"Excuse me, O King of Beasts," cries the mouse. She asks the lion to let her go, and she promises to help him just as he has helped her.

The lion really likes the idea that the mouse could help him. So he lifts his paw, and the mouse runs off.

A few days later some hunters have the lion in a trap. The hunters want to bring him to the king. So they tie him to a tree with a rope and go get a cart to carry him in. Just then the little mouse comes by and notices the dangerous situation the lion is in. She approaches the lion, takes the rope with her teeth and begins to cut it.

"Oh thanks, little mouse!"

"You see I told you the truth, didn't I?" answers the mouse.

Small friends can become big (great) friends.

SUGGESTIONS FOR TEACHING

Day 1:

Presenting the context (Your goal today is to establish the context and to locate the *er* verbs.)

Tell the story in French, using pictures or puppets. Ask basic content questions, using the props.

Distribute copies of an abbreviated, illustrated text, and discuss through questions, true/false statements, etc.

Distribute entire text and vocabulary reference.

Ask students to make a list of all the *er* verbs in the text. This can be done as individuals, with a partner, or as a four-person team.

Le lion et la souris

Un lion dort et une petit souris commence à courir sur lui.

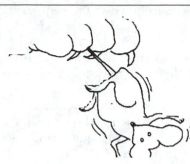

Le lion met sa grande patte sur la souris.

Il ouvre sa gueule pour la manger.

La souris demande au lion de la laisser partir et elle lui promet de l'aider exactement comme il l'a aidée.

Le lion aime bien cette idée—l'idée que la souris peut l'aider.

Plus tard . . .

Des chasseurs prennent le lion dans un piége.

Ils l'attachent à un arbre avec une corde.

La souris prend la corde dans ses dents et commence à la couper.

As students tell you the verbs, write them on a transparency, leaving enough space to write the entire sentence from which the verb was taken.

Day 2:

Focusing on the structure (Your goal is to get the students to tell you how the *passé composé* is formed.)

Review the list of verbs from the transparency, and write the sentences from which they were taken, using a different color marker so the *er* verb is still distinguishable.

Retell the story in the *passé composé,* asking students to concentrate on listening to the sentences that are on the overhead.

Ask students what difference they heard and how they think it is written.

Write a few on a new transparency until they see a pattern developing.

Ask students to complete the list of *er* verbs, changing each to *passé composé.*

Day 3:

Practicing the structure (Your goal is to get students to use the *passé composé* correctly.)

Use two or three contextualized activities to practice. This is best accomplished in a cooperative learning setting, either in partners or in teams of four.

EXAMPLES

Activity 1

Rearrange the sentences in the order in which the story takes place.

La souris a demandé au lion de la laisser partir.
(The mouse asked the lion to let her go.)

Les chasseurs ont attaché le lion à un arbre.
(The hunters tied the lion to a tree.)

La souris a commencé à courir sur le lion.
(The mouse began to crawl on the lion.)

Le lion a bien aime l'idée de la souris.
(The lion really liked the mouse's idea.)

La souris a coupé la corde.
(The mouse cut the rope.)

Le lion a attrapé la souris sous la patte.
(The lion trapped the mouse under his paw.)

La souris a remarqué la situation dangereuse du lion.
(The mouse noticed the lion's dangerous situation.)

Le lion a levé la patte pour laisser partir la souris.
(The lion lifted his paw to let the mouse go.)

1. _____

2. _____

3. _____

4. _____

5. _____

6. _____

7. _____

8. _____

Activity 2

(This activity is designed for partners, but it can be expanded to a four-person team activity when students are familiar with the future and the conditional. See Activity Sheet, opposite page.)

Task:

1. Partner one is responsible for the first row, partner two for the second.
2. Write a question in each block, starting with words given.
3. Ask your partner each of your questions.
4. Paraphrase your partner's answers. (Il dit que...)
5. Combine your answers into one or two sentences.

Write the sentences.

The Lion and the Mouse

When is . . .	*Where is . . .*	*Why is . . .*	*What is . . .*	*Who is . . .*
When was . . .	*Where was . . .*	*Why was . . .*	*What was . . .*	*Who was . . .*

Activity 3
Listen to an audiotape of the story, and fill in the missing verb forms.

Days 4–5
Presenting more structure of *passé composé*.

Using the same context, you can present *ir, re* verbs and eventually those using *être*. Of course, this will mean more practice activities, two of which follow.

Activity 1: (Opposite page.)

Activity 2: Scrambled Sentences
Rearrange the words to make a sentence.

1. attaché le lion Ils à arbre ont un
2. sa Il ouvert gueule a
3. corde coupé la a Elle
4. à le La courir commencé lion a souris sur
5. a bien Le aimé idée lion cette
6. patte pauvre lion la Le petite a sa sur souris mis
7. corde ses La la dans pris dents a souris
8. a la partir demandé La lion laisser souris au de
9. piège Les le pris un ont lion chasseurs dans

Scrambled Sentences (translation)
1. tied/the/lion/they/to/tree/a
2. his/he/opened/mouth
3. rope/cut/the/she
4. on/the/the/crawl/began/lion/mouse/to
5. really/the/liked/idea/lion/this
6. paw/poor/lion/the/the/little/his/on/mouse/put
7. rope/his/the/the/in/took/teeth/mouse
8. the/let/to/asked/lion/the/go/mouse/him
9. trap/the/the/had/a/lion/hunters/in

Day 6 or later

Expanding the structure to a new context
This activity is designed for a four-person team.

Distribute copies of the poem on page 314.

Using it as a model, help students create a shorter original version. Write it on a transparen-

cy or board as they create.

Ask teams to create a poem of their own. This may take part of the next day's class.

Ask students to copy their poem, along with appropriate illustrations.

Make copies of all the poems, and staple them in a booklet to give to class members.

(Translation of poem, page 310)

BREAKFAST

He put the coffee
In the cup
He put the milk
In the cup of coffee
He put the sugar
In the coffee with milk
With a teaspoon
He stirred
He drank the coffee with milk
And he put back the cup
Without speaking to me
He lit
A cigarette
He made rings
With the smoke
He put the ashes
In the ashtray
Without speaking to me
Without looking at me
He got up
He put his hat on his head
He put on
His raincoat
Because it was raining
And he left
In the rain
Without a word
Without looking at me
And I took
My head in my hand
And I cried.

Suggested Expansion Activities for Whole Language Approach

1. Human sentences: Make up cards (5 X 8 index cards work well) with components of simple sentences. Concentrate on verb forms.

Dites-moi ce que le lion a fait et ce que la souris a fait:

(Tell me what the lion did and what the mouse did)

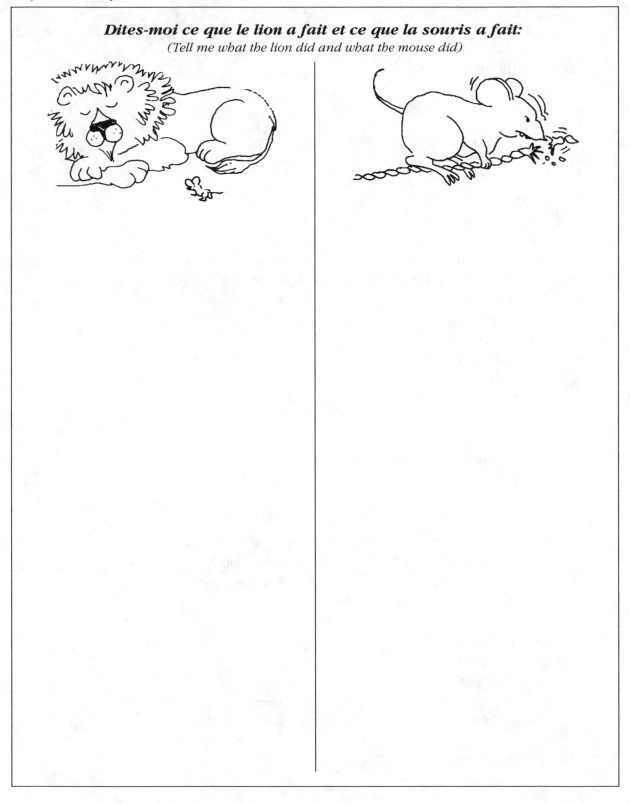

Poème

DÉJEUNER DU MATIN

Il a mis le café
Dans la tasse
Il a mis le lait
Dans la tasse de café
5 Il a mis le sucre
Dans le café au lait
Avec la petite cuiller°   la cuiller = la cuillère
Il a tourné
Il a bu° le café au lait   il a bu: *he drank*
10 Et il a reposé° la tasse   reposer: *to put back*
Sans me parler°   sans me parler: *without speaking to me*
Il a allumé°   allumer: *to light*
Une cigarette
Il a fait des ronds°   le rond: *ring*
15 Avec la fumée°   la fumée: *smoke*
Il a mis les cendres°   la cendre: *ash*
Dans le cendrier°   le cendrier: *ashtray*
Sans me parler
Sans me regarder
20 Il s'est levé°   il s'est levé: *he got up*
Il a mis
Son chapeau sur sa tête°   la tête: *head*
Il a mis
Son manteau de pluie°   le manteau de pluie = l'imperméable
25 Parce qu il pleuvait°   il pleuvait: *it was raining*
Et il est parti°   il est parti: *he left*
Sous la pluie
Sans une parole°   la parole = le mot
Sans me regarder
30 Et moi j'ai pris
Ma tête dans ma main°   la main: *hand*
Et j'ai pleuré.°   pleurer: *to cry*

Jacques Prévert, *Paroles*. ©Editions Gallimard, 1949

Divide class into teams. Teacher reads a sentence. Students form the sentence. First team to form the sentence correctly wins a point.

2. Rearrange sentences from a story in proper order.

3. Scrambled sentences: Rearrange components to form a correct sentence.

4. Retell the story, changing the time.

5. Act out the story with puppets or other props.

6. Play a tape or read the story to students while they complete missing words.

7. Describe the story through pictures.

8. "Find someone in the class who...."

9. Graphic organizers: For variety, use different shapes to retell the story or tell facts about the grammar point, etc.

10. Give students a list of verbs. Ask them to use the verbs on the list to tell you what they did over the weekend.

11. Freeze frame: While some students are role playing, stop the action while students at their seats describe the action either orally or in writing.

12. Write a poem, using a model which emphasizes the grammar point.

As the teacher creates more activities, ideas will flow more readily. The following are suggestions for context:

Textbook	Children's stories
Songs	Poems
Recipes	Advertisements
Cartoons	Letters
Invitations	Labels
Magazines	Newspapers
Audiocassettes	Videocassettes

Source: Original material from P. Cumo 1992

Presentation of a Reading Using the Interactive Model for Teaching Listening and Reading

I. Pre-reading:

In preparation for reading this article, look at the title and illustrations. Then answer the following questions in English or Spanish.

1. What do you think this article is about?

_____

_____

2. Write down at least three pieces of information you might learn concerning the topic.

_____

_____

_____

II. Identify main elements:

Skim the article without reading word for word. Can you identify the three main categories of information? Use the organization of the article as a clue.

   OR

Skim the article without reading word for word. From the list of alternatives given below, select the three main categories of information. Use the organization of the article as a clue.

1. ___ Planning vacations with your travel agent
2. ___ Doing your packing before the trip
3. ___ Planning activities when you reach your destination
4. ___ Preparing for your trip back home
5. ___ Handling emergencies during the trip

III. Identify details:

Now scan the article to find two details for each of the three categories you identified in Part II above. Make a chart of main categories and supporting details in Spanish.

   OR

Now scan the article for supporting details. Which of the following pieces of information does the article include? Organize the details under each of the main categories you identified in Part II above, using a chart format. Find other details not listed below.

1. ___ Pack prescription medicines.
2. ___ Pack anything that might spill in your carry-on bag.
3. ___ Take your prescription for your contact lenses along on the trip.
4. ___ Take a first-aid kit with you.
5. ___ Take extra food along if traveling by car.
6. ___ Avoid going out in the evenings.
7. ___ Ask your travel agent for names of competent doctors who speak English.
8. ___ Seek help immediately if someone is injured, even if you're not sure it's an emergency.

IV. Organize/revise main ideas/details:

Compare your chart with that of a classmate. Make changes as necessary, organizing the ideas in a logical manner and using language from the article.

V. Recreate text:

For homework: Write a summary of the article in an 8–10 sentence paragraph. Use your chart as a guide, but create ideas in your own words in Spanish.

In class the next day: Exchange paragraphs with a classmate and read summaries for content and linguistic accuracy. Make suggestions for revision/correction.

VI. React to text/explore intertextuality:

In this stage, the teacher might enter into oral discussion of the article in an attempt to elicit opinions and ideas.

For a follow-up written assignment, students might make a list of other things they would do to prepare for a trip abroad and/or give other advice for taking an enjoyable vacation.

Intertextuality: Students might compare this article to a taped public service announcement they heard earlier dealing with vacation planning. They might discuss similarities and differences (discourse, organization, etc.).

Consejos para unas vacaciones saludables

Por Monica Perez, Copley News Service

Cualquiera puede tratar el efecto del avión o el mareo. Pero para los millones de turistas planificando sus vacaciones soñadas, un poco más de planificación puede ser el resultado entre unas vacaciones placenteras o una pesadilla médica.

Afortunadamente hay varias cosas que usted puede hacer de antemano para reducir esos problemas de salud y proveerse usted mismo la paz mental. He aquí una lista de cotejo.

Antes del viaje

Al preparar su maleta incluya un surtido amplio de medicinas recetadas. Lleve parte de éstas consigo en su maletín de mano en caso de que es extravíe su equipaje.

Si usted usa lentes de contacto, lleve consigo una copia de la receta en caso de que se le extravíen o se le rompan. Lleve siempre consigo en su maleta un pequeño maletin de primera ayuda que incluya aspirinas, antibióticos, tabletas antihestamínicas, vendajes adhesivos y gaza, la loción para protegerse del sol y el repelente de insectos.

Si su viaje es en carro, lleve botellas de agua así como mantas en caso de que sufra su carro una avería en el largo viaje en un sitio desolado.

Al llegar al destino

Usted quizás querrá proveer para los malestares que le pueda ocasionar la comida extraña y el agua. Consulte a su médico para que le aconseje la medicina que debe usar en caso de diarrea o estreñimiento.

Evite participar en actividades afuera durante las horas más calurosas del día ya que el calor lo puede afectar especialmente en áreas donde la humedad es bien alta.

Si está viajando al exterior, pregunte a su agente de viajes los nombres de médicos competentes que hablen inglés. La embajada o consulado puede ayudario en caso de que se enferme.

De surgir una emergencia

Las autoridades médicas informan que cada año miles de turistas norteamericanos mueren o son incapacitados sin necesidad por falta del tratamiento adecuado inmediatamente luego de la emergencia. Minutos, aun segundos puede ser la diferencia para salvar una vida.

Si alguna persona está herida y aún respira, busque ayuda inmediatamente aun cuando no esté seguro que la situación sea una emergencia. El personal de emergencia médica está adiestrado para estimar el grado de emergencia.

English translation

Advice for a Healthy Vacation

Anyone can cure the ill effects of air or sea sickness, but for the millions of travelers planning their vacations, a bit more planning could be the difference between a pleasant vacation and a medical nightmare.

Fortunately, there are various steps that you can take beforehand to reduce such health problems and to give yourself peace of mind.

Here is a checklist:

Before the trip:

When packing your bags, be sure to include an ample supply of prescription medications. Bring some of these medications with you in a carry-on bag in case your luggage is lost.

If you wear contact lenses, bring a copy of your prescription with you in case you lose one of them, or in case one breaks. Always carry a small first-aid kit with you in your suitcase. Inside the kit you should have aspirin, antibiotics, antihistamines, band-aides, medical gauze, sunblock, and insect repellent.

If you are traveling by car, bring bottled water as well as blankets in case your car breaks down in an isolated area.

Upon arrival at your destination:

You will want to prepare for the discomforts that you may encounter with the food and the water. Consult your doctor for professional medical advice on some medicines that you should use in case of diarrhea or constipation.

Avoid exercising outside during the hottest hours of the day. Such activities could be harmful to your health, especially in areas where the humidity is very high.

If you are traveling abroad, ask your travel agent the names of competent doctors who speak English. The American embassy or consulate can help you in case you become sick.

In case of an emergency:

Medical authorities report that each year thousands of tourists from the U.S. die or are unnecessarily incapacitated due to inadequate immediate treatment. Minutes, even seconds could be the difference in saving a life.

If someone is hurt and still breathing, look for help immediately even if you're not quite sure that the situation is an emergency. Emergency medical personnel are trained to estimate the degree of any emergency.

Source: Glisan and Shrum 1991.

APPENDIX A13

The Chronological Development of Language Teaching

ERA	TIME PERIOD	METHOD	BASIC TENETS
I. Influence of Teaching of Latin and Greek	until late 19th century	Grammar–translation	The mind needs to be trained by analysis of the language, memorization of rules, paradigms; application of these rules in translation exercises (Rivers 1968).
II. Reaction to Grammar-Translation Method	late 19th–early 20th century	Direct	Learners should acquire rules of grammar inductively through imitation, repetition, speaking, and reading. The best way to teach meaning is to use visual perception (Titone 1968).
III. Result of Structural Linguistics and Behavioral Psychology/ National Emphasis on Oral skills	1940–1950	Audiolingual (ALM)	L2 should be taught without reference to L1. Students learn through stimulus-response (S-R) techniques. Pattern drills should precede any explanation of grammar. The natural sequence LSRW should be followed in learning the language (Chastain 1976).
IV. Reaction to ALM	1960s	Cognitive (Code)	Students must attain control over the rules of the target language so they can generate their own utterances. The teacher should move from known to new information. Creative use of the language should be promoted. Grammar should be explained so that students understand the rules. Language practice should always be meaningful (Chastain 1976).
V. Result of Studies in First Language Acquisition	1974	Total Physical Response	Comprehension must be developed before speaking. Speech will emerge naturally as students internalize language. Students learn to understand best through physical movement in response to commands (Asher 1974).
	late 1970s, early 1980s	Natural	Students should acquire language before being forced to learn it. Affective factors merit much attention in language instruction. Communicative competence should be the goal in beginning language instruction. Students need to acquire a great deal of vocabulary to understand and to speak (Terrell 1977).

TECHNIQUES	PROPONENT(S)
translation; learning of grammar rules; memorization of bilingual word lists; little or no emphasis on oral skills	No one person; German scholar Karl Plotz (1880–1891) very influential
exclusive use of L2; use of visuals; grammar rules taught through inductive teaching; emphasis on correct pronunciation	Comenius, Gouin, Jespersen, de Sauzé
stimulus-response pattern drills; memorization of dialogues; correction a must; comparison of L1 and L2; exclusive use of L2; grammar rules learned through induction; skills learned in the sequence of listening, speaking, reading, writing; focus on culture	Fries, Skinner, Bloomfield, Brooks
meaningful language use; deductive teaching of grammar in native language; grammar practice follows mechanical, meaningful, communicative sequence	Chomsky, Ausubel
listening and responding physically to oral commands for first ten hours of instruction; exclusive use of target language; creative language use	Asher
creative, communicative practice; limited error correction; "foreigner talk"; acquisition activities: comprehension, early speech production, speech emergence; inductive teaching of grammar	Terrell

ERA	TIME PERIOD	METHOD	BASIC TENETS
VI. Focus on effective Development of Individual: Humanistic Methods	1972–1973	Silent Way	Teachers can help students most by allowing them to take more responsibility for their own learning. Learning is not relegated to imitation and drill. Students learn from trial and error and are capable of making their own corrections (Gattegno 1983).
	1976	Community Language Learning	The teacher, in the role as "knower" or "counselor," should remain passive in order to reduce anxiety among students. Students learn when working in community with others who are trying to achieve similar goals (Curran 1983).
	1978–1979	Suggestopedia	Relaxation techniques and concentration assist learners in releasing the subconscious and in retaining large amounts of language (Bancroft 1983).
VII. Effects of Drama on Language Teaching	1980	Dartmouth Intensive Language Model (DILM)	The teacher must help students to overcome their inhibitions so that they can live the language experience more fully. The teacher should be an actor and possess vitality in the classroom. The target language should be spoken exclusively, and all errors should be corrected. The language must come to life in the classroom (Rassias 1983).
VIII. Proficiency	1980–Present	No particular method	Knowing a language means being able to use it in communication. Students use the language to perform functions in a range of contexts and with a level of accuracy in grammar, vocabulary, pronunciation, fluency and pragmatic competence, and sociolinguistic competence.

Source: Original material from Shrum and Glisan (1993).

TECHNIQUES	PROPONENT(S)
use of Cuisenaire rods to denote words and structures; students more responsible for learning; self and peer correction; early writing practice	Gattegno
translation by teacher from native language to target language in early lessons; theme of each class determined by students; analysis of group conversations from tape	Curran
"suggestive" atmosphere (living room setting, soft lights, baroque music, dramatic techniques by teacher); dialogues accompanied by music in background; role-plays and activities to "activate" the material in dialogues; grammatical explanations given in native language	Lozanov
drama and action by teacher; immediate correction of grammar and pronunciation errors; skits and games; "micrologue" for teaching culture; master teacher and apprentice teachers (who conduct drill sessions); inductive teaching by master teacher	Rassias
opportunities for self-expression and creativity; use of language in a variety of contexts; exposure to authentic texts; interaction with others; integration of culture and language	Proficiency Guidelines established by ACTFL/ETS

"Talk Scores": Monitoring and Evaluating Group Speaking Activities

What: An uncomplicated way to assess student performance during small group activities.

When: As often as possible and as much as you can observe during a group activity.

Why: Often we have subjective impressions (often correct!!!) about a student's level of participation, cooperation, performance. The TALK SCORES allow you to compare your impressions with real classroom performance.

How: Each letter of the word TALK represents one PERFORMANCE OBJECTIVE to be observed during small group activity. During an activity the teacher should select only ONE objective to observe. The goal should be that at the end of one or two weeks, the students have been observed for ALL FOUR performance objectives (a round).

PERFORMANCE OBJECTIVES:

(T) = <u>TALKING</u>
Is the student TALKING?
Is the student TRYING to communicate?
Is the talk TASK RELEVANT?

(A) = <u>ACCURATE</u>
Is the student performing at an ACCEPTABLE level of ACCURACY?
Does the student demonstrate the point of the lesson that is being used in the activity?

NB Total accuracy not to be expected but you should have a clear idea of what language elements you will observe for. For example, in an activity that requires the students to use "time," the teacher could observe for how accurately the students are constructing time expressions (It's 2:30, 3:45, etc.)

(L) = <u>LISTENING</u>
Is the student ON TASK?
Does the student LISTEN to her partner or partners?
Does the student LISTEN to directions?

(K) = <u>KIND</u>
Is the student KIND and COOPERATIVE? Does the student KILL the activity by his lack of cooperation? Does the student work with his group?

Procedures:

During an activity, circulate around the room observing for ONE performance objective for each activity (T, A, L, or K). Record in your grade book the objective you are observing, the date, and the activity:

Example:

Obj. – T
date – 9/18/92
Act. – ex c. page 12—partner practice

In other words, on September 18, 1992, you decided that this activity was a good one to use for observations on TRYING TO TALK.

You should try to cover all 4 objectives over a two week period. Covering all four objectives is called a "round." As your grade book fills up with scores for students, you *will begin to see* students who need more observation and students who maybe you should observe less often. For example, if at the end of the week Mary Leech has been observed for three objectives while John Arnold has been observed for only one that will indicate that John needs more of your attention. The goal is that when it is time to compute scores you have an equal number of "rounds" for each student (e.g., 2 T scores, 2 A scores, 2 L scores, 2 K scores).

Scoring:

For each objective score with either a "+", " √ ", or "–"

example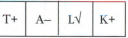

Plus ("+") scores are worth 2 points ⟶ EXCELLENT
Check ("√") scores are worth 1 point ⟶ GOOD TO FAIR
Minus ("-") scores are worth 0 points ⟶ NEEDS WORK

For *one round of scoring* (one T, A, L, K) the following grade conversions can be used:

Points

7–8	=	A
5–6	=	B
3–4	=	C
1–2	=	D
0	=	F

At the end of a round you will have a PROFILE of a student's activity during pair or group work (See sample grade book page). You may want to experiment with observing for more than one objective per activity or per student.

CLASS: Spanish 1 1992-1993

NAMES	T 9/9	A 9/11	L 9/13	K 9/17	Round One	Grade
Jason	T√	A–	L–	K+	3	C
Ann	T–	A–	L√	K+	3	C
John	T+	A+	L+	K–	6	B+
Kelly	T+	A–	L+	K√	5	B
Mark	T–	A–	L+	K+	4	C+
Kelly	T+	A+	L+	K+	8	A+
Jen	T√	A+	L+	K+	7	A
Robert	T+	A–	L–	K√	3	C
Sharon	T√	A+	L+	K+	7	A
	ex. C p. 12 partner practice	Time activity	info-gap activity	peer correction of HW assign.		

Source: Permission of Richard Donato, University of Pittsburgh, 1992, personal communication.

APPENDIX A15 Essay Correction Code (ECCO)

Aux Use of an improper *aux*iliary verb, e.g., *haben* in place of *sein*; also included may be constructions involving *werden* or a modal verb (+ infinitive).

C A part of speech has been assigned the wrong *c*ase.

G Wrong *g*ender assignment to a noun or pronoun, e.g., *Die Mädchen sieht schön aus.*

L A *l*exical or dictionary error, e.g., *wohnen* for *leben*; includes cognates.

M The verb has been placed into the wrong *m*ood; usually subjunctive will need to be replaced by the indicative or vice versa.

N Incorrect *n*umber assignment to a noun or pronoun, e.g., *Er trägt zwei Buch.*

Nag *N*oun-*a*djective-*g*reements are faulty in some way, e.g., *Meiner guter Vater.*

NS A completely *n*ew *s*tructure is needed to convey the proper meaning, e.g. in the sentence *Paul hatte einen Vetter hieß Eduard*—the sentence may be corrected by using any one of several structural alternatives. The structure in need of replacement could be underlined.

PP *P*rincipal *p*art of the verb is incorrect (usually the stem) .

R *R*ewrite successfully completed.

Ref If written as a *ref*lexive construction, change to non-reflexive or vice versa. The code may also indicate use of an incorrect reflexive pronoun.

Sp *Sp*elling error, e.g., *Gestern kame er mit,* or *Ich kenne deisen Mann.*

SV *S*ubject *v*erb agreement is faulty in some way, e.g., *Er kommen morgen.*

T *T*ense selection is in some way inappropriate; usually the student has not been consistent, e.g., *Er setzte sich an den Tisch, grüßt und bestellt ein Bier.*

UN *UN*MÖGLICH! No such word or construction exists in German; includes the use of English words where German versions are not known, e.g., *Ich studierte im Library.*

WO Any error involving *w*ord *o*rder.

X One or more words are missing and must be inserted (exception = reflexive pronouns).

+ Any especially nice touch for which the student may be awarded extra points, e.g., use of the subjunctive or passive.

// Double lines through a word indicate that it is not necessary and must be deleted, e.g., *Ich möchte nach Hause zu gehen.*

? A question mark adjacent to a word, clause, or sentence that is *underlined* indicates that the reviewer could make no sense of the passage whatsoever. The student should consult a teacher, native speaker, etc.

Please note: If the student commits the exact same error more than two times (e.g., he misspells *Fräulein* as *Fraulein*), then he shall not lose additional points and there shall be no additional tallies entered onto the EASE.

Source: Lalande, T.F. II. "Reducing Composition Errors: An Experiment." *Foreign Language Annals* 17 (1984), pp. 116-117.

APPENDIX A16 Error Awareness Sheet (EASE)*

Name _____

Course/Section _____

	Essay #1	Essay #2		Essay #3	Essay #4	Essay #5
SV 2–3						
PP 3						
UN 3						
M 1–3						
WO 1–3						
NS 1–5						
? 1-5						
Aux 2						
G 1–2						
T 1–2						
X 1–2						
C 1						
L 1						
N 1						
Nag 1						
Ref 1						
Sp 1						
// 0–1						
* 1–5						
Points Off						
Grade/R						
Total Errors						

	Time #1	Time #2	Time #3
Which *three* types of errors have you probably made the most on your last two essays?	a) _____ b) _____ c) _____	a) _____ b) _____ c) _____	a) _____ b) _____ c) _____

*The numbers indicate the point values for each error made. For example, for each error in subject-verb agreement, 2 or 3 points are deducted, depending on the gravity the teacher assigns to the error. In each large box, the total number of errors is recorded with the use of tally marks (example:). In the small box appearing in the right-hand corner, the number of points deducted appears (example: 2 errors in subject-verb agreement, with each weighing 2 points, would equal 4 points to be deducted. The box "Grade/R" is used to indicate the grade on the original composition and to show whether or not the composition was rewritten with corrections; R = rewrite completed.

Source: Lalande, J.F., II. "Reducing Composition Errors: An Experiment." *Foreign Language Annals* 17 (1984), p. 117.

Student_____ Date_____ Topic _____

Score	Level	Criteria	Comments

Content

30-27   EXCELLENT TO VERY GOOD: knowledgeable • substantive • thorough development of thesis • relevant to assigned topic

26-22   GOOD TO AVERAGE: some knowledge of subject • adequate range • limited development of thesis • mostly relevant to topic, but lacks detail

21-17   FAIR TO POOR: limited knowledge of subject • little substance • inadequate development of topic

16-13   VERY POOR: does not show knowledge of subject • non-substantive • not pertinent • OR not enough to evaluate

Organization

20-18   EXCELLENT TO VERY GOOD: fluent expression • ideas clearly stated/supported • succinct • well-organized • logical sequencing • cohesive

17-14   GOOD TO AVERAGE: somewhat choppy • loosely organized but main ideas stand out • limited support • logical but incomplete sequencing

13-10   FAIR TO POOR: non-fluent • ideas confused or disconnected • lacks logical sequencing and developing

9-7   VERY POOR: does not communicate • no organization • OR not enough to evaluate

Vocabulary

20-18   EXCELLENT TO VERY GOOD: sophisticated range • effective word/idiom choice and usage • word form mastery • appropriate register

17-14   GOOD TO AVERAGE: adequate range • occasional errors of word/idiom form, choice, usage *but meaning not obscured*

13-10   FAIR TO POOR: limited range • frequent errors of word/idiom form, choice, usage • *meaning confused or obscured*

9-7   VERY POOR: essentially translation • little knowledge of English vocabulary, idioms, word form • OR not enough to evaluate

Language Use

25-22   EXCELLENT TO VERY GOOD: effective complex constructions • few errors of agreement, tense, number, word order/function, articles, pronouns, prepositions

21-18   GOOD TO AVERAGE: effective but simple constructions • minor problems in complex constructions • several errors of agreement, tense, number, word order/function, articles, pronouns, prepositions *but meaning seldom obscured*

17-11   FAIR TO POOR: major problems in simple/complex constructions • frequent errors of negation, agreement, tense, number, word order/function, articles, pronouns, prepositions and/or fragments, run-ons, deletions • *meaning confused or obscured*

10-5   VERY POOR: virtually no mastery of sentence construction rules • dominated by errors • does not communicate • OR not enough to evaluate

Mechanics

5   EXCELLENT TO VERY GOOD: demonstrates mastery of conventions • few errors of spelling, punctuation, capitalization, paragraphing

4   GOOD TO AVERAGE: occasional errors of spelling, punctuation, capitalization, paragraphing *but meaning not obscured*

3   FAIR TO POOR: frequent errors of spelling, punctuation, capitalization, paragraphing • poor handwriting • *meaning confused or obscured*

2   VERY POOR: no mastery of conventions • dominated by errors of spelling, punctuation, capitalization, paragraphing • handwriting illegible • OR not enough to evaluate.

Total Score   Reader   Comments

Source: Jacobs, H.L., S. Zingraf, D. Wormuth, V. Hartfield, and J. Hughey, *Testing ESL Composition: A Practical Approach*. Rowley, MA: Newbury House, 1981, pp. 30, 92-96.

How to Write a Composition

I. *Work method*
1) Read and study the necessary texts.
2) Study the principles presented below (in sections II, III, IV).
3) Take notes on your ideas.
4) Organize your notes in a clear and logical manner.
5) Write the first draft at least 4 days before the due date.
   — Use your notes.
   — Don't stop to look up a word you don't know or to correct your grammar. You will do those things when you review the whole thing.
   — Mark your questions about grammar and vocabulary with a question mark (?).
   — Then, review what you have written.
     State your ideas as clearly as possible.
     Be sure the organization is logical.
     Look up words you don't know.
     Correct grammar errors that you find.
   — Using a dictionary:
     For every word that you look up in a dictionary, consult the dictionary from two points of view, that is, look up the word in the English/French section and check it in the French/English section. The meaning of a word often depends on the context in which you use it.
6) Set this draft aside for one or two days.
7) Review, revise, and rewrite the second draft. Pay attention to:
   — logic of ideas and organization;
   — clarity of presentation
   — accuracy of grammar and vocabulary
8) Type the final draft; pay attention to the presentation (see below, section IV)

II. *Ideas: Take notes on:*
   main ideas;
   supporting ideas;
   examples, of the author's thoughts or of your own logic

III. *Organization: Don't forget to organize your composition with:*
1) an introduction
   — Identify the text (and the author) about which your are writing.
   — Give a summary of your necessary arguments.
2) a development of your ideas
   — Put different ideas in different paragraphs.
   — Identify each idea clearly.
   — Give all necessary examples and arguments.
3) a conclusion
   — Give the conclusion you reached after reasoning through the development.
   — The conclusion *is not* a repetition of the ideas in the introduction.
4) a title
   — Choose a title that is clear.
   — Choose a title that gives some indication of the direction or focus of the composition.

IV. *Presentation: Consider these details:*
1) If you quote the words of the author, put them between quotation marks (or the equivalent form for the language in which you are writing), and note the page on which they are located (p. 000).
2) Margins at least 1" wide on all sides.
3) Composition typed or printed on a word processor, double spaced.
4) Submit the original copy.
5) Pay attention to spelling, accents, and punctuation.

V. *To be submitted:*
1) notes that you took
2) first draft
3) second draft

VI. *Grade will depend on:*
1) ideas and organization: 50%
2) accuracy of grammar, vocabulary, spelling, punctuation, presentation: 50%

Source: Translation from Barnett's "Comment écrire une composition," 1989.

Writing as Process and Product:
Scoring Guide

This chart is designed to be used by the student in the process of writing a final version of his or her composition. It can then be stapled to the composition and used by the teacher for evaluation.

Your task; how to demonstrate your accomplishment of it; and percentage of grade	What grade you earned; teacher comments
Formulating ideas and developing organization; turning in your notes and first draft; setting forth ideas in a logical manner; using transitions between ideas, building to summaries. (50%)	_____ # of points earned Did you turn in your notes? Did you turn in your first draft? Does the introduction draw the reader's interest? Does each paragraph contain a key idea that is elaborated within the paragraph? Does each paragraph connect to the previous one and to the next one? Do all the paragraphs lead to a summary or conclusion?
Appropriate Use of Vocabulary; use vocabulary you have learned in this lesson; appropriate use of dictionary, 10%	_____ # of points earned Have you used as many words from this lesson as possible? Are there others you could have looked up to supplement? If so, did you check both sides (English and target language) of the dictionary? If more than one choice was given in the dictionary, did you check the context and the grammatical use of the word, e.g. noun, verb, adjective, etc.? Are there synonyms you could have used for variation in vocabulary?

Grammar; Appropriate use of grammar that is the focus of this (these) lesson(s); appropriate use of previously learned grammar; 10%	_____ # of points earned Did you check that all grammar use from this lesson was used correctly? Is grammar from previous lesson used correctly? Did you check for simple grammatical errors such as singular and plural agreement of nouns, verbs, adjectives, accents, etc.? If your sentences are short and choppy, are there ways you can combine or elaborate to make them more interesting?
Spelling; check spelling for accuracy; 10%	_____ # of points earned Did you check spelling for simple reversals of letters, omission of letters, double letters, etc.?
Punctuation; check punctuation for accuracy; 10%	_____ # of points earned Be sure all question marks, exclamation points, periods, commas, semicolons, colons, quotation marks and reference citations are included.
Presentation; check appearance of composition for compliance with the requirements for length, typing, etc.; 10%	_____ # of points earned Does the physical appearance of the composition meet the requirements set forth (for instance, typed, double-spaced, suitable length, etc.)?

Checklist for Preparing the Writing Task

Does the task:

[   ] require writers to *compose* a piece of connected discourse?

[   ] establish a clear purpose for communicating, especially by indicating the intended reader and a context for the task?

[   ] motivate writers to communicate their knowledge and perception of the topic?

[   ] reflect the kind of writing students will normally be expected to do in their academic programs or the real world?

[   ] provide a subject that will interest students of this age, sex, educational level, field of study, and cultural background?

[   ] present a topic about which these students will have knowledge?

[   ] appear to be the right level of difficulty for students of this proficiency range?

[   ] provide a topic that is free of hidden elements of bias?

[   ] present a clearly defined task that cannot easily be misinterpreted?

[   ] provide a topic that is broad enough for every writer to approach from some angle?

[   ] use as few words as possible, and definitions if necessary?

[   ] give clear and concise instructions that indicate also the time allowed for writing and the approximate number of words or length of composition expected?

[   ] present a writable and readable topic, pretested with students similar to the test group?

[   ] include as many modes of discourse as are appropriate to the purpose of the test and to the actual writing needs of the students?

[   ] provide at least two writing occasions, in order to produce an adequate sample of a student's ability?

[   ] require all students to write on the same topic, unless skill at choosing a topic is a part of the abilities being tested?

[   ] allow enough writing time for a reasonable performance?

[   ] provide ruled paper for writing?

[   ] use a coding system for identifying writers so that authorship will be anonymous during the evaluation?

[   ] Is the writing task appropriate to the specific purpose(s) of this test?

Source: Jacobs, H.L., S. Zingraf, D. Wormuth, V. Hartfield, and J. Hughey. *Testing ESL Composition: A Practical Approach*. Rowley, MA: Newbury House, 1981, p. 22.

How to Teach Students to Evaluate the Writing of Others

The instructions that follow are designed to prepare a class for the peer essay sharing described in this strategy. However, they can be modified to include the following variations. Members of the dyads can outline on paper each other's essay structure, pointing out the thesis or main point and specifying how that point was developed or substantiated. Or, in triads, one student can act as editor and one as proofreader.

The task for today is to read closely the papers of class members to both give and receive feedback on the papers; and (optional) to ask for any areas that the reader of your paper could suggest for improving the written communication. The steps are as follows.

1. Read each other's paper carefully.
2. Without looking at the paper, tell the author what you think he or she is saying, or, if it is a narrative, tell the story back to the author as precisely as you can.
3. Then your partner(s) should give you the same type of feedback on your paper.
4. After this, if you want to ask your partner(s) about anything which seems unclear, you may do so; if you wish to ask for constructive suggestions, you may. You might want to ask for such information as:
   a. Was there any place in my story that was hard to follow? (narrative)
   b. Is there any point that you just did not really understand?
   c. Was there any place in which my examples, reasons, or explanation needed developing?
   d. Was there any place where I should add more details to my description?
   e. Is there any place where I seemed to wander from my topic?
   f. Were there any transitions that were unclear or missing?
   g. Anything else that you want feedback on: spelling, sentence fragments, run-on sentences, punctuation, sentence variety, style, etc.
5. After each of you has given and received feedback on the essays, you may decide to rework your essay. If so, you may turn it in at the next class meeting; if not, turn in your essay at the end of class. Remember that good feedback is specific, not general. Constructive: "I think that this sentence could be more clear if you added some color words in your description of the trees." Destructive: "Your sentences are lousy." Also remember to check with your group members to make sure your comments are clear. The attitudes which make this sharing helpful are (a) mutual trust; (b) recognition that the helping situation is a joint situation of trust; (c) a real listening to each other; (d) a mutual recognition that whatever is said is merely how we subjectively see things and not necessarily the absolute, objective truth; and (e) a mutual recognition that we want to communicate effectively and that to do this we need reaction from others.

Source: Koch, C., and J. Brazil, *Strategies for Teaching the Composition Process*. Urbana, IL: NCTE, 1978, pp. 86-87.

Strategies to Extend Student Thinking

■ **Remember "wait time I and II"**
Provide at least three seconds of thinking time after a question and after a response.

■ **Utilize "think-pair-share"**
Allow individual thinking time, discussion with a partner, and then open up for the class discussion.

■ **Ask "follow-ups"**
Why? Do you agree? Can you elaborate? Tell me more. Can you give an example?

■ **Withhold judgment**
Respond to student answers in a non-evaluative fashion.

■ **Ask for summary to promote active listening**
"Could you please summarize John's point?"

■ **Survey the class**
"How many people agree with the author's point of view?"
("thumbs up, thumbs down")

■ **Allow for student calling**
"Richard, will you please call on someone else to respond?"

■ **Play devil's advocate**
Require students to defend their reasoning against different points of view.

■ **Ask students to "unpack their thinking"**
"Describe how you arrived at your answer."
("think aloud")

■ **Call on students randomly**
Avoid the pattern of only calling on those students with raised hands.

■ **Encourage student questioning**
Let the students develop their own questions.

■ **Cue student responses**
"There is not a single correct answer for this question. I want you to consider alternatives."

Source: Cited in Kuykendall, C. *Improving Black Student Achievement by Enhancing Students Self-Image*. Washington, DC: Mid-Atlantic Equity Center, 1989, p. 41

An Interactive German Test Based on a Reading

LESEN SIE DEN FOLGENDEN ARTIKEL ÜBER CONRAD SCHUMANN, DESSEN BILD GESCHICHTE MACHTE.

I. Finden Sie in dem Text die Stichwörter, die in diesem Artikel eine wichtige Rolle spielen.

- wer
- wann
- was
- wo
- warum

II. Verwenden Sie die Stichwörter in Nummer I in einen Satz, der die Hauptidee des Artikels erklärt.

III. Eklären Sie die folgenden Ausdrücke in Beziehung zu dem inhalt des Artikels.

- absichern und bewachen
- die letzte Chance
- in die Freiheit springen
- ihm zujubeln

IV. Schreiben Sie vier oder fünf Sätze, die die Hauptereignisse des Artikels beschreiben.

V. Das erste Bild wurde "in aller Welt zum Symbol für die Teilung Deutschlands". Das zweite Bild ist auch symbolisch. Erklären Sie, was es bedeuten könnte.

(Translation)

READ THE FOLLOWING ARTICLE ABOUT CONRAD SCHUMANN, WHOSE PICTURE MADE HISTORY.

I. Find the key words in the text that play an important role in this article.

- who
- when
- what
- where
- why

II. Use the keywords in number I in a sentence that explains the main idea of the article.

III. Explain the following expression/phrases in relation to the content of the article.

- secure and guard
- the last chance
- to jump to freedom
- to cheer him on

IV. Write four or five sentences that describe the main events of the article.

V. The first picture became "throughout the world a symbol for the division of Germany." The second picture is also symbolic. Explain what it might mean (represent).

Source: Original material from Thekla Fall 1993

Die Mauer Fällt

Nach 28 Jahren: Vopo Schumann springt wieder

AZ war mit dem Wahl-Bayern an der Mauer

Von Ildiko von Kürthy

Dieses Bild ging um die Welt: Ein junger Volkspolizist springt in die Freiheit. Von Ost- nach West-Berlin. Das historische Bild ent- stand vor 28 Jahren, 1961, als die Mauer gebaut wurde. Und als die Mauer langsam höher wurde, da begriffen viele: Das ist die letzte Chance. Und diese letzte Chance nutzte auch Conrad Schumann, der 19-jährige Volkspolizist, dessen Bild Geschichte machte.

Was ging in diesem jungen Mann var, als er innerhalb weniger Sekunden seine Heimat hinter sich ließ? Wir alle kennen das Foto, wie sahen seine Gedanken aus? Conrad Schu- mann lehnt sich in seinem Sessel zurück und läßt seine Gedanken schweifen, bis zu dem Tag, als er sprang.

"Absichern und bewachen, das ist euer Auftrag", sagt der Offizier. "Schumann, Sie gehen zur Bernauer Straße, wenn es Probleme gibt, schießen Sie." Schumann sieht, wie die Mauer wächst. Er springt. Es ist 16 Uhr. Auf der anderen Seite begrüßen ihn die Menschen mit Beifall. Sie jubeln ihm zu. Conrad Schumann hat es geschafft. Er ist frei.

28 Jahre später: Menschen liegen sich weinend in den Armen. Heute wird wieder gejubelt—auf beiden Seiten der Mauer. Conrad Schumann ringt um Worte: "Ich kann es noch gar nicht glauben (ed.: daß die Mauer weg ist)", sagt er.

Conrad Schumann 1961 und 1989: Als er vor 29 Jahren in die Freiheit sprang (kl. Foto) wurde sein Bild in aller Welt zum Symbol für die Teilung Deutsch- lands. Für die AZ sprang der ehemalige Volkspolizist an derselben Stelle in der Bernauer Straße ein zweites Mal—und bekam Rückenschmerzen.

Foto Ludwig Hübl.

Source: *Die Abendzeitung,* Journal 1/90 & 2/90, Munich, Germany.

Procedures for an ACTFL Oral Proficiency Interview

american council on the teaching of foreign languages, inc.

ACTFL

6 Executive Plaza, Yonkers, NY 10701-6801 • (914)963-8830 • FAX: (914)963-1275

CERTIFIED ORAL PROFICIENCY TESTING

ACTFL has licensed Language Testing International (LTI) to provide certified foreign language speaking proficiency testing in 23 languages. Those serviced by LTI include: universities, boards of education, state teacher certification boards, government agencies, municipalities, major corporations and private individuals. LTI arranges testing exclusively with ACTFL and government certified testers. All official testing is certified by ACTFL via the issuance of an ACTFL Oral Proficiency Rating Certificate.

Oral proficiency testing is available in:

Arabic	German	Korean	Russian
Bulgarian	Hebrew	Mandarin	Spanish
Czech	Hindi	Norwegian	Tagalog
Dutch	Hungarian	Persian	Thai
English (ESOL)	Italian	Polish	Vietnamese
French	Japanese	Portuguese	

LTI can arrange for telephonic or face-to-face interviewing. To request an OPI, one needs only to call and within 24–72 hours a telephonic oral proficiency interview can be scheduled with a certified tester. Face-to-face interviews usually involve more time to arrange, and are dependent upon whether a tester is available in the candidates area.

The oral proficiency interview lasts approximately 10–30 minutes and is tape recorded by the tester. The taped interview is later reviewed and rated by the tester and then forwarded to a second tester for rating confirmation. Once the second rating is received by LTI, the candidate's name and test result data are entered into the testing data base and an ACTFL certificate of the candidate's oral proficiency rating is issued within two weeks.

For further information, please call LTI at 914-235-8400 or write:

Language Testing International
1 Ramada Plaza, Suite 707
New Rochelle, NY 10801-5217

Teacher Observation Form

APPENDIX B1

CHESTERFIELD COUNTY PUBLIC SCHOOLS
OBSERVATIONS/FOREIGN LANGUAGES

Text _____   Page No. _____   No. of Students _____

+ — Outstanding   OK — Satisfactory   NI — Needs Improvement   NA — Not Applicable

	Date	Date	Date
Lesson Planning	Visit No. 1	Visit No. 2	Visit No. 3
Variety of techniques/activities			
Several skills worked on			
Length of activities (15–20 min. except for upper level Latin translations)			
Mixture of new & familiar material			
Warm-up used			
Transitions between activities			
Overview given to each activity			
Evidence of lesson plans			

Techniques Used			
Amount of teacher talk/to/student talk			
Mixture of choral/group/individual work			
Small group activities included			
Use of visuals			
Target language used throughout period (NA for Latin)			
Personalization of materials			
Learning checks (comprehension and transfer)			
All students called on			
Meaning reinforced via visuals, intonation, etc.			
Correcting: cues for student self-correction			

Class Climate

	Visit No. 1	Visit No. 2	Visit No. 3
Amount of student volunteering?			
Students prepared?			
Students active during hour?			
Students relating to each other?			
Teacher's rewards: varied? sincere? partial (accepting what's right in answer)?			
Target language used as communication (T. greets ss. in target language, comments in target language; ss. speak to each other in target language)—NA for Latin.			

Comment On

1. Learning during the hours: Did students make progress?

2. Clarity of goals and whether they were attained:

3. Thoroughness of planning:

Teacher's Signature/Self-Assessment*/Date   Teacher's Signature/Date   Jane J. Baskerville
Foreign Language Program Specialist

*Teacher is encouraged to discuss this **working medium** with superiors ☐

Sample Letter of Expectation Between Cooperating Teachers and Student Teacher

Letter A—Student Teacher's Section

1. I will teach 4 classes (two French II and two French III) at 8:20, 9:30, 1:30, and 2:30, plus home-room at 9:20. I will be in the building from 8:00 a.m. till 4:00 p.m., M–F during the block period.

2. I will begin full teaching responsibilities by the second week, October 25. Up until then, I will observe and then gradually begin teaching more, perhaps one dialogue on Wednesday, two half-classes on Thursday, two full classes Friday of the first week.

3. The cooperating teacher and I will outline material to be covered; I will be responsible for individual lesson plans, using the materials students will learn from.

4. I will model tests after the cooperating teacher's tests, but make my own.

5. I will follow the "+, OK, –" homework policy, and return homework the day after turned in.

6. I will encourage my students to use only French, by setting the model myself.

7. I hope that the cooperating teacher observes me often, but fades out in the fourth week so that I am not aware she has left the class. I hope she observes intermittently after that.

8. After the cooperating teacher and I confer, I will prepare lesson plans by Friday for the following week.

9. I will try to attend at least one extra-curricular activity at Memorial High.

10. From the cooperating teacher I will hope for positive as well as negative constructive criticism, since everybody needs both. Likewise, I will feel open to criticism and will accept it as constructive, instructive, experience-based help.

11. I will try not to be frustrated about sharing others' materials. I will not feel obligated to make up all new exercises of my own.

12. On the weeks of no visit from the University supervisor, I will expect to tape and analyze one of my classes, report on it, and send in a report with the cooperating teacher's help.

13. I will expect to be able to go to the cooperating teacher for help on resources, discipline problems, and questions regarding methodology.

14. I will be open to suggestions and criticisms and will try to integrate those ideas into the next day's teaching.

Letter A—Cooperating Teacher's Section

1. During the first week of the student teaching block, I will teach my normal sequence of classes, with the student teacher sitting in and observing all activities. During this period, we will spend time together discussing the goals, methodology, success, or failure of the lesson plans, strong and weak points of the lesson, materials used, and student response to the lesson. Toward the end of week one, the student teacher will have done at least one activity in each class on Thursday, perhaps two activities on Friday. Monday of the second week at least one class will be assumed completely by the student teacher.

2. I will remain in classes initially, taking notes pertaining to methodology, use of the French language, discipline and control of the class, and preparation. These will be shared with the student teacher, discussed, and commented upon by both of us.

3. Lesson planning will be a joint venture throughout the student teaching block. My materials (e.g., overhead transparencies, pictures, files, slides, etc.) will be available for use by the student teacher if he or she so desires.

4. Initially, at least, I will help with the taking of attendance, parent contracts, and determining grades. These areas will also be discussed and acted upon by both of us, with the student teacher taking more responsibility in these areas as the student teaching block continues. By the third week of the block, the student teacher will be given full responsibility for attendance-taking procedures in his or her classes.

5. As the block continues, I will visit most, but not all, classes. These visits will be announced. The notes taken during all class visits will be shared and discussed by both myself and the student teacher. The notes will be given to the student teacher for reference.

6. One of the student teacher's classes will be videotaped; this videotape will be discussed in a post-observation conference by myself and the student teacher.

7. Toward the end of the student teaching block, I will ask the student teacher for his or her appraisal of each student's daily participation during the block and general comments about the student's achievement during this period.

8. Initially, I will assist the student teacher in the homeroom with attendance taking and handling of other pertinent business. By the third week, the student teacher will assume full responsibility for keeping homeroom advisees' records up to date with regard to attendance, cuts, and other pertinent data. We will share the responsibility of dealing with problems related to advisees.

9. I will be available for assistance at school between 8:00 a.m. and 4:00 p.m. and evenings by phone at my home.

Source: Kay Cipperly, Madison Memorial High, Madison, Wisc. (cf. Knop, C. *Teaching a Second Language: Guide for the Student Teacher.* Washington, D.C.: ERIC Clearinghouse on Languages & Linguistics. 1980, pp. 39–46.)

Etiquette Guidelines for the Nonsupervisory Observation of L2 Classrooms

Background

1. The observation/visitation of classroom teachers is serious business; it should not be approached casually.
2. Classroom observations are not easy for the classroom teachers involved.
3. Knowing how to teach a second language (L2) and knowing how to observe L2 classroom dynamics competently are two very different abilities. An experienced L2 teacher is not necessarily an effective or well-informed observer.
4. Learning how to observe in a manner acceptable to all parties involved is a slowly developing ability. It takes time, careful reflection, personal tact, and creativity. Visiting and visited teachers should expect that this ability will develop, change, and improve over time.
5. An observer is a guest in the teacher's and the students' classroom. A guest in the classroom should not attempt to take away even a modest degree of classroom responsibility, control, or authority from the classroom teacher or L2 students.
6. A guest's purpose for visiting is not to judge, evaluate, or criticize the classroom teacher; it is not necessarily even to offer constructive advice.
7. One option is for the guest to envision his/her role as that of an interested visitor, someone who has entered into a long-term process of learning to observe.
8. One potentially useful, though provocative, theme of the literature on L2 teacher education suggests that observing others as they teach provides invaluable opportunities for "visiting" teachers to learn to see more clearly in order to increase awareness of their own classroom practices. Reflecting upon what we see other teachers do in classroom settings sometimes helps us to become more aware of our own classroom behaviors. As Fanselow (6) puts it, "seeing you allows me to see myself differently and to explore variables we both use" (p. 115).

Procedures

9. Visitors should contact the teacher well in advance whose class they would like to visit; a minimum of 24 hours in advance is recommended. This is a crucial procedural concern that prospective visitors need to work out with the classroom teacher directly. Some teachers may prefer significantly more than 24 hours' lead time.
10. A visitor who is planning to observe a class should arrive in the classroom a few minutes ahead of time.
11. The classroom teacher should always reserve the right to say, "No," when a nonsupervisor inquires into the possibility of visiting his/her class. A teacher who withholds permission on one occasion might change his/her mind at a later date.

12. Visitors need to discuss with the classroom teacher how long they are planning to stay in the classroom. It is important to negotiate a suitable length of time that is acceptable to both the visitor and to the classroom teacher. Once the teacher and visitor have agreed upon a suitable length of time, the visitor should stay in the classroom for at least that long.

13. If something unexpected comes up and the visitor is not able to observe a class at the agreed upon time, the visitor needs to explain this to the classroom teacher at his/her earliest convenience. If the visitor has said that s/he is coming to the class, and then s/he does not show up, classroom teachers sometimes feel rejected. It is a visitor's responsibility to keep the classroom teacher informed.

14. Once having entered a classroom, the visitor should try to be as unobtrusive as possible. If possible, s/he should try to "blend into the woodwork."

15. If an L2 student in the class asks the visitor a direct question (e.g., What are you doing here? Are you a teacher, too?), the visitor should answer as briefly as possible. The visitor should not monopolize classroom time. It is important for a visitor to bear in mind that s/he is not a regular member of the class. Visitors should not initiate or pursue conversations unnecessarily.

16. The role of the participant observer is a special exception to numbers (14) and (15) above. This role can be adopted but only if it is initially suggested and encouraged by the classroom teacher directly. In this regard, a general rule of thumb is for the visitor to wait for an unsolicited cue from the classroom teacher.

17. A visitor should be appreciative and polite. At the earliest opportunity, s/he should thank the classroom teacher for having made possible this generous opportunity to visit an L2 classroom. In order to be unobtrusive, it is often necessary to express this appreciation in a setting other than the classroom setting.

18. A visitor who is taking written notes or collecting information in some other way should do this as unobtrusively as possible. The visitor must make sure that the teacher and students are comfortable with any procedures s/he may follow for data collection (e.g., audio or video taping).

Post-Visitation

19. It is imperative for visitors to keep whatever impressions they have of a visited teacher's style, effectiveness, or personal demeanor to themselves. These impressions should remain private and confidential.

20. Visitors should explain to the classroom teacher that his or her name will not be used in any discussions with other people. Visitors should let a visited teacher know that their policy is to keep any direct references to teachers, in either formal or informal settings, anonymous.

21. If visitors produce any retrievable artifacts (e g., written notes, audio or video recordings) during a classroom visit, the classroom teacher should have access to these materials.

22. Even well intentioned feedback to classroom teachers often misfires. Visitors need to bear this point in mind during their post-visitation interactions with teachers.

23. For this reason, visitors should monitor carefully and keep in check the natural inclination to offer advice. Unless visitors are observing in the capacity of a professionally trained supervisor, their role is not to assist, evaluate, or judge.

24. At times, discussions and collaborations between a visitor/observer and a classroom teacher are appropriate and useful. In fact, teachers sometimes expect and even request feedback from classroom visitors. The point is that such exchanges should only be pursued if they are initially suggested and encouraged by the classroom teacher. It is not the visitor's place to initiate or overemphasize the role of such exchanges.

25. Bearing items (23) and (24) in mind, visitors should be aware that if a post-observation discussion with the visited teacher does take place, it needs to be approached with great care, sensitivity, and tact.

26. Those who plan to visit L2 classrooms should read and discuss with others the literature on classroom observation etiquette. Becoming familiar with this tradition in the literature is important for visiting and visited teachers alike.

Source: Murphy, John M. "An Etiquette for the Nonsupervisory Observation of L2 Classrooms." *Foreign Language Annals* 25 (1992): pp 223–225.

APPENDIX B4 Information from the SWCOLT Language Teacher's Resource Book 1992

SOURCES OF INFORMATION

Foreign Countries

Agencies, Consulates, Embassies, Cultural Attachés, Tourist and other offices

For a more complete listing see the latest edition of "Foreign Consular Offices in the United States" (Publication 7846), and the Diplomatic List (Publication 7894), both published by the U.S. Department of State and available through the U.S. Government Printing Office or in many libraries. Other important addresses can be found in the *World Chamber of Commerce Directory* published annually by the World Chamber of Commerce Directory, Inc., P.O. Box 1029, Loveland, CO 80539 (also in libraries).

Argentina (Argentine Republic)

Office of the Embassy
1600 New Hampshire Ave., N.W.
Washington, DC 20009

Argentine-American Chamber of Commerce
50 W. 34th St., 6th Flr.
New York, NY 10001

Austria, Republic of

Office of the Embassy
3524 International Ct., N.W.
Washington, DC 20008-3035

Austrian Press and Information Service
31 East 69th Street
New York, NY 10021

Austrian Institute
11 East 52nd Street
New York, NY 10022

Austrian National Tourist Office
11601 Wilshire Blvd., Suite 2480
Los Angeles, CA 90025

U.S.-Austrian Chamber of Commerce
165 W. 46th Street
New York, NY 10036

Belgium

Office of the Embassy
3330 Garfield St., N.W.
Washington, DC 20008

Belgian-American Chamber of Commerce
350 Fifth Ave. #703
New York, NY 10118

Tourist Information Bureau
Hotel de Ville
Grand Place
1000 Brussels, Belgium

Bolivia

Office of the Embassy
3014 Massachusetts Ave., N.W.
Washington, DC 20008

Instituto Boliviano de Turismo
Av. 6 de agosto 2424
La Paz, Bolivia

Brazil

Office of the Embassy
3006 Massachusetts Ave., N.W.
Washington, DC 20008

Brazilian-California Trade Association
900 Wilshire Blvd. #1434
Los Angeles, CA 90017

Brazilian-American Chamber of Commerce
22 W. 48th St., #404
New York, NY 10036

Funtur-Brazilian Tourism Foundation
551 Fifth Ave., #421
New York, NY 10176

Canada

Office of the Embassy
501 Pennsylvania Ave., N.W.
Washington, DC 20001

Canadian Government Office of Tourism
1251 Ave. of the Americas
New York, NY 10020

Tourism Quebec
P.O. Box 20 000
Quebec City QU G1K 7X2
Canada

Chile

Office of the Embassy
1732 Massachusetts Ave., N.W.
Washington, DC 20036

North American-Chilean Chamber
220 E. 81st St.
New York, NY 10028

Servicio Nacional de Turismo de Chile
Avenida Providencia 1550
P.O. Box 14082
Santiago, Chile

China, People's Republic of

Office of the Embassy
2300 Connecticut Ave., N.W.
Washington, DC 20008

China International Travel SVC, Inc.
60 E. 42nd St., Rm. 465
New York, NY 10165

Colombia

Office of the Embassy
2118 Leroy Place, N.W.
Washington, DC 20008

Costa Rica

Office of the Embassy
1825 Connecticut Ave., N.W., Suite 211
Washington, DC 20009

Costa Rica National-Tourist Bureau
1100 Brickell Ave
BIV Tower #801
Miami, FL 33131

Cuba

Cuba's interests are handled through the Swiss Embassy.

Dominican Republic

Office of the Embassy
1715 22nd St., N.W.
Washington, DC 20008

Ecuador

Office of the Embassy
2535 15th St., N.W.
Washington, DC 20009

Egypt, Arab Republic of

Office of the Embassy
2310 Decatur Place, N.W.
Washington, DC 20008

El Salvador

Office of the Embassy
2308 California St., N.W.
Washington, DC 20008

European Community

Delegation of the Commission of the European Community
2100 M Street, N.W., 7th Flr.
Washington, DC 20037

France

Office of the Embassy
4101 Reservoir Rd., N.W.
Washington, DC 20007

French-American Chamber of Commerce
6380 Wilshire Blvd., #1608
Los Angeles, CA 90048

French-American Chamber of Commerce
509 Madison Ave., #1900
New York, NY

French Film Office
745 Fifth Avenue
New York, NY 10151

French Government Tourist Office
9454 Wilshire Blvd.
Beverly Hills, CA 90212

French Government Tourist Office
610 Fifth Avenue, # 222
New York, NY 10020

French News Hotline
Telephone news in French and English
Houston:
(713) 653-8361
Los Angeles:
(213) 653-8361
San Francisco:
(415) 981-7999

MinitelNet
French computer network for Minitel in U.S.
Information:
(800) 822-MNET

Germany, Federal Republic of

Office of the Embassy
4645 Reservoir Rd, N.W
Washington, DC 20007

German-American Chamber of Commerce of Los Angeles
3250 Wilshire Blvd. #1612
Los Angeles, CA 90010

Goethe Institute
530 Bush Street
San Francisco, CA 94108

German-American Chamber of Commerce
666 Fifth Avenue, 21st Flr.
New York, NY 10103

German National Tourist Office
444 S. Flower St., #2230
Los Angeles, CA 90017

Goethe Institute
3120 Southwest Fwy, #100
Houston, TX 77098

German National Tourist Office
747 Third Ave
New York, NY 10017

Guatemala

Office of the Embassy
2220 R Street, N.W.
Washington, DC 20008

Haiti

Office of the Embassy
2311 Massachusetts Ave., N.W.
Washington, DC 20008

Honduras

Office of the Embassy
3007 Tilden St., NW
Washington, DC 20008

Israel

Office of the Embassy
3514 International Dr.
Washington, DC 20008

Office of Tourism
6380 Wilshire Blvd., #1700
Los Angeles, CA 90048

Italy

Office of the Embassy
1601 Fuller Street
Washington, DC 20009

Italy-American Chamber of Commerce
350 Fifth Avenue, #3015
New York, NY 10118

Japan

Office of the Embassy
2520 Massachusetts Ave., N.W.
Washington, DC 20008

Japanese Chamber of Commerce of Southern California
244 S. San Pedro St. #504
Los Angeles, CA 90012

Korea, Republic of (South)

Office of the Embassy
2370 Massachusetts Ave., N.W.
Washington, DC 20008

Korean Chamber of Commerce
3000 W. Olympic Blvd #200
Los Angeles. CA 90006

Mexico

Office of the Embassy
1911 Pennsylvania Ave., N.W.
Washington, DC 20006

Mexican Government Tourism Office
405 Park Avenue, #1002
New York, NY 10022

U.S.-Mexico Chamber of Commerce
1900 L St., N.W. #612
Washington, DC 20036

Panama

Office of the Embassy
2862 McGill Terrace, N.W.
Washington, DC 20008

Paraguay

Office of the Embassy
2400 Massachusetts Ave., N.W.
Washington, DC 20008

Peru

Office of the Embassy
1700 Massachusetts Ave., N.W.
Washington, DC 20036

Peru Tourist Office
1000 Brickell Ave. #600
Miami, FL 33131

Portugal

Office of the Embassy
2125 Kalorama Rd., N.W.
Washington, DC 20008

Portuguese Tourism Office
590 Fifth Avenue
New York, NY 10036

Portugal-U.S. Chamber of Commerce
590 Fifth Ave., 3rd Flr.
New York, NY 10036

Puerto Rico (USA)

Puerto Rico Tourism
575 Fifth Avenue
New York, NY 10017

Russia

Russia also represents the republics of the former Soviet Union.

Office of the Embassy
1125 16th St. N.W.
Washington, DC 20036

Intourist
630 Fifth Ave., #868
New York, NY 10111

Saudi Arabia

Office of the Embassy
601 New Hampshire Ave., N.W.
Washington, DC 20037

Spain

Office of the Embassy
2700 15th Ave., N.W.
Washington, DC 20009

Spanish National Tourist Office
8383 Wilshire Blvd., #960
Beverly Hills, CA 90211

Spain-U.S. Chamber of Commerce
350 Fifth Ave., Rm. 3514
New York, NY 10118

Switzerland

Office of the Embassy
2900 Cathedral Ave., N.W.
Washington, DC 20008

Swiss-American Chamber of Commerce
347 Fifth Ave., Rm. 1008
New York, NY 10016

Swiss National Tourist Office
608 Fifth Ave.
Swiss Center
New York, NY 10020

Uruguay

Office of the Embassy
1918 F Street, N.W.
Washington, DC 20006

Uruguay Tourist Information
541 Lexington Ave.
New York, NY 10012

Venezuela

Office of the Embassy
1099 30th St., N.W.
Washington, DC 20007

Venezuelan-American Association of the U.S.
150 Nassau, #2015
New York, NY 10038

PROFESSIONAL ORGANIZATIONS AND AGENCIES

International, National and Regional Organizations and Agencies

Academic Alliances in Foreign Languages and Literatures
Dr. Ellen Silber, Coordinator
Marymount College Tarrytown
Box 1368
Tarrytown, NY 10591-3796

Advocates for Language Learning (ALL)
P.O. Box 4964
Culver City, CA 90231

African Language Teachers Association (ALTA)
Pres. Lioba Moshi
Dept. of Anthropology and Linguistics
Baldwin Hall
University of Georgia
Athens, GA 30602

Alpha Mu Gamma
National Collegiate FL Honor Society
Los Angeles City College
855 N. Vermont Avenue
Los Angeles, CA 90029

**American Association for the Advancement
of Slavic Studies (AAASS)**
128 Encina Commons
Stanford University
Stanford, CA 94305

**American Association for Applied Linguistics
(AAAL)**
1325 18th St., N.W. #211
Washington, DC 20036-6501

**American Association of Teachers of Arabic
(AATA)**
Dilworth Parkinson, Exec. Dir.
Dept. of Asian and Near East Languages
4072 JKHB
Brigham Young University
Provo, UT 84602

**American Association of Teachers of French
(AATF)**
Fred M. Jenkins, Exec. Sec.
57 E. Armory Drive
Champaign, IL 61820

**American Association of Teachers of German
(AATG)**
Helene Zimmer-Loew, Exec. Dir.
112 Haddontowne Court #104
Cherry Hill, NJ 08034

**American Association of Teachers of Italian
(AATI)**
Prof. Giuseppe Battista
Foreign Language Dept.
Islip Arts Building
Suffolk Community College
Selden, NY 11784
or
Dept. of French & Italian
Ohio State University
Columbus, OH 43210

**American Association of Teachers of Slavic
and East European Languages (AATSEEL)**
Sandy Couch, Exec. Sec.-Treas.
Foreign Languages
Arizona State University
Tempe, AZ 85284

**American Association of Teachers of Spanish
and Portuguese (AATSP)**
James R. Chatham, Executive Director
Drawer 6349
Mississippi State, MS 39762-6349

American Classical League
Miami University
Oxford, OH 45056

**American Council of Teachers of Russian
(ACTR)**
1619 Massachusetts Ave., N.W., Suite 527
Washington, DC 20036

**American Council on the Teaching of Foreign
Languages (ACTFL)**
C. Edward Scebold, Exec. Director
6 Executive Plaza
Yonkers, NY 10701-6801

**American Literary Translators Association
(ALTA)**
Box 830688
Univ. of Texas at Dallas
Richardson, TX 75083-0688

American Translators Association (ATA)
109 Croton Avenue
Ossining, NY 10562

Association of Asian Studies (AAS)
1 Lane Hall
University of Michigan
Ann Arbor, MI 48109

**Association of Departments of Foreign
Languages (ADFL)**
John W. Cross, Director
10 Astor Place
New York, NY 10003-6981

Association of Teachers of Japanese (ATJ)
Hiroshi Miyaji, President
Hillcrest 1
Middlebury College
Middlebury, VT 05753-6119

Canadian Association of Second Language Teachers, Inc. (CASLT)
369 Montrose Street
Winnipeg, MB R3M 3M1
Canada

CASLT President (1991–92):
Denise Bourassa
6 St. Vital Ave.
St. Albert, Alberta T8N 1K2

Canadian Linguistics Association
Association canadienne de linguistique
Experimental Phonetics Lab
New College
University of Toronto
Toronto, ON M5S 1A1
Canada

Center for Applied Linguistics (CAL)
1118 22nd St., N.W.
Washington, DC 20037

Central States Conference on the Teaching of Foreign Languages (CSC)
Jody Thrush, Exec. Dir.
Madison Area Technical College
3550 Anderson Street
Madison, WI 53704

Chinese Language Teachers Association (CLTA)
Dept. of East Asian Studies
211 Jones Hall
Princeton University
Princeton, NJ 08544

Computer-Assisted Language Learning & Instruction Consortium (CALICO)
Frank L. Borchardt, Exec. Dir.
014 Language Building
Duke University
Durham, NC 27706

Consortium of Teachers of Southeast Asian Languages (COTSEAL)
School of Language Studies
Foreign Service Institute
1400 Key Blvd.
Arlington, VA 22209

Deutscher Akademischer Austauschdienst (DAAD)
950 3rd Ave., 19th Fl.
New York, NY 10022

English Plus Information Clearinghouse (EPIC)
220 Eye Street, N.E., #220
Washington, DC 20002

Esperanto League for North America (ELNA)
P.O. Box 1129
El Cerrito, CA 94530

Fédération Internationale des Professeurs de Langue Vivantes (FIPLV)
Head Office
Seestraße 247
CH-8038 Zurich
Switzerland

Hispanic Society of America
613 W. 155th St.
New York, NY 10032

International Association of Learning Laboratories (IALL)
Dr. Robin Lawrason
IALL Business Manager
Media Learning Ctr 022-31
Temple University
Philadelphia, PA 19122

Joint National Committee for Languages (JNCL)
National Council for Languages and International Studies (NCLIS)
J. David Edwards, Exec. Dir.
300 Eye St. NE, Ste. 211
Washington, DC 20002

Language Acquisition Resource Center (LARC)
San Diego State University
San Diego, CA 92182-0230

Linguistic Society of America
1325 18th St., N.W., Suite 211
Washington, D.C. 20036-6501

Modern Language Association (MLA)
10 Astor Place
New York, NY 10003-6981

Mountain States Association for Language and Technology (M-SALT)
Marie Sheppard
ALTEC
Campus Box 239
Univ. of Colorado
Boulder, CO 83039-0239

National Association for Bilingual Education (NABE)
810 1st St., N.E.
Union Center Plaza, 3rd Fl.
Washington, DC 20002-4205

National Association of District Supervisors of Foreign Language (NADSFL)
Dr. Paul Garcia, Co-president
The School District of Kansas City
1211 McGee St.
Kansas City, MO 64106

National Center for Research on Cultural Diversity and Second Language Learning
399 Kerr Hall
UC Santa Cruz
Santa Cruz, CA 95064

National Clearinghouse for Bilingual Education
1118 22nd St., N.W.
Washington, DC 20037

National Council of State Supervisors of Foreign Languages (NCSSFL)
Pres., Susan M. Grier
Dept. of Education
State Educ. Bldg. 4, Capitol Mall
Little Rock, AR 72201-1071

National Foreign Language Center (NFLC)
Richard D. Lambert, Director
1619 Massachusetts Ave., N.W.
Washington, DC 20036

National Foreign Language Resource Center
University of Hawaii
Webster Hall 203
2528 The Mall
Honolulu, HI 96822

National Resource Center for Translation and Interpretation
Div. of Interpretation and Translation
School of Langs and Lings
Georgetown University
Washington, DC 20057

Northeast Conference on the Teaching of Foreign Languages
200 Twin Oaks Terrace, #16
South Burlington, VT 05403

Pacific Northwest Council on Foreign Languages (PNCFL)
Ray Verzasconi, Exec. Sec.
Foreign Languages & Literatures
Kidder Hall 210
Oregon State University
Corvallis, OR 79331-4603

Rocky Mountain Modern Language Association
Charles G. Davis, Exec. Dir.
Dept. of English
Boise State University
Boise, ID 83725

Southern Conference on Language Teaching (SCOLT)
Lee Bradley, Exec. Sec.
Modern Foreign Languages
Valdosta State College
Valdosta, GA 31698

Southwest Conference on Language Teaching (SWCOLT)
Jan Herrera, Exec. Dir.
10724 Tancred
Northglenn, CO 80241

Teachers of English to Speakers of Other Languages (TESOL)
1600 Cameron St., Ste. 300
Alexandria, VA 22314

U.S. Department of Education
400 Maryland Ave., S.W.
Washington, DC 20202

PROFESSIONAL DIRECTORIES AND GUIDES

The Administrator's Guide to FLES Programs
Dr. Gladys Lipton, Chair
National FLES Commission of AATF
Modern Languages/UMBC
Baltimore, MD 21228

Advisory List of International Educational Travel and Exchange Programs, 1992
Council on Standards for International
Educational Travel (CSIET)
3 Loudoun Street, S.E.
Leesburg, VA 22075
(703) 771-2040

Directory of Professional Preparation Programs in TESOL in the United States, 1992–1994
TESOL Publications
1600 Cameron St., Suite 300
Alexandria, VA 22314-2751

Federal Funding Guide for Language and International Education
ACTFL
6 Executive Plaza
Yonkers, NY 10701

Foreign Students as Resources: Cross-Cultural Learning in K–12 Schools
NAFSA: Association of International Educators
1875 Connecticut Ave., N.W. #1000
Washington, DC 20009
(202) 462-4811

INTERNATIONAL

CABLE
Plaza de los Reyes Magos 9, 5º C
28007 Madrid, Spain
• Twice yearly periodical on the teaching of Spanish as a foreign language

The Canadian Modern Language Review
237 Hellems Avenue
Welland, Ontario L3B 3B8
Canada

World Englishes
Journal of English as an International and
Intranational Language
Pergamon Press
Maxwell House
Fairview Park
Elmsford, NY 105323

NATIONAL

AATF National Bulletin
American Association of Teachers of French
57 E. Armory Avenue
Champaign, IL 61820

AATG Newsletter
Die Unterrichtspraxis
German Quarterly
American Association of Teachers of German
112 Haddontowne Ct. #104
Cherry Hill, NJ 08034

AMACADMY
Newsletter of the American Academy in Rome
41 East 65th Street
New York, NY 10021-6508

ACTR Letter
American Council of Teachers of Russian
Betty Leaver, Editor
747 St. Regis Way
Salina, CA 93905

ADFL Bulletin
Association of Departments of Foreign Languages
10 Astor Place
New York, NY 10003-6981

ATA Chronicle
Newsletter of the American Translators Association
109 Croton Avenue
Ossining, NY 10562

ATJ Newsletter
Naomi Hanaoka McGloin, Editor
Association of Teachers of Japanese
Dept. of East Asian Languages & Lit.
University of Wisconsin
Madison, WI 53706

Athelstan Newsletter
Michael Barlow, Editor
P.O. Box 8025
La Jolla, CA 92038-8025

CALICO Journal
Duke University
014 Language Building
Durham, NC 27706

The Classical World
Department of Classics
Duquesne University
Pittsburgh, PA 15282

CLTA Newsletter
Chinese Language Teachers Association
Seton Hall University
South Orange, NJ 07079

Collaborare
Ellen Silber, Editor
Marymount College Tarrytown
Box 1368
Tarrytown, NY 10591-3796

The ELNA Newsletter
Esperanto League for North America, Inc.
P.O. Box 1129
El Cerrito, CA 94530

ENLACE
Newsletter of the AATSP
Irving P. Rothberg, Editor
Dept. of Spanish and Portuguese
The University of Massachusetts
Amherst, MA 01003

ERIC/CLL News Bulletin
1118 22d Street, NW
Washington, DC 20037

Foreign Language Annals
6 Executive Plaza
Yonkers, NY 10701-6801

French Review (AATF)
Ronald W. Tobin, Editor
Dept. of French & Italian
University of California
Santa Barbara, CA 93106

Hispania (AATSP)
Theodore Sachett, Editor
Dept. of Span. & Port.
University of Southern California
Los Angeles, CA 90089-0358

IALL Journal
Read Gilgen, Editor
Learning Support Systems
Univ. of Wisconsin
279 Hise Hall
1220 Linden Drive
Madison, WI 53719

IALL News Review Newsletter
Trisha Dvorak, Editor
2018 MLB
Univ. of Michigan
812 Washington
Ann Arbor, MI 48109

MLA Newsletter
Modern Language Association (MLA)
10 Astor Place
New York, NY 10003

The Modern Language Journal
David P. Benseler, Editor
Case Western Reserve University
Ohio State University
Cleveland, OH 44106

NABE Journal
NABE Newsletter
National Association for Bilingual Education
Room 405
1201 16th Avenue, NW
Washington, DC 20036

Newsletter of Japanese Language Teachers'
Network
Japanese Language Teachers' Network
University High School
1212 W. Springfield Ave.
Urbana, IL 61801

PMLA
Publications of the Modern Language Association
10 Astor Place
New York, NY 10003

SCOLA Global
Satellite Communication for Learning Worldwide
2500 California Street
Omaha, NE 68178-0778

Technology and Language Learning
Yearbook
Athelstan
P.O. Box 8025
La Jolla, CA 92038-8025

TESOL Newsletter
TESOL Quarterly
1600 Cameron St., Ste. 300
Alexandria, VA 22314

INDEX

Emotional development, 58
Emotion/motivational strategies, 202, 204
English as a Second Language. *See* ESL
Episode Hypothesis (Oller), 28, 30
Error Awareness Sheet (EASE), 188
Error correction
 indirect, 188
 in speaking, 167
 in writing, 188
Error tracking system, 169, 188
Escape From Utopia program, 265
Eskey, D.E., 119
ESL (English as a Second Language), 31
 top-down lesson, 37
Essay Correction Code (ECCO), 188
Ethnic bias, 209–210
Exam results, poor, 14–16
Explicit grammar instruction, 91–92
 deficiencies of, 92–93

Fall, T.F., 31, 149, 150–152
Family, unit on, 79–81
Fantasy experiences, 65
Feedback, 167–169
First language acquisition, 8, 93
 Krashen's definition of, 8
 research, 93
Fjeldstad, Lucie, 248
Fleak, K., 162
FLES (Foreign Language in the Elementary School), 31, 61
 content-enriched programs, 62
 past and present, 61
FLEX (Foreign Language Exploratory) programs, 61
Floaters, outside groups, 147
Flower, L., 185
Folktales, 63, 81
Foreign Language Exploratory programs. *See* FLEX programs
Foreign Language in the Elementary School. *See* FLES
Foreign language learning, defined, 7
Foreshadowing
 of language elements, 94
 using songs, 105–108

Form, focus on, 96, 98
Formative testing, 226
Freeman, D., 4
French instruction
 CBI and, 31
 with culturally diverse students, 216–219
 culture-based syllabus for beginning level, 46
 evaluation of speaking, 242
 first grade level, 71
 middle school level, 84, 100, 104, 105–108
 objective setting, 51
 and physical education, 66–72
 reading aloud for pronunciation, 134
 sample textbook exercises, 33–35
 software, 263–264
 whole language approach to, 100, 104, 105–108
Functionally based curriculum, 78
Functions, expected learner outcomes in, 45

Gaitan, S., 1
Gallimore, R., 98
Galloway, V., 30, 94
Gaming, 163–164
Garfinkel, Barry, 209
Garrett, N., 247, 248, 260, 264, 265
Garza, T.J., 256
Gaudiani, C., 186
Gebhard, J., 1
Gender bias, 209–210
Gender/Ethnic Expectations and Student Achievement (GESA) Program, 210
Gendron, B., 247
German instruction
 alternative teaching philosophies, 123–133
 combined levels in, 170
GESA (Gender/Ethnic Expectations and Student Achievement) Program, 210
Gifted students, 211–213
 defined, 211
 strategies for instruction, 212–213

Glisan, E.W., 31
Global students, 199–200, 202
Global units, 64–65
Goodman, K.S., 93, 113
Grading
 testing and, 225
 of writing, 187–188
 see also Testing; Tests
Grammar instruction
 bottom-up approach, 24
 explicit and implicit methods, 91–92
 interacting dimensions of, 96
 presentations in textbooks, 101–103
 rationale for, 90–91
 role of the teacher in, 91, 92
 traditional approach, 99
 using songs to foreshadow, 105–108
 whole language approach to, 90–108
Grammatical competence
 in listening and reading, 113
 in speaking, 141
 in writing, 181
Grammatical structures, 90–91
Grayson, D.A., 210
Greenfield, P.M., 182
Grouping students, 146–147
 for cooperative learning, 202
Group interaction skills, teaching, 147–148
Groups, small, working in, 78, 146
Group tasks, structuring, 148
Guessing, in context, 114
Guessing games, 164
Guided participation, 92, 93, 97–98

Handicapped students, 205–209
Hands-on students, 200, 201
Hanesian, H., 94
Harper, S.N., 120
Hayes, J.R., 185
Hearing impaired students, 208
Heritage Project (Oxford), 159
Herron, C., 92

vacation and travel, 26, 47
weather, 45
Ur, P., 163

Vacation, unit on, 26, 47
Variable Competence Model
(Bialystok), 8–9
Video, 251–259, 267–269
captioned reading material, 256
integrating into language
instruction, 256–259
interactive, 256
modes and descriptions, 255–256
selecting materials, 252–256
viewing guides, 258–259
Videocassettes, 252
Videodiscs, 252, 256
Video split, 259
Videotexts, 252
for listening and reading, 117, 119
selecting, 252, 253–255, 265–269
use of, 257
Vigil, N., 167
Vigil, V.D., 117
Villegas Rogers, C., 30
Visually impaired students, 208
Visuals, culturally appropriate, 214.
See also Video
Visual students, 200, 201
Vocabulary, building, 116
Vygotsky, L.S., 9–11, 92, 182

Walz, J., 25
Weather, unit on, 45
Whole language approach, 26,
90–108
basic principles of, 93–94
compared to traditional
approach, 99
cyclical approach, 95–96
designing contextualized
activities, 100–101
explicit/implicit controversy,
91–92
guided participation, 92
key elements of, 99–100
PACE model for integrating form,
96–99
reformulating grammar
instruction, 92–93
sample lesson (Cumo), 304–311
Wiseman, D.G., 78
Writing
as a communicative skill, 184
competencies for, 181
journal, 185, 186
and language development, 180
as a process, 180–182, 185–187
as a product, 187–188
purposes for, 184–185
role of, 183–185
as a tool for learning, 180, 182
see also Writing instruction;
Writing skills

Writing instruction, 180–194
correcting and grading, 187–188
at different grade levels, 181
elementary level, 183, 189
grammar–focused, 184
middle school level, 183, 189
peer editing, 186, 192
post-secondary level, 184
pre-writing stage, 186
process-oriented approach to,
186
rating systems for, 188
revising, 181
re-writing stage, 186
secondary level, 184–185, 189
traditional activities, 184
use of authentic materials in, 187
see also Writing; Writing skills
Writing skills, 184
comparison of skilled and
unskilled, 181
development of, 180–181
three stages of, 185–186
see also Writing; Writing
instruction

Zamel, V., 181
Zone of Proximal Development
(Vygotsky), 9–11, 96
defined, 10